# Popular Music in Leeds

# Urban Music Studies

**Series editors:**
Alenka Barber-Kersovan, Lisa Gaupp, Volker Kirchberg and Robin Kuchar
**Print ISSN:** 2752-4442 | **Online ISSN:** 2752-4450

Urban Music Studies aims at an inter- and trans-disciplinary exchange between researchers working on the relationship between music and the city. The series covers a broad range of topics and musical practices, current as well as historical. With its cross-cultural point of departure and the focus on cities, countries and geographical regions which are normally excluded from the scholarly discourse this series will bring fresh perspectives on the role of music in accelerated urbanization processes.

The theoretical model of Urban Music Studies is based on the assumptions that: there is a vital exchange between the music and the city; music is a part of the intrinsic logic of cities; music contributes to the image design of a city; music is an important part of the economy of cities and urban regeneration; music can become an issue of urban politics and policies; music is an essential component of the cultural heritage of cities; and music is a pivotal part of urban culture and the Creative Industries.

In this series:

*Sonic Signatures: Music, Migration and the City at Night*, edited by Derek Pardue, Ailbhe Kenny and Katie Young (2023)
*Popular Music in Leeds: Histories, Heritage, People and Places*, edited by Brett Lashua, Karl Spracklen, Kitty Ross and Paul Thompson (2023)

# Popular Music in Leeds

Histories, Heritage, People and Places

EDITED BY

*Brett Lashua, Karl Spracklen,
Kitty Ross and Paul Thompson*

Bristol, UK / Chicago, USA

First published in the UK in 2023 by
Intellect, The Mill, Parnall Road, Fishponds, Bristol, BS16 3JG, UK

First published in the USA in 2023 by
Intellect, The University of Chicago Press, 1427 E. 60th Street,
Chicago, IL 60637, USA

Copyright © 2023 Intellect Ltd
All rights reserved. No part of this publication may be reproduced,
stored in a retrieval system, or transmitted, in any form or by
any means, electronic, mechanical, photocopying, recording, or
otherwise, without written permission.

A catalogue record for this book is available from
the British Library.

Copy editor: MPS Limited
Cover designer: Tanya Montefusco
Cover image: Leeds Libraries
Production manager: Sophia Munyengeterwa
Typesetter: MPS Limited

Hardback ISBN 978-1-78938-805-3
Paperback ISBN 978-1-78938-861-9
ePDF ISBN 978-1-78938-806-0
ePUB ISBN 978-1-78938-807-7

To find out about all our publications, please visit our website.
There you can subscribe to our e-newsletter, browse or download our current
catalogue and buy any titles that are in print.

www.intellectbooks.com

This is a peer-reviewed publication.

# Contents

List of Figures ... ix
Acknowledgements ... xi
Foreword ... xiii
   *Jez Willis*
Introducing Leeds ... 1
   *Brett Lashua, Karl Spracklen, Kitty Ross and*
   *Paul Thompson*

## PART 1. PLACES OF LEEDS' POPULAR MUSIC ... 13

1. Dance and Drink the Fenton: Fighting for Territory in Leeds' Culture Wars ... 15
   *Rio Goldhammer*
2. When Mr Fox Met Kit Calvert, the Maker of Wensleydale Cheese: Constructing Yorkshireness in the Sixties Leeds Folk Scene ... 31
   *Karl Spracklen*
3. Park Life: When Roundhay Went Pop ... 43
   *Peter Mills*
4. 'Everything Is Brilliant in Leeds': Venues in the Leeds Indie Scene 1992–2012 ... 57
   *Dan Lomax*
5. Noise, Power Electronics and the No-Audience Underground: Place, Performance and Discourse in Leeds' Experimental Music Scene ... 70
   *Theo Gowans, Phil Legard and Dave Procter*

## PART 2. PEOPLE: LEEDS' MUSICAL COMMUNITIES AND CULTURAL IDENTITIES — 85

6. La-Di-Dah: Some Thoughts on Jake Thackray and British Popular Culture — 87
   *Stephen Wagg*
7. Home Is Where the Music Is: Migrants and Belonging in Leeds — 102
   *Jonathan Long*
8. A Tale of Two Artists: Thinking Intersectionally About Women and Music in Leeds — 117
   *Beccy Watson*
9. Leeds Punk through a Feminist Lens — 130
   *Mallory McGovern*
10. Americana and Leeds: Narrating the American South with Northern Grit — 144
    *Dave Robinson*

## PART 3. HISTORIES OF POPULAR MUSIC IN LEEDS — 159

11. Leeds City Varieties in the 1950s and 1960s: Decline, Nudity and Nostalgia in the British Variety Industry — 161
    *Dave Russell*
12. The Evolution of DIY Venues as Dancing Spaces in Leeds from the 1940s to 2020s — 176
    *Stuart Moss*
13. Music of the Leeds West Indian Carnival — 191
    *Danny Friar*
14. Jazz in Leeds, 1940s–50s — 205
    *Michael Meadowcroft*

## PART 4. POPULAR MUSIC HERITAGE, LEGACIES AND FUTURES — 215

15. *Sounds of Our City* Exhibition: Music and Materiality in Leeds' Abbey House Museum — 217
    *Kitty Ross and Paul Thompson*

16. Where You're From *and* Where *They're* At: Connecting Voices, 235
    Generations and Place to Create a Leeds Hip Hop Archive
    *Sarah Little and Alex Stevenson*
17. A Splendid Time is Guaranteed for All: A Psychogeography 250
    of Leeds' Popular Music Heritage
    *Brett Lashua and Paul Thompson*
18. Music:Leeds – Supporting a Regionalized Music Sector and Scene 264
    *Paul Thompson and Sam Nicholls*

Conclusion: Putting Popular Music in Leeds 'On the Map' 279
  *Brett Lashua, Paul Thompson, Kitty Ross and Karl Spracklen*
Notes on Contributors 287
Index 299

# Figures

| | | |
|---|---|---|
| 1.1: | A Google Maps view of the University of Leeds campus, showing the Fenton nearby. | 19 |
| 3.1: | Mick Jagger on stage during the Rolling Stones' 1982 performance at Roundhay Park. | 47 |
| 3.2: | Ed Sheeran performing at Roundhay Park in 2019. | 54 |
| 5.1: | Poster for an experimental music event at Chunk, 14 November 2019. | 74 |
| 5.2: | Meanwood Park Noise Walk. | 78 |
| 11.1: | The City Varieties in 1949, viewed from the gallery. | 162 |
| 11.2: | 'The theatre with the double life,' a recording of 'The Good Old Days' interrupts the run of a Paul Raymond nude show in 1954. | 165 |
| 14.1: | A session at Studio 20 in 1954. | 208 |
| 14.2: | George Melly signing the 'Gallery of Fame for Uninhibited Idealists' at Studio 20, 1955. | 209 |
| 15.1: | The Dearlove Orchestra outside the Royal Baths, Harrogate, c.1891. | 220 |
| 15.2: | The bedroom displayed in the *Sounds of Our City* exhibition. | 223 |
| 15.3: | Ceramic figure of Ivy Benson and her band, made by Katch Skinner, 2017. | 229 |
| 16.1: | A Freshjive flyer, c.2010. | 243 |
| 17.1: | Leeds 'Song Tunnel' (left), with close-up view (right). | 256 |
| 17.2: | The gravestones of Susannah (standing) and William Darby (and with Brett Lashua, foreground). | 260 |
| C.1: | Putting popular music in Leeds on the map; the installation at Ginger Works, 2022. | 280 |
| C.2: | A close-up of the mapping at Ginger Works. | 281 |

# Acknowledgements

We are grateful to the many musicians, music venues and venue staff, and music fans of Leeds, past and present. Kitty would like to acknowledge Marek Romaniszyn, an assistant community curator and the main impetus behind most of the contemporary collecting at Leeds Museums and Galleries post-2008. Thanks go to Louise Birch at Leeds Libraries for use of the book's cover image, and to the Terry Cryer Archive Collection for permission to include the photographs in Chapter 14. We are very appreciative of all the support from Tim Mitchell and Sophia Munyengeterwa at Intellect.

# Foreword

### Jez Willis (Utah Saints)
*Leeds, March 2022*

Leeds has been my home for over 35 years, and I've been involved with music the whole time, including 31 years as half of Utah Saints. I've always seen Leeds as 'having one of everything'. That's not to say Leeds is small, but that pretty much everything in the city has its own Unique Selling Point (USP). For me, this also applies to the music in the city. Historically, you could find whatever music scene you were drawn to; no one was really competing directly with anyone else – everything musical had its own character in Leeds.

I'm often asked why Utah Saints never moved to London when our career took off, and the simple answer is the importance of the place for music. We had three top-ten records, and another five in the top 40, that were written and produced here in Leeds – highly unlikely to have been written in any other city. The sheer number of unique influences that fed into our writing process wouldn't have happened anywhere else.

I came to Leeds from Carlisle, with the ambition to become Entertainments Secretary at the university. That didn't happen, but in my first week I joined Music for the Masses, a university society run by Simon Denbeigh from The March Violets and, a year later, I took over the running of that society. We had 400 members, a communal sound system (its claim to fame was that it was used by The Wedding Present), a fanzine and a Roland TR606 drum machine, which lived at my house when it wasn't being lent out to other members. This is where I learnt drum programming and I spent sixteen-hour days copying the drums from my favourite records so, when I played the track, I could start the drum machine at the same time and it would play along – kind of karaoke for electronic music aficionados.

Music for the Masses also provided me with the opportunity to put on gigs, interview bands and business people for the fanzine, and network like never before – for ten years I felt like I was at the epicentre of all sorts of musical moments in Leeds. There are way too many to fully list, but here are some for starters:

- Seeing The Clash busk in the car park of The Royal Park; Crewing Bruce Springsteen at Roundhay Park;
- Driving Henry Rollins and Ian Mackaye to a studio in Kirkstall;
- A Sigue Sigue Sputnik gig (I co-promoted) with five people in the audience;
- U2 in the University of Leeds Refectory;
- Interviewing John Peel at Leeds Beckett University for our fanzine;
- Elastica at The Duchess;
- Bad Brains at Brannigans;
- Daft Punk at The Pleasure Rooms;
- Swedish Mike and his flight cases;
- Providing cymbals for Grandmaster Flash & The Furious 5;
- Filming the video for our track 'Something Good' at a gig at the university;
- Seeing bands and DJs early in their career – U2, Front 242, The Young Gods, Faith No More, Siouxsie and The Banshees, The Sisters of Mercy, Propaganda, The Sugarcubes, The Three Johns, Jo Whiley, Sasha, Carl Cox, March Violets, Nightmares On Wax, LFO, Chumbawamba …;
- Seeing legends actually 3 metres away on stage – Bobby Byrd, Alan Vega, Sly and Robbie, Yellowman, Motorhead, Public Enemy, The Ramones!

I lived in the LS6 neighbourhood, which was where a lot (but by no means all) of Leeds bands rehearsed and I spent a lot of time making noise in various cellars around Hyde Park. Random meetings at gigs led to me joining a Surf band (Surfin' Dave) and two Electro Punk bands (Cassandra Complex and MDMA), before forming Utah Saints in 1991. I also promoted weekly club nights in the city, starting at a function room above a restaurant in the late 1980s, and overseeing the venue to transform into a 1400-capacity, four-room nightclub during the birth of Rave.

By 1991, I was promoting four nights a week at the club (The Gallery, later to become The Pleasure Rooms). All nights were different: Tuesdays were Indie, Thursdays Disco, Fridays House and Mondays, er … 10p a pint (Mondays are tricky to promote!). On my nights off I would still go to that club for the music – Wednesday was Jazz night, called The Cooker, which was presented by Gip Dammone and the Dig! Family. As well as the best Funk and Jazz music, the promoters brought in amazing international names: often bands would play Ronnie Scott's in London and The Cooker in Leeds as their only UK dates. Saturdays were also House nights, and with the addition of the legendary Back To Basics night, the club pretty much hosted a 'who's who' of dance music. Sundays were the 'alternative' music nights, which were members-only to get around the 'no dancing on a Sunday' law that was in place at the time; ridiculous as that sounds now. There were so many successful nights in 1991 that ten of us, all promoters, got together with the idea to put on a festival called 'United Club Federation'. But, going back to the 'one of everything' idea, the whole thing was abandoned because there were too many ideas to formulate one coherent direction.

None of this, like a lot of Leeds' music history, was ever properly documented. There will be many reasons for this, but, for us, it was all about the crowds coming week after week to our club nights that was enough – we didn't need any more attention. There was a period when rave was in the tabloids and we had interview requests on a weekly basis and turned them down – we were doing fine, thank you. Whilst other cities were shouting about what was going on, Leeds, in typical style, understated everything and so it's often overlooked, even though the city, in the words of Dave Beer from Back To Basics, goes 'two steps further than any other fucker'.

There has always been a strong link between academia and local music, even if it took a while for both sides to realize it. Every music-maker I know has carried out deep research into music, and every academic I have encountered through my recent work in Higher Education has been immersed in music. That is why it is such an amazing thing to pull together a book like this, a valuable addition to academic literature. Written with passion, accuracy and a deep local knowledge, this book has far-reaching importance, well beyond the reader with a focus on Leeds. This collection demonstrates the importance of place when it comes to music – nothing exists in a vacuum, of course, but each place becomes its own melting pot of creativity, history, legacy and forward-thinking.

If you care about music, this book will be inspiring, entertaining and informative – each chapter has a 'wow' element, like powerful music, built around moments. There will always be omissions because it is impossible to fit everything in, but this hopefully paves the way for further volumes.

So, Leeds. Music, research, academia and above all an accurate history, to the authors and publishers – Thank you!

# Introducing Leeds

*Brett Lashua, Karl Spracklen, Kitty Ross and Paul Thompson*

Rebecca Solnit contends that 'every place deserves an atlas' (2010: vii) and this book is intended as a kind of atlas of popular music in Leeds. It is the first academic collection dedicated to mapping Leeds' popular music histories, heritage, people and places. As each of the contributing authors uniquely argues, Leeds is deserving of, and long overdue for, serious attention. The city has spawned crooners, folk singers, punks, post-punks, Goths, DJs, popstars, rappers, indie rockers and more. Yet – with a few exceptions (Butt 2022; O'Brien 2012; Riches and Lashua 2014; Spracklen et al. 2016; Spracklen et al. 2013; Thompson and Nicholls 2021) – Leeds has not been studied for its musical cultures like other UK cities, such as Liverpool, Manchester, Birmingham and Sheffield. Having lived, worked, studied and even performed here, we have found the absence of literature about Leeds' popular music histories and heritage curious. In some ways, Leeds is a city with a 'lost' local musical heritage (Carr 2019), hidden even to those who reside there. While a number of bands from Leeds remain beloved by fans – late 1970s punk and post-punk groups Gang of Four, Delta 5, Scritti Politti and the Mekons; early 1980s goth-rock group The Sisters of Mercy, indie rock band The Wedding Present, dance duo Utah Saints, and in the early 2000s, Kaiser Chiefs – recent events including the death of Gang of Four guitarist Andy Gill (1 February 2020) have sparked renewed interest in the city's musical heritage. This book aims to give Leeds the atlas that it deserves and put popular music in Leeds firmly 'on the map'.

This introductory chapter is designed to help contextualize the book, give the reader an overview of Leeds and establish the sociohistorical context of the chapters that follow. It also offers an overview of some of the theoretical developments in scholarship on popular music, cultural heritage and music geographies (Baker et al. 2018; Bennett 2022; Draganova et al. 2021; Lashua et al. 2019). Finally, it provides a snapshot of the book's eighteen chapters, delineating and linking some of the shared and contrasting threads among them. The collection has been developed from the work of a diverse range of contributors, including interdisciplinary scholars, musicians, local historians, journalists and community members. Significantly, elements of it have been drawn from a major public museum exhibition *Sounds of Our City: Leeds' Music History* (January 2020–December 2021) led by social historian and curator (and co-editor) Kitty Ross (see Chapter 15), in partnership with Music:Leeds (lead by Sam Nicholls; see Chapter 18), with contributions by academics (see Chapter 3 by Peter Mills), community historians such as Danny Friar (see Chapter 13) and musicians such as Michael Meadowcroft (see Chapter 14). All chapters in this collection build upon contemporary research.

The breadth and range of contributions help to map something of the complexity and diversity in perspectives of this city. As Solnit (2010: vii) pointed out:

> A city is a particular kind of place, perhaps best described as many worlds in one place; it compounds many versions without quite reconciling them, though some cross over to live in multiple worlds […]. An atlas is a collection of versions of a place, a compendium of perspectives, a snatching out of the infinite ether of potential versions a few that will be made concrete and visible.

In ways that each of the book's chapters explores, Leeds' popular music exemplifies and informs complex understandings of the materiality and intangibility of the city. Leeds has a rich musical history and heritage, a long tradition of vibrant music venues, nightclubs, dance halls, pubs and other sites of musical entertainment. Through these, the book traces broader social, cultural and urban changes – both across Britain and in wider global contexts – of the historical significance of music as mass entertainment; of music and migration; of music and social equity; of industrialization and de-industrialization, regeneration and the rise of the 24-hour city (Chatterton and Hollands 2003) and more. Charting moments of stark musical politicization and de-politicization, the chapters concomitantly trace arguments about 'heritagising' popular music (Roberts and Cohen 2014) within discussions of music's 'place' in museums (Baker et al. 2016) and in the city's economy. Importantly, this book contributes to debates about why music matters (Hesmondhalgh 2013), has mattered, and continues to matter – in Leeds and beyond.

## *Locating Leeds*

Although Leeds is considered the fourth largest metropolitan area (by population) in the United Kingdom, it remains peripheral to better-known British cities in many ways. Chartered in 1207 and granted city status in 1893, Leeds became a major industrial centre in the North of England in the nineteenth century, primarily in manufacturing textiles such as wool and flax. During the mid nineteenth century, Marshall's Mill in Leeds was one of the largest factories in the world. Spanning the River Aire, the city benefitted from waterways and canals, and later rail links, across the north of England to port cities such as Liverpool and Hull. With 95,000 residents in 1801, a century later Leeds' population had reached over 550,000. Although its growth slowed after the First World War, the district had approximately 750,000 residents in 2011, and Population UK (2022: n.pag.) predicted that Leeds reached around 840,000 residents in 2022.

Its manufacturing base saw the city through the Second World War and, like many UK cities, waves of migration from South Asia, Africa, the Caribbean and Europe transformed the demographics of metropolitan Leeds in the post-war years. Industrial decline and a shift to a service economy, coupled with more recent moves to turn Leeds into a '24-hour city' of nightlife and entertainment, saw the remaking of the city centre and visions of Leeds as the 'capital of the North' (Chatterton and Hollands 2004: 266). Once 'a grim industrial city on the edge of the Yorkshire coalfields' (Connell 2014: 97), Leeds has been transformed into a centre for retail, leisure and entertainment since the 1990s (Unsworth and Stilwell 2004). With five universities, Leeds has a large student population, which has impacted and influenced its nightlife and popular music scenes (Lashua and Skeldon 2023). Despite its long working-class history and abundance of students, Leeds has not received mainstream music industry attention beyond a small handful of celebrated bands and artists such as The Wedding Present, Gang of Four, the Mekons, Kaiser Chiefs, Utah Saints, Corinne Bailey Rae, Chumbawamba, Soft Cell, The Sisters of Mercy and more recently, Yard Act. Yet, as this book's chapters showcase, the city has supported vibrant folk, jazz, punk, post-punk, goth, metal, African-Caribbean, electronic dance music and hip hop scenes. Although not renowned for producing global music superstars, Leeds nonetheless has a reputation as 'a good place to do and see music' (Spracklen et al. 2016: 149). But what makes a 'good place' for music?

## *Placing popular music and heritage*

In the last 25 years, scholars have increasingly given attention to questions of music and place (Leyshon et al. 1998); for example, why are some cities viewed as more musical than others? Connected to these are further questions of cultural heritage and the ways in which understandings of the past inform the present (Smith 2006). There is an established body of scholarship on popular music, place and cultural heritage (e.g. Baker et al. 2018; Bennett 2022; Cohen 2007; Connell and Gibson 2003; Lashua et al. 2019; Lashua et al. 2014; Leyshon et al. 1998; Mahoney and Schofield 2021), and the potential for further explorations in this nexus remains vast. From specific in-depth studies of single venues or local scenes to neighbourhoods, cities, regions and nations, 'place' matters in popular music heritage. The relations of music and place – politically, culturally and economically – offer important registers of cultural identity and meaning-making, particularly during times of intense debates about the loss, forgetting or erasure of these distinctions (Waxer 2002; Whiteley et al. 2004). This is especially the case for debates about cultural heritage, cities and urban cultural regeneration, where music is very much a part of what makes a city unique and helps to give it character (Lashua et al. 2010).

With a view towards the past, numerous cities have sought to capitalize on their popular music heritage (e.g. Liverpool, Memphis, Detroit, Nashville and others; see Cohen 2007; Cohen et al. 2014; Fry 2017), with varying degrees of success amidst broader attempts to regenerate urban centres, especially in smaller or regional post-industrial cities such as Sheffield (UK), Cleveland (USA), Melbourne or Wollongong (Australia) (Brabazon and Mallinder 2006; Cantillon et al. 2021; Homan et al. 2021; Lashua 2019; Long 2014).

Some interventions to regenerate urban centres through musical activities have been part of a larger cultural policy (Hutton 2009; O'Connor and Shaw 2014) or may have been part of a strategy to address noise, gentrification or zoning of the night-time economy within a local authority's urban planning policy (e.g. Gibson and Homan 2004; Homan 2014; Strong et al. 2017) rather than specific attempts to capitalize on a city's notable music history. As a result, some of these strategies have sidelined local creators and artists. They may have emphasized short-lived, rather than sustainable cultural activities, or exacerbated the instability of an already unstable local musical economy (Scott 2006). Leeds encapsulates and epitomizes these debates, with its new arena (2016) and iconic venues, such as the Brudenell Social Club (established in 1913, rebuilt in 1978, and hosting local musicians and professional touring bands since 1992) in the heart of the student district, and longstanding pubs such as the Fenton (which has been a pub since at least 1872, although it is better known since the 1970s as a punk, post-punk, alternative and metal venue – see Chapter 1 by Rio Goldhammer), or vanished venues such as the Duchess of York (1987–2000; with events put on by John Keenan, including pre-fame Nirvana). Accordingly, our focus on Leeds also necessitates a shift away from a broader mapping of the city to explore what Long (2014: 51) referred to as 'obscure places' in popular music heritage. These explorations include the stories of people and places that have been largely overlooked as well as those that, although neglected, serve as points of entry into explanations of larger events and wider historical processes.

So, why dedicate a book to the popular music histories and heritage of Leeds? As noted above, the musical cultures of Leeds have not been the focus of intensive studies as in other UK cities, such as Liverpool, Manchester, Bristol or Canterbury. We are curious why Leeds – arguably similar to many British post-industrial cities with large student populations such as Sheffield, Newcastle and Birmingham – has remained an 'obscure place' in popular music history. Despite being home to many fascinating musical scenes and cultivating a number of globally recognized artists and bands, Leeds is not widely perceived as a 'music city', and not widely viewed as having its own distinctive (if mythologized) 'sound'. Yet, in some ways the popular music heritage of Leeds is hiding in plain sight, hidden by its perceived ordinariness. A sense of rediscovery is at the heart of this book: to recognize and remark upon Leeds, in some ways an 'ordinary' UK city, yet in other ways an extraordinary one. Perhaps we had failed before to see and appreciate its extraordinariness because it is widely perceived through the lens of the ordinary and unremarkable.

The book extends wider discussions and debates about music, place and heritage in Leeds and beyond. As one of our contributors, Jonathon Long, commented, this book is 'about Leeds and of Leeds, but it is about more than that' (see Chapter 7: 103). For example, the book is about the radical politics of post-punk, collective activism, anti-racist and anti-sexist politics, and the power of music as art. In this context, Leeds serves as a remarkable case. The book is also about the flourishing of creative entrepreneurialism, for example, in do-it-yourself (DIY) dance music and DJ cultures in Leeds stretching back into the 1940s and read across 80 years of the changing city. In this sense, the book captures wider urban changes in connection with innovations and shifts in the music of the city. The book also presents numerous niche scenes in the city – e.g. jazz, hip hop or noise music – read through global musical flows with strong local inflections. In this, several chapters evoke the changing relationships between the local and the global. Additionally, the book is about the ways that the city remembers itself. In official civic discourse and wider media narratives, Leeds seems reluctant to celebrate itself, to embrace and retell its own musical stories. This is, in part, what made the *Sounds of Our City* exhibition so refreshingly vital, because it showcased many stories of why music has mattered in Leeds and, in telling those stories, it said something more about why music (and music heritage) matters in other cities, too. Invariably, it takes special attention to focus and draw out such significances and resonances; as each of our contributors explains – whether in folk, music hall, Americana, calypso, electronic music, hip hop or punk – Leeds is perhaps not a unique musical city, but it is a fascinating city to explore the relations of popular music, places, people, histories and heritage.

## Introducing the chapters

As an atlas of popular music in Leeds, this book is structured in four parts: places, people, histories and heritage. The chapters have been contributed by an array of authors – academics, a museum curator, historians, a politician, a journalist and musicians – and this variety of voices and views is a notable strength of the collection. Part 1 presents chapters that primarily map places of popular music in the city and the wider Yorkshire region. While the chapters in Part 2 maintain geographical perspectives, they shift focus to musical communities and cultural identities – Leeds' people – and the music that informs a sense of belonging in Leeds. Part 3 features histories that showcase broader eras in the city's musical past, from music hall and dance venues to its Caribbean carnival, as well as the city's twentieth-century jazz scenes. Finally, in Part 4, the chapters explore cultural heritage, popular music legacies and the current (re)configurations of music in the city. The concluding chapter draws upon an art installation led by two of the co-editors (Lashua and Thompson) that aimed to map the book overall – as a full-sized wall mapping – to bring together the diverse themes of the collection, while also pointing to gaps and directions for future scholarship. The book's parts and the chapters that comprise them are introduced in further detail, below.

Focused primarily on places of popular music in Leeds, Part 1 also acknowledges the ebb and flow of people and cultural changes in Leeds. The first chapter by Rio Goldhammer takes us into The Fenton, where musical pioneers such as The Mekons, Gang of Four, Delta 5, The Three Johns, March Violets and a host of others contributed to the cultural significance of the post-punk era in Leeds during the late 1970s and early 1980s. The Fenton was also a birthplace of Rock Against Racism, and Goldhammer locates this venue within the sociopolitical crises of post-industrial decline and decay, the Yorkshire Ripper and National Front activity. In Chapter 2, Karl Spracklen shares the history of Mr. Fox, a group that emerged from the 1960s Leeds folk music scene. Situating Leeds in a regional context, the chapter recounts how Mr. Fox constructed an imaginary Yorkshire-ness, blending elements of the historical, spatial and cultural relationships between Leeds, Yorkshire and the Yorkshire Dales. Spracklen locates Mr Fox's attempt to recreate an authentically northern sound through the myth, folklore and magic of Yorkshire. Chapter 3 by Peter Mills takes readers into the suburbs of Leeds, tracing the exceptional history of popular music concerts in Roundhay Park, one of the largest urban parks in Europe. Attracting megastars like The Rolling Stones, Bruce Springsteen, Michael Jackson, U2 and Ed Sheeran from the 1980s through the present, Roundhay Park's open-air arena became an international pop venue and arguably helped to put Leeds on the map as a significant music city. In Chapter 4, Dan Lomax takes us into the underground of the 1990s, with an exploration of key venues in the Leeds indie scene during that time. Although they have vanished from the city's popular musicscape (Cohen 2012), Lomax explores how indie venues, such as The Town & Country Club (est. 1992), The Well (est. 1992) and The Cockpit (est. 1994), offered spaces for a new generation of music promoters and entrepreneurs to develop an interconnected music ecology in the city that continues to endure. Chapter 5 completes Part 1 by venturing into iconoclastic experimental music. Here, Theo Gowans, Phil Legard and Dave Procter introduce the underground noise and power electronics scene of Leeds through a specific focus on the Termite Club, which served as a location for an influential promoter of 'difficult musics' between 1983 and 2010. Although controversial, often confrontational and always niche, the music that featured at the Termite Club found an audience in Leeds' student population, and its legacy in Leeds also endures, if arguably in 'safer spaces' than during its heyday.

Building upon Part 1's geographic foundations, Part 2 of the book explores the people of Leeds by putting the spotlight on varying musical identities and communities. The biography of the Leeds-born singer Jake Thackray (1938–2002) is examined in Chapter 6 by Stephen Wagg. Thackray rooted his music in French chanson and the 'satire boom' of the 1960s. He often sang of women, unfulfilled sexual desires and a mythical Yorkshire. Wagg remarks upon the conflicts that characterized Thackray's life, as well as the recent renewed interest in Thackray as a performer. Jonathan Long (Chapter 7) looks at migration and the role that it has played in the musical makeup of Leeds. Leeds has longstanding Irish and Jewish communities, well-established populations that have roots in the Commonwealth countries of the Caribbean and southern Asia, and more recent migrant flows, from places like Eastern Europe and the Horn of Africa. Long's interlocutors share the ways in which migrants commonly come to the city with few material possessions, but carry within them a cultural repository, including the musical traditions of their country of origin. For Chapter 8, Beccy Watson shares a tale of two Leeds women, Sara and Fuzzy, who became musicians, DJs and producers. Viewed through an intersectional lens that accounts for gender, race, class and place, Watson explores how Leeds has shaped the routes Sara and Fuzzy have taken and ways that intersectional forces have influenced their professional pathways. Chapter 9 returns focus to Leeds punk and post-punk music, but through a feminist lens. Mallory McGovern charts the anti-sexist, anti-elitist and anti-racist principles that characterized elements of this scene in the city. Spotlighting the music and politics of groups such as Gang of Four, the Mekons, Delta 5 and The Catholic Girls, McGovern illustrates how some of the actions taken by feminists and punks during this time found particular resonance with one another. Next, Dave Robinson takes us inside the Americana scene as an ongoing and often vibrant site of counter-hegemonic resistance at the heart of

Leeds in Chapter 10. As some venues have closed, new ones have opened, and a few – like The Grove – continue on. Robinson illustrates how music of the rural American south has come to form part of the musical narrative, and grit, of this northern English city.

Part 3 shares some longstanding yet lesser-known musical histories of Leeds. It begins with music hall, and in Chapter 11, Dave Russell tells the unique story of Leeds City Varieties, set against the broader national decline of the music hall tradition and changing media landscape of music and entertainment as spectacle in the 1950s. Established in 1865, Leeds City Varieties continues to offer a tangible link to a rich performance heritage, and it remains one of the UK's most historically significant live entertainment venues. Chapter 12 shares the remarkable, expansive history of DIY dance music spaces and the rise of DJ cultures in Leeds. From 1940s tearooms and 1950s milk bars through to 1980s warehouses and 1990s raves, then into house parties in the 2010s, Stuart Moss charts how DJs have provided music for audiences who wanted somewhere to dance, using found spaces to make events happen, often in non-traditional spaces for musical performance. In doing so, the chapter traces Leeds' significant role in the development of UK youth (sub) cultures within the changing terrain of music entrepreneurialism. Music journalist and community historian Danny Friar presents an account in Chapter 13 of the Leeds West Indian Carnival (LWIC) and chronicles the ways in which LWIC has played a vital role in preserving, promoting and developing Caribbean music in Britain since the 1960s. The chapter shares the often forgotten and unknown story of Caribbean carnival music in Leeds and its importance to the Leeds West Indian Carnival, the black community in Leeds and the broader musical landscape of Britain. Michael Meadowcroft closes Part 3 of the book and explores Jazz communities in Leeds (Chapter 14). He introduces the post-war Jazz revival that was largely inspired by the influx of records from the United States and notes key musicians and places around Leeds – such as Studio 20. These venues hosted Jazz in the city in the 1940s and 1950s, before entering a period of decline and largely disappearing from view, except for a core of Jazz enthusiasts, like Meadowcroft, who continue to perform in remaining venues.

Part 4 is concerned with popular music heritage in Leeds. It begins where the idea for this book began, at Leeds Museums' exhibition *Sounds of Our City* which opened at Abbey House Museum in January 2020. In Chapter 15, lead curator Kitty Ross (along with co-editor Paul Thompson) guides us through the exhibition, which spans music in Leeds over two centuries – from a 1769 cello used in Hunslet Parish church before they installed an organ, a mix of musical artefacts that may have been found in a Leeds teenager's bedroom ranging from the 1960s to 2000s, to event flyers collected to give a snapshot of the Leeds music scene in 2019. Sarah Little and Alex Stevenson (Chapter 16) explore the Hip Hop scene in Leeds through a unique archival partnership between a recently formed community-led organization, the Hip Hop Historian Society (HHHS) and Leeds Museums. They argue that although Hip Hop in Leeds has been overshadowed by attention to other UK cities, Leeds provided a fertile environment for early pioneers to forge their 'glocal' interpretations of Hip Hop culture. Leeds was a creative base for multiple generations of Hip Hop practitioners. Little and Stevenson introduce the Hip Hop archive as a way of connecting voices, generations and places in Leeds. In Chapter 17, Brett Lashua and Paul Thompson hit the streets of Leeds and take the reader on a psychogeographical tour of the city. Going on a series of walks, they explored the materiality of the city to attempt to answer the question: where is popular music heritage in Leeds? Walking and drifting through the city, they stumbled across some tangible material artefacts of the city's popular music heritage, on the ground and on the walls, including a song tunnel and a surprising connection to the Beatles in a cemetery close to the University of Leeds. Part 4 concludes with a look at Leeds' popular music present and future, in which Paul Thompson and Sam Nicholls (Chapter 18) provide an overview of the cultural, economic, political and environmental factors that have contributed to Leeds' diverse and eclectic music sector and communities, despite lacking a coherent infrastructure to develop new talent or retain established artists. Thompson and Nicholls survey the stakeholders in the private and public sectors, celebrate achievements and remarkable music events and projects, and explore how the variable institutional support over the last 40 years has left the potential for music as a driver in the city unfulfilled.

Finally, in the Conclusion, we return to the notion of the book as an atlas of Leeds popular music. Here, we recount the creation by two of us (Lashua and Thompson) of an art installation (March–April 2022) at a Leeds art gallery, Ginger Works. In this installation, Lashua and Thompson produced a wall-sized mapping of the city that plotted the sites noted in this book's chapters – over 150 venues, pubs, clubs, records stores and other sites of popular music heritage. Yet, even a mapping of this size fails to adequately evoke the historical depth and social complexity of the city, just as a book limited to eighteen chapters can only include a few facets of Leeds' musical histories and heritage, and its people and places. Nevertheless, both the art installation and this book offer different and powerful kinds of cultural mappings. In these, we have sought to 'bring alternative and local perspectives' (Crawhall 2009: 7) to wider attention and showcase distinctive accounts, or mappings, of Leeds. Like the museum exhibition (*Sounds of Our City*) and art installation that served as bookends for this collection of chapters, we believe this book also makes moves to 'transform the intangible and invisible into a medium that can be applied' (Crawhall 2009: 11) to put Leeds and its people, places, histories and heritage 'on the map' as a noteworthy musical city.

# REFERENCES

Baker, Sarah, Istvandity, Lauren and Nowak, Raphael (2016), 'The sound of music heritage: Curating popular music in music museums and exhibitions', *International Journal of Heritage Studies*, 22:1, pp. 70–81.

Baker, Sarah, Strong, Catherine, Istvandity, Lauren and Cantillon, Zelmarie (eds) (2018), *The Routledge Companion to Popular Music History and Heritage*, London: Routledge.

Bennett, Andy (2022), *Popular Music Heritage: Places, Objects, Images and Texts*, Cham: Palgrave Macmillan.

Brabazon, Tara and Mallinder, Stephen (2006), 'Popping the museum: The cases of Sheffield and Preston', *Museum and Society*, 4:2, pp. 96–112.

Butt, Gavin (2022), *No Machos or Pop Stars: When the Leeds Art Experiment Went Punk*, Durham: Duke University Press.

Cantillon, Zelmarie, Baker, Sarah and Nowak, Raphaël (2021), 'Music heritage, cultural justice and the Steel City: Archiving and curating popular music history in Wollongong, Australia', in L. Mahoney and J. Schofield (eds), *Music and Heritage: New Perspectives on Place-making and Sonic Identity*, Abingdon: Routledge, pp. 103–13.

Carr, Paul (2019), 'Lost musical histories: Curating and documenting local popular music-making in the UK', *Popular Music History*, 12:1, pp. 5–14.

Chatterton, Paul and Hollands, Robert (2004), 'The London of the North? Youth cultures, urban change and nightlife', in R. Unsworth and J. Stilwell (eds), *Twenty-first Century Leeds: Geographies of a Regional City*, Leeds: Leeds University Press, pp. 265–91.

Cohen, Sara (2007), *Beyond the Beatles: Decline, Renewal and the City in Popular Music Culture*, Aldershot: Ashgate.

Cohen, Sara (2012), 'Urban musicscapes: Mapping music-making in Liverpool', in L. Roberts (ed.), *Mapping Cultures*, Basingstoke: Palgrave Macmillan, pp. 123–43.

Cohen, Sara, Knifton, Rob, Leonard, Marion and Roberts, Les (eds) (2014), *Sites of Popular Music Heritage: Memories, Histories, Places*, London: Routledge.

Connell, John (2014), 'Sport, leisure and the postmodern city' (book review), *Australian Geographer*, 45:1, pp. 97–99.

Connell, John and Gibson, Chris (2003), *Sound Tracks: Popular Music Identity and Place*, London: Routledge.

Crawhall, Nigel (2009), *The Role of Participatory Cultural Mapping in Promoting Intercultural Dialogue – 'We Are not Hyenas': A Reflection Paper*, United Nations Education Scientific and Cultural Organisation (UNESCO), http://www.iapad.org/wp-content/uploads/2015/07/nigel.crawhall.190753e.pdf. Accessed 1 August 2022.

Draganova, Asya, Blackman, Shane and Bennett, Andy (eds) (2021), *The Canterbury Sound in Popular Music*, Bingley: Emerald Publishing.

Fry, Robbie W. (2017), *Performing Nashville*, Basingstoke: Palgrave.

Gibson, Chris and Homan, Shane (2004), 'Urban redevelopment, live and public space: Cultural performance and the re-making of Marrickville', *International Journal of Cultural Policy*, 10:1, pp. 67–84.

Hesmondhalgh, David (2013), *Why Music Matters*, New York: John Wiley & Sons.

Homan, Shane (2014), 'Liveability and creativity: The case for Melbourne music precincts', *City, Culture and Society*, 5:3, pp. 149–55.

Homan, Shane, O'Hanlan, Seamus, Catherine, Strong and Tebbutt, John (2021), *Music City Melbourne*, London: Bloomsbury Publishing.

Hutton, Thomas (2009), *The New Economy of the Inner City: Restructuring, Regeneration and Dislocation in the 21st century Metropolis*, London: Routledge.

Lashua, Brett (2019), *Popular Music, Popular Myth and Cultural Heritage in Cleveland: The Moondog, the Buzzard and the Battle for the Rock and Roll Hall of Fame*, Bingley: Emerald.

Lashua, Brett, Cohen, Sara and Schofield, John (2010), 'Popular music, mapping and the characterisation of Liverpool', *Popular Music History*, 4:2, pp. 127–46.

Lashua, Brett and Skeldon, Gabby (2023), 'Youth, music and the city: A mapping of Leeds in five scenes', in A. Bennett (ed.), *The Bloomsbury Handbook of Popular Music and Youth Culture*, London: Bloomsbury, pp. 491–510.

Lashua, Brett, Spracklen, Karl and Wagg, Stephen (eds) (2014), *Sounds and the City: Popular Music, Place, and Globalization*, Basingstoke: Palgrave Macmillan.

Lashua, Brett, Wagg, Stephen, Spracklen, Karl and Yavuz, Selim (eds.) (2019), *Sounds and the City: Volume 2*, Cham: Palgrave Macmillan.

Leyshon, Andrew, Matless, David and Revill, George (eds) (1998), *The Place of Music*, New York: Guilford Press.

Long, Philip (2014), 'Popular music, psychogeography, place identity and tourism: The case of Sheffield', *Tourist Studies*, 14:1, pp. 48–65.

Mahoney, Liam and Schofield, John (eds) (2021), *Music and Heritage: New Perspectives on Place-Making and Sonic Identity*, Abingdon: Routledge.

O'Brien, Lucy (2012), 'Can I have a taste of your ice cream?', *Punk & Post-Punk*, 1:1, pp. 27–40.

O'Connor, Justin and Shaw, Kate (2014), 'What next for the creative city?', *City, Culture and Society*, 5:3, pp. 165–70.

Population UK (2022), 'Leeds population 2022', https://www.ukpopulation.org/leeds-population/. Accessed 17 February 2022.

Riches, Gabby and Lashua, Brett (2014), 'Mapping the underground: An ethnographic cartography of the Leeds extreme metal scene', *International Journal of Community Music*, 7:2, pp. 223–41.

Roberts, Les and Cohen, Sara (2014), 'Unauthorising popular music heritage: Outline of a critical framework', *International Journal of Heritage Studies*, 20:3, pp. 241–61.

Scott, Allen J. (2006), 'Creative cities: Conceptual issues and policy questions', *Journal of Urban Affairs*, 28:1, pp. 1–17.

Smith, Laurajane (2006), *Uses of Heritage*, Abingdon: Routledge.

Solnit, Rebecca (2010), *Infinite City: A San Francisco Atlas*, Berkeley: University of California Press.

Spracklen, Karl, Henderson, Steve and Procter, Dave (2016), 'Imagining the scene and the memory of the F-Club: Talking about lost punk and post-punk spaces in Leeds', *Punk & Post-Punk*, 5:2, pp. 147–62.

Spracklen, Karl, Richter, Anna and Spracklen, Beverley (2013), 'The eventization of leisure and the strange death of alternative Leeds', *City*, 17:2, pp. 164–78.

Strong, Catherine, Cannizzo, Fabian and Rogers, Ian (2017), 'Aesthetic cosmopolitan, national and local popular music heritage in Melbourne's music laneways', *International Journal of Heritage Studies*, 2:2, pp. 83–96.

Thompson, Paul and Sam Nicholls (2021), 'Music:Leeds – Supporting a regionalised music sector and scene', in R. Hepworth-Sawyer, J. Paterson and R. Toulson (eds), *Innovation in Music: Future Opportunities*, Abingdon: Routledge, pp. 432–34.

Unsworth, Rachel and Stilwell, John (eds) (2004), *Twenty-First Century Leeds: Geographies of a Regional City*, Leeds: Leeds University Press.

Waxer, Lise A. (2002), *The City of Musical Memory: Salsa, Record Grooves and Popular Culture in Cali, Colombia*, Middletown: Wesleyan University Press.

Whiteley, Sheila, Bennett, Andy and Hawkins, Stan (eds) (2004), *Music, Space and Place: Popular Music and Cultural Identity*, Aldershot: Ashgate.

# PART 1

## PLACES OF LEEDS' POPULAR MUSIC

# 1

# Dance and Drink the Fenton: Fighting for Territory in Leeds' Culture Wars

*Rio Goldhammer*

Home to John Keenan's seminal Futurama festivals, genre pioneers such as The Mekons, Gang of Four, Delta 5, The Three Johns, March Violets, a host of others, and the birthplace of Rock Against Racism (Leeds Libraries 2019), Leeds is a place of immense cultural significance to the post-punk era of 1978–84. Against the backdrop of post-industrial decay, the Yorkshire Ripper (O'Brien 2012) and National Front activity, Leeds was primed for the oppositionality and politicism that became the hallmark of the aforesaid artists.

In Goldhammer (2019), I argued that the prominence of Leeds in this era was overshadowed in the collective consciousness, and in academia, by an approach to 'the north' which is often Manchester-centric (its groups, such as Joy Division/New Order, Magazine, The Fall and The Smiths, are often considered synonymous with the era). Over recent years though, through O'Brien (2012), and the works of Spracklen et al. (2016), Spracklen and Spracklen (2018), Trowell (2016) and others since the Leeds band the Kaiser Chiefs topped the charts during the 2000s 'Post-Punk Revival' period, the city has been under a renewed interest in both academia and popular culture. In April 2019, Dave Simpson published an article in *The Guardian* celebrating Leeds' post-punk bands of the late 1970s, stating: 'against the backdrop of the Yorkshire Ripper and Fascist thugs, bands in late-1970s Leeds started creating the most dynamic DIY music in the UK – and all from a single pub' (2019: n. pag.). Later that year, Leeds Libraries (2019) published a piece on Rock Against Racism on their heritage blog, drawing together archival evidence from the eponymous series of concerts in the era and setting the scene for a politically charged and highly influential period in the city's history. The following year, both independent and mainstream press mourned the passing of Gang of Four guitarist Andy Gill, with unwavering praise for the group's legacy (see Sweeting 2020).

However, it is this 'single pub' that is the focus of this chapter. The pub in question, the Fenton, on Woodhouse Lane, is more than a journalistic convenience. Although 'all from a single pub' is too simplistic, the Fenton is ubiquitous in the testimony of key participants in the scene of this era. In Dooley (2018), Rachel (2016), Heylin (2007) and Reynolds (2005), and in numerous hours of interviews recorded as part of my own research, the Fenton is brought up time and time again. The home of a number of Leeds' leftist do-it-yourself (DIY) bands, the pub was also the target of an infamous 1978 'attack' by the National Front, who themselves claimed to have a 'stranglehold on [Leeds'] punk scene' (Forbes and Stampton 2015: 10).

But what is so important about the Fenton? Could its proximity to university campuses make it of strategic geographical importance? Through a review of existing testimony, a re-examining of the data collected in my doctoral research, and additional data collected from two further key participants – one new and one interviewed previously – with a specific focus on the Fenton, this is what this chapter will seek to determine.

## *The Fenton in post-punk memory and mythology: A physical permanence in a constructed landscape*

In both the theoretical and methodological approaches to this chapter, there is a close resemblance to Spracklen et al. (2016), who performed an ethnographic social discourse analysis of the memory and mythology of Leeds' F-Club: a punk and post-punk club night in the 1970s and 1980s. The memory and mythology of the Fenton explored in this chapter take place in the same era, in the same city, and often refer to the same bands and fans as the F-Club. Their mythology is therefore necessarily intertwined in the memories of Leeds' musical heritage, and this chapter is likewise concerned with 'structural accounts of identity and community' (150). Subsequently, it is similarly informed by cultural theorists such as the likes of Gramsci (1971), Hebdige (1979) and Hall (1993), alongside Bourdieusian notions of habitus and cultural capital (1986). In the case of the latter, there is an important strain within the cultural theory that refers specifically to *sub*cultural capital, notably in Thornton's (1996) research on 'club' cultures. As a perspective that effectively navigates the seminal subcultural theory of Hebdige and Hall in the Gramscian and Bourdieusian context of class and capital, Thornton's work has an unwavering influence on research such as mine and forms an important part of the theoretical framework for my doctoral research: an ethnography of cultural identity and heritage in the Yorkshire post-punk scene, for which purpose the bulk of the primary research presented in this chapter was taken, but in the specific case of this chapter it is not of primary importance. The reason for this is largely methodological, which will become clearer in the next section, because the participants featured in this chapter are among those that memories of post-punk are constructed *around*, and there is therefore no discernible need for them to construct an identity of 'belonging' to the subculture (although there is the additional consideration of personal and professional legacy). However, the constructed narratives of community and identity through imagination and myth (Pickering and Keightley 2013; Anderson 1983) are just as important to this chapter as in Spracklen et al.'s (2016) F-Club paper.

Where the Fenton and the F-Club fundamentally differ, though, is a matter of geographical permanence. Physical geography plays an important part in the mythology of place (see O'Brien 2012: 28, Connell and Gibson 2003: 14), and in the case of Leeds in the 1970s and 1980s, it represents a bleak post-industrial city in the midst of Thatcherite neo-liberal reform. This is why Spracklen et al. wrote: 'in the face of capitalism and in these contested leisure spaces, we have to be Marxists' (2016: 150); moreover, the physical space of Leeds – and more specifically its university campus – is credited with influencing the music of the city's seminal post-punk groups. O'Brien stated the music of bands such as The Mekons and Gang of Four 'echoed the stark campus architecture' of the university (2012: 29), and furthermore that the spectre of serial killer Peter Sutcliffe contributed not only to the political charge of post-punk at this time but also began to influence the built environment of the city itself. She writes: 'walls and cars were daubed with slogans like "CASTRATE ALL MEN" and "DISARM RAPISTS" […] many postpunk performers embodied that tension' (O'Brien 2012: 36).

In Goldhammer (2019), I argued, using the example of Keighley, a town that was absorbed by the metropolitan area of nearby Bradford and for where this distinction is either ignored or reinforced depending on the intent of the narrator, that even the physical geography of place has a fluidity through memory that can adapt to suit its mythology. This chapter will use this approach to unpick the mythology of a single pub and to test the hypothesis that the fraught, violent and volatile culture of Leeds in the 1970s and 1980s, which provided the backdrop for the original post-punk movement – arguably the most enduring music legacy of the north of England – manifested in territorial claims to the city's pubs on behalf of far-right and left-wing activists.

### *What it means to be a post-punk ethnographer …*

As stated previously, the starting point for this chapter was existing primary data gathered as part of a mixed-method ethnography of post-punk identity in Yorkshire, with a specific focus on the 1978–84 period which tends to be regarded as the defining epoch of the genre (see Reynolds 2005, 2010). Hodkinson's research on the goth subculture (2002) has been an important methodological influence on this research. Beyond the fact that the genres of post-punk and goth have significant overlap, to the extent that the boundaries between the two are often blurred, Hodkinson utilized his insider status to begin the snowball sampling of participants for qualitative data collection – via semi-structured interviews – and to conduct participant observation without first having to gain access (2002: 5). My own insider status comes from my role as the vocalist in 1919: a Bradford band formed in 1980, who played a notable role in the post-punk scene of the era in question, if somewhat on the fringes compared to some of the band's contemporaries. One of the important things about my role here, though, is that I am not an original member of the group, and in fact was not born until 1990, six years after they originally disbanded. Whether I can definitively be considered an 'insider', then, is not certain, and this question of authenticity is a vital epistemological concern in this research (see Goldhammer 2021), especially as I seek to analyze the interview data alongside autoethnographic field notes. However, as 'insider accounts have been criticized for their over-reliance on insider knowledge and their necessary subjectivity' (Spracklen et al. 2016: 148; see also Bottero and Crossley 2011; Jarman et al. 2014), it is also my hope that some of these limitations will be mitigated in a research perspective that is both outside and in.

Where there are potential methodological limitations in this research, though, are in sample size and a reliance on interviews. But these are inevitable. As previously alluded to with reference to Thornton (1996), participant observation is not possible in matters of memory. Additionally, in attempting to gain the perspectives of post-punk performers rather than fans, there are necessarily far fewer potential respondents and many of the more prominent voices are well documented. However, reliance on such accounts, as Spracklen et al. highlight above, is rightfully open to suspicion, and is furthermore a fertile environment for the propagation of a mythology which places these voices in high esteem. It is for this reason that I sought to focus on key participants who, whilst influential in their own right, are below the surface of popular narratives of post-punk. Through an analysis of secondary perspectives, a re-examining of two previously recorded interviews with musicians from this era, a third performed with the Fenton in mind, and finally with notes made from an informal conversation with a key participant, it is my hope that while the snapshot of the era and place will be relatively small, it should be enough to shed new light on an important narrative in Leeds' cultural history.

## The importance of the Fenton in Leeds post-punk discourse

*Against the backdrop of the Yorkshire Ripper and fascist thugs, bands in late-70s Leeds started creating the most dynamic DIY music in the UK – and all from a single pub.*

(Simpson 2019: n.pag.)

The pub in question, the Fenton, is on Woodhouse Lane in Leeds, West Yorkshire, England. It sits on the main road in front of the University of Leeds' city centre campus, just a few hundred metres from the heart of the campus itself (see Figure 1.1). As stated in the introduction to this chapter, the pub is frequently name-checked in accounts of Leeds' post-punk scene of the 1970s and 1980s, and its importance to influential groups of the time is summarized in the aforesaid newspaper article: 'Gang of Four initially rehearsed in the university's film society, which adjoined the Fenton. When they nipped to the pub, their friends picked up their instruments and called themselves Mekons' (Simpson 2019: n.pag.).

Simpson's article also sets the scene for the era in striking terms: of violence, sociopolitical unrest and artistic innovation – a narrative reinforced by the Leeds Library blog, which cites Soft Cell's Marc Almond (among the most commercially successful artists with ties to the city in this era) by stating that between 1977 and 1981, Leeds 'was such a heavy town for the National Front […] skinheads, they were scary' (2019: n.pag.; see Stubbs 2014). In academic literature, Lucy O'Brien

FIGURE 1.1: A Google Maps view of the University of Leeds campus, showing the Fenton nearby.

(2012) offers a detailed account of Leeds at this time, and this is further reinforced by the testimony collected by Spracklen et al.:

> the National Front was a fixture in city streets and outside the Elland Road football ground of Leeds United. Some of that extreme Right-Wing politics filtered into the Leeds punk scene, and some [of our] respondents recalled the presence of these neo-Nazis at gigs and outside gigs. At the same time, much of the alternative punk scene was driven by Radical Left-Wing politics, especially associated with the students […] there was a strong awareness by many of our respondents of this Left/Right politics divide in the scene.
>
> (2016: 153)

Frequently, accounts of the scene in this era refer to a specific incident of violence at the Fenton, perpetrated by the far-right National Front (see Simpson 2019; Worley and Copsey 2016: 37). Gang of Four's Hugo Burnham recounted in Heylin (2007) that the Fenton 'occasionally attracted the British Movement element' (341), while, referring to the night of the 'attack', the Mekons' Kevin Lycett recounted to Dave Simpson:

> One night the Fenton was attacked. 'I think they thought: "There's a load of weirdos and anarchists there and we're going to hurt them" […] "Somebody picked up a beer glass and threw it across the room and it hit Dick, a political activist. Everyone got up and we chased them down the street. After a short running battle, it was over, but it was shocking, because this was the only place we had"'.
>
> (2019: n.pag.)

Gang of Four's Andy Gill highlights the same incident in Rachel (2016): 'It was shocking when the National Front smashed up the Fenton. Friends of ours were there: lots of chairs flying, glass smashing, people getting hit. They targeted art students and bohemian types and gays' (2016: 208–09).

There are few accounts of this night, though, from the perpetrators. One exception is former National Front organizer Eddy Morrison, whose self-published memoir (Morrison 2005) is cited frequently by Forbes and Stampton (2015) as they attempt to depict a right-wing perspective on the era. Morrison refers to the incident at the Fenton too, though by his account, it was potentially less organized than could be suspected:

> On a very warm night in August 1978, I was at the head of a group of 40 NF members, all from Leeds, who gate-crashed a Sham 69 concert at the F Club – we had been banned. The F Club was still situated in Chapeltown, the Afro-Caribbean

area of the city. We halted the concert which escalated into a mini street battle with some rastas outside the venue. Stacks of police arrived and we scattered, meeting up again at a pub called the Fenton in the student area. Unbeknownst to us, the [Anti-Nazi League] were having a gay/lesbian social in the Fenton that night. The evening turned into a really bloody fight with 29 injured.

(2015: 13)

For someone such as Morrison, who is no stranger to grandiosity, this is a surprisingly muted account. Elsewhere in his account of the era, Morrison is keen to stress the dominance of the far-right in post-punk spaces. For example, there is a note of pride in his claim that leftist bands, 'in particular The Mekons […] stopped playing the F Club because we brought every one of their gigs to a halt' (Forbes and Stampton 2015: 10–11).

We controlled the F Club, basically […] We also held a weekly Friday Bowie/Roxy night at the Adelphi Pub in Leeds city centre with some nationalist stuff in between – strictly 'All-White Music Night' we billed it. Those Friday night events were 100% NF whereas at the F Club, although we dominated, a lot of normal punks came along too. The reds attacked the pub three times, but the landlord was very pro-NF and we kicked them out of it each time. The Adelphi, the Prince of Wales and the Scarborough Taps were all NF/RAC pubs. The Prince of Wales was basically 100% NF customers. Alan the manager was totally reliant on our customers to the extent that once when John Tyndall came up and we had lost the main city centre venue, we went to the Prince and put the pool table out into the street to give room inside for John Tyndall to speak!

(Forbes and Stampton 2015: 10–11)

There are a few considerations, then, to make of his account of the Fenton 'attack'. The Fenton is quite far from Chapeltown: around a mile and a half, which though not necessarily prohibitive on foot makes it an unlikely next destination without some kind of foresight, and certainly no closer than the purported city centre strongholds to their point of origin. It's possible that, as a student pub, the Fenton may have been considered a kind of neutral territory by Morrison and his affiliates but were simply unable to resist causing trouble when confronted by a 'gay/lesbian social'. However, it is also unlikely that a group of far-right 'soldiers' (to use the titular terminology of Morrison's account) would be happy to admit, after an organized attack, to being chased 'down the street' (Simpson 2019: n.pag.) by a group of 'art students and bohemian types and gays' (Rachel 2016: 209). Though with these considerations in mind, it should be stated that the real motivation and level of organization that preceded the event can never be definitively known. Instead, we have two narratives: left-wing students under attack from neo-Fascists and emerging as cultural pioneers, and the immediate hegemony of the latter which could take or leave the fleeting resistance of the former. These are the narratives at play in the memory of the Fenton, and it must be the focus of this research to – rather than fruitlessly attempt to separate fact from fiction – shed light on how this interplay contributes to cultural mythology.

### Who gets to tell the story of Leeds? New perspectives from this research

*We all lived in the same house: Mekons, Delta 5, Gang of Four, Me and Marian ['Kitty' Lux] [...] Cromer House. End of Cromer Terrace.*
(John, interview, 4 September 2018)

Although fact and fiction in memorialized accounts cannot be separated categorically, there are nonetheless some fixed points of reference. For example, there is additional evidence, from my primary research, to support the assertion that the Fenton was indeed at the heart of the Leeds counterculture of the era. The above quote, from an interview with a member of the Three Johns, demonstrates the hyperlocalized habitus of a number of seminal Leeds groups. As March Violets' Rosie puts it: 'we all kind of hung around the University – went to the Fenton, the Faversham. There was a pub culture' (interview, 10 July 2018). My interview with John also credits the pub as the setting for the formal inception of the group:

> Everybody in the year above us, which was Mekons, they all went back to London cos they finished their course. Except for John Langford. And so, basically, there was me, John Langford, and John Diamond left in Leeds, and we were in the Fenton and Ralph (from Ralph & the Ponytails, whose real name's Michael) – we were having a pint in the Fenton and decided we might as well form a band because we were left and called it Three Johns and a Michael. But Michael never turned up, so it got shortened!
> (interview, 4 September 2018)

One of the main considerations in my doctoral research is to uncover, if it exists, a kind of essential Yorkshireness, and attempt to dissect how this might manifest in the music produced in the region. A prominent perception of Yorkshire identity has to do with birthright, with Yorkshire's cricket captain stating in 2010: 'I dream of leading out a team of players born and bred in the county' (Hopps 2010: n.pag.;

see also Fletcher 2012). Eventually suggesting in Goldhammer (2019) that such goalposts are moved freely in the name of furthering the mythological heritage of a given place, I had wondered whether the university bands – almost exclusively non-native to Leeds – had felt a specific attachment to the city. As the above quote had suggested a relatively short existence in the city, the subsequent part of the conversation carried on in this ballpark:

**Did you stick about after your courses had ended?**
We did.

**How come?**
Dunno … Well I didn't wanna go back to Wolverhampton cos I'd had enough of it. Langford I guess didn't want to go back to Newport in Wales. Brenny was on his way to India, as were a lot of people in Leeds who'd come from Belfast.

**[Oh] Right? Why?**
They'd left Belfast to escape the troubles, got as far as Leeds and their money'd run out. But they were actually on their way to India!

**I never knew that! Never heard of that before…**
There was a whole crowd of Belfast lads…

**Tranna get to India!?**
… spend all their money, get completely paralytic, and stay that way for years!

**Why India?**
Well that's what you did in those days.

(John, interview, 4 September 2018)

This particular anecdote reminded me of Davy, an Irish Leeds resident who is a good friend through music and political circles. I remember him telling me some years ago that he used to pester the Three Johns to let him replace their drum machine in the band (to no avail), and the alignment of these things identified him as having the potential to be able to give some additional focus to this paper. After introducing the research and telling Davy I'm writing about the Fenton, I start with John's description of the Irish diaspora landing in Leeds, ostensibly en route to India:

Yeah, yeah […] I know John Hyatt very well anyway, because Brenny from the Three Johns, we had a band together. We played the Fenton. We were called the

Super Mystics; it was a fuckin awesome band [...] we were doing really well but the bass player died. Spencer, he was a beautiful guy, just a chronic alcoholic. But yeah we had the band called the Super Mystics. Brenny was one of them, he was the Three Johns; I was playing in another Leeds band, and then with [...] a blues fella, but also the Mekons – obviously [John] Langford – I dipped into that thing. So we had these crossover bands.

**When you say you dipped in, were you in a band with John Langford for a bit?**
Kevin Mekon [Lycett], and the accordion player Eric [Bellis], we had this sort of offshoot band – almost alive about two years ago - called the Hill Bandits: sort of a rockabilly band from that. So we all knew each other in that sort of big circle of what was goin on in the 80s, the back end of the 80s, maybe even early 90s.

(Davy, interview, 6 November 2021)

Davy had moved to England from Belfast in late 1979 to early 1980, initially to pursue music in London before joining his girlfriend in Leeds in 1981–82 who was a student in the city. However, this wasn't necessarily to 'escape' the troubles as such. Despite performing at the Europa Hotel during a bomb attack, he said it 'didn't really bother' him, although the relentless sectarianism – in particular from British loyalists – was a significant concern for an ardent leftist. Asked about Morrison's claim to certain pubs in the city, and in particular the Adelphi:

I didn't, myself, see that. I knew they were around. But I never, by coincidence or whatever, 'got' to see them. I knew they were there. We confronted them once or twice in the middle of Leeds, just because they used to sell that fucking book – I can't remember what it's called – and some of them had Leeds United caps on, but that's easy pickin for them [...] even the Gang of Four, I don't really remember seeing the Gang of Four – [though] I probably have seen [them] – around everything else that was going on [...]

I know the Adelphi [...] I know it was a fantastic fuckin venue, but I mainly knew it for bonkers jazz! It was like a free jazz thing and I had mates goin on in there. But I remember Nick Griffin being chased [down there] by a couple of friends of ours [...]

Coming back to the Fenton, playing fucking riotous music there n whatever else, but nobody ever came in to give us a hiding. Maybe they knew we were there: two fuckin Irishmen! Sorry, three Irishmen! No, they never did show up and fuck us about that's for sure. But I knew they were out there.

**But was it kind of a leftist hangout, the Fenton?**
It was a student hangout … […] There was the Fenton, the Eldon […] The Adelphi was the other end of town. That's an easy one. But the ones up near Headingley? Never used to get any truck with any of that.

**[…] It feels like there's maybe an idea that certain pubs belonged to certain groups?**
I'll tell you what, if there was I'd have known about that. But no, I don't think that was a thing. Maybe the odd one or two of them creeping in, trying to corrupt young minds.

**The Adelphi, Scarborough Taps […] there was never anywhere you thought "we can't go in there, it's a fash [fascist] pub" or whatever?**
Scarborough Taps I've only been into a few times […] Again, the bottom end of town. All the workers would drink in there and that. But no, never got that. The Adelphi, never got that. In fact, Republica [a left-wing amateur football team in Leeds, of which Davy and I are both members] we used to meet down there […] If I'd have had thought that was there, one of two things would have happened: 1, we'd have been down there just to get in their faces, and 2, we'd have avoided the fuckin' place cos they're just arseholes.

[…] We'd have known about it. In the 80s we'd have known about it no problem. Saying that, I was very, very drunk!

When I was ready to submit this chapter initially I was at a gig with Wolfy, a prominent musician from the era through his work with Expelaires and Red Lorry Yellow Lorry. He is a key participant in my doctoral research, though we didn't discuss the Fenton in our recorded interview. When I mentioned this chapter he had a lot to say and was happy for me to note down the key points as best I could. In summary:

- Expelaires were a 'town' band, not a student band. So they didn't go up to the Fenton.
- Talked about the National Front (NF) 'going after' it. People in hospital, people in prison. It was horrible.
- In 1978, Expelaires used to drink in the Guilford in the city centre. The pub became a popular NF spot, but he and his mates were left alone. That was true even when they'd played Rock Against Racism gigs. It was 'all there', 'all nasty', but 'we didn't wanna give it up' (the pub).
- Mentioned the F-Club, and the night they'd put the (far-right) dentists on. He says John Keenan (the promoter) wanted the night to be inclusive, but this was too much.
- Had a run-in with the NF lot at Elland Road. Thought they'd be ok because they're Leeds fans but were beaten up to chants of 'we all hate punks'.

Crucial here is the mention of the Guilford, which was not listed in Morrison's claimed NF territory. Returning to Rosie, there are some signs that the Fenton was just one of many student haunts in Leeds at this time:

**So you kind've met one or two of the others at uni [...] Wo' they at the Fenton?**
Well no [...] It was at uni, mates of mates, I knew Si [Denbigh's] current girlfriend [...] You know, everyone seemed to be in and out of everyone's houses, student parties …

**Normal Hyde Park stuff?**
Normal Hyde Park stuff! Student parties, everyone goes round to everyone else's houses, you hang around for hours and hours, sometimes you stay the weekend …

**That was my first experience of Manchester! [...] I 'ad some mates who were a couple of school years above me and they'd just started uni here, so I used to come down on the Friday [...], walk down to Fallowfield, get a kebab and a bottle of cider, and then we'd go to Jilly's!**
Ooh, Jilly's! Yeah …

**[Now] a Tesco Express!**
I'm not sure if it's a complete urban legend, but just after it converted to the Tesco, a friend of a friend – so it's probably an urban legend – was arrested for moshing in one of the aisles!

**It's more fun to believe that!**
It is! But no, many years spent at Jilly's.

(Rosie, interview, 10 July 2018)

From these accounts alone, the Fenton, if not interchangeable with other pubs favoured by students at the University of Leeds, certainly there does not appear to be much in the way of elevated status. The others mentioned, the Eldon and the Faversham, are a few hundred yards up Woodhouse Lane and across the university campus, respectively, and are frequented by students to this day. But at the end of this exchange, referring to the now-closed Manchester rock bar Jilly's, it is possible to identify some of the 'daily myth-making' referred to by Spracklen et al. (2016: 159) as a key contributor to identity through idealized notions of the past. Although in this case the myth is asserted as likely just that, an 'urban legend', it is nonetheless a romanticized account given by one of the club's former dwellers for the enjoyment of another: one that is more appealing to both parties than any likely truth as it better fits the shared imaginary of the bygone community. It is plausible, therefore, that this could be at play in the memories of the Fenton, especially among those for whom political oppositionality plays an important part in personal identity. I would like to emphasize, though, that this is not to be sceptical of any events cited by primary or secondary sources, and certainly to acknowledge that the violence of post-punk-era Leeds is of far greater sensitivity and severity than the myth of supermarket moshing, but is something that should be taken into account when considering whether any cultural significance should be placed specifically on the Fenton pub. In this regard, there are two final pieces of primary data that I will present before my concluding thoughts: first, a suggestion from Rosie that it might be oversimplistic to consider students as a homogenous group:

**You're never kind've been seen as one of the "university" bands, in the same way I suppose as Delta 5 …**
… Gang of Four […] Yeah, it's funny. We never felt like a university band, and also we felt very different to things like the Delta 5 and Gang of Four–

**Because they were attached to the art department as well?**
They were. And art students didn't mix with mere mortals! In fact one of the only art students we did know was the lovely John Hyatt! I found a lot of art students thought that we were kind of lesser forms – somewhere lower down on the evolutionary scale! But you know, it's like […] I was never ashamed of going to university – it's not like I pretended that I didn't – but we didn't feel particularly attached to the university. We were a Leeds band.
(Rosie, interview, 10 July 2018)

## *What can we learn from all of this?*

The first point of note is one of ethnographic methods. Although existentially faced with, as I have addressed in Goldhammer (2021), the notion of authenticity as a critically reflexive insider researcher, the manner of Wolfy's contribution to this chapter demonstrates rather convincingly my proximity to my area of research interest. For the most part, my participants are friends, acquaintances and friends of friends, and as such, it is difficult to draw a definitive line under the research process or the potential for ontological development. This is one of the reasons why ethnographers such as Ben Carrington (2016) and Liza Grandia (2015) advocate for 'slow' ethnographies, of years or decades in length, and even then, 'even the best ethnographies can only ever produce partial knowledge' (Carrington 2008: 442, see also 434 and Anderson 2002: 1548).

With this in mind, there are a number of directions research such as this could take, and indeed there have been two unexpected turns in the process: first, Davy having no real memory of a far-right presence in any of his (many) trips to the pub, and ,second, Wolfy's determination to keep the same local, in spite of the 'nasty' encroachment of the same. There are questions to be asked of memory and identity, especially given the combination of alcohol and passing decades, but fundamentally the notion of habitus, of social space 'from which ordinary agents [ ] see the social world' (Bourdieu 1984: 169; 1973: 56; see also Branch 2014: 22), is at its core. Spracklen et al. state:

> there was an awareness of a split between students and locals in the scene, but different memories about the consequences of that split. For some of the respondents, the students were identified as being more 'artsy' or more (Left-Wing) political, whereas the locals were more into punk for the music.
>
> (2016: 153)

Although this type of 'split' is supported by my participants, to split between students and locals alone appears to be too simplistic. As Rosie's testimony shows, among students there was something of a split between art students and non-art students; Wolfy's testimony, compared to the account of Morrison, suggests multiple habitus among the NF, and as Davy shows it's possible for the myriad habitus of students and non-students to exist in the same space, without each becoming aware of the other. What's clear, though, is that non-student punks seemed to attract less unwanted attention from the far-right than their student counterparts – save for Wolfy's experience at Elland Road – perhaps out of some sense of local pride or perhaps simply because, as Davy suggested, they were perceived to be a more difficult target. If that's the case it may explain the emboldened attack at the football ground, and if the Fenton is (or was) considered more or less an extension of the University campus, culturally or geographically, then this could be an important part of Leeds' cultural mythology.

## APPENDIX: INTERVIEWS AND PERSONAL COMMUNICATIONS
Davy. Interview (online – WhatsApp), 6 November 2021.
John. Interview (in-person – Liverpool), 4 September 2018.
Rosie. Interview (in-person – Manchester), 10 July 2018.
Wolfy. Personal communication (in-person – Baildon), 17 December 2021.

## REFERENCES
Anderson, Benedict (1983), *Imagined Communities*, London: Verso.
Anderson, Elijah (2002), 'The ideologically driven critique', *American Journal of Sociology*, 107:6, pp. 1533–50.

Bottero, Wendy and Crossley, Nick (2011), 'Worlds, fields and networks: Becker, Bourdieu and the structures of social relations', *Cultural Sociology*, 5:1, pp. 99–119.

Bourdieu, Pierre (1973), 'Cultural reproduction and social reproduction', in R. Brown (ed.), *Knowledge, Education and Cultural Change: Papers in the Sociology of Education*, London: Tavistock.

Bourdieu, Pierre (1984), *Distinction: A Social Critique of the Judgement of Taste* (trans. R. Nice), Cambridge: Harvard University Press.

Branch, André (2014), '"Stop flexing your roots, man": Reconversion strategies, consecrated heretics and the violence of UK first-wave punk', *Punk & Post-Punk*, 3:1, pp. 21–39.

Carrington, Ben (2008), '"What's the footballer doing here?" Racialized performativity, reflexivity, and identity', *Cultural Studies ↔ Critical Methodologies*, 8:4, pp. 423–452.

Carrington, Ben (2016), 'Slow ethnography: A political and methodological manifesto', Lecture delivered at the University of Leeds, Leeds, 1 June, https://www.eventbrite.co.uk/e/dr-ben-carrington-slow-ethnography-a-political-and-methodological-manifesto-tickets-25235897248?utm-medium=discovery&utm-campaign=social&utm-content=attendeeshare&aff=estw&utm-source=tw&utm-term=listing. Accessed 21 September 2022.

Connell, John and Gibson, Chris (2003), *Sound Tracks: Popular Music, Identity and Place*, London: Routledge.

Dooley, James (2018), *Red Set: A History Gang of Four*, London: Watkins.

Fletcher, Thomas (2012), 'All Yorkshiremen are from Yorkshire, but some are more "Yorkshire" than others: British Asians and the myths of Yorkshire cricket', *Sport in Society*, 15:2, pp. 227–45.

Forbes, Robert and Stampton, Eddie (2015), *The White Nationalist Skinhead Movement: UK & USA, 1979–1993*, Port Townsend: Feral House.

Goldhammer, Rio (2019), 'Provincial towns and Yorkshire cities: Post-punk sounds, suburban escape, and metro-hegemony', in B. Lashua, S. Wagg, K. Spracklen and M. Yavuz (eds), *Sounds and the City: Leisure Studies in a Global Era*, Cham: Palgrave Macmillan.

Goldhammer, Rio (2021), 'Authenticity in an insider-in ethnography of post-punk', *Punk & Post Punk*, 10:3, pp. 439–61.

Google Maps (2021), 'University of Leeds campus', https://www.google.com/maps/place/The+Fenton/@53.806213,-1.5545522,17z/data=!4m5!3m4!1s0x48795c02582c1ea5:-0xac00934b42db0895!8m2!3d53.8057246!4d-1.5495432. Accessed 1 December 2021.

Gramsci, Antonio (1971), *Selections from Prison Notebooks*, London: Lawrence and Wishart.

Grandia, Liza (2015), 'Slow ethnography: A hut with a view', *Critique of Anthropology*, 35:3, pp. 301–17.

Hall, Stuart (1993), 'Culture, community, nation', *Cultural Studies*, 7:3, pp. 349–63.

Hebdige, Dick (1979), *Subculture: The Meaning of Style*, London: Routledge.

Heylin, Clinton (2007), *Babylon's Burning: From Punk to Grunge*, London: Penguin.

Hodkinson, Paul (2002), *Goth: Identity, Style and Subculture*, Oxford: Berg.

Hopps, David (2010), 'Captain Andrew Gale would welcome return to Yorkshire-born tradition', *The Guardian*, 19 April, https://www.theguardian.com/sport/2010/apr/19/andrew-gale-yorkshire-county-cricket. Accessed 10 November 2021.

Jarman, David, Theodoraki, Eleni, Hall, Hazel and Ali-Knight, Jane (2014), 'Social network analysis and festival cities: An exploration of concepts, literature and methods', *International Journal of Event and Festival Management*, 5:3, pp. 311–22.

Leeds Libraries (2019), 'Rock Against Racism', *The Secret Library | Leeds Libraries Heritage Blog*, 25 October, https://secretlibraryleeds.net/2019/10/25/rock-against-racism/. Accessed 10 November 2021.

Morrison, Eddie (2005), *Memoirs of a Street Soldier: A Life in White Nationalism*, London: British People's Party.

O'Brien, Lucy (2012), 'Can I have a taste of your ice cream?', *Punk & Post Punk*, 1:1, pp. 27–40.

Pickering, Michael and Keightley, Emily (2013), 'Communities of memory and the problem of transmission', *European Journal of Cultural Studies*, 16:1, pp. 115–31.

Rachel, Daniel (2016), *Walls Come Tumbling Down: The Music and Politics of Rock Against Racism, 2 Tone and Red Wedge*, London: Pan MacMillan.

Reynolds, Simon (2005), *Rip It Up and Start Again: Post Punk 1978–84*, London: Faber & Faber.

Reynolds, Simon (2010), *Totally Wired: Post-punk Interviews and Overviews*, New York: Soft Skull Press.

Simpson, Dave (2019), 'Pubs, disco and fighting Nazis: How Leeds nurtured British post-punk', *The Guardian*, 19 April, https://www.theguardian.com/music/2019/apr/19/pubs-disco-and-fighting-nazis-how-leeds-nurtured-british-post-punk. Accessed 10 October 2021.

Spracklen, Karl, Henderson, Stephen and Procter, David (2016), 'Imagining the scene and the memory of the F-Club: Talking about lost punk and post-punk spaces in Leeds', *Punk & Post Punk*, 5:2, pp. 147–62.

Spracklen, Karl and Spracklen, Beverley (2018), *The Evolution of Goth Culture: The Origins and Deeds of the New Goths*, Bingley: Emerald.

Stubbs, David (2014), *Future Days: Krautrock and the Building of Modern Germany*, London: Faber & Faber.

Sweeting, Adam (2020), 'Andy Gill Obituary', *The Guardian*, 2 February, https://www.theguardian.com/music/2020/feb/02/andy-gill-obituary. Accessed 10 November 2021.

Thornton, Sarah (1996), *Club Cultures: Music, Media and Subcultural Capital*, Middleton: Wesleyan University Press.

Trowell, Ian (2016), 'Hard floors, harsh sounds and the northern anti-festival: Futurama 1979–1983', *Popular Music History*, 10:1, pp. 62–81.

Worley, Matthew and Copsey, Nigel (2016), 'White youth: The far right, punk and British youth culture', *JOMEC Journal*, 9:1, pp. 27–47.

# 2

# When Mr Fox Met Kit Calvert, the Maker of Wensleydale Cheese: Constructing Yorkshireness in the Sixties Leeds Folk Scene

*Karl Spracklen*

In *Electric Eden: Unearthing Britain's Visionary Music,* journalist Rob Young (2011) argues that there is a long history of myth-making in English music, rooted in the late nineteenth century and the art of William Morris, present in Frederick Delius and Edward Elgar and brought to prominence in folk music. Young shows how folk-rock bands such as Fairport Convention, The Incredible String Band and Mr Fox all attempted to construct their own visions of England and Englishness while simultaneously being part of the post-war folk music revival, itself a return to the initial work of Ceil Sharp and other collectors of folk song and dance. Young is cynical about English folk music's attempts to find the authentic songs of a rural, premodern culture untainted by industrialization, a scepticism shared by many critiques of English folk music (Keegan-Phipps 2017; Spracklen 2013). For Young, the only truly authentic English music is mystical, hallucinogenic and weird.

In 1970, Mr Fox released their first, eponymous album on Transatlantic Records (Mr Fox 1970). Marketed as folk rock – being released just a year after Fairport Convention re-constructed the genre with *Liege and Leaf,* and two years after Pentangle popularized it – the album became a commercial and critical success, winning folk album of the year in *Melody Maker*. In 1971, Mr Fox released their second album, *The Gipsy,* which included the epic title track, an adventure up the Yorkshire Dales by the narrator in pursuit of a gipsy he has fallen for in a pub in Leeds or Bradford (Mr Fox 1971). This second album was not as well-received, and the band split soon after. In this chapter, I want to explore how Mr Fox emerged from the Leeds folk music scene. The band's key musicians, the young married couple Bob and Carole Pegg, had moved to Leeds in 1963 as musicians already building a reputation on the national scene at the time. It was in Leeds that Bob and Carole started to explore the traditional music of the Yorkshire Dales, and this exploration led to them attempting to capture something authentically northern and rural Yorkshire (Spracklen 2016), while simultaneously re-producing it in a folk-rock style. After showing how the band came to be, I will move on to discuss the lyrical and musical themes that the Peggs used across both albums to construct their own imagined Yorkshire. In particular, I will return to the journey narrated in 'The Gipsy'. Before I return to Mr Fox, however, it is necessary to discuss the spatial and cultural relationship between Leeds, Yorkshire and the Yorkshire Dales, and a brief historical account of the latter.

## Leeds, Yorkshire and the Yorkshire Dales

Leeds, the city at the focus of this book and chapter, is situated in the historic county of Yorkshire, the largest county in England, which stretches from the eastern coast of northern England to a point far over the Pennine watershed very close to the west coast. More precisely, Leeds was in the West Riding of Yorkshire, which was the third of the traditional county that extended from the mines and factories of what is now South Yorkshire all the way through modern West Yorkshire and into the southern part of the Yorkshire Dales (now the Craven and Harrogate Districts of North Yorkshire). Leeds is on the River Aire, one of the rivers of the Yorkshire Dales. But Leeds is not in Airedale or within the boundaries of the National Park: Leeds is in the low-lying floodplain of the coal measures, a possibly Roman foundation built to protect the river crossing. Modern Leeds now extends to cover the lower reaches of the River Wharfe, one of the other rivers that form the Yorkshire Dales. So it was never far by Roman road or by river from the limestone and millstone grit pastures of the Pennines and the Yorkshire Dales, and there was much interaction between Leeds and its hilly hinterland for hundreds of years.

Leeds was never the capital of the West Riding, but in the nineteenth century it competed with Sheffield and Bradford for the prize of being the most enterprising and the richest (Briggs 2014). In 1904, Leeds beat Sheffield by one year to be the first Yorkshire city to have a University, and both of these cities attracted professionals, academics and students who gentrified the university districts through the twentieth century and before the growth of higher education in the post-war period (Whyte 2015). Leeds in the twentieth century was also at the centre of the growth of the railway industry, textiles and chemical engineering, all of which demanded large numbers of workers. As a consequence, the population and the size of the urban district of Leeds grew enormously from the 1930s to the beginning of the 1970s. The black smoke of the factory chimneys made people in Leeds yearn to escape up into the Yorkshire Dales, especially in the 1950s and 1960s when many green fields and farms in Leeds not protected by planning laws were built on by new houses.

At the same time, traditional life in the Yorkshire Dales was under threat. Quarrying and lead-mining had finished. Farming was becoming unprofitable, especially for upland sheep farms, and the mechanization of farming removed opportunities for employment. In Hawes in Wensleydale, the Dale north of Wharfedale, the creamery that made the eponymous cheese was being run-down and threatened with closure by the managers who preferred central factories close to the new motorways. For many of the people born in the Yorkshire Dales in the 1920s and 1930s, there was nothing to keep them in the area. This was a time, then, when people migrated to Bradford and Leeds, where there were still opportunities for employment and education. As villages such as Grassington, Hawes, Kettlewell and Buckden lost permanent residents, empty cottages were bought as second homes and holiday lets (Williams and Hall 2000). Throughout the twentieth century, the Dales were marketed to tourists and active recreation enthusiasts as spaces in which one could escape the city and find the freedom to walk green fields in the shadow of hills (Dewhurst and Thomas 2003; Spracklen and Robinson 2020). By the Second World War, walking and cycling tourism had become key forces in re-shaping the domestic economy, with lobbying groups such as the Ramblers Association and the Youth Hostel Association campaigning for better access to the beautiful places of Britain (Birkett 2014; Sheail 1995). Labour backed this movement and its post-war government ensured national parks became established throughout England, including the Yorkshire Dales National Park in 1954. The original and long-established boundaries of the Yorkshire Dales National Park took in all the hills and fells the major valleys that cut through them: Swaledale, Wensleydale, Dentdale, Littondale, Wharfedale and Airedale. It stretched as far as the old West Riding border in the Howgill Fells above Sedbergh but did not include the towns and cities in the southern and eastern valleys. To anyone in Leeds in the 1960s, though, the Dales could be found on OS maps that stretched towards the city, on bus and train timetables,[1] in walking books and in newspapers. And one might even glimpse Rombald's Moor, beyond which lay Ilkley and Wharfedale.

### *Bob and Carole Pegg become Mr Fox*

According to the sleeve notes of the 2004 compilation re-release CD *Join Us In Our Game* (Wells 2004: 1), Bob and Carole Pegg were both born in the northern counties of the Midlands, 'on either side of the Derbyshire/Nottingham border'. Bob's personal website[2] tells us that he was born in Long Eaton Derbyshire, a place very close to Nottingham and far from the moors of the Dark Peak and the green valleys of the White Peak. We can assume that Carole was the one born on the Nottinghamshire side of the border. They met each other at the Nottingham Folk Worksop, became a double act, fell in love and eventually married in 1964.

In 1963, Bob moved to Leeds to study English Literature at the University. Carole chose to follow her professional and personal partner to Leeds, abandoning her own degree at Southampton. Now married and living in Leeds, the couple became regulars on the local scene, and with others 'ran a folk club at the Royal Sovereign pub in Kirkstall' (Wells 2004: 1). Kirkstall at this time was an industrial inner district of Leeds, but one with the blackened stones of a medieval abbey sitting in idyllic parkland by the River Aire. It was also adjacent to Burley and Headingley, the main university district where Bob Pegg must have attended lectures. From his personal website,[3] we know that Bob was active in the University folk music society as well, as he edited its magazine. While Bob was still an undergraduate, Bob and Carole Pegg were becoming known on the national folk scene, and after submitting a demo to Transatlantic, they appeared on a 1965 compilation. But by this point, their music had not been transformed into what became Mr Fox.

The key moment happened when Bob Pegg started work on a postgraduate research project recording the folk musicians of the Yorkshire Dales. Pegg recalled (in Wells 2004: 2):

> By that point I'd moved on at university to train as a folklorist, recording various fiddlers and squeezebox players from the Yorkshire Dales. We incorporated elements of that sound into what Carole and I were doing in the clubs [...] Whenever [Fairport Convention] played in Leeds [...] [Ashley Hutchings[4] and I] spent a lot of time together listening to the recordings I was making of traditional musicians in the Yorkshire Dales.

On his own website, Bob Pegg himself recalls the inspiration of those musicians and the locations:[5]

In 1967 we spent a week in Moor End farmhouse, high on a hill above Wharfedale, overlooking the villages of Kettlewell and Starbotton. We were working with a group of talented teenagers from Buttershaw Youth Club in Bradford, and their visionary leader Trevor Sharpe. Moor End had no running water and no electricity. We sang and played music into the candlelit night, just like folk used to do. Songs inspired by that magical sojourn appeared on later recordings - The Hanged Man on Mr Fox [...] Jackie Beresford of Buckden, Wharfedale, playing the accordion, with his son Peter on fiddle – around 1967. Jackie was, among other things, a village dance musician, taxi driver, and barman at the Buck Inn. He is one of the characters mentioned in the song The Gipsy, on the Mr Fox album of the same name. Also featured in The Gipsy is Richard Alderson, better known as Neddy Dick, a farmer from Keld in Swaledale, playing his invention the harmonium and bells. He has his own song, The Ballad of Neddy Dick, on the first Mr Fox album.

The Yorkshire Dales and the musicians of Upper Wharfedale, then, were a direct influence on the musical turn in the music of the Peggs. In the anecdote offered to Wells, Pegg conjures up an image of a research assistant setting out into the Dales and recording the musicians in a formal academic interaction, collecting data for a project. In his own invocation of this spirit of the Dales, the interaction is more playful. We can imagine the young people from the council estate in south Bradford becoming enraptured by the majesty and the misery of the hills above Kettlewell, the hours of sun and rain, night and day. Moor End is still present on the western edge of Upper Wharfedale. Pegg does not tell us that Jackie and Peter Beresford were actually present at Moor End with the Bradford youngsters in that formative week (nor does he say Carole was there, apart from the ambiguous 'we' at the start of his story). Buckden is just a few miles up at the top of Wharfedale, so Moor End would have been easily accessible for the Beresfords. Pegg remembers their playing being an influence on the week and the musical turn of the Peggs. And he frames his recollection in such a way that there is no doubt the Beresfords were two of the musicians he had seen and recorded. But of course, this turn was equally shaped and negotiated by the urban mundanity of middle-class Leeds: the folk clubs, the coffee shops around the University, and especially the University itself. There were academics who were keen to capture the folklore of the Dales, and students like Bob Pegg were happy to be employed to record musicians because they shared a belief that folk music was an important part of English culture (Young 2011). Bob himself clearly believed that the music of the Dales had to be recorded and protected as an authentic representation of rural Yorkshire popular culture, at a time when radio and television were commodifying music and mechanization was commodifying sheep farming – the basis of the economy of the Dales (Spracklen and Robinson 2020).

In 1969, the Peggs left Leeds and moved to Hertfordshire, the commuter belt of London, far from Yorkshire, where Bob had secured a position as a lecturer in English and music at Stevenage College of Further Education. Just after that move, according to Wells (2004: 2), Bob and Carole worked with Bill Leader, 'old Leeds pals, country pickers Nick Strutt and Roger Knowles, Stevenage musicians Barry Lyons and Pete Wagstaff' to record an album for Trailer called *He Came from the Mountains* (Pegg and Pegg 1971). Again, according to the story by Wells (2004), friends in the industry gave a copy of this to Transatlantic, which had released their demo in 1965 but had then refused to sign them professionally at the time. Five years on, the Peggs had built a strong reputation on the live circuit and had vocal supporters in the music press. Transatlantic signed up the Peggs in 1970, but by that point the Peggs had become Mr Fox.

## *Mr Fox* and Mr Fox

Mr Fox was born in Stevenage, but the band was deliberately put together by the Peggs to reflect the arrangement of bands that had played the chapels and dance events in the Yorkshire Dales in the first half of the twentieth century (Wells 2004: 3, 4). Barry Lyons came into the band from the *He Came from the Mountains* session to play electric bass and was joined by Alun Eden on drums, Andrew Massey on cello, and John Myatt on flute, clarinet, bass clarinet and bassoon. Carole continued to play the fiddle and sing, but Bob extended his range to include organ, melodeon, tin whistle and terrapin alongside his vocals. This band went into Livingstone Studios in Barnet, far from Leeds or the Dales. Carole and Bob nonetheless reproduced their imagined Yorkshire folk rock to perfection. Most of the ten songs on this debut album were written by the Peggs together or individually, with one song brought to the band and another two co-written with Ashley Hutchings. In other words, none of these songs were traditional English folk music or even Yorkshire folk music, even though they are constructed to sound like they are.

On the front cover of the eponymous first album (Mr Fox 1970), there is a picture credited to Bob Pegg, which we might assume, to be of Mr Fox[6] himself, a wizard or spirit of the woods with a black hat, scraggly beard and demonic eyes. He stood in a wild landscape holding a naked woman close to him. On the back, there is a picture of the Peggs standing across an outcrop of Millstone Grit. Below this, we are told:

> Mr Fox came out of the Yorkshire dales [sic]. Hard-bitten farmland cut bare of trees centuries ago – a landscape which controls the men who live in it […] Three years spent working in the dales; treading out their emotional and geographical contours; making friends with warm and defeated people; meeting their ghosts, listening to their music and their tales […] Three years re-creating a past when the lead mines were still producing ore […] And all the time, everywhere, the landscape: hills bare but for rocks and sheep, rivers waiting to catch you unawares, crags waiting to fall and innocent field that might swallow a man.

The album begins with the creepy whistle and keyboards of 'Join Us in Our Game', written by the Peggs, which sounds like nothing except perhaps an impossible combination between a late-Victorian Methodist revival meeting and the Goblin soundtrack to *Dawn of Dead* – as if Mr Fox had travelled forward and backwards in time. Then comes 'The Hanged Man', where Bob Pegg starts to sing in a Yorkshire accent about a hanged man 'in a valley that never saw the sun'. He sings of rocks, rivers and the moor, then says:

> Waking in the forest, beneath the spreading pine,
> I saw my body hanging like a shirt upon a line.

Every word evokes the Dales, reinforced by the folk arrangement around them and the way Bob is obviously imitating the Yorkshire accent and style of the singers he recorded. The music is mournful and nostalgic for the places he tells us about in the chorus: the valley, the stones, the church and the pathway. At the end of the song we discover that the villagers found his body and took it away, but 'I remain here still'.

The rest of the first side reproduces the feel of the opening two songs. 'The Gay Goshawk', written by Carole Pegg, is driven by her ethereal vocal and unsettling fiddle playing. Then Bob's 'Rip Van Winkle' has the harmonium and the Yorkshire enunciations in a song that evokes mountains, sheep, rivers and valleys and a 'flower that has withered in my hand'. 'Mr Trill's Song', with words by Hutchings and tune by Bob Pegg, feels like a live recording of a Morris band doing a ceilidh in Skipton town hall.

The second side begins with 'Little Woman', written by Dave Mason. It is slow and does not have the obviously Yorkshire vibe of the rest of the album, even if the musical arrangement does. 'Salisbury Plain' with words by Hutchings and music by Carole Pegg is even slower than 'Little Woman'. The name, referencing the South-West of England, is not a promising start, but the music and the feel are strangely correct. The album continues with Bob's 'The Ballad of Neddy Dick' which brings us clearly back to the Dales and Pegg's description of the song's inspiration, the musician and Swaledale farmer Richard Anderson. The lyrics again take us through the landscape evoked in the songs on the first side of the album and described on the back of the album. This is followed by the lament 'Leaving the Dales', written by Bob, which identifies the decline of the traditional communities there. The album ends with Bob's 'Mr Fox', another pagan evocation of the spirit of the Yorkshire Dales.

The debut album was a critical success, as I explained earlier in this chapter. According to Pegg,[7] this was when they 'tour[ed] Britain playing folk clubs, concert halls and festivals'. But commercial success was another matter. The band had to lose Massey and Myatt as the line-up was too expensive. One can imagine the label and its management team scratching their heads at these strange tales of hanged men, and who was Mr Fox anyway? Almost immediately, the band was back in the studio: the pressure was on to create an album that would keep the band in the business.

## The Gipsy (Mr Fox 1971)

*The Gipsy*, produced again by Bill Leader and recorded at Livingstone Studios in Barnet, has a cover on which the gipsy girl herself is portrayed in traditional Romany costume. On the back is a cartoon of the four members of Mr Fox, and Carole is wearing the same dress as the gipsy. Three of the seven songs are written by Bob, one by Carole, and two are traditional songs arranged by the Peggs. The album begins on side one with Carole's 'Mendle', a start as equally unsettling and awesome as 'Join Us In Our Game'. Her ethereal vocals are accompanied perfectly by Bob's sinister church organ. The story is inspired by the then popular book *Mist Over Pendle* (Neill 1951), about the famous witches of Pendle Hill, who were tried and executed in 1612, though Carole has made a weak pun about being pissed over Pendle (Wells 2004: 8). Then the rest of side one is dedicated to the thirteen-minute epic 'The Gipsy', Bob's finest moment discussed in more detail below. The second side begins with 'Aunt Lucy Broadwood', Bob's Yorkshire Dales proto-rap song. This side includes 'The House Carpenter' and 'All The Good Times', traditional folk songs made traditional or invented Yorkshire Dales songs. But nothing on the second side can compare to the combination of 'Mendle' and 'The Gipsy'.

'The Gipsy' itself is built on the English folk narrative tradition of musicians falling in love with beautiful but deadly women: witches, fairies and gipsies (Joosen 2011). In these tales, these otherworldly lovers can be deadly for the musician, or they can provide inspiration or gifts. Gipsies belong to this tradition because they have been viewed as exotic and dangerous outsiders ever since they arrived in this country with their culture of movement (Kenrick and Clark 1999). Many conservative people still view Romany and Irish travelling communities with suspicion because these communities want to maintain their freedom to move from site to site. Bob's tale is a modern iteration. His story begins, sung in a broad Yorkshire accent to a jaunty organ riff:

> I'd like to tell you people I met her at a fair,
> But I met her in a pub down by the far side of the square.

This is Mary Lee, the gipsy, and he falls in love with her immediately, drawn to the 'fires of India' in her eyes. She tells him that her family used to have horses, 'but now they lived in Bradford where her father dealt in scrap'. We never know explicitly which city Bob meets the gipsy in, but since he is drinking 'Tetley's Ales' in the evenings he spends 'court[ing]' her 'from Autumn into Spring', so we can guess it is Leeds, the home of Tetley's. Leeds is also close to Bradford where Mary Lee lives, though the courting may be taking place in Bradford in a Tetley's pub. Bob wants to ask for her hand in marriage but is too nervous. Then he fears that his lover is becoming 'restless with the budding of the trees'. One day he turns up at her father's and receives the news that Mary Lee is gone, travelling to Scotland. Bob laments:

> And I knew that I must travel on the road that she'd gone on
> Even if it took me to the dark side of the sun.

'The road' is the old way to Scotland through the Yorkshire Dales. At this point in the song the music changes, slowing down and becoming as unsettling as 'Mendle'. This is a magical road, but one marked by real places. Bob travels from the 'silent' city to Ilkley, on the River Wharfe. He hitches a lift to Bolton, which is Bolton Abbey. Then he tells us he walks past 'the low hills of Wharfedale' and the 'black top of Kilnsey' Crag, before meeting a farmer who tells him the gipsies 'were camped up at Langstrothdale', the far end of the valley carved out by the Wharfe. Bob is of course walking the tarmac road, not a public footpath. This is the old way pedestrians reached these dales, as the road follows the old tracks by the rivers that take the easiest way from village to village – although it is possible he took the paths that go on either side of the valley below Moor End farm between Kettlewell at Buckden. At Buckden, Bob stays the night presumably at the Buck Inn, where his 'friend Jackie' (Beresford, mentioned earlier in this chapter) works, where he is told the gipsies have moved on 'over the top' to Wensleydale. The next day Bob follows them:

> So next morning I took the road into Wensleydale,
> Moorland before me, stretched out like a dream.
> Up by the boulders and over the bridge
> Where the White Lady walks into the stream.

Where this happens, and who the White Lady is, is unclear. The road to Wensleydale from Langstrothdale goes high over rough moorland, but the direction and description in the third line suggest to me the road in Langstrothdale – limestone country scattered with erratics – before it turns up to the moors. There is a bridge in Wensleydale before the road reaches Hawes at Gayle, but this is in a village by a mill. Wherever the White Lady crosses the water may not be possible to mark on a map that is not in the fairy realm. But the magical tone is balanced by the first person Bob meets in Wensleydale: 'Kit Calvert, the Maker of Wensleydale Cheese'. Kit is the person who saved Hawes Creamery and Wensleydale Cheese, and at the time in the 1950s and 1960s, he had some regional fame for his involvement in

Dales culture, folklore and dialect. His presence raises a smile for those who know the story of how he saved the local cheese – even if the music is still in the same slow, spooky tone. Kit warns Bob that the gipsies have already set off towards Keld in Swaledale over the Buttertubs Pass, one of the most difficult climbs in the north of England. Bob pursues them onto the rise between the two dales, where is alone. At this point, the music changes and there is a fiddle solo, a tin whistle and a more furious drumbeat.

Then the slow music returns as Bob tells us he has come to Thwaite by the River Swale, before reaching Keld where he tells us 'Neddy played his harmonium and bells'. He then spies the horses and wagons and realizes he has found the gipsies. The music returns to the jaunty riff of the first part, and he sees Mary Lee again. He knows this is 'the closing of a love affair' but spends the night with her 'under the haloed moon'. When he wakes up she is gone and has left him a note. Later, he hears she has a baby and is living in Dundee with a 'tinker'. He ends his tale by wondering whether she still remembers him. At this point, there is a magnificent instrumental coda that remains joyful.

*The Gipsy* did not receive critical acclaim, nor did the album sell enough records to allow the band to become the next Fairport Convention. Rather than reach out to a bigger audience by making their music accessible and relatable, *The Gipsy* was defiantly, regionally Yorkshire, seemingly appealing only to people who had walked themselves up and around the low hills of Wharfedale. The band struggled on until 1972 then broke up at the same time as Bob and Carole's marriage ended. Carole tried to establish herself as a singer-songwriter, then became an ethnomusicologist when that career path failed. Bob returned to Leeds and tried to recapture the magic of Mr Fox in a series of idiosyncratic recordings, but nothing came close to having the impact of the debut album. And none of those recordings invent and play with rural Yorkshire so effectively as either Mr Fox album. Indeed, in Leeds in the late 1970s, Bob's music was becoming more grim, more real and more reflective of the (post)industrial city scape of that time.[8]

## Conclusion

Everything released by Mr Fox was clearly a confection, a re-imagined construction of songs and tunes. There was nothing in either of the two albums that were authentic Yorkshire folk music. Neither of the Peggs came from Yorkshire, and neither lived there when they were making the Mr Fox albums. Listening to the records now, one can hear romantic notions of identity and place, of meaning and purpose and belonging that are as real as the ghost of the White Lady.

All Bob Pegg wanted to do was to take the songs and tunes he had heard and recorded and somehow reproduce them in a way that captured some idea he had about what genuine Yorkshire Dales folk culture or popular culture actually was: church music, bands playing organs and singing songs of the decline of mining, of farming and of the villages and communities that had been thriving at the turn of the last century.

And yet there is much in this collage of Yorkshireness that rings true (Spracklen 2016). The musicians who inspired Mr Fox were real people making real music, which Bob and Carole channelled into what they believed to be a true reproduction of the sound and the place. The Dales exist, and people live in it still, as farmers, taxi drivers and pub landlords. People visit the Dales as tourists and pass through these places and wear down every stile with the weight of their boots. When Bob and Carole Pegg moved to Leeds the Dales were there on the horizon, for them and for every other citizen of the city, so it is not surprising they found pleasure and belonging for themselves in exploring the fields and the hills and the moors. And it is not surprising that people now listen to Mr Fox and identify completely with the Yorkshire Dales evoked by the ritual magic at the heart of their albums.

## NOTES

1. A railway went from Leeds to Skipton via Ilkley and Bolton Abbey in Wharfedale. This popular line was axed as far as Ilkley, as there was a second railway to Skipton from Leeds.
2. https://www.bobpegg.com/life. Accessed 6 June 2021.
3. https://www.bobpegg.com/life. Accessed 6 June 2021.
4. One of the important professional musicians in the folk-rock movement, and one of the founders of Fairport Convention.
5. https://www.bobpegg.com/songs. Accessed 6 June 2021.
6. The name Mr Fox was chosen because the fox often appears in folk songs (Young 2011).
7. https://www.bobpegg.com/life. Accessed 6 June 2021.
8. In 1978, Bob was interviewed by police in Leeds as he released a single called 'The Werewolf Of Old Chapeltown' at the height of the hunt for the Yorkshire Ripper: the police thought the lyrics were suspiciously true to what the actual killer Peter Sutcliffe had been doing (Wells 2006: 7, 8).

## REFERENCES

Birkett, Norman (2014), *National Parks and the Countryside*, Cambridge: Cambridge University Press.

Briggs, Asa (2014), *The Age of Improvement: 1783–1867*, Abingdon: Routledge.

Dewhurst, Helen and Thomas, Rhodri (2003), 'Encouraging sustainable business practices in a non-regulatory environment: A case study of small tourism firms in a UK national park', *Journal of Sustainable Tourism*, 11:5, pp. 383–403.

Joosen, Vanessa (2011), *Critical and Creative Perspectives on Fairy Tales: An Intertextual Dialogue Between Fairy-Tale Scholarship and Postmodern Retellings*, Detroit: Wayne State University Press.

Keegan-Phipps, Simon (2017), 'Identifying the English: Essentialism and multiculturalism in contemporary English folk music', *Ethnomusicology Forum*, 26:1, pp. 3–25.

Kenrick, Donald and Clark, Colin (1999), *Moving On: The Gypsies and Travellers of Britain*, Hatfield: University of Hertfordshire Press.

Mr Fox (1970), *Mr Fox*, LP, London: Transatlantic.

Mr Fox (1972), *The Gipsy*, LP, London: Transatlantic.

Neill, Robert (1951), *Mist Over Pendle*, London: Hutchinson.

Pegg, Bob and Pegg, Carole (1971), *He Came from the Mountains*, LP, London: Trailer.

Sheail, John (1995), 'John Dower, national parks, and town and country planning in Britain', *Planning Perspectives*, 10:1, pp. 1–16.

Spracklen, Karl (2013), 'Nazi punks folk off: Leisure, nationalism, cultural identity and the consumption of metal and folk music', *Leisure Studies*, 32:4, pp. 415–28.

Spracklen, Karl (2016), 'Theorising northernness and northern culture: The north of England, northern Englishness, and sympathetic magic', *Journal for Cultural Research*, 20:1, pp. 4–16.

Spracklen, Karl and Robinson, Dave (2020), 'Putting faith in vinyl, real ale and live music: A case study of the limits of tourism policy and a critical analysis of new leisure spaces in a northern English town', *Tourism, Culture and Communication*, 20:2&3, pp. 151–61.

Wells, David (2004), 'Sleeve notes in Mr Fox', *Join Us in Our Game*, CD, London: Castle.

Wells, David (2006), 'Sleeve notes in Bob Pegg', *Keeper of the Flame*, CD, London: Castle.

Whyte, William Hadden (2015), *Redbrick: A Social and Architectural History of Britain's Civic Universities*, Oxford: Oxford University Press.

Williams, Allan M. and Hall, C. Michael (2000), 'Tourism and migration: New relationships between production and consumption', *Tourism Geographies*, 2:1, pp. 5–27.

Young, Rob (2011), *Electric Eden: Unearthing Britain's Visionary Music*, London: Faber and Faber.

# 3

# Park Life: When Roundhay Went Pop

*Peter Mills*

This chapter introduces the series of large-scale pop music concerts mounted in Roundhay Park in Leeds between 1982 and 2019, from The Rolling Stones to Ed Sheeran. It also considers the outlier in this narrative, the BBC-sponsored 'Love Parade' (2000), and by taking a closer look at these huge public events, it can reveal much about changes in staging, ticketing and performance of concerts and the industry that surrounds them. I also reflect on Leeds as a musical environment and how comfortable, or otherwise, it is in presenting itself to the gaze of the world. After all, this was the city that in 1973 imposed a 96-decibel limit on live music concerts, prompting a lyrical barb from Ian Hunter after a Mott the Hoople gig at Leeds Town Hall was the first major gig to enforce the limit: 'And if the going gets rough, don't you blame us, you 96 decibel freaks!' (Mott the Hoople 1974: n.pag.).

To get a sense of the meaning of Roundhay to the city of Leeds as a shared social and public space, it's useful to first consider the wider function and character of the park. At over 700 acres, Roundhay is one of the largest civic spaces in Europe. Burt (2000) provides an excellent summary of the park's history and how it came to be bought on behalf of the city from the Nicholson family in 1871 and opened in 1872 by Prince Arthur, the third son of Queen Victoria. This event provided the park with its own theme tune ('This Is Our Opening Day') and a foretaste of the late twentieth-century concerts in attracting nearly 100,000 people to the park and getting the name of Roundhay (and, thereby, Leeds) into the national eyeline. Proof that if you build it, they will come, the park quickly became a key part of the city's life, a green, open space available to all amid an era of heavy industrialization. Leeds remains blessed with many parks but Roundhay has always been first among equals. Music was built into the park's new role as the city's playground: bandstands were incorporated into the park furniture between the two lakes and this wide distribution meant that visitors could hear music wherever they went.

At the park's centre lies the Arena, a huge bowl originally earmarked as the site for a third lake, which in 1894 was designated as a sports arena with a cycling track, in response to the boom in cycling clubs in the late nineteenth century. No one grew up in Leeds in the mid twentieth century without knowing about the week-long Military Tattoos and the legendary Children's Day which ran from 1920 to 1963, a near-half century which saw an extraordinary social and cultural change, its final iteration coming in a year earmarked by Philip Larkin as something of a watershed. It even hosted an episode of the BBC show *Jeux Sans Frontières* in July 1976. So Roundhay was not a complete novice in hosting large field-days, but its use for a world-class musical event was still something of a radical thought.

In 1982, Roundhay joined the roster of civic parks in the United Kingdom used for huge musical events, providing a Northern English location for concerts on this scale between London and Scotland (Russell 2004; Mazierska 2018). Central London's Hyde Park has a longer concert history, from 1968 to the present (Rabbitts 2015; Frith et al. 2019), but interestingly during the busiest era for Roundhay – the 1980s – Hyde Park hosted only one show. Finsbury Park in North London is perhaps a closer fit – a well-used civic space within a community which has a long and sometimes problematic concert history (Smith et al. 2022). So, the scale is vast, yet the whole story of these concerts in Roundhay Park can arguably be traced to the door of one man: Michael Johnson.

## *Roundhay Park and Leeds City Council*

Michael Johnson was music officer for Leeds City Council 1979–87 and ramped up the civic musical offering, running over 250 concerts a year and making Leeds the UK's most 'musical' city in terms of civic provision for several years in the 1980s. With this civic context in mind, I asked him in July 2019 (Johnson 2019) how the first concert was mooted:

> **Michael Johnson (MJ):** I was approached by Kennedy Street Enterprises, Manchester-based promoters, and a scout from them came over in the Spring of '82. They were looking for a venue in Yorkshire, or at least the east side of the country, to put on this rock band. They didn't want to tell me who it was, but I got it out of them that it was the Stones, who were probably still the biggest rock band in the world at the time. So, I said I might have something that would be of interest to them. The scout came over, I drove him up to Roundhay Park and showed him the bowl there.

**Peter Mills (PM):** So, they didn't ring you saying they were interested in Roundhay?

**MJ:** No, no. They said did I know of anywhere in my role in charge of musical activities. Most of that was classical and easy listening because there was no indoor venue in Leeds for the promotion of pop and rock at the time. They said it would have to be an outdoor venue because of the sheer size of it.

They'd also looked at Old Trafford in Manchester and St. James's Park in Newcastle, the football grounds, I recall. Roundhay is different from those kinds of stadia of course. So, the scout went back and Danny Betesh, the boss of Kennedy Enterprises came over, we went for a stroll in the park, no more than half an hour, he had a look and we went on from there.

So, the lengthy run of world-class events at Roundhay, and all the money and memories made at them, have their root in two men walking around the oval of the Arena one quiet afternoon. Indeed, Betesh and Kennedy Street proved central to this story as they were involved in virtually all the shows over the next decade. While the city was not a complete stranger to big one-offs – Queen had played at Elland Road on 29 May 1982 – a concert in a public park was a new idea. How prepared, and willing, was Leeds to set off down this particular road?

**MJ:** Not particularly – it had never happened before. It all came down to money actually, that was the thing that swayed it in the end. We agreed they would give us £60,000 for putting the event on, which enabled us to restore a restaurant down by the lake. It was thought the event would make quite a big improvement to Roundhay, and it did. We had complaints and pressure from local residents too, many worries – noise, vandalism, drugs, everything.

**PM:** How did the event deal with security issues?

**MJ:** The promoters engaged a lot of stewards, who weren't terribly reliable and came from all over the country. We had many meetings with West Yorkshire Police who had a very strange idea about penning the site, we'd have put people in pens and Hill 60 would have been one pen, the Arena itself another and so on. It would have been a disaster. We managed to persuade them not to proceed with that. The safety of people climbing over these low barriers would have been a nightmare.

**PM:** How would you characterize the attitude that it sounds like you had to push against?

**MJ:** It wasn't exactly hostility, but the *Yorkshire Post* and *Yorkshire Evening Post* (the dailies produced in Leeds) were desperate for any copy because this was such a big thing at the time, and because of all this attention the administration was happy to go along with it. Once I was able to convince them there was a sizable facility fee in the offing and over a million pounds' worth of tickets sold, it was a nice little earner. It wasn't all profit because the department had to make good the site afterwards, but it *was* a good earner. More importantly we were able to add it to our range of events and it put the city council in a good light. It showed they were quite ahead.

Despite all the material benefits to the city, there was local politics mixed in alongside the commercial considerations.

**PM:** Did you meet any political resistance?

**MJ:** Peter Sparling was the leader of the council at the time, it was a Tory council. He was pushing back throughout, but once I presented to the Tory group that the event would result in a substantial net profit and make the city look good on a world stage, they changed their minds. Mr. Sparling kept insisting in the press that he would not be going near the event but on the day, he turned up. I remember seeing him standing outside of the cricket pavilion, where we had been asked to make an enclosure for members of the council who had insisted on having their own area!

The local press gave the event a cautious endorsement setting the tone for future coverage of such events, focusing on cost, traffic issues, the 'clean-up' and policing matters alongside the sniff of 'potential for other supergroups' to visit (Bungey 1982: 4).

As for the concert itself, the bill on Sunday, 25 July 1982 was The Rolling Stones, the J. Geils Band, Joe Jackson, and George Thorogood and the Destroyers. The gates opened at noon, as an early start was one of the many conditions of the show going ahead. The Rolling Stones arrived on stage at 6 p.m. and the whole event was over by 8 p.m. (see Figure 3.1); it was from start to finish a daylight concert – as may be seen from the now commercially issued CD/DVD *Live at Leeds* (The Rolling Stones 2015). Around 120,000 people attended, well over the actual projected 80,000 capacity. This figure was superseded due to the decision to open the gates, in preparation for the crowd's departure, about twenty minutes into the Stones' set, allowing those without tickets to enter the Arena unchecked. Even then this seemed reckless, especially after previous worries about overcrowding and disorder. Before the Hillsborough disaster of 1989, issues of overcrowding were seen differently – Michael Johnson noted the advocacy of penning by police.

FIGURE 3.1: Mick Jagger on stage during the Rolling Stones' 1982 performance at Roundhay Park. Courtesy of Peter Mills.

In light of this experience, security was reconsidered for future events; the park's agreed capacity was set at 80,000 and had to be applied for on an event-by-event basis. The next visitor to the Arena was Bruce Springsteen, on 7 July 1985, another Sunday event. After a decade as a cult hero, Springsteen had broken through on a global level with 1984's *Born in the USA* album; the booking tells us about the reputation of Roundhay but also the requirement on an artist to make the event work in such a space and to a crowd of such a size – the onus is on them to reach the people at the back as well as the groundlings stage front. Mick Jagger worked hard in '82 with his fluorescent outfit, catwalks to the sides of the stage and the cherry picker that swooped him and guitarist Ron Wood over the crowd. Springsteen's less showy but warmly charismatic presence was able to draw the crowd in and his gig – again, a tour finale – is probably the most happily remembered show in the park.

This show was aided by the innovation of two large video screens, now a concert staple but cutting-edge technology at this time and twice as many as the Stones had in 1982. Even a performer as effective as Springsteen benefitted from the changing modes of staging; indeed, Roundhay serves as a kind of indexical guide to the way large-scale pop concert performances were both constructed and mediated between 1982 and 2019. Despite laments in the press about traffic – 'still queues on the Ring Road at 11.30 pm' (Anon. 1985: 1) – there were signs the city was getting into its stride with these events and a powerful economic argument could be made for them to keep on coming: 'What happened at Roundhay Park at the weekend held elements of comfort for those who have come to believe that big crowds mean bad news [...] unlike other heavily subsidized art forms, rock pays its way, and handsomely' (Wellington 1985: 14).

The benefits were starting to be seen to outweigh the problems.

## *L'Age D'or, or 50 Jets Landing On The Roof*

Annual events at a venue like Roundhay can't be guaranteed – a number of elements need to align. An act of a certain stature, able to attract a huge audience, needs to be touring the United Kingdom between May and September, and open for booking. They also need to be able to deal with Roundhay's relative lack of infrastructure. As Steven Thomas, part of the Genesis crew in 1987 told ITV's *Calendar*: 'When you get Roundhay Park that's what you get; a park. Not even a lightbulb' (Thomas 1987: n.pag.).

Despite this, two of the world's biggest acts visited in summer '87. Genesis and Madonna came to Roundhay; U2 played at Elland Road on 1 July 1987, using the city's football stadium because three events at Roundhay in one summer was deemed an excessive burden on the area. Genesis visited on 28 June, and on 15 August the park welcomed Madonna for a lively and raucous show: frank exchanges of opinion between her and the front rows may be heard on the bootleg recording that still circulates. Remarkably this was her first ever full live show in the United Kingdom and functioned as a kind of warm-up to a sold-out week at the old Wembley Stadium: Roundhay was by now keeping illustrious company on tour itineraries. Madonna was the biggest-selling artist in the world that year, so the booking could not have been more prestigious. Some residents were still not happy, whoever was playing, but a highly professional organization, crowd management and free tickets for locals had reduced the refusers to a rump.

Both shows cut through in the local press, being hailed as 'a great advert for the city and its businesses' (Wellington 1987: 6) and the *Yorkshire Evening Post* (*YEP*) review of the Genesis show had a message for the dissenters:

> I only wish some of the stay-at-home critics and detractors were there to share it. Perhaps then they would stop carping about rates and privacy, shattered peace and

> litter [...] the cash can be used to subsidise other less well supported branches of the arts or help to provide much needed amenities. The new lakeside café in the park is visible proof of that.
>
> (Corry 1987: 6)

The numbers were indeed compelling: the city earned £70,000 from both shows, roughly £1 from each ticket sold. The '87 concerts were a tremendous success and coincided with a rising sense of confidence in the city – the Leeds International Film Festival was first mooted this year – and a steady process of civic reinvention seemed to be underway.

In terms of the park's pulling power, Michael Jackson's visit on 29 August 1988 was arguably the peak; the world's biggest pop star entertaining a crammed, adoring park on a late summer's evening moving through a long, slow dusk to darkness. The brief 'POV' clip of Jackson performing 'Human Nature' available online gives a sense of the atmosphere, illustrating what a superb natural venue the Arena is. The first clouds on his horizon were still some way off, although the *YEP* found time to wonder a little about 'the enigma' of Jackson, even as it declared the event 'A Thriller in the Park' and recorded Jackson's improbable encounter with the city's Lady Mayoress before the show. It was also Jackson's thirtieth birthday. To add to the bizarre feel, a light aeroplane swooped over the Arena (the pilot was later prosecuted) and Jackson himself was spotted on Ilkley Moor hours before the show filming for a tour documentary. The show shared the Bank Holiday Monday with the Leeds West Indian Carnival down the road in Chapeltown, and while the *YEP* acknowledged that local residents of LS8 endured 'a measure of inconvenience', it emphasized that the 'Roundhay Park concert has now become an established event in the area and is bolstering Leeds' worldwide image as an exciting, developing city' (Wellington 1988: 6).

By the time Simple Minds arrived on 23 July 1989, the Park was fully in its stride as a first-look venue for any act operating at the highest commercial level. Simple Minds opened their triumphant 'homecoming' UK tour in Roundhay. As a schoolboy I had seen them play a much loved if somewhat notorious venue down the road in Harehills and, amazingly, vocalist Jim Kerr remembered that show too:

> The first place we played in Leeds was the Fforde Grene pub, it was the kind of place where you expected chairs to be thrown at you. Anyway, we played a new song called 'Life In A Day' and the place erupted and I've never forgotten that – that's why the tour is starting in Leeds.
>
> (Hurst 1989: 8)

Processes for staging such an event were still developing; for this concert, the gates were opened at noon to prevent huge queues developing on the Soldiers Field: this, after all, was just a few weeks after the Hillsborough disaster and queues had been an issue in previous years. Similarly, the show closed at 22:30, allowing the audience to appreciate the band's light show in full. A few years earlier the Stones and Bruce Springsteen had to end their sets in daylight, so here was another shift in policy, which smoked out comment: a local resident, 'who did not wish to be named', unwittingly flattered the music by describing it as 'like 50 jets landing on the roof' (Cooper 1989: 2).

## Achtung Roundhay

The Simple Minds show was arguably the end of an era: the next gigs were repeat visits from well-established acts. Genesis called in on their 'We Can't Dance' world trek on 31 July 1992, followed on 16 August by another visit by Michael Jackson. Both acts had, arguably, peaked commercially and creatively and this change in the appeal was reflected in the sanguine attitude of the city to the events – feathers, civic and residential, were less ruffled – and reflected in the scale of the crowds. In both cases, trouble was looming, even if this wasn't yet apparent. Genesis were even called 'middle-aged superstars' by the *YEP*, and Jimmy Savile walked down the hill from his flat overlooking the park to introduce them to the stage. 'Top marks for concert planning' commented the *YEP*: 'Bliss at the park [...] the event did Leeds proud' (Spencer 1992: 3).

Michael Jackson's appeal had waned somewhat by the time he returned to Roundhay and he attracted around 65,000 as opposed to the 80,000 plus who had squeezed into the park in '88. Indeed, adverts were placed in the local press before the show, a promotional push unnecessary in 1988 when all tickets were sold (pre-internet, lest we forget) in a single day. 'Wizardry fails to hide a decline' a *YEP* headline read (Whitworth 1992: 3) while the cursory report made a brief reference to 'well-behaved fans' and 'traffic problems' after the concert, revealing how routine these events had become.

U2 were the next visitors, almost exactly one year later, on 14 August 1993, revealing how the huge summer gig at Roundhay had become a part of the city's 'season'. Much was made of the technology which delivered the show – 'the most hi-tech set ever created for a rock concert' gasped the *YEP* (Whitworth 1993: 3) – and U2 presented a new kind of staging to which the space of the Arena was well suited. Emphasizing the theme of sensory overload, the screens were pumping out images and slogans as opposed to simply giving a close-up of the singer or drummer. Coupled with this 'total experience', the structure of the stage itself was a key part of the performance rather than a neutral platform for it.

The *YEP*'s front page on the day of the show provided my favourite headline in all my research on this topic: 'Achtung Roundhay' (Anon. 1993a: 1). Their next front page praised the show but also accidentally revealed a changing musical culture – adjoining the picture of Bono was an article about the break-up of an illegal rave on Otley Chevin, a rural beauty spot some ten miles outside of Leeds (Bruce 1993: 1). The next wave of pop musicians didn't need an arena to work in; the new dance music required a club with a dancefloor or, as Jarvis Cocker put it, a field in Hampshire (Anon. 1993b: 1).

Any venue is prey to changes in musical taste, style and fashion and the early 1990s showed a partial turn away from the type of mega-concerts that Roundhay specialized in. The free Heineken and Shine festivals (1992–95) had superb bills catering to both rock and dance audiences but this shift in demand – and of what was current, innovative and popular – meant that the next single artist show at Roundhay would prove to be the last for nearly a decade. It was a repeat visit from U2, the only act to have performed successive shows at the park. Their 'PopMart' tour arrived on 28 August 1997, on the far side of rave culture and just past the peak of Britpop, three months after the election of Tony Blair and just three days before the death of Princess Diana. A total of 53,000 paying customers saw an extravagant stage show. Roundhay took its place on their UK itinerary alongside Wembley and the national stadia of Scotland and Ireland.

There wouldn't be another pop concert on this scale for nearly a decade. In 2000 came an event that actually realized all the fears of the residents that had almost blocked the way in 1982: 'The Love Parade'. Despite the event being sponsored by the BBC, there was much wrangling in the weeks leading up to the event and Roundhay residents were sufficiently perturbed to hire their own security, including patrolling guards with dogs – the environs of the park include some of the city's most expensive streets. Attendees could come and go as they pleased and this led to an unprecedented level of interaction between the participants and the local environment, one that lasted for a long weekend. Furthermore, a drug-related death took place in a city centre club but was squarely blamed on The Love Parade. It remains the Park's only music event-related fatality (Jeeves 2000).

The Love Parade was actually very successful in terms of numbers – estimates varied between 300,000 and 500,000 attendees – yet that margin of error is indicative of the way the event slipped away from its organizers. It's no exaggeration to say Leeds was ill-prepared for the event, partly because the city had become used to these huge events, possibly blasé; however, The Love Parade was a different animal altogether. Suddenly seeing all their fears realized, there was a substantial backlash from locals and the wider community, voices by now expressed in online forums as well as via letters published in the local press. 'City suffers a party hangover' lamented a *YEP* editorial (Anon. 2000: 10), criticizing 'penny pinching' and 'amateurish organisation' from the BBC and the promoters. Nearly two decades after the Stones called in, the city was now inclined to expect much better. For the first time, a pop-related event in Roundhay Park was perceived as a failure.

It would take six years and the power of a modern-day family entertainer to allay the fears of locals and let the heat out of the system. Robbie Williams played two consecutive nights, 8 and 9 September 2006. It was a return to the 'classic' model of Roundhay concert staging – a structured, 'single act' performance by a world best seller. It was staged according to the principles laid down in the 1980s but boosted by the enhanced performative media technologies available in the early twenty-first century. Massive lighting rigs stood in the Arena itself and an array of digital screens flashed pixel-perfect close-ups of Williams; this was a long way from Mick Jagger's fluorescent jacket and the single screen atop the stage of 1982. Ticketing had changed too: instead of people being able to watch from wherever they chose once inside the Arena – squeezed against the crash barriers stage front, or having a picnic on Hill 60 – the tiering of prices meant paying more to stand in the 'Golden Circle' close to the catwalks which protruded into the arena. The ring of steel which surrounded the park was a marked contrast to the chicken wire and wood panels dotted around the perimeter for the first concert in '82. Watching the opening number 'Radio' online is to see how well Roundhay as a venue showcases the generational shift in the representation of pop celebrities, from Jagger to Williams.

No one could mistake a Robbie Williams audience for a weekend rave crowd, but controversy arose because a decision was taken to close schools in the area on the day of the first concert, Friday 8 September. Children were thrilled; adults less so, even if they were going to the show, as evidenced by heat in online forums and a flurry of letters to the *YEP*, gathered under the heading 'Everything Stops For Robbie' (Anon. 2006: 1). Williams himself referred to this issue onstage, with his customary mix of egotistic brashness and self-effacement: 'How great am I? That never happened when I was at school. Michael Jackson never came to Stoke on Trent'. Councillor John Proctor, the LCC executive member for Leisure, fell back on a favoured mantra: 'If anyone feels adversely affected by the closures I sincerely apologise. That said, this was a fantastic showcase for the city not just nationally but internationally' (McTaggart 2006: 2). Despite this controversy – and the fact that Williams had arguably peaked commercially a year or two earlier – the concerts were a substantial success and this was a great relief for the city.

## On, Roundhay?

The absence of shows post-2006 was a consequence of changes both in the civic mood and the music industry itself; the city had in some ways tired of the events, and there was a dearth of acts who could function in the vast space Roundhay offers. The concerts had generated a lot of money which had helped renovate parts of the park from its low point in the early 1980s and now the conservation of those gains became of central concern. Alongside the well-established sports clubs, it was used much more regularly for all sorts of more modest events – food festivals, outdoor theatre, a flirtation with Mela (South Asian diasporic festivals) – which monetized the space more rapidly in straitened times, and these smaller, more regular events were not as disruptive as the 'big bang' concerts. The cultural landscape and the position of pop music within it was very different too; pop had moved from still being something of an outsider in the early 1980s, through a period of apparently unlimited profitability, to dealing with the big smash of the internet: filesharing, streaming, and YouTube. The old music industry certainties no longer seemed so stable.

Competition had grown in the region too: Leeds Fest, the city's Millennium Square and Harewood House have all hosted Roundhay-sized acts (Bryan Adams, Kaiser Chiefs, KT Tunstall and Simple Minds), while thanks to huge indoor venues across the north of England the show could go on all year round, whatever the weather. When Leeds finally got its own arena in 2013 (opened by park veteran Bruce Springsteen) Roundhay's summer window of opportunity started to look very limited indeed. Having a venue of a scale capable of welcoming the biggest touring acts became a key part of a civic offering and Leeds Arena – a purpose-built 14,000-seater just at the edge of the city centre, easily accessible to all – made the idea of further events at the infrastructure-light Roundhay increasingly unlikely.

Indeed, this proved the case until promoter Harvey Goldsmith parked his touring 'On' festival in Roundhay for a weekend in September 2016. This offered a much broader cultural experience than the one-off mega-gigs, described as a 'family friendly experience', featuring a choice of stages and a wide array of food outlets, and wristband passes allowing comings and goings. This all took place in an enclosed area to the north of the Arena itself and offered a relaxed, low-key atmosphere. The On festival targeted those who were of an age to feel nostalgic about their own former festival going but now wanted a more comfortable experience, and delivered via the quietly professional nature of the organization and the acts booked, with top billing going to 1990s survivors James and Primal Scream – both successful and esteemed by a certain demographic, but not million sellers.

One of *those* would turn up in 2019: Ed Sheeran played Roundhay on 16/17 August, at the very end of his 260-date '÷' tour. Sheeran had spent some of his childhood in Hebden Bridge and wanted to do some gigs in West Yorkshire before the final four shows in his hometown of Ipswich. It had been so long since the park had staged an event on this scale that a whole new set of requests and permissions had to be submitted to the city by the promoters; the previous standing arrangements were long lapsed. An application was posted on notices around the Leeds 8 postcode area several months in advance and a temporary capacity of 79,999 was granted, although not without the council receiving some objections from local residents which were remarkably similar to those submitted in 1982: traffic congestion, litter and waste issues, restricted access to the park, and what was by 2019 called 'anti-social behaviour'.

As in 1982, the concerts went smoothly, and while lights and screens did their work there was no elaborate staging, no catwalks and no multimedia assault (see Figure 3.2). For the first time, the main attraction was a one-man band. The packed Arena provided evidence, not of the magnitude or sophistication of the stage show but simply the scale of Sheeran's appeal. That a local promoter, Futuresound, was instrumental to the gigs happening, reveals much of how music culture has changed in the city: 'Futuresound's concerts during 2019 handed a major contribution to the Yorkshire tourism economy this summer, most notably with the Ed Sheeran shows in Leeds which sold a total of 140,000 tickets' (Caasci 2019: 24).

FIGURE 3.2: Ed Sheeran performing at Roundhay Park in 2019. Courtesy of Eva Mills-Thomas.

Sheeran paid tribute to Futuresound onstage by reminiscing how he had played at the promoter's old venue, the Cockpit (see Lomax, this volume), several times en route to Roundhay: the two faces of live music in Leeds coming together at last.

## *Conclusion*

So, what is the future of the park as a venue? Roundhay has only a brief window in which it could host acts. There are pros and cons: as was noted in 1987, when someone books the park, that's what they get – a park. There are always changes in taste and style and there is not necessarily the same demand for huge outdoor shows of the kind seen in the park as once was the case. Yet, possibly even more so post-COVID-19, it is still perfect for 'special occasion' shows of a certain kind of genuinely popular act who can work with the opportunity Roundhay Park offers them: of the old guard, perhaps Paul McCartney or Stevie Wonder and, of the younger acts, Taylor Swift, Dua Lipa, or Adele … make your own list. And watch this infinitely adaptable space.

## REFERENCES

Anon. (1985), 'Rock fans hit out at traffic chaos', *Yorkshire Evening Post*, 8 July, p. 1.
Anon. (1993a), 'Achtung Roundhay', *Yorkshire Evening Post*, 14 August, p. 1.
Anon. (1993b), 'Rock in the park', *Yorkshire Evening Post*, 18 August, p. 1.
Anon. (2000), 'City suffers a party hangover', *Yorkshire Evening Post*, 10 July, p. 10.
Anon. (2006), 'Everything stops for Robbie', *Yorkshire Evening Post*, 8 September, p. 10.
Bruce, David (1993), 'Police foil the Chevin rave', *Yorkshire Evening Post*, 18 August, p. 1.
Bungey, John (1982), 'A day in the park … for a party with the Stones', *Yorkshire Evening Post*, 26 July, p. 4.
Burt, Steven (2000), *An Illustrated History of Roundhay Park*, Leeds: Steven Burt.
Caasci, Mark (2019), 'Company behind massive Ed Sheeran and Kaiser Chiefs shows in Leeds set for record year', *Yorkshire Post*, 24 October, p. 24.
Cooper, Pauline (1989), 'Park noise pop furore', *Yorkshire Evening Post*, 22 July, p. 2.
Corry, Howard (1987), 'Singin' in the rain', *Yorkshire Evening Post*, 29 June, p. 6.
Frith, Simon, Brennan, Matt, Cloonan, Martin and Webster, Emma (2019), *The History of Live Music in Britain, Volume 2: 1968–1984: From Hyde Park to the Hacienda*, London: Routledge.
Hurst, Mike (1989), 'Thousands thrill to simple minds', *Yorkshire Evening Post*, 24 July, p. 8.
Jeeves, Paul (2000), 'Love parade drug death', *Yorkshire Evening Post*, 10 July, p. 1.
Johnson, Michael (2019), in-person interview with P. Mills, Leeds, 12 July.

Mazierska, Ewa (2018), *Sounds Northern: Popular Music, Culture and Place in England's North*, London: Equinox.

McTaggart, Suzanne (2006), 'A Robbie dazzler!', *Yorkshire Evening Post*, 9 September, p. 16.

Mott the Hoople (1974), *The Golden Age of Rock 'N' Roll*, vinyl record, New York: CBS Records.

Rabbitts, Paul (2015), *Hyde Park: The People's Park*, Stroud: Amberley Publishing Limited.

Russell, Dave (2004), *Popular Music in England 1840–1914: A Social History* (Music and Society series), Manchester: Manchester University Press.

Smith, Andrew, Osborn, Guy and Vodicka, Goran (2022), 'Private events in a public park: Contested music festivals and socio-spatial justice in Finsbury Park, London', in *Whose Green City?* Heidelburg: Springer.

Spencer, Richard (1992), 'Rock of ages', *Yorkshire Evening Post*, 1 August, p. 3.

The Rolling Stones (2015), *The Rolling Stones: From the Vault – Live in Leeds 1982*, CD/DVD, Amsterdam: Promotone/Eagle Rock.

Thomas, Steven (1987), *Calendar*, Yorkshire TV, 25 June.

Wellington, John (1985), 'Crowd praised', *Yorkshire Evening Post*, 9 July, p. 14.

Wellington, John (1987), 'Bliss in the park', *Yorkshire Evening Post*, 29 June, p. 6.

Wellington, John (1988), 'Boosting the city's image', *Yorkshire Evening Post*, 30 August, p. 8.

Whitworth, Damian (1992), 'Wizardry fails to hide a decline …', *Yorkshire Evening Post*, 17 August, p. 3.

Whitworth, Damian (1993), 'The heavy mob invade Roundhay', *Yorkshire Evening Post*, 13 August, p. 3.

# 4

# 'Everything Is Brilliant in Leeds': Venues in the Leeds Indie Scene 1992–2012

*Dan Lomax*

Whilst it is tempting to view a city's music scene through the stories of the bands that rose to prominence, the infrastructure and places of a city can tell a longer story of the impact of social and cultural developments. The 1990s and 2000s saw substantial changes in how the experience of music was produced, shared and consumed, and the story of this change in Leeds reflects the experience of other cities and regions of the United Kingdom more generally. This chapter focuses on the indie/alternative scene in Leeds, in particular the venues and organizations that made up the infrastructure of the scene, allowing both creators' and consumers' spaces to interact with one another. It should be noted that at the same time, and often in the same spaces, both the dance and rock scenes in Leeds were also dominant parts of the city's music landscape, and whilst this chapter focuses on indie, these scenes would at times grow together and at others remain firmly separated. First, the chapter will define key terms of scenes and music ecosystems along with their components including venues, gatekeepers and finances, before then turning to an account of the Leeds indie scene in three phases 1992–98, 1998–2001 and 2001–10.

Studying the loss of venues and leisure spaces associated with the alternative cultures of the 1980s (punk, Goth and the radical Left), Spracklen et al. (2013) suggested that as a result 'the urban centre [of Leeds] is no longer a space in which alternative scenes can easily socialise and organise' (176). Their study takes a retrospective view to look back on the decline of the venues and spaces that were frequented in the 1980s. However, it ignores the more holistic perspective that whilst individual scenes rise and fall with a specific lifespan (Bennett and Peterson 2004), they are replaced by new ones, populated by new and younger agents and centred on different spaces. As this narrative will show, although the geography of where scenes were located within the city changed, the ability of the city to develop diverse musical cultural scenes and infrastructure remained strong through the 1990s and 2000s. The decline of both 'indie' and the nightclubbing part of the scene in the 2010s has led to a significant loss of venues and whilst this chapter looks at some of the reasons behind this, the story brings with it the hope that cultural consumption and creation has moved into new forms, even if these are not immediately recognizable to previous generations.

## *Music scenes and ecosystems*

The idea of music scenes is a popular and well-researched approach with Cohen (1999) identifying them as the people, events, organizations and situations related to the production and consumption of music of a particular style. When looking at a specific location or grouping of actors, particularly in the production and curation of music, the ecosystem approach (Hitters 2018) is a useful method to identify which elements of the wider scene can be identified. Writing from a contemporary perspective, Hitters identifies the intermediaries between makers (musicians) and the wider sector (consumers, audiences) as venues, festivals, bookers and 'pop education'. By looking at this list of intermediaries from the perspective of Leeds during the 1990s and 2000s, it makes sense to remove festivals, as they have only risen to prominence in the 2010s (Robinson 2015), and to define 'pop education' as the ways by which consumers found out about music at that time. During this period in Leeds, this was centred around the music press (nationally, plus local publications such as *Leeds Guide*, *Vibrations* and *Sandman*), record stores (particularly independent stores Crash Records and Jumbo Records) and nightclub DJs, as radio was still mainly a national concern, although as I will discuss, the rise of free access to music through illegal downloading (in the 2000s), and then streaming (in the 2010s) altered this aspect of the system significantly and had a major impact on music consumption.

While much of the literature around music scenes focuses on the production and consumption of live music, it should also be noted that other music-related media ecosystems, which include radio, nightclubs and even background music in pubs via jukeboxes, were important means by which musical and associated cultural products were shared and mediated within a scene. Indeed, given the higher cost and infrequent nature of live shows by both local and touring artists, the importance of jukeboxes in alternative pubs, including The Fenton and Faversham, and nightclubs such as The Phonographique can be seen as central to the introduction of new songs, styles and artists to audiences. The live show was often the culmination of an interest in an act leading to a deeper relationship between the artist and the audience, not the initial spark of interest.

## Venues

What is meant by a venue is not clearly defined, but generally includes spaces where scene members can socialize in a set location. In the case of music-based scenes, this included live music venues, pubs and nightclubs, although younger members of the scene also adopted other peripheral spaces. It would be interesting to track all venues within the Leeds indie scene but for the purposes of space and narrative this chapter will focus most closely on those associated with the 'indie' scene in the 1990s (The Duchess of York, The Town and Country Club, The Cockpit and Joseph's Well) and the 2000s (The Cockpit, The Well, The Hi-Fi Club, The Faversham and The Brudenell Social Club). This ignores many important pubs and nightclubs such as The Phonographique, The Fenton, The Warehouse, The Bassment, Café Mex/Wire, The Packhorse and live venues such as The Irish Centre, Carpe Diem and notably both Leeds University's and Leeds Metropolitan University's Students Unions, which hosted gigs, event nights and jukeboxes that at one time or another were part of the indie scene in the city.

## Gatekeepers

*Beyond artists and (venue) owners, key gatekeepers, or 'cultural intermediaries' (Bourdieu 1984), allow scenes to flourish within venues. Intermediaries use cultural knowledge to influence consumer behaviour and control 'taste' and style, occupying authoritative positions between production and consumption spheres.*

(Gallan 2012: 49)

In the 1990s and 2000s, the two most significant gatekeepers associated with venues were band bookers and club DJs as they curated the soundtrack of the venues in which they operated, especially as access to the music itself was much more limited than it has become in an era of music streaming. Whilst music fans could buy records, to have a large and current enough collection to have a contemporary view on a scene was expensive and time-consuming and it is not surprising that many bookers and DJs also had connections with, or worked at, local record shops.

The methods and requirements of these two gatekeeper groups varied significantly which meant that it was the club DJs that had a more immediate role in terms of introducing new sounds and trends. The DJ's challenge was to identify new content and then find a way of introducing it to an existing audience, in a way that was exciting yet still made sense in terms of what was currently popular. Indeed, there has always been a major tension in the DJ's role between entertainment (existing hits) and education (new sounds). This would involve finding appropriate places in an existing set where a new track made sense both sonically and culturally. For the experienced DJ, this was a challenge yet could be managed swiftly, with the introduction of new tracks taking a few weeks as the audience got to know the song, although in some cases DJs would take months building songs from obscurity to cult status to scene defining.

The band booker's challenge was different, with a need to build relationships with music industry contacts, such as agents, and then to sell shows with a significant lead time. This was a greater investment in terms of time, money and effort and carried with it a significant risk of failure. A wrong call by a DJ means an empty dancefloor; a bad live booking can cost a great deal of money and threaten a relationship with an important agent. As a result, as found by Foster et al. (2011), bookers will tend to share knowledge and rely on extensive relationships in wider music scenes about what is selling and what to book and as such have a much wider reach beyond the local scene both regionally and nationally. Whiting (2021) also suggests that the relationship between different gatekeepers and the venue is in fact two way, with the gatekeepers mobilizing the cultural value of the venue and each other's effort to create a positive feedback loop of reputation between the venues and the events they host. This in turn leads to positive reinforcement and drives certain venues to become central to scenes.

## Financial realities

As well as understanding the importance of venues, and those that use them to promote cultural content relevant to the scene, it is important to understand the financial imperative behind managing a venue. As with all businesses, making sure that a space is used efficiently is crucial to survival and profitability. Music venues are large spaces with significant fixed costs and a venue that is closed is not efficient with the role of the venue management to ensure that it is open and generating income as much as possible. It is rare to find venues that can operate in one format, or to one audience, and remain financially viable. A common thread through the story of Leeds music venues through the 1990s and 2000s is how this issue is addressed and, in many instances, it is this challenge that drives change, and often leads to (terminal) failure as new opportunities are sought or existing ones are impacted by external cultural or social change. It is also a reason the two student unions, with their different funding models, are not included in this narrative as centrally as they might be.

## Indie/alternative music in Leeds

The terminology on what constitutes various scenes and how they are connected is contested, but for the purposes of this narrative, the indie/alternative scene encompasses a reasonably wide range of mainly guitar-based music that followed from punk in the late 1970s but doesn't include overtly heavy rock or electronic/dance aesthetics. Whilst varied, the Leeds 1980's post-punk scene had two major threads, both of which can be regarded as internationally resonant and high points in Leeds alternative culture; the Leeds Polytechnic Art School scene centred on The Fenton pub threw up bands such as The Gang of Four, The Mekons and Soft Cell whilst the Goth scene based at The Phonographique, The Warehouse and The Faversham became regarded as the spiritual home of the subculture globally. Indie, a development from the post-punk era that preceded it with a more individualistic, and less overtly anti-establishment political message (Dale 2008) grew through the late 1980s and reached prominence with the Madchester Baggy scene and London's Shoegaze movement, and whilst some Leeds bands such as The Wedding Present, Cud and Chumbawamba were nationally successful, Leeds was not seen as a central part of the scene at that time.

## 1992–98: All you good good people

1992 represented the beginning of a new era for Leeds venues, but at the same time was one of declining interest in the Leeds indie scene. The year saw a peak of interest in grunge and a sharp contraction of the indie scene of the late 1980s. At the same time, as grunge acts such as Nirvana were dominating the alternative music sphere, a new generation of dance clubs inspired by the rave culture of the late 1980s including Leeds nights Back to Basics (see Chapter 12 by Stuart Moss) and The Orbit, was also in their prime. By 1994 an indie rebirth in the form of Britpop had emerged and would grow through the city over the following four years; however, Leeds could not boast one major Britpop act, and the region only delivered Brighouse's Embrace and York's Shed Seven (Millward et al. 2017).

Live music, both indie and alternative, in the early 1990s was centred on both of Leeds' main university student unions and The Duchess of York ('The Duchess'). The Duchess, a pub on Vicar Lane with a 250-capacity gig space, had started putting on live music during the mid 1980s and had teamed up with legendary Leeds promoter John Keenan, meaning it was the venue of choice for all smaller or upcoming bands to play in the city and was sustained by having live bands most days of the week. Given the need to tour to build a following, this meant that many bands that would become global stars would play there including Nirvana, Pixies, Oasis, Blur, Radiohead and Muse, alongside many local, tribute and other bands that would go no further. What mattered was that the venue was full six or seven nights a week.

The Leeds Town and Country Club (T&C) opened in October 1992 as a partner venue to a London sister venue. This allowed its owners to book acts for both the North and South of the country, although this plan only survived for a year when the Mean Fiddler group bought the London venue and opened it as the London Forum. The T&C included an 1800-capacity main room, 300-capacity upstairs bar and 400-capacity separate basement venue called The Underground. In addition to its extensive live music aspect, the T&C was also very dependent on its use as a nightclub venue. The main room was too large for alternative club nights and focused on mainstream retro-pop; however, the other two spaces are more closely related to this story of indie. From 1994 and 1995 with the rise of Britpop, the upstairs room became an important indie venue, with long queues within the venue to get upstairs as soon as the club doors opened. Meanwhile in The Underground, a new community was forming around soul, funk and jazz nights, allowing the venue to develop its own identity, with music students from the nearby Leeds College of Music (now Leeds Conservatoire) using the venue for rehearsal and impromptu performances.

The Cockpit opened in September 1994 as the Cock o' the North, a pub with a 500-capacity function room that was available for gig and club promoters to hire. The venue comprised three arches under Leeds Railway Station, with a pub occupying the smallest arch, the middle arch originally used as a small bar and bar cellar and the third arch housing the function room. Saturday nights were initially a rave night 'Propaganda', and Fridays an indie night, 'Brighton Beach', promoted by Richard Todd, ex-bass player of Leeds Goth band Salvation. Brighton Beach arrived just as Britpop moved from the underground to the mainstream during the winter of 1994–95, the club, with DJ Red Helen (Baron) and in-club performances from up-and-coming Britpop bands, became an important indie hub in the city and the wider region. Propaganda did not last long and in May 1995 the Saturday night was taken over by 'The Garage', a rock/metal club night promoted by Colin Oliver with stalwart rock/metal DJ Electrichead (Marcus Waite). Within a couple of years, Richard and Colin would merge their interests and buy the venue under their new business name Futuresound. This partnership of rock and indie would be at the heart of the venue and the companies it spawned, providing a crucial means by which the business could manage the variation of music scenes and fashion.

The live venue was not initially successful, partly due to the strong reputation of the Duchess and partly due to the in-between size of the main room: a 500-capacity venue that was hard to fill and fell between different gig circuits. Indeed, it took a few years, remodelling and a reopening of the middle arch as The Rockit (or The Venue or Cockpit 2 as it was variously renamed over the years) to provide a workable business model. This 250-capacity venue then acted as a feeder space, allowing promoters to book in bands at an earlier stage of their development and then welcome them back to the bigger main room later.

## 1998–2001: Take the long road and walk it

By the late 1990s, whilst the indie scene was still popular in terms of record sales and established bands, its relevance in terms of new musical trends was waning. It was felt that major labels and the wider music industry had driven indie music into a safe and marketable space. Large acts that had broken through would still sell well at larger Leeds venues such as the T&C and the Universities, and indie featured in the more mainstream club settings. Indeed, Saturday club nights at the T&C changed in 1998 to 'Sorted' a hybrid chart/pop/indie night where you could hear Take That, The Spice Girls and Blur back-to-back.

The impact of indie's mainstream success on smaller Leeds venues was significant, with the 'new' talent that drove smaller live venues and club nights no longer as exciting or credible. Brighton Beach was reduced to a monthly event and other indie nights adopted competing alternative sounds from dance (such as The Chemical Brothers and Underworld) and nu-metal. By being a shared indie and rock space, the Cockpit could cope with this change in fashion and as Brighton Beach faded The Garage grew, adapting to the new three-room layout by introducing metal and alternative rock rooms. In addition, new mid-week nights started covering pop-punk and hip hop (Dust, then Slam Dunk) as well as longstanding and well-respected indie-queer night Poptastic. Yet, by 2000 the last two remaining indie nights in the city were Brighton Beach and Gigantic (Thursdays at Leeds University), both of which were under threat due to falling numbers.

Through the late 1990s, the rise of The Cockpit as a live venue and its reputation and relationships with a new generation of bands, bookers and agents meant that it was becoming the first choice as a space for new bands to play in the city. The Duchess was supplementing its remaining interesting bands with more cover bands, meaning that its relevance and ambience diminished. Alongside this, Joseph's Well, a similar-sized venue had developed a good relationship with the punk, do-it-yourself and hardcore scenes meaning these acts had their own place to play. As a result, the Duchess was struggling and had lost its once dominant position by the time its lease was sold in March 2000, with the venue being redeveloped as part of the high-end County Arcade redevelopment that also saw the arrival of Harvey Nichols to the city.

In June 2000 the T&C also unexpectedly shut its doors when the venue lease was bought by leisure corporation First Leisure, who had embarked on a significant national expansion strategy. The venue was redeveloped as a mainstream nightclub and significantly increased its capacity by building a new floor across the main auditorium. At the time most large scale gigs moved over to the Leeds University Refectory venue, a space unloved by bands and audiences alike due to poor acoustics and the inability to disguise its main use as a dining hall.

With the loss of the Duchess and the T&C, and with The Cockpit and Joseph's Well both focused more closely on the rock scene, 2000 was another low point in the indie scene in Leeds. In early 2001 the Harvey Milk Bar (later Mine) at Leeds University Students' Union was also closed as the whole SU building was redeveloped, meaning Gigantic also lost its home and existed as a monthly night in the Bassment Club, a rock venue newly opened to accommodate the Dust club night after it had left The Cockpit. Finally, Brighton Beach was paused in spring 2001 to make way for a new pop/indie hybrid night at The Cockpit, albeit with a dedicated second room with Red Helen still as DJ. The scene consisted of two monthly club nights operating in rock venues, one second room and whatever gigs came through to the university students' unions.

## 2001–10: 'Everything Is Brilliant in Leeds'

Rebirth in indie came from America in 2001 with the arrival of The Strokes and The White Stripes and what was dubbed at the time the 'New Rock Revolution', a reintegration of indie with its post-punk and alternative past. A buzz had started to build over that summer with The White Stripes playing the Cockpit's second room in August and The Strokes scheduled to play the venue at the beginning of October to support the release of their debut album 'Is This It?' that month. An important date in the transformation of the Leeds indie scene was 11 September 2001. The World Trade Centre attacks in New York City, and at the Pentagon in Washington DC, even from as far away as Yorkshire, signalled significant changes. The increasingly cartoonish pop-punk and nu-metal scenes suddenly seemed very out of sync with the times, and the stripped-back new indie sound was taken up by a new generation as the sound of the new millennium.

Given the near death of the Leeds Indie Scene by the summer of 2001, there were initially few places to adopt this new indie sound. Gigantic returned in September 2001 as a weekly club night whilst at the Cockpit it was initially the third room of The Garage that first adopted the sound, especially as it seemed to chime much more closely with 1980s post-punk and the 1990s alt-rock sound than the Britpop sound that still dominated the Cockpit's Friday offering. Live music was also disrupted, with international flight bans, post-9/11, meaning the postponement of The Strokes' October show until February 2002. When the show did take place, having been upgraded to the much larger Refectory, it marked the confirmation of a new age in the city. By the summer of 2002, The Cockpit opened a new weekly Friday night 'The Session' with DJs Gigantic Dan (Lomax) and Red Helen, dedicated to the new indie sound and the new wave of acts including Yeah Yeah Yeahs, Interpol and The Rapture all playing the venue by the spring of 2003. Indeed, when American bands came to Leeds, they would talk enthusiastically about The Gang of Four, who they regarded as a key influence, but who had been all but forgotten by the Leeds indie scene (see Chapter 9 by Mallory McGovern), raised on a diet of 1990s bands from Manchester and London.

If Gigantic and The Cockpit represented the response of the existing indie survivors to the new scene, then a new generation first seized the reigns at the PIGS club night that launched late in 2002. Initially, a collaboration between art/graphic student and DJ Nick Scott and more established Brighton Beach regular Nick Hodgson (then drummer of indie band Parva, soon to be The Kaiser Chiefs) the collective expanded to include Nick's bandmate Ricky Wilson and local promoter Ash Kollakowski.

The venue for this infamous night was the Hi-Fi club, which had arisen from the almost complete relocation of The Underground from the T&C to a space close to the Leeds Corn Exchange. The Hi-Fi was a soul/jazz club and its décor reflected this; it did not look or feel like a traditional indie club. Musically the club did not sound like a traditional indie club either. New indie sounds would be mixed with 1980s pop and electroclash in a conflicting mash-up, inspired by the two Nick's (Scott and Hodgson) experiences in London clubs such as Erol Alkan's 'Trash'. PIGS was held monthly on a Tuesday night, meaning that it became a destination and an event, rather than a standard club night. An extensive queue resulted due to selective entry with an increasingly fashion-driven door policy. Also, in a first for Leeds alternative clubs, PIGS generated extensive online discussion using the proto-social media of the day, the PIGS chatboard.

Realizing that to scale up PIGS would probably dilute and destroy it, the organizers pursued additional opportunities, all of which would play an essential role in the development of the Leeds scene as it grew to national prominence. The two Nicks were approached to take over the third room at The Session at The Cockpit, cementing it as a weekly night in the new scene. With the main room now covering the new indie post-punk sound, the second room showcased the best of Britpop, and the new third room brought the new eccentricity from PIGS. In addition, in early 2004, they started a much more low-key mid-week gathering at Milos, the bar managed at that time by Ricky Wilson. The night was not a club night but a gathering, with the Nicks playing vinyl, and local bands playing short and often chaotic sets in the small and overcrowded space. This night, 'The Village Green Preservation Society' became the social hub for many bands and artists who would become the heart of the Leeds indie scene, including The Cribs, The Long Blondes, Black Wire and Grammatics. It would only last a year, as the success of The Kaiser Chiefs would make it untenable, but it became the ultimate insider's place, notably turning away Pete Doherty from the Libertines for being too wasted, but welcoming The Smiths' Johnny Marr and Blur's Graham Coxon.

In 2004, the owners of the Hi-Fi, Soundblast, who also had a stake in the longstanding Leeds pub/venue The Faversham (a centre of the Goth scene in the 1980s and the dance scene in the 1990s), collaborated with Ash Kollakowski in staging Nastyfest. This soon evolved into a biannual all-day live event highlighting new talent from the emerging indie scene, including an early headlining slot for Sheffield's Arctic Monkeys. The relationships developed from these events also led to a new Saturday club night at The Faversham, 'Bad Sneakers', that would bring back Nick Scott from PIGS as DJ and give Ash a venue to book bands into.

By 2005, both Futuresound/The Cockpit and the collaboration between Ash Kollokawski/Soundblast had established themselves as the main players of the new Leeds scene, just as the interest generated by the success of the likes of The Kaiser Chiefs and The Cribs brought the scene into national focus. Interest in the city would draw many young indie fans to the city, and clubs and gigs were numerous and busy. This success gave those working in the scene, particularly those booking live acts, better connections nationally, and cemented the position of their organizations in the wider music industry. Both organizations started to diversify their business, booking bands into larger spaces as they outgrew their own venues, starting festivals (Ash running Beacons festival 2011–14, and Futuresound running Live at Leeds from 2006). Both also started record labels (Bad Sneakers/Soundblast and Dance to the Radio/Futuresound) to capture the local talent. By the middle of the decade indie bands from Leeds such as The Kaiser Chiefs, The Cribs (from Wakefield), The Sunshine Underground and The Pigeon Detectives (signed to Dance to the Radio) were at the forefront of the national scene.

As the scene developed it become an open, creative environment drawing inspiration from many new sources including dance music (nu-rave), and Leeds became a place that aspiring bands, including Wild Beasts (initially signed to Bad Sneakers), Little Boots and Alt-J, and a generation of students would relocate to the city because of the perceived strength of the scene, positively characterized by The Kaiser Chiefs rallying cry: 'Everything is Brilliant in Leeds'.

The last piece of the Leeds indie jigsaw from this era was the rise of the now iconic Brudenell Social Club. Current manager Nathan Clark took over the venue in the early 2000s and focused on building strong relationships with bands, audiences, and promoters such that the venue became the pre-eminent small to mid-sized live space in the city by the latter part of the decade. As other venues struggled or moved away from the indie and alternative live scenes, The Brudenell has worked hard to ensure its survival, both in its live space and its pub/bar that has become a central part of the Leeds scene. In a circular sense, The Brudenell has adopted a similar approach to the Duchess and is its heir in the city.

## *Conclusion*

The Leeds indie scene dissipated after 2010, and whilst new bands emerged, the critical mass of both numbers and creativity was very much in retreat. With key venues closing or refocusing on new scenes, The Brudenell was the centre of what was left. Whilst the reasons for the decline of the individual venues of the 2000s Leeds scene vary, they all relate to the changing patterns of how music was consumed and how this affected the business models they were based upon. Richard Todd of Futuresound highlighted the rise of streaming and how music is consumed as a major issue for the decline of nightclubs, with DJs and clubs no longer acting in gatekeeper roles. Instead, fans and artists have different relationships mediated through social networks and streaming sites. In addition, he identified a change in consumption habits both of live music and alcohol, and a move to the 'eventization' of music and the rise of festivals as irregular sites of activity, meaning that many venues could no longer offer the differentiation required to sustain themselves as businesses.

The Cockpit closed in 2014, partially due to structural issues with the railway arches that housed it, but arguably because it was no longer a valuable or viable part of the Futuresound business model. The decline in nightclubs as leisure spaces (Davies 2013) had removed an important revenue stream which was impossible to replace. Futuresound itself no longer needed the venue to stage live music as, due to their established relationships with acts and the wider industry, they now booked acts into a variety of spaces, large and small, across the city and beyond, including Leeds Arena, the O2 Academy, Millennium Square, as well running their own festivals Slam Dunk and Live at Leeds. This separation of promoter and venue meant that the remaining venue owners, including The Brudenell, could be more efficient with bookings from multiple promoters ensuring gigs almost every night, whilst promoters were no longer tied to the success of their own venues.

If Futuresound's diversified business model offers one approach, then The Faversham/Soundblast approach highlights an alternative. The Faversham withdrew from indie events around 2010 realigning to its 1990s dance roots and then refocusing as a more upmarket events space. They restricted their venue offering to smaller and dance-focused clubs (Wire and the Hi-Fi) and a multi-use event space, Canal Mills (now also closed due to development pressures). This approach was mirrored by ex-Futuresound booker Simon Stevens and Ash Kollakowski's new ventures, the Belgrave Music Hall (opened 2013) and Headrow House (opened 2015), similar hybrid venues that included music only as part of a more varied events and hospitality business model.

The wider conclusion that can be drawn from the indie era in Leeds, 1992–2012, is that live music is just one aspect of a music ecosystem and that for music venues to survive they need to be as efficient as possible. As patterns of consumption have changed, such as the decline in nightclubs and the rise in casual dining and events, so too event spaces have needed to adapt. Venues that were reliant on pub/nightclub business, and tied to individual promoters, have made way for spaces open to a range of more diverse leisure activities, or like The Brudenell (or indeed the larger O2 Academy and Leeds Arena) have become a focal point for a wider range of promoters. Conversely, promoters less tied to venues and able to charge higher ticket prices can book acts into a range of spaces, as well as diversify their businesses into festivals and other locations. But from 1992 to 2012, the Leeds indie music scene was indeed brilliant and arguably became the last geographically orientated UK music scene in the pre-social media era.

ACKNOWLEDGEMENTS

The author would like to thank Richard Todd, ex-Futuresound co-owner, and Nick Scott, DJ and graphic designer, for their time and input into this chapter.

REFERENCES

Bennett, Andy and Peterson, Richard A. (eds) (2004), *Music Scenes: Local, Translocal, and Virtual*, Nashville: Vanderbilt University Press.

Cohen, Sara (1999), 'Scenes', in B. Horner and T. Swiss (eds), *Key Terms in Popular Music and Culture*, Malden: Blackwell, pp. 239–50.

Dale, Pete (2008), 'It was easy, it was cheap, so what? Reconsidering the DIY principle of punk and indie music', *Popular Music History*, 3:2, pp. 171–93.

Davies, Paul (2013), *Nightclubs – UK – May 2013*, London: Mintel, https://reports.mintel.com/display/664809/. Accessed 1 December 2021.

Foster, Pacey, Borgatti, Stephen P. and Jones, Candace (2011), 'Gatekeeper search and selection strategies: Relational and network governance in a cultural market', *Poetics*, 39:4, pp. 247–65.

Gallan, Ben (2012), 'Gatekeeping night spaces: The role of booking agents in creating "local" live music venues and scenes', *Australian Geographer*, 43:1, pp. 35–50.

Hitters, Erik (2018), *Live Music Ecologies and Value Creation for Musicians, Industries and Cities*, Rotterdam: Erasmus University Rotterdam, https://www.poplive.nl/wp-content/uploads/2018/09/Hitters-VMBRD16x9.pdf. Accessed 29 October 2021.

Millward, Peter, Widdop, Paul and Halpin, Michael (2017), 'A "different class"? Homophily and heterophily in the social class networks of Britpop', *Cultural Sociology*, 11:3, pp. 318–36.

Robinson, Roxy (2015), *Music Festivals and the Politics of Participation*, London: Ashgate.

Spracklen, Karl, Richter, Anna and Spracklen, Beverley (2013), 'The eventization of leisure and the strange death of alternative Leeds', *City*, 17:2, pp. 164–78.

Whiting, Sam (2021), 'The value of small live music venues: Alternative forms of capital and niche spaces of cultural production', *Cultural Sociology*, 15:4, pp. 558–78.

# 5

## Noise, Power Electronics and the No-Audience Underground: Place, Performance and Discourse in Leeds' Experimental Music Scene

*Theo Gowans, Phil Legard and Dave Procter*

Four men in pig masks stalk the dark cellar of the Royal Park pub. Harsh electronic tones and churning high-volume feedback fill the small space. One pig shrieks the refrain 'DO YOU LIKE THE FILM BILLY ELLIOT?' The delivery is both absurd and menacing. A genuine pig's head is pulled from a plastic bag. One of the man-pigs clumsily rolls over it. The others attempt to smash it with a sledgehammer and ignite it with lighter fluid. Eventually, the snout combusts, and the noise churns on. Moments after the performance ends the landlord storms in: 'Alright everybody, you've got about 30 seconds to get out me pub – I'm not having this shit in here!'

This appearance by the group Smell & Quim notoriously opened and closed the Termite Club's 2007 'Deaf Forever' festival within ten minutes of the event beginning. This was a performance of 'noise'. Tracing a lineage from the Italian Futurists through to the industrial music of the 1970s (Taylor 2016), noise describes a genre of music usually with no conventional instrumentation, structure, rhythm or tonality, which instead relies on sheer volume and visceral confrontation to make its impact. From the mid 1990s to early 2000s, noise – and its even more aggressive sub-genre 'power electronics' – became synonymous with the types of uncompromising music promoted by Leeds' Termite Club, which served as an influential promoter of experimental music between 1983 and 2010.

This chapter presents two practitioner accounts by co-authors Theo Gowans and Dave Procter concerning place – real and virtual – and the contemporary Leeds noise scene. These accounts are prefaced by an analysis of the present scene's heritage from the Termite Club: particular attention is paid to how discourses around the ethos of noise in Leeds have shifted since the Termite Club ceased its activities, primarily as a consequence of the venues in which these performances now take place.

## *No bigots: Shifting venues and shifting discourse*

Leeds has a longstanding reputation as the home of a vibrant experimental and improvised music scene owing to the historic influence of the Termite Club. Founded in 1983 by guitarist Paul Buckton and saxophonist Alan Wilkinson, 'the Termite' began as an eclectic promoter of left-field music, filling bills with indie bands and more experimental fare, before dedicating itself to the promotion of free-jazz, improvisation and other self-described 'difficult' music (Graham 2016: 18; see also Atton 2012; Foist 2016). Although many Termite gigs of the 1980s took place upstairs at the Adelphi Hotel, the Termite never had a permanent home in Leeds, describing itself as a 'moveable feast of improvised and related musics' (Termite Club 2001: n.pag.). Despite the music being self-described as niche, the Termite Club found a healthy audience particularly with Leeds' student population, drawn from two universities and the music and arts colleges, with events regularly promoted and reviewed in the *Leeds Student* paper throughout the 1980s and 1990s.

Amongst the music promoted by the early Termite Club were occasional representatives of the UK's underground noise scene, including Mike Dando, *alias* Con-Dom. In 1992, Dando relocated from the midlands to Leeds, becoming a prominent organizer for the Termite from 1995 (Foist 2016). Although the Club had promoted occasional noise gigs during the 1980s, the idea of the Termite as Leeds' *de facto* home of noise became firmly embedded over the decade in which Dando headed the committee, owing to his own associations with the global noise scene.

Foist (2016) has provided a detailed overview of the Termite Club and its place in the development of the British underground noise scene between 1983 and 2010, which is supported by significant oral testimony from organizers and participants. As a corollary to Foist's work, this section focuses on the discourses surrounding noise in Leeds and their transformations from the mid 2000s to the present.

Combining harsh electronic timbres, punishing feedback and confrontational performances, noise and its sub-genre power electronics took the abrasive sound and the oppositional and antinomian stances of prior industrial music to new extremes. Although 40 years have elapsed since Philip Best of power electronics group Whitehouse released the seminal compilation *White Power*, debate continues around the meanings and motivations of noise and power electronics symbolism whose use of visual and lyrical imagery relating to serial killers, death camps, sexual abuse, fascism, torture, racism, misogyny, deformity and abjection are well chronicled – as are attempts to rationalize or justify it (Bailey 2013). The concept of the noise artist 'holding a mirror up to the sickness of society' has often been invoked (Blenkarn 2019: 120, see also Stevenson 2016; Candey 2016), while Throbbing Gristle's assertion that taboo images could be utilized as a part of an agenda for cultural deprogramming also persisted in noise subcultures (Bailey 2013: 52). Dando himself echoed this latter position:

> Confrontation is the chosen method of education. Con-Dom generates brutality, pain, fear, hate (the instruments of control), *so that the existence of the forces of control may be acutely felt, experienced and recognised.* The aim is to provoke resentment / confusion / ambivalence, to upset and challenge conditioned expectation, to shatter preconceptions. [...] *The creation of blankness may be a necessary step towards enlightenment.*
>
> (cited in Taylor 1993, emphasis added)

Other Termite regulars did not necessarily adopt justifications as cerebral as those of Dando. Davy Walklett of Smell & Quim considers the adolescent shock value of power electronics to be thoroughly tongue-in-cheek: 'It's so important to realise and enjoy the ludicrous absurdity of guys screaming filth and hate-speak over washes of electronic shite' (Walklett in Grady 2016: n.pag.). Whether apologists for power electronics invoke appeals to enlightenment or absurdity, we can bracket such defences of the indefensible with Keith Khan-Harris' concept of reflexive anti-reflexivity (2007: 151), which describes how members of subcultural scenes knowingly use offensive discourses, while simultaneously distancing themselves from their wider cultural and social implications.

Of his time as the coordinator of the Termite Club Dando said: 'We were there to provide a platform for anything extreme [...] I don't care if people pillory me for that' (cited in Foist 2016: n.pag.). The anti-reflexive creed of 'anything extreme' was explicit during the 2004 Termite Festival held at East Street Arts: a studio space situated in an old mill building on the outskirts of the city centre. The extreme ends of the political spectrum were represented by Nocturne, a French martial-industrial project whose performance incorporated recordings of Nazi speeches and footage from concentration camps, and Militia: a group of eco-anarchists from Belgium who used junk percussion and footage sourced from animal liberation activists. Bradford zine *Idwal Fisher* recalled Nocturne's humourless performance as underwhelming to those who sought an absurd spectacle in their extreme music:

a French bloke called Nocturne who played for an hour in a beret to a totally bored and uninterested audience. A drunk Walklett shouts in his ear 'You're dying a fucking death mate' which has absolutely no effect on him whatsoever.

(Idwal Fisher 2014: n.pag.)

Dando retired from organizing gigs in the wake of the 2006 Termite Festival, which failed to secure Arts Council funding and swallowed the Club's finances. Experimental musician Melanie Ó Dubhshláine assumed the role as head of the committee, organizing shows for the subsequent three years and marking a shift in the Club's discourse around 'extreme' music.

The 2007 Deaf Forever festival at Royal Park Cellars was indicative of a shift in the types of noise presented by the Termite Club: acts using explicitly right-wing aesthetics were absent, although visceral performers were still present, such as Justice Yeldham who performed using amplified broken glass placed in his mouth. Performers combining noise and absurdity were also represented, such as Filthy Turd, Kylie Minoise, Puke Brigade, The Jim Morrisons and Dogliveroil. Although the opening performance by Smell & Quim resulted in the swift cancellation of the festival at its original venue, Deaf Forever resumed hours later at The Common Place: a collective-run social centre associated with Leeds Action for Radical Change, situated on the edge of the city centre in what was once a pork pie factory.

In early 2011, Common Place collective member Lynn Watson was identified as an undercover police officer, tasked with infiltrating environmental justice campaigns (Lewis et al. 2011). This led to the venue closing and relaunching as Wharf Chambers towards the end of the same year. While only a few Termite events had taken place at the Common Place, Wharf Chambers would become a significant venue for the post-Termite Leeds noise scene.

Despite attempts to raise the Termite's public profile through collaborations with Leeds Ladyfest and Light Night events in 2007, the Club's Arts Council funding applications were consistently rejected and Ó Dubhshláine declared the Termite Club 'mothballed' in a November 2010 letter to *The Wire* (Ó Dubhshláine 2010). Although this instigated a fallow period for the Leeds experimental music scene, a generation of younger performers such as Feghoots (Pete Cann), Guttersnipe and Territorial Gobbing (Theo Gowans) began regularly organizing gigs and one-day festivals from 2013. These events were held at Wharf Chambers and the collectively run rehearsal space Chunk in Woodhouse, which became the primary venues for post-Termite experimental music in the city.

Both Wharf Chambers and Chunk follow safer spaces agreements. Hill and Megson (2020) have highlighted the proliferation of these policies in feminist, do-it-yourself (DIY) and punk spaces over the last decade, and cite the policies of both Wharf Chambers and Chunk in their research. While Wharf Chambers' policy concentrates on how to tackle occurrences of violence, prejudice and harassment, Chunk explicitly enacts an exclusive policy, summed up by the inclusion of the words 'no bigots' on many of their event posters (see Figure 5.1):

> *We will also try to ensure that groups with harmful political positions will not be asked to participate in our events* [...] essentially this means *no bigots*. If you feel that something has slipped through the net, please let us know.
> (Chunk cited in Hill and Megson 2020: 68–69, emphasis added)

FIGURE 5.1: Poster for an experimental music event at Chunk, 14 November 2019. Courtesy of Theo Gowans.

A consequence of the association between the post-Termite experimental scene and venues with safer spaces policies is that the demographics for both performers and audience have diversified with a significant number of prominent female performers (both cis- and transgender) in what was previously a male-dominated environment. The use of reflexive anti-reflexivity to justify promoting groups with problematic political stances and imagery has also been deprecated as a result. In fact, many performers are vocally opposed to earlier power electronics discourse and its potential for harm. In *The Wire*, Urocerus Gigas of Guttersnipe described a moment when she confronted the use of fascist imagery beyond the Leeds scene:

> [The Adolf Hitler World Tour T-shirt man] was just another clueless privileged noise bro who thought it would be funny to shock people. I told him that […] he was either a fucking idiot, or a fucking asshole, or both.
>
> Several women from the audience, one of whom was Asian, came up to me afterwards to tell me they had also taken serious offence […] it is terrifying, engaging in a confrontation with some dude […] who, for all you know, might follow you out of the venue and assault you.
>
> (Gigas cited in Guttersnipe 2018: 32)

The diversification of performers and audiences within the Leeds noise scene and its tacit adherence to the ethos of safer space agreements do occasionally encounter opposition from representatives of the wider UK noise and power electronics scene who still follow the anti-reflexive ethos. The controversies surrounding Matthew Bower, a Yorkshire-based noise-rock guitarist who regularly played Termite gigs between the mid 1990s and early 2000s are illustrative of this. In 2019, Bower provoked controversy when his band Skullflower shared a bill with Bizarre Uproar at Leeds venue Temple of Boom. Bizarre Uproar is the project of Finnish noise artist Pasi Markkula, who also performs as the explicitly racist and misogynistic Xenophobic Ejaculation. The gig, organized by Scottish noise musician William Watts, was also intended to include Hal Hutchinson's Zyklon SS project, although the presence of Markkula alone caused a significant response. Rob Hayler, a former Termite Club organizer and performer, tweeted: 'Oh FFS! Just somehow lost a 14 tweet draft thread about Bower, that Bizarre Uproar show […] etc. In summary: 1. Skullflower review deleted from radiofreemidwich, 2. NAZI PUNKS FUCK OFF' (Hayler 2019: n.pag.).

The controversy surrounding Bower also emerged the following month when the London-based Raw Power festival cancelled his appearance after attention was drawn to imagery associated with Nazism on Bower's personal blog

(Miller 2019), prompting discussions that echoed wider societal discourses on the so-called Culture War. The following exchange is illustrative:

> **Commenter:** This scene seems to have been infiltrated by very 'safe' people when it should always fly in the face of it – the world isn't utopian and we are lucky to be involved in a broad mix of sounds and people who understand this.
>
> **Respondent:** Safe people? Or people who feel the need to challenge right wing etc views? Is it still considered edgy – or the opposite of safe – to trade in the same old tropes: totalitarianism, nativism, yadda yadda yadda?
>
> (Anon. 2019: n.pag.)

A recurrent suggestion that 'safe' people have infiltrated a scene implies that for many the anti-reflexive discourse of power electronics persists beyond the tight-knit Leeds noise scene, evoking a nostalgia for an antinomian imaginary that posited extreme music as 'dangerous', despite their performance to a homogenous audience where any implied resistance was itself performative. The shift in discourse within the Leeds scene itself, variously enacted through the policies of the venues central to the scene, Ó Dubhshláine's tenure with the Termite Club and shifting cultural values in the present generation of noise musicians indicates that performers leveraging an anti-reflexive ethos to justify the language and imagery of hate are currently unlikely to find a platform within the spaces that host the majority of experimental music events in the city.

## *Beyond venues: Noise walks and public space*

While Wharf Chambers and Chunk provide a stable home for the post-Termite noise and experimental music scene, unconventional music has a tradition of escaping into public spaces, for example Lol Coxhill's 2004 tour conducted from a skip, or Sophie Cooper's 2017 'Dial-a-bone' performances from an old phone box (Bath 2017).

Leeds-based noise musician Dave Procter had his first encounter with noise at the Termite's 2007 Deaf Forever festival. Subsequently, he became active in the post-Termite noise scene through his own project (Legion of Swine), regular 'difficult music' shows (Hogwash), occasional festivals (Swinefest) and collective events beyond gig spaces, known as noise walks. This section presents Dave Procter's account of these noise walks, and the artistic, social and political implications of noise music displaced from private spaces (e.g. performance venues) into what are ostensibly public spaces:

During the 2010s, my own performance practice was developing and I wanted to test ideas in non-traditional spaces: specifically spaces that were outdoors. Noise and experimental music shows usually take place in squats, venues, houses – the same places other types of music are performed in. Inspired by the Hamburg noise collective Kommerzbow, I wanted to try other approaches. Kommerzbow had subverted the idea of 'sound walks', where people follow a specific route and discover or rediscover the urban soundscape. Their idea was to add their own voices to that soundscape via the use of noise-making gadgets, human and non-human, as part of a mobile intervention into Hamburg's audio panorama.

Hayler (2015: n.pag.) has described post-Termite Club Leeds and similar experimental micro-scenes around the UK as comprising what he calls a No-Audience Underground: a term that describes a DIY ethos in which the audience is highly likely to be comprised of fellow musicians. My Leeds Noise Walks took the concept of the No-Audience Underground above ground – inviting anyone to play, and any observer to cross over from audience to performer. I wanted to try three different parks on weekday evenings in August 2015 and advertised for willing collaborators on social media with two rules only – '(1) if you turn up, you can perform (2) if you don't perform, you audio/video record and review'.

My decision was to perform as my noise act Legion of Swine with whoever showed up to participate. Legion of Swine is a playful, non-verbal communicative pig-man hybrid, who encourages collaboration by hand signals and squeals/grunts. It was important to create something visually appealing and absurd to attract people: a pig-man hybrid consisting of latex pig-head-on-lab-coat-clad-human seemed a possible way to at least stir curiosity, and an echo of Smell & Quim's notorious performance – minus the implied malevolent threat of violence (see Figure 5.2).

What was the point in these noise walks? Was it to provoke spontaneity in art production, dissemination and participation? Was it a mechanism to stretch performance creativity to new areas? Both of these are valid questions to an extent. My main intention was to repurpose and reclaim public space for spontaneous artistic performances. Public space in many so-called democracies is being slowly but surely sectioned off, commercialised and privatised. My ambition was to create something that fought back against the passivity offered by the market: to create something that costs nothing and encourages active participation and imaginative use of public space. If we put it on, (maybe) they will come.

The first noise walk took place in Burley Park, starting and ending at the bandstand – we will return to this place later in the text. Legion of Swine was joined by one collaborator, who also filmed the process. 30 or so joggers seemed unconcerned that this was a "noise walk and there was no need to run" and limited their interaction. Several dogs showed a passing interest in the pig as he completed a circuit around the park and tennis players asked 'Mr Pig' where he

FIGURE 5.2: Meanwood Park Noise Walk. Courtesy of Dave Procter.

was going. The performance finished after around fifteen minutes and we left the park to reflect.

The second noise walk took place a week later on Woodhouse Moor (Hyde Park) with a different collaborator in tow. The duo performed both on the move and statically. An interesting interaction occurred when the pair were approached by two members of a religious order who were intrigued by what was taking place. We explained our ideas and processes and our wish to create art spontaneously and to encourage others to join in and interact. Our visitors used some of the equipment we had for a while and went on their way. At the end of the performance it became clear that there is potential for participation if something is taking place. People (maybe) want to join in and be involved, even in an art form that they may not have previously known about or appreciated.

We would test this idea the next day on the final Leeds leg in Meanwood Park. This time with another new collaborator and a lot of homemade electronic noise making devices. Meanwood Park was fairly busy that day, especially with people walking dogs. Our noise making activities alerted the hounds and they pulled their owners towards our party. The dogs seemed really enthusiastic about the sound and the performance, but their owners definitely weren't. These humans would not be asking questions on contact microphones, 3W amps and feedback loops. It struck me at this point that this was the one occasion on the three walks where there seemed to be actual animosity towards what we were doing. Nothing was said, but the speed and intensity of trying to withdraw their animals and their facial expressions told a story – that we should not be doing this in a park, or near/in 'their' space.

Whilst Leeds has many great areas of green, natural space, it is also a city dogged by traffic pollution and the lack of any properly integrated public transport system, with the local bus service provided by FirstBus being nicknamed 'WorstBus' by many long-suffering residents. Becoming bored with the lack of punctual services and annoyed at the perpetually increasing price of a single ticket to town I started walking the 3.5 kms or so from my home at Burley Hill to the city centre, but found following the same route uninspiring and unhealthy because of the roads. I began walking along the Leeds-Liverpool canal instead, which took longer, but seemed healthier and pleasant on the eye, especially after the work on restoring the towpaths and cleaning the canal area over the prior decade. There is an impressive collection of different types of bridges and viaducts crossing the canal between Armley Ridge Road, where I joined the towpath, and the [Leeds] railway station, which is more or less the terminus of the canal.

This gave rise to an idea for public performance using the acoustic properties of the bridges and viaducts as part of the creative process. *Canal Bridges of Noise* took place over May and June 2016. Again, collaborators were requested on social media and suitable spaces were chosen for performances. A few gatherings took place with different performers attending each time. A favourite recording space was bridge 225H just outside Leeds railway station. This bridge has many rail tracks running over it, reverberating sound through the concrete and steel and contributing to any sound being created by performers beneath. Many people stopped to listen and to ask questions about the performances. The second event at midsummer by the stone bridge 221A near Kirkstall Bridge attracted several passers-by to watch. Further events were planned, but these quickly developed into the next project, which responded to tumultuous political events.

After the Brexit vote in summer 2016, I spent some time wondering what would happen next, both for myself and the wider country. The split in the Leave/Remain vote was almost reflected in Leeds, but in the opposite direction. There were, and still are, divisions in UK society widened by the flag-waving nihilism of the current government. Buoyed by ongoing opposition to Brexit and responses to the austerity politics of the Right, I wanted to create something regular and that would bring people together: collective live performance in public, free of market considerations with all welcome to watch and perform. This led to the equinox and solstice set of concerts starting with *Drone for the Spring* in March 2017 at the bandstand in Burley Park. These are still taking place now in Leeds (reinstated under COVID-19 conditions in midsummer 2021 by Theo Gowans and others) and with my SEMF

(Svenska Experimentell Musik och Film) collective in Värmland, Sweden in autumn 2021 in the park near the flat where I recently relocated.

Noise disrupts, but can also be welcoming. These projects have similar underlying ideals: encouraging collaboration, creativity, participation, nonsensical practice and performance and unusual experimentation. Earlier noise musicians often put their lack of conventional musicality at the service of opposing hegemonic morality through anti-reflexive positioning. The contemporary No-Audience Underground perspective simply asks a willingness to have a go, make noise and participate with no bar to entry, providing an alternative and potentially liberating experience.

## *Beyond physical space: Stream it yourself*

Dave Procter imagined the potential for noise and the No-Audience Underground to enact a surreal, utopic vision of a liberated anti-capitalist space. Utopia, of course, can be literally rendered as 'no place', which could equally apply to the virtual spaces that the micro-scenes associated with the No-Audience Underground found themselves in response to the COVID-19 pandemic.

Most musicians in DIY scenes do not rely on revenue from performances and music royalties for their primary income, usually producing cultural goods for little or no remuneration (Threadgold 2018), with ticket profits for gigs usually being passed to any touring performers (Bealle 2013). Although the financial stakes of participants in the No-Audience Underground may be lower than those of performers whose primary income depends on paid performances, the scene still runs in a state of terminal financial precarity as a consequence of its DIY ethos. While the COVID-19 lockdown measures of 2020 had a multitude of implications for live music in general, the Leeds noise underground was able to sustain itself despite the limited assets of its participants. Here, Theo Gowans gives an account of his experience translating gigs at Wharf Chambers and Chunk into virtual spaces as a consequence of the lockdown:

> The switch to virtual gigs was almost immediate once lockdown had been introduced in the UK. While I'd been organising noise and weird music gigs in Leeds for the last few years, the transition of No-Audience Underground logic to online gigs was a chaotic and slightly awkward one. As far as I'm aware I was one of the first promoters in the UK to organise an online virtual gig once Covid measures were introduced. I had arranged a gig for David Liebe Hart (a US musician and comedian who was touring the UK) on the 18 March. However, with lockdown introduced we had to organise an alternative. David had his entire UK tour cancelled and I'd refunded all the pre-ordered tickets. I was symptomatic at the time, but, between

myself and a team of friends, sets by each of the acts were filmed either at Wharf Chambers or from their houses. These were then streamed the next evening and people were encouraged to donate online to cover David's losses from the other cancelled shows. Twitch.tv, a website predominantly for streaming games enabled us to show these videos, along with a set by Petronn Sphene filmed at home (to replace their planned Guttersnipe set at the gig), and a live chat where anyone with a Twitch account could comment. Overall we had 810 people attend the gig. This figure was a tenfold increase on those who would have attended the gig in person, and people both across the UK and globally were able to watch. David Liebe Hart is certainly a better-known figure than most noise musicians but it's a clear example of the possible reach granted through streaming, compared to the 50 to 100 people I was expecting based on ticket sales.

Having our hand forced and streaming a gig through necessity showed that it was a more rewarding experience than I would have presumed. Of course this wasn't isolated to Leeds: within the same week fellow noise artists and organisers were hosting similar events of their own, such as Isolated Mass hosted by Kerry Hindmarch in Sheffield and the TOPH Housebound series by The Old Police House in Newcastle. After the success of the David Liebe Hart stream I decided to continue using this arrangement with a series of virtual gigs called *Heinous Whinings* as a way to replace other booked gigs throughout the spring and summer which I'd had to cancel. This involved asking artists to produce pre-recorded video sets that I would then stream on Twitch every Saturday night.

I hosted 13 of these gigs initially running from 28 March to 11 July 2020. Pre-recording allowed flexibility for people to prepare and produce their sets while avoiding the logistics and demands of live streaming. It expanded the possibility of participating acts from anywhere in the world without time zone or accessibility issues, although most acts were UK and Europe based, with many being regulars at Leeds noise shows specifically. Additionally *Heinous Whining* was able to host sets from acts in Mexico, New Zealand, the USA, Canada & Australia, such as Arboles Mentirosos, The Doll, Crank Sturgeon, Brian Ruryk and Justice Yeldham. In many ways the organisational demands of virtual gigs were similar to what had come before, though the event's requirements had dramatically changed.

Audiences fluctuated but we had between 30 and 90 viewers at a time, with viewers from all over the world on both the initial streams and the archives on YouTube. This immediately felt distinct from the experience of gigs prior: though it's hard to state statistics as a whole, in my experience of promoting and touring both the UK and Europe turnout for DIY noise shows would normally be between five and thirty punters, or for all-dayers and more well-known acts, maybe 50, though these were notable exceptions rather than the norm (Hayler 2015). This was probably the most immediate notable difference, though an obvious consequence of the untethering of the event from a specific place. The momentum for virtual gigs within the noise community persisted and through the spring and even writing now, in October 2021, virtual gigs are still happening and some spaces (such as Wharf Chambers) offer hybrid livestreaming gigs from the venue on their own Twitch channel. Many of the in person noise gigs I've organised or played since lockdown restrictions lifted have been streamed simultaneously, with viewers internationally being able to engage with what is happening in Leeds.

In general the No-Audience approach to music integrates with virtual platforms pretty seamlessly. The community aspect to participation in the No-Audience Underground was demonstrated to be of more importance than any sense of professionalism within the content itself. Videos varied between edited green screen footage and animation, to unedited sets filmed straight onto people's phones. Most viewers of these streams were themselves contributors to other streams or at least creatively involved within the 'scene'. Of course the immediacy and indeterminacy of performance within a physical space disappears due to the temporal and physical divide between the pre-recorded videos and the live streamed engagement, but this did little to hinder what makes the No-Audience Underground a self-sustaining community.

## *Conclusion*

Although noise and power electronics were not the sole domain in which the Termite Club operated, the persistence of the underground noise scene is the most visible legacy of Dando and Ó Dubhshláine's efforts to establish Leeds as a hub for 'difficult' music. The subsequent concentration of the noise scene from a wide variety of venues during the Termite Club's heyday to a smaller number of venues with explicit safer spaces policies does not necessarily mean that noise in Leeds itself has become 'safe' in a pejorative sense. Aspects of anti-reflexive practice are still present, for example in the use of pornography by acts like Filthy Turd (Mooney and Wilson 2013), or Pete Cann's work as Half an Abortion. The lower-hanging fruits of Nazism, violent misogyny and racial hatred may be shunned, but the volume and intensity of the performances remain unchanged.

Dave Procter's noise walks and the embrace of gigs in online spaces during the COVID-19 lockdowns of 2020 query what constitutes performance space beyond established venues. Theo Gowans' decision to move to hybrid live-streaming gigs can also be read in accord with the safer spaces and accessibility concerns of the venues like Wharf Chambers that host the performances. The continuing opportunities to attend Leeds noise gigs both physically and online through platforms such as Twitch also echo the conclusion of Harris (2021) that lockdown measures assisted the enculturation and legitimization of the 'online stage'. However, the use of platforms such as Twitch, and the wider underground scene's reliance on Bandcamp to distribute and sell music suggest that contemporary DIY has an entangled relationship with the corporate technological sphere: one which may be beneficial in terms of increased accessibility, while the reliance to which may antagonise the DIY ethos. Looking beyond this brief chapter, the question of how these tensions will manifest in the discourses surrounding the noise scene suggests an interesting avenue for further research.

## REFERENCES

Anon. (2019), Anonymised Facebook exchanges in response to Miller. Accessed 8 February 2019 [link no longer available].

Atton, Chris (2012), 'Genre and the cultural politics of territory: The live experience of free improvisation', *European Journal of Cultural Studies*, 15:4, pp. 427–41.

Bailey, Thomas Bey William (2013), *Micro Bionic: Radical Electronic Music & Sound Art in the 21st Century*, n.p.: Belsona Books.

Bath, Tristan (2017), 'Spool's out: The best releases on cassette this October', *The Quietus*, 23 October, https://thequietus.com/articles/23435-tape-column-sophie-cooper-worriedabout-satan-wild-card-pye-corner-audio. Accessed 18 November 2021.

Bealle, John (2013), 'DIY music and scene theory', in *Midwest Chapter of the Society for Ethnomusicology*, Cincinnati, Ohio, 13 April.

Blenkarn, Michael (2019), '*Confronting the shadow: A power electronics praxis*', Ph.D. thesis, Newcastle: Newcastle University.

Candey, Scott E. (2016), 'Chronicling US noise and power electronics', in J. Wallis (ed.), *Fight Your Own War: Power Electronics and Noise Culture*, London: Headpress, pp. 42–61.

Foist, D. (2016), '"The Horror! The Horror!": Leeds Termite Club and British Noise History', in J. Wallis (ed.), *Fight Your Own War: Power Electronics and Noise Culture*, London: Headpress, pp. 93–111.

Grady, Spencer (2016), 'The servitudes of slapstick: A comedy of violence', in J. Wallis (ed.), *Fight Your Own War: Power Electronics and Noise Culture*, London: Headpress, pp. 199–211.

Graham, Stephen (2016), *Sounds of the Underground: A Cultural, Political and Aesthetic Mapping of Underground and Fringe Music*, Ann Arbor: University of Michigan Press.

Guttersnipe (2018), 'Guttersnipe', interviewed by A. Bliss, *The Wire*, 417, November, pp. 30–32.

Harris, Taran (2021), 'Covid-19 as a catalyst for the enculturation of online video performance: The online stage during the coronavirus lockdown', *Sonic Scope: New Approaches to Audiovisual Culture*, no. 2, https://www.sonicscope.org/pub/cwuic4ju/release/2. Accessed 20 November 2021.

Hayler, Rob (2015), 'What I mean by the term "no-audience underground"', radiofreemidwich blog, 14 June, https://radiofreemidwich.wordpress.com/2015/06/14/what-i-mean-by-the-term-no-audience-underground-2015-remix/. Accessed 7 October 2021.

Hayler, Rob (@radiofreemidwich) (2019), 'Oh FFS! Just somehow lost a 14 tweet draft thread about Bower, that Bizarre Uproar show (which I went to knowing nothing about BU, just wanting to say hi to Stokoe) etc. In summary: 1. Skullflower review deleted from radiofreemidwich, 2. NAZI PUNKS FUCK OFF.', Twitter, 10 February, https://twitter.com/radiomidwich/status/1094659335924387841. Accessed 7 October 2021.

Idwal Fisher (2014), 'Recon special', *Idwal Fisher*, fanzine, Bradford, n.pag.

Khan-Harris, Keith (2007), *Extreme Metal: Music and Culture on the Edge*, Oxford: Berg Publishers.

Lewis, Paul, Evans, Rob and Wainwright, Martin (2011), 'Second police officer to infiltrate environmental activists unmasked', *The Guardian*, 12 January, https://www.theguardian.com/environment/2011/jan/12/second-undercover-police-officer-unmasked. Accessed 16 November 2021.

Miller, Dylan (2019), 'Does my black sun look big in this? Skullflower's patterns of predjudice', *The Quietus*, 11 February, https://thequietus.com/articles/26024-skullflower-matthew-bower-fascism-racism. Accessed 16 November 2021.

Mooney, James and Wilson, Daniel (2013), 'Beyond auditive unpleasantness: An exploration of noise in the work of Filthy Turd', in M. Goddard, B. Halligan and N. Spelman (eds), *Resonances: Noise and Contemporary Music*, New York: Continuum, pp. 312–25.

Ó Dubhshláine, Melanie (2010), 'Swingin' Leeds', *The Wire*, 321, November, p. 6.

Stevenson, Richaard (2016), 'Questionable intent: The meaning and message of power electronics', in J. Wallis (ed.), *Fight Your Own War: Power Electronics and Noise Culture*, London: Headpress, pp. 176–84.

Taylor, Phil (1993), 'Con-Dom', *EST*, 4 (Summer), http://media.hyperreal.org/zines/est/intervs/con-dom.html. Accessed 3 November 2021.

Taylor, Philip (2016), 'The genesis of power electronics in the UK', in J. Wallis (ed.), *Fight Your Own War: Power Electronics and Noise Culture*, London: Headpress, pp. 10–18.

Termite Club (2001), Termite Club website (archived), https://web.archive.org/web/20010518184306/http://www.geocities.com/sunsetstrip/pit/5725/. Accessed 18 February 2022.

Threadgold, Steven (2018), 'Creativity, precarity and illusio: DIY cultures and "Choosing Poverty"', *Cultural Sociology*, 12:2, pp. 156–73.

# PART 2

## PEOPLE: LEEDS' MUSICAL COMMUNITIES AND CULTURAL IDENTITIES

# 6

# La-Di-Dah:
# Some Thoughts on Jake Thackray and British Popular Culture

*Stephen Wagg*

This essay discusses the singer Jake Thackray, particularly in relation to his upbringing in Leeds and its likely influence on his art; his place in British popular culture of the 1960s and 1970s; and the resurgent and continuing interest in his work that has followed his death. Depictions of women and ideas of a mythical Yorkshire are central to this. A biography of Thackray, in press while the research for this essay was conducted and published in the autumn of 2022 (Thompson and Watterson 2022), reveals a good deal more in the way of facts about Jake Thackray the man, but, in any event, as the historian E. H. Carr (quoting Italian dramatist Luigi Pirandello) once said 'a fact is like a sack – it won't stand up till you've put something in it' (1990: 11). Into this sack this essay places the following suggestion: Thackray was troubled throughout his life by deeply damaging experiences of Roman Catholicism, visited upon him variously by a brutal father, bullying educators and a loving mother. While unable to free himself of the strictures imposed by this Catholicism, he took refuge in his art and, within that, in a mythical Yorkshire wherein women, historically often both the chief objects and the chief agents of Catholic repression, become cartoonishly sexualized and run rampant in a Yorkshire bacchanalia of the imagination. However, in the song for which he is best known and most celebrated, the female, this time not placed geographically and identified only as the apparent wife, ceases to be a sexual subject and instead becomes an intolerable, chattering intrusion upon male life. The lyric does not spare her.

### Jake Thackray: Performing dick, performing 'Jake'

Jake Thackray died in 2002. Four years later an impressive documentary about his life and work had been completed and was broadcast on BBC2 (Warburton

2006). For many watching it, possibly the most startling piece of information it contained was that the songs for Thackray's first album, released in 1967 when he was nearly 30, had been written in a school exercise book while he was still living with his mother in Leeds. Moreover, at the instruction of his mother, a devout Roman Catholic, he had written 'TTGOG', which stood for 'To the glory of God' at the top of every page. This, of every observation made of Thackray, has to be the most telling. As his widow Sheila pointed out, it meant that Jake 'hadn't to take any personal pride in his gift'. Thackray was said to be close to his mother and, as a student at Durham University had sent part of his grant money home to her (Bell 2016). However, the brutal nature of his early life seems uncontested. His father, a policeman, was 'not loving' and would 'knock them [presumably Jake and his siblings] about', said Sheila, and he received a punitive education at a local Jesuit college. His friend John Ethridge, who had also been to a Catholic school, recalled: 'we used to compare the kind of beatings we'd had as children' (Warburton 2006: n.pag.). 'Our form master was head of English', Thackray had once written,

> and he put the fear of God into people. That was his job: fear of God into people. He put a lot into me and, although I've since got rid of some of it, there's still a good bit left [...] He was a man who developed and worked hard on his scorn, flexed it like a bodybuilder does his muscles. And then he used to beat us up with it.
> (Thackray 1977b: n.pag.)

His widow also hinted at an emotional reticence, widely attributed to Yorkshire males in local Muck-or-Nettles mythology (Wagg 2003) – Sheila recalled his chat up line when they had first met at a local folk club as 'What d'they call you then?' These experiences stayed with Thackray: 'I can't see myself', he says in the documentary, 'rising above my raising [...]' (Warburton 2006: n.pag.).

Dealing with the enduring problems of his raising may have led to a fondness for drink; a contributor to jakethackray.com wrote:

> Intake School was/is a secondary school in West Leeds where Jake used to teach. He was popular with his colleagues except when he had a few drinks at lunchtime and decided not to come back for the afternoon and they had to take his classes for him.
> (Pace n.d.: n.pag.)

Thackray died an alcoholic (Newell 2011). It seems that he dealt with it (insofar as he dealt with it at all) chiefly through a reinvention of himself. Like many public figures, he developed a persona for performance purposes, which was distinct from his private self while bearing the same name. This was done predominantly through his music. He was a skilled, self-taught guitarist and, during his time in Europe following university had been taken by the work of two singer/songwriters: the Frenchman Georges Brassens and Belgian Jacques Brel. This had led him to develop his own English north country version of the French chanson.

Jake the performer also affected a rural Yorkshireness, albeit that his experience had been largely urban (in Kirkstall, Leeds). He was actually born (in 1938) in Pickering (Academic Dictionaries and Encyclopedias n.d.), 50 miles north-east of Leeds, where his father was the village policeman, and the family moved to Leeds when he was still a boy. Speaking about his background in 1976, Jake said that 'we were a working-class family from Leeds, *which is in Yorkshire*' (Warburton 2006: n.pag., emphasis added). His precise placing of Leeds here may have been because he was not confident that his interviewer knew where Leeds was; equally, and perhaps more probably, he was keen to stress his identification with Yorkshire, rather than specifically with Leeds. The Yorkshire moors of his birth are, after all, repositories of myth. According to local lore, they are inhabited by hardy, honest-to-goodness, plain-spoken folk, unencumbered by personal pride – as the Sheffield-born Labour politician Roy Hattersley (1991: 15) once said: 'Yorkshire is an idea, not a place'. Thackray the artist liked to see himself as a man of the dales. Indeed in 1971, Independent Television News (ITN) sent him to Swaledale, 70 miles north of Leeds, to make a documentary film (see Dodge Devil 2016). Here his apparent lack of self-esteem makes him an occasionally awkward interviewer and he seems uncomfortable meeting the flesh-and-blood Yorkshire people he has mythologized in song. Predictably, they aren't always as he's imagined them: 'No life is this', he suggests to a veteran, weather-worn sheep farmer tending his flock. 'Best job in the world', replies the shepherd.

Jake also sings songs written especially for the programme. He frequently escaped in song to his fabled Yorkshire and one song, *Old Molly Metcalfe*, is sung with a choir of village school children. *Molly* featured on Jake's third album *Bantam Cock* (1972) and in another TV appearance in 1971, Thackray introduced the song with an explanation of the lyric: it contained references to the traditional way of counting sheep on the Yorkshire moors and was a tribute to his great aunt Molly, who had died young, having begun minding sheep at the age of 7 (TallPiler 2009). The counting method was authentic, but as his friend northern playwright Alan Plater made clear, the great aunt was an invention (Warburton 2006).

Jake Thackray's alter ego took charge, it seems, only when he was singing. Here his impassive face, remarkable command of the language, precise Yorkshire-inflected diction and witty delivery of often risqué (for the time) punchlines gave him an air of mastery. But Jake the private individual was never comfortable with Jake the performer. Perhaps this was Catholic guilt over his, invariably erotic, artistry. Maybe, having as a young man had his creativity scorned, he felt unworthy of public acclaim – his manager Alex Armitage said that Jake liked to perform for as few people as possible (Warburton 2006). Certainly, he was uneasy with some of the conventions of show business – he refused, for example, to play encores 'saying something along the lines of, "if it pleases you to see a grown man walking on and off stage with a guitar, I would have started earlier"' (Thackray 1977b: n.pag.). In 1977, Jake Thackray recalled with affection the first eleven songs that he'd written but rued the day that he'd become a 'performing dick' (Thackray 1977b: n.pag.).

## A wry look at the week

While still working as a teacher (and encouraging pupils in their own performance [Warburton 2006]), Jake tried his music out locally. 'In the morning', he remembered with relentless self-effacement, 'I was a mediocre teacher [...] In the evening, a mediocre singer, coming on after Vi Tye (housewife and stripper) at the music hall in Leeds' (Thackray 1977b: n.pag.). Changes in British television brought his (emphatically not 'mediocre') work to a wider public.

The 1950s had seen important political developments in British broadcasting. Following the entry into parliament of a number of Conservative MPs linked to the world of impression management (advertising, public relations…) in the general elections of 1950 and 1951, a campaign for a commercial television channel led to the establishment of Independent Television (ITV) in 1954 (Wilson 1961). From 1955 onwards, a swathe of British TV viewers would be exposed to explicitly commercial discourse. A dimension of this entailed commercial advice or purported vigilance on behalf of 'the consumer' – as dispensed on *Braden's Week* (ITV 1962–67) – was presented by expatriate Canadian comedy actor Bernard Braden. There were parallel moves at the BBC, the (invariably high-handed) public service broadcaster, for a less constrained style of programming, which addressed its audience as consumers and spoke on their behalf. An early manifestation of this new thinking was *That Was the Week That Was*, briefly broadcast late on Saturday nights in 1962 and 1963, which subjected current (Conservative) ministers to a degree of ridicule and cast a caustic (and generally socially liberal) eye over the week's news. The programme's producer Donald Baverstock had suggested that 'on Saturday night people are more aware of being persons and less of being citizens than at any other time of the week' (Milne 1988: 32). This rationale was of course already being applied on the commercial channel and in 1969 the BBC introduced *Nationwide*, an early evening magazine programme that mingled news, consumer affairs and light entertainment. *Nationwide*, and more specifically its audience, became the subject of a landmark sociological study by researchers at

Birmingham University's influential Centre for Contemporary Cultural Studies, and concerned that ideological themes were now being fed to viewers under the mantle of consumer-friendly TV bonhomie (Morley and Brundson 1999).

The paradigm for these broadcasting developments was the so-called 'satire boom' wherein comedic scepticism was being woven into current affairs reportage. More and more people were being called in to take what journalist and ex-Conservative MP Matthew Parris recently called 'a wry look at the week' (Great Lives 2020) – a task that has long since become a media staple. Most recruitment for this task centred on the 'smoker' evenings at Cambridge University which, as Clive James (2001) records, attracted London agents, particularly when comedy writer, performer and entrepreneur Peter Cook was a student there, between 1957 and 1960. Cook had worked on the pilot for *That Was the Week ...* and appeared several times on *Braden's Week*. He offered exactly what was now in demand: a capacity for sophisticated, irreverent commentary that was at the same time not 'party political' and certainly did not treat directly with the ongoing strife between capital and labour. So did Jake Thackray, who following some guest appearances on the comedy sketch show *Beryl Reid Says Good Evening* in the spring of 1968 joined *Braden's Week* later that year. When *Braden* was discontinued in 1972 he moved to *That's Life*, probably the definitive British consumer TV programme, begun the following year by BBC and fronted by Braden's researcher Esther Rantzen.

Those who knew Jake have talked about his politics, formed in part during the time spent in Algeria during its war of independence (1954–62), which, they say, melded socialism, Catholicism and anarchism. He was very much 'a supporter of the underdog and ordinary people', said his friend Ian Gliddon (Warburton 2006). But Jake's art was such that it permitted little direct expression of these politics, and this would have attracted TV producers. Besides, as his brother-in-law Richard Irons attested, when he worked for the BBC, his songs, written that week in order to be topical, were closely scrutinized, and when deemed necessary, doctored, by BBC censors (Warburton 2006). Sat on a stool with startling good looks (he resembled the French actor Jean-Paul Belmondo), a blank expression and a polo-necked sweater, Thackray looked every inch the iconoclast and his 'wry look at the week' reflected this, as did most of his *oeuvre*. One song may illustrate this point: On 7 October 1970, Jake sang 'The Municipal Workers' Strike' on *Nationwide*. The strike by local authority manual workers had begun the previous month and in October was to be the subject of angry exchanges in the House of Commons between Conservative government minister Robert Carr and Labour frontbencher Barbara Castle (Hansard HC Deb., 29 October 1970). This indeed was an historically tempestuous time in the history of British industrial relations. The previous year Castle, as Secretary for Employment and

Productivity in the then Labour government, had split the labour movement with her proposal (in the White Paper *In Place of Strife*) to impose settlements in industrial disputes; Labour had lost the General Election the following June. Jake's song acknowledges none of this: BBC guidelines and the *Nationwide* ethos would not have permitted it and Jake's art, in any event, had a different mainspring. Instead, Thackray did what he would so often do: he created a fantasy in which female libido ran rampant, and for the time being would not be serviced by the absent council workers. The song is a comic lament for the absent parkies, jolly rat catchers, grave diggers, public bath attendants ('Many a female cleavage heaves for your massage') and lusty dustbin men: 'There's many a bulging dustbin / That craves your touch / Many a bulging housewife / Would be glad of half as much'.[1] The song also includes a throwaway remark about local politicians – 'Lowly sewer men shovelling sewage, take no notice of sniffs and jeers / We all know that, down at the town hall, they have all been / Shovelling it for years'. There are one or two similarly passing references to politics: a dismissive allusion to the 'Rural District Council / Where they'll all talk a load of clap-trap' from *Little Black Foal* (Thackray 1967), and in *The Hole* (Thackray 1969) the narrator was 'in the British worker's classic pose I was leaning on a door' – a minor betrayal, surely, for a socialist and rooter for the underdog. There is also, remarkably, *God Bless America*, a coruscating indictment of US culture in which an imaginary American tourist reflects thus on the British:

> Their French-fried potatoes only make me smile / And they can't grill niggers quite the way that we do – / Southern style / God bless, God bless America, God will because God's okay / God will save, God will save America, if he's cleared with the CIA.[2]

Here, arguably, the private Jake and the public one for once embrace. Thackray certainly wouldn't have been allowed to sing it on television and the majority of his work seems to be centred on women: women feature strongly in his songs and so does their sexual desire, but his females, ideologically speaking and literally, come in all shapes and sizes.

## *Jake and the women*

Thackray's songs were predominantly what might be called carnivalesque. In BBC2's documentary, there is a reference to his 'Rabelaisian earthy humour' and Plater aptly summarizes the landscape inhabited by Jake's invariably lusting characters as a 'parallel northern universe […] a second cousin to the real world, a wonderful place to escape to and have fun in' (Warburton 2006:

n.pag.). This seems to underplay the complexity of Thackray's range: the songs aren't all fun and his catalogue embraces a huge range of imaginary women and girls.

Females sometimes feature as oppressive figures, slaves to snobbery or convention or as harridans, inflicting sheer marital cruelty; these traits are invariably accompanied by a physical ugliness. *Lah-Di-Dah* (Thackray 1968), for instance, is, on the face of it, a love song and was improbably covered in a duet by mainstream singers Rod McKuen and Petula Clark in 1971. As the title suggests the song is primarily about suburban pretension, peddled in the main by females: in the song, the narrator professes devotion to his betrothed, despite the insufferable nature of her relatives, who include 'your gruesome Auntie Susan' and the bride's mother who is characterized as 'crabby old batface'. He promises 'I won't run amuck when the females chuck / Confetti in my ears'. In *Little Black Foal*, the narrator pines for a higher-born girl who has a mother 'with the huge hindquarters / Which she's tried disguising at considerable expense / Off to dig the dirt with the local ladies? / Well, it's all a load of stuff and nonsense'. On his third album, *Bantam Cock* (1972) Thackray sang of a *Jolly Captain* who was 'A simple man, and a good man, but the bane of his life / Was his ill-tempered, bad-hearted bitch of a wife'. The wife falls downstairs and breaks her neck. Before expiring of her injuries she vows to hound him from beyond the grave. The jolly captain retorts: 'No, she won't come to haunt me and taunt me, I know / Cause I buried her face downward, she's a long way to go'. When Jake sang the song to an audience at St Thomas Aquinas Catholic School in Birmingham in 1968 each of these couplets drew a huge laugh from the audience (Jake Thackray Unseen 2016). Sometimes they are obvious symbols of class privilege, as with Roedean-educated *Caroline Diggeby-Pratte* (Thackray 1969), who 'likes marzipan and pussycats / Caroline's the latest in a very long line of aristocratic Prattes / Somebody may love you, Caroline, hopefully / Caroline, oh, callow Caroline, I know it won't be me'.

Often sex and/or the female longing for it insinuate themselves into songs that are primarily about something else. A tribute on his first album to a rickety north 'Country Bus' notes that it's suitable for copulation: 'We've got the springs in our backsides to ride out your bounce / Though you may stumble / After the dance on a Sat'day night / Backseat lovers don't grumble / They seem to manage alright' (Thackray 1967). Sex is interrupted ('We were getting to a very important bit') by lovable but intrusive dog *Ulysses* (Thackray 1967) and sex is even invoked in his *Last Will and Testament*, Thackray's (1967) witty dismissal of the bourgeois niceties of funeral observance: having decreed that there be 'no forget-me-nots, no epitaphs, no keepsakes; you can let my memory slip / You can say a prayer or two for me soul then, but make it quick, boys', he adds 'Lady, if your bosom is heaving don't waste your bosom on me / Let it heave for a man who's breathing, a man who can feel, a man who can see'.

Occasionally, sex is the reward for Thackray's cherished underdog, who is privately desired and taken by the socially superior female. Such, for example, is the fate of the didecai (or 'didecoy', meaning 'tinker') in *It Was Only a Gypsy* (Thackray 1972) who is beaten by a policeman but beds the policeman's wife, the proud possessor of 'breasts of alabaster'. The lady in question finishes the song thus: 'Between her breasts a hedgerow nosegay / In between her teeth a tell-tale whisker / The house is full of clothes-pegs'. A similar fate was accorded to another, earlier creation, *Scallywag* (Thackray 1967), 'blackguard of the neighbourhood': 'You smoke your evil-smelling shag, and you get drunk as a newt / To boot, and this mortifies the Ladies' Institute'. 'It's no wonder when you wash your back down by the riverside', the song ends,

> Even the local countess finds it hard to look away as you scrub / She's only got to give you the eye, eye, eye, and in the by and by/You'll pussyfoot through the squire's rhododendrons on tippy-toe / Tapping at her window when it gets dark.

The theme of illicit sex across the social class divide is, of course, an old-established one – one thinks, for instance, of the traditional folk song *Matty Groves* (Fairport Convention 1969) and inevitably of D. H. Lawrence's (1960) *Lady Chatterley's Lover*; it's perhaps not a coincidence that Jake in the Box (2021), a double act that sings Thackray's songs, includes both *It Was Only a Gypsy* and a song called *The Trial of Lady C* in their repertoire.

The Scorn-Him-By-Day/Have-Him-By-Night hypocrisy aside, the women in many of these songs (along with the men) get what they want and are sexually active on their own account. These are most likely the songs that Plater had in mind when he spoke of Jake's *oeuvre* as a parallel universe in which to have fun (Warburton 2006), and a number of other songs, including those that were/are probably Thackray's most popular, spring to mind. In these, the women are defined primarily by their desires and, in some cases, by the fervent realization of these desires. An early and striking example is *The Statues* (Thackray 1967), in which the narrator and his equally inebriated uncle witness a statue of Britain's first Prime Minister Sir Robert Walpole – 'Shaking with a century of petrified desire' – ravishes a shy female bronze statue stood in the adjoining lake. She does not initiate this, and the drunks try unsuccessfully to protect her, but 'Today she wears a smile, her face is alight, and her eyes are bright / Ever so bright / Awfully bright'. The *Country Girl* (Thackray 1969) – 'Milking the goats, her legs open wide / All springtime blows inside her petticoat' – dreams of, and is fulfilled by, sex: 'Putting on her pinafore / Combs from her hair all the straw that was there from the night before / Smiles to herself now and then'. *The Lodger* (Thackray 1971) is seduced in turn by his landlady's three sex-hungry daughters, followed by the landlady herself; he declares then that he has no strength left to accommodate Grandma. There is also the garish tale of Isobel, who makes love on national monuments: 'The Forth Bridge, The Cenotaph, Balmoral and Wembley / The British Museum and the House of Lords / So many ticks in her National Trust catalogue' encompass the places 'Where Isobel's white shoulder blades have briefly reposed' (Thackray 1972). Similarly, in *The Castleford Ladies' Magic Circle*, while their husbands are playing snooker purportedly respectable ladies 'in Sunday coats and flowerpot hats' convene to observe 'unspeakable pagan rites' and 'frantically dancing naked for Beelzebub' (Thackray 1969). But perhaps Thackray's most eloquent and finely crafted song about a female striking out against suburban prejudice is *The Hair of the Widow of Bridlington* (Thackray 1977a). Here a widow of 42, living in this genteel resort on the north Yorkshire coast, does as she pleases, buying a motorbike and using it to conduct affairs with the local fishermen:

> And she was fond of fishing boats and all their beardy crew / And partial to a salty kiss or two / And some of them would gruffly whisper, 'Marry me and stay'/But blackbirds do their singing from a different bush each day.

Locals angered by her promiscuity attack her and shave her head, but she is undeterred. She buys a wig, consoles herself that the hair will grow again and moves to neighbouring Scarborough, where more fishermen await her.

Jake Thackray's songs mainly describe women through their bodies (their cleavage, their alabaster breasts, their white shoulder blades and so on) and, in general, the implication is that those bodies should be enjoyed. But, as an artist and as a person, he seems to have had difficulty in going beyond that. For example, he wrote a song about the Miss World contest (*Miss World*, featured on his live album; Thackray 1971) and sang it on *Braden's Week* in November 1968. The song has some droll fun at the expense of imaginary 'Miss Dogger Bank' and 'Miss West Bromwich', but the joke is on the women who are, once again, reduced to their (here unwieldy) component parts: 'Breasts and thighs that hypnotise me / Galvanise me, so agonisingly / But such a size that, not surprisingly / She can hardly move at all'. Instead, the song makes more palpable hits on international politics – a Thackray rarity – making wry asides about the American invasion of Vietnam and the Cold War: 'And what does Miss USA say? / She says that she's everyone's sister / But she don't give a damn for Miss Vietnam / And she reckons Miss Russia's a Mr' (the latter remarks a reference to claims often made during the Cold War that female Soviet Olympic athletes were actually men). As for women's liberation, Thackray homed in on one of the lesser milestones in the history of this movement:

> The Women's Liberation Movement, of which, let it be said, I am a violent admirer, held, in 1970, a branch meeting at which it was decided to a man [*sic*] that it was about time they took matters into their own hands. They marched out of the meeting hall on to the cobblestones and pavements of West London, where they began to pinch men's buttocks, publicly and lasciviously, to show how equal they could be if they really wanted. It was a bit silly, so I did a silly song, *The Ladies' Basic Freedoms Polka*.
>
> (Thackray 1977b: n.pag.)

Many listeners to this song will want to take it at the author's estimation: Thackray always seemed more comfortable with imaginary women who use their bodies for physical gratification than for political gestures. What is probably Thackray's best-known song about women, however, is also his most contentious and is seemingly unlike any of the others.

### *Jake and legacy: The next misogynist?*

'On Again! On Again! ... yes we do that', says Ron Middleton (2021) of tribute act Jake in the Box unprompted, 'but only where we are confident that it will be well received. It was of its time, but there are other fabulous songs to fill a set with!' He's referring to a song written by Thackray and sung on *That's Life* in January 1977; it became the title track on his fourth studio album, issued by EMI the same year. BBC2's documentary begins with a tribute to this song. Writer and broadcaster Danny Baker praises the song's first line 'I love a good bum on a woman, it makes my day'; when it comes to a discussion of the greatest ever opening line to a song this, he says, is 'the marker' (Warburton 2006). Ian Watson, producer of *Sister Josephine Kicks the Habit*, a musical based on Thackray's work and performed in Leeds in 2005,[3] judges the second line to be 'every bit as good'. He recites it: 'To me it is palpable proof of God's existence, *a posteriori*'. 'And that's a pun in Latin', he points out. 'It's just a very, very beautifully crafted line' (Warburton 2006: n.pag.). The verse moves into a familiar Thackray tribute to the female anatomy: 'Also I love breasts and arms and ankles, elbows, knees'. However, he continues,

> It's the tongue, the tongue, the tongue on a woman that spoils the job for me / Please understand I respect and admire the frailer sex / And I honour them every

bit as much as the next misogynist / But give some women the ghost of a chance to talk and thereupon / They go on again, on again, on again, on again, on again, on again, on.

The song is, thus, in the first person; contrary to Thackray's usual *modus operandi* neither the connoisseur of women's bums, nor the female chatterbox is given a character. The woman in the song natters 'on a Sunday when I go singing hymns and drinking heavily', 'when I'm saying my rosary' – even when they're having sex 'I might just as well have been posting a letter or stirring up the tea!' Any resemblance to Thackray's own life might be coincidental, but he made no effort to avoid it.

This, understandably, is likely to be Thackray's most argued-over song. Its sentiments, when distilled (women can be nice to look at but, oh dear, try shutting some of them up) could have been expressed, even at the time it was written, by the most tiresome of male saloon bar bores. For its defenders, the skilled construction of the song transcends such considerations. For example, blogger Andrew Hickey reflects 'Personally, I don't see the song as misogynist at all, even though it contains the line "I honour them every bit as much as the next misogynist." The song is much, much too clever for that' (Hickey 2007). Equally, the song is liable to have confirmed Jake's standing among contemporary opponents of 'political correctness' and those given remarks like 'Honestly, you can't say *anything* nowadays'. 'Jake Thackray was a dyed in the blood Yorkshireman', said an anonymous purchaser of the Thackray retrospective box set on the eBay website in 2008.

> He lived in an era before 'Political Correctness' was invented. And that is one of the great joys of this collection of his music and lyrics. He wrote songs about love, relationships, politics, class divisions, sex, hypocrisy and corruption. All the things that went on then and still go on today. But in Jake's day they called a spade a spade. Nagging wives, irritating in-laws, scabby cats, scruffy dogs, disrespect for figures of authority.
> 
> (Anon. 2021: n.pag.)

Elsewhere discussion could be more nuanced. A trawl of the internet suggests that most of the people writing and/or performing in tribute to Jake Thackray have been male. By contrast, for a discussion of Thackray's work in 2020, BBC Radio 4 invited actress and writer Isy Suttie to comment. Suttie, born the year after 'On Again!...' had first been performed, said that Jake's work had both depth and darkness (Great Lives 2020). Evidence of this darkness isn't hard to find. It's difficult, for example, not to read *Bantam Cock* (the title track on his 1972 album) as a celebration of abusive male sexuality. Announced with heavy-handed *double entendres* ('a fine upstanding bantam cock / So brisk and stiff and spry') the cock forces himself on every animal in the farmyard before feigning death in order to attract the vultures now circling overhead: 'He gave me a wink and a terrible grin / The way that rapists do / He said you see them big daft buggers up there / They'll be down in a minute or two'. And the song *Family Tree* (Thackray 1969) includes the verse 'Up my, my family tree / No blue blood, no nobility / No trace of aristocracy / Except for Uncle Sebastian / Who once raped a duchess'. 'The only censorship I impose', says John Watterson (who performs Jake's songs as 'Fake Thackray) 'is to replace the word "rapist" in the *Bantam Cock* and "raped" in *Family Tree* – those words are too toxic now and would destroy the humorous effect' (Watterson 2021: n.pag.). Where and when were these words less toxic? One possible answer was provided by the feminist writer and York University academic Nicole Ward Jouve who perceived a culture of masculinity in Yorkshire at the time of the Ripper murders (1975–80) wherein women were seen as strictly 'for frying bacon and for screwing' (Jouve 1986: 91). Neither Thackray nor his audience is likely to have endorsed such a notion, but the Yorkshire ethos to which Thackray seems to have subscribed left little room for the misty-eyed – Plater emphasizes in his summation of Jake's work as 'not sentimental' (Warburton 2006). Besides, in the 1970s and 80s, anyone who winced at the celebration of a farmyard rapist would likely have fallen back on the thought that, no, Jake was just too clever to condone rape. As time has gone on, though, it's probable that more and more of Jake's public – especially, perhaps, its female members – would laugh at the sheer gall of some of his lyrics and/or would, like Suttie (Great Lives 2020), forgive their unconcealed sexism (a description, one has to say, that fits *On Again! On Again!*) as one would a favourite uncle, who didn't know any better. That's because discussions of gender depictions in popular music have become a common coin, both in academic debate (see, e.g., Whiteley 2000) and in public conversation. And the issue of Jake and his imagined women was briefly raised once again in 2022 when the first biography of Thackray was published (Thompson and Watterson 2022). 'These could be feminist songs', insisted Manchester folk singer and Thackray drinking buddy Mike Harding (Male 2022) and, to an extent, this argument can be sustained: Jake's women are, as I've argued, often sexual agents, acting on their own account – albeit that, in other songs, they are objectified and become only their breasts and thighs. But 'On Again, On Again' remained (and remains) a fly in the ointment. Biographer Paul Thompson once again invoked Thackray's socialism, pointing out that he refused a request to advertise Dulux paint, and suggested that Jake might have been writing 'in character' when he composed 'On Again…' (Male 2022). Comparisons were made with American musician-satirist Randy Newman's *Good Old Boys* album (1974) on which Newman often sings in the character of a racist from the Deep South. But there's no reason to suppose that an avowed socialist on the British folk scene of the 1970s – accustomed to ballads about the 'cuckoo's nest'[4] – could not write a sexist song. And, whereas Newman was clearly making a liberal intervention in America's ongoing culture wars,[5] there's nothing in 'On Again…' to suggest that this was Jake's purpose. While some (mainly male) admirers redeem the song (e.g. 'of its time', 'brilliant opening lines') female devotees are, as I say, more likely to forgive a lapse in taste from a man who allowed women to have fun in many of his other songs.

Many Thackray fans knew, or knew of, Thackray as a humble, troubled and kindly man who couldn't wait to get off stage and enjoy a pint and a chat with members of the audience. They agreed that Jake-on-stage was funny and clever and, when not actually singing, plagued with self-doubt. They almost certainly appreciated that this was all somehow bound up with religion – in his final years he refused to sing anything but the Angelus at his local church (Warburton 2006). They may be also sensed that his songs were his escape and saw that in his art he was always playful about religion. 'At some point', remembers Peter Gray,

> during a Folk Club set way back in the '70s, he announced that he was going to do an impersonation, of course prefaced by telling us he was a less than talented impersonator. He started doing a sort of John Cleese silly walk thing only not walking but simply changing his posture and the position of his arms and legs, twisting and turning, stooping, crouching, turning […] all very odd. He finally said: 'It's an impersonation of God, you know – he moves in mysterious ways!'.
>
> (Gray n.d.: n.pag.)

## ACKNOWLEDGEMENTS
Thanks to Thackray devotee Malcolm Butcher for introducing me to Jake's work. Thanks also to Thackray revivalists John Watterson and Ron Middleton for answering my questions.

## NOTES
1. I'm grateful to John Watterson for supplying these lyrics. The song is on his album *The Lost Will and Testament of Jake Thackray* (2016).
2. Thackray doesn't seem to have recorded this song. It is however sung by John Watterson on his album *The Lost Will…*
3. The title refers to *Sister Josephine*, a song on *Bantam Cock*, in which a nun bears a strong resemblance to a male fugitive being sought by police.
4. This phrase referred to female pubic hair and genitalia. The song 'The Cuckoo's Nest' is centuries old and was generally sung by men. Lately more women have begun to record it,

but with feminist critique and revision. For example, English folk singer Kelly Oliver sang it on *Botany* Bay, her album of 2018. 'I refused to sing all the traditional misogynistic lyrics of this song', she said, 'so I altered some of the lyrics. They now tell a story of female defiance against unwanted affection'. See https://mainlynorfolk.info/guvnor/songs/cuckoosnest.html, Accessed 14 November 2022.

5. For good discussion, see Hart (2014) and Cook-Wilson (2016).

## REFERENCES

Academic Dictionaries and Encyclopedias (n.d.), 'Jake Thackray', *Academic Dictionaries and Encyclopedias,* n.d., https://en-academic.com/dic.nsf/enwiki/636858. Accessed 13 November 2021.

Anon. (2021), 'Comment: Product reviews, Jake Thackray – Jake in a Box (The EMI Recordings 1967–1976, 2006)', 21 April, https://www.ebay.co.uk/urw/Jake-Thackray-Jake-in-a-Box-The-EMI-Recordings-1967-1976-2006-/product-reviews/52648689. Accessed 8 November 2021.

Bell, Michael (2016), 'Comment: Jake Thackray', *The Opening Sentence*, 13 June, https://theopeningsentence.wordpress.com/2015/08/11/jake-thackray/. Accessed 12 November 2021.

Carr, Edward H. (1990), *What is History*, London: Penguin.

Cook-Wilson, Winston (2016), review of *Good Old Boys* by Randy Newman, 16 October, https://pitchfork.com/reviews/albums/22308-good-old-boys/. Accessed 14 November 2022.

Dodge Devil (2016), 'Jake's Scene – Swaledale', YouTube, 29 December, https://www.youtube.com/watch?v=0PlBzWXY9Xk. Accessed 14 November 2021.

Fairport Convention (1969), *Liege and Lief*, London: Island Records.

Gray, Peter (n.d.), 'Comment: Jake Thackray', Memories, https://jakethackray.com/memories/. Accessed 15 February 2023.

Great Lives (2020), 'Jake Thackray', BBC Radio 4, UK, 14 February, https://www.bbc.co.uk/programmes/b042jhlm. Accessed 20 November 2021.

Hansard HC Debate (1970), 'Local Authority Manual Workers (STRIKE)', House of Commons Debate, 29 October, vol. 805 cols 418–26', https://api.parliament.uk/historic-hansard/commons/1970/oct/29/local-authority-manual-workers-strike. Accessed 16 November 2021.

Hart, Steven (2014), 'He may be a fool but he's our fool: Lester Maddox, Randy Newman, and the American culture wars', in Steven Hart (ed.), *Let the Devil Speak: Articles, Essays, and Incitements*, Highland Park: Black Angel Press.

Hattersley, Roy (1991), *Goodbye to Yorkshire*, London: Pan Books.

Hickey, Andrew (2007), 'Jake in the Box: Thackray reconsidered', *The Hi Hat*, 8, http://www.thehighhat.com/Potlatch/008/hickey_thackray.html. Accessed 23 June 2021.

Jake in the Box (2021), 'The Trial of Lady C', composed by M. Knott, *Jake in the Box,* https://jakeinthebox.co.uk/music/trial-lady-c/. Accessed 18 November 2021.

Jake Thackray Unseen (2016), '04 Thackray Unseen The Jolly Captain', YouTube, 13 May, https://www.youtube.com/watch?v=Y7xdh8-2KMI. Accessed 17 November 2021.

James, Clive (2001), *Always Unreliable: The Memoirs*, London: Picador.

Jouve, Nicole Ward (1986), *The Streetcleaner: The Yorkshire Ripper Case on Trial*, London: Marion Boyars.

Lawrence, David Herbert (1960), *Lady Chatterley's Lover*, London: Penguin.

Male, Andrew (2022), 'Beware of the bull: The extraordinary life of singer Jake Thackray revealed', *The Guardian*, 10 August, https://www.theguardian.com/music/2022/aug/10/beware-of-the-bull-the-extraordinary-life-of-singer-jake-thackray-revealed-paul-thompson-john-watterson. Accessed 14 November 2022.

Middleton, Ron (2021), e-mail to author, 5 November.

Milne, Alasdair (1988), *DG: The Memoirs of a British Broadcaster*, London: Hodder & Stoughton.

Morley, David and Brundson, Charlotte (1999), *The 'Nationwide' Television Studies*, London: Routledge.

Newell, Martin (2011), 'The legend of Jake', *The Independent*, 6 October, https://www.independent.co.uk/arts-entertainment/music/features/legend-jake-490086.html. Accessed 29 June 2021.

Newman, Randy (1974), *Good Old Boys*, Burbank: Warner Brothers.

Pace, Ian (n.d.), 'Memories', https://jakethackray.com/memories/. Accessed 15 February 2023.

Tallpiler (2009), 'Jake Thackray "Molly Metcalfe"', YouTube, 28 July, https://www.youtube.com/watch?v=TiXINuf5nbI. Accessed 14 November 2021.

Thackray, Jake (1967), *The Last Will and Testament of Jake Thackray*, London: EMI.

Thackray, Jake (1968), *Lah-Di-Dah*, London: EMI.

Thackray, Jake (1969), *Jake's Progress*, London: EMI.

Thackray, Jake (1971), *Live Performance*, London: EMI.

Thackray, Jake (1972), *Bantam Cock*, London: EMI.

Thackray, Jake (1977a), *On Again! On Again!*, London: EMI.

Thackray, Jake (1977b), *Jake's Progress*, London: Star Books, https://jakethackray.com/archive/media/books/277-jakes-progress.html. Accessed 12 November 2021.

Thompson, Paul and John Watterson (2022), *Beware of the Bull: The Enigmatic Genius of Jake Thackray*, Leeds: Scratching Shed.

Wagg, Stephen (2003), 'Muck or nettles: Men, masculinity and myth in Yorkshire Cricket', *Sport in History*, 23:2, pp. 68–93.

Warburton, John (dir.) (2006), *Jake on the Box*, England: Associated-Rediffusion Television.

Watterson, John (2021), e-mail to author, 5 November.

Whiteley, Sheila (2000), *Women and Popular Music: Sexuality, Identity and Subjectivity*, London: Routledge.

Wilson, H. Hubert (1961), *Pressure Group: The Campaign for Commercial Television*, London: Secker & Warburg.

# 7

# Home Is Where the Music Is: Migrants and Belonging in Leeds

*Jonathan Long*

Especially if they are refugees, migrants arriving in their new country typically carry few possessions with them. One thing they may have is 'their' music. In the past this would have been in their head, now it may be on their mobile phones. Some are musicians themselves, while others seek to surround themselves with familiar music. Music offers a connection with their past, which may of course prompt very ambivalent feelings if they have fled persecution; nostalgia may be counterposed with anger and resentment. Even for subsequent generations music may provide similar connections. One of the contributions to the BBC Radio programme, *Soul Music*, was a Black British woman talking about the version of John Denver's 'Take Me Home, Country Roads' by Toots and the Maytals (Soul Music 2021), which substitutes West Jamaica for West Virginia. She explains that it brings her comfort and is medicine and therapy.

> It reminds me of a place I've never been to, of a life I've never known, only heard of [...] It's a history; it's a prayer. He says West Jamaica, but each and every one of us could take that, just like he did, and replace it with our own vision of home, whatever that is for people.

This paper is not about the experiences of an individual, nor even of one ethnic group, but is an attempt to consider commonalities of experience across various minoritized groups. As such, it is not the story of successful bands/musicians but of quotidian music. Like other forms of leisure, music is fundamental to the practice of identity and belonging, providing a link with people's cultural backgrounds (Cain et al. 2020). Indeed, it is central to a culture's most profound social occasions and experiences (Lidskog 2016) and as Rojek (2000: 37) argues, 'our participation in leisure activity is a way of demonstrating to others who we are and what we believe in'. The paper lies outside mainstream writing about migrant communities in the United Kingdom, which typically views them through a policy lens of 'problems'. Apart from issues of entitlement to be in the United Kingdom, the emphasis of the policy community is unsurprisingly on housing, finance and language. Of course, one of the appeals of music is that it does operate outwith the operational sphere of institutions of authority, and most people can recognize the emotive power of music.

Writing as someone who arrived in Leeds 35 years ago and made it his home, the chapter is not about Leeds and of Leeds, but about more than that. On the basis of the local, I want to make more general claims about the nature of the experiences involved. I shall use the experiences of migrants to Leeds, and others of subsequent generations who identify with ethnic groups originating outside the United Kingdom, to reflect on the effects music might have on the nature of being 'other'.

## *Migration to Leeds*

Currently, with a population of just under 800,000 people, Leeds is a place that has long offered immigrants the prospect of employment. It also offers a destination where there are many others who have had the experience of migrating from another country. In the 2011 Census, the proportion of people self-defining as not being White British was 19 per cent, about the same as the United Kingdom average, and 11.5 per cent were born outside the United Kingdom (12.6 per cent in 2020 according to the Intercultural Cities Programme of the Council of Europe). Notably, in Leeds people have come from a very diverse range of countries; 170 nationalities with varying migration histories (Council of Europe 2020a). Significant, long-established Jewish and Irish communities in the city were supplemented by wartime (Second World War) and 1950s migration, respectively; postwar Commonwealth migration came mainly from the Caribbean and the Indian sub-continent; East Europeans fleeing Nazis or Communists at the time of the Second World War were later joined by compatriots given the right to free entry by the European Accession Treaties of 2003 and 2005; and more recently refugees have arrived from the Middle East, the Horn of Africa and West Africa. Although the number of nationalities is large, kinship ties have meant that there are strong connections with particular parts of some originating areas, for example Mayo/Sligo (Ireland); St Kitts and Nevis (Caribbean): Sylhet, Mirpur, Punjab (Indian sub-continent); and Krakow (Poland).

The reputation of Yorkshire County Cricket Club and some Leeds United fans notwithstanding, Leeds likes to consider itself a welcoming city. 'Whilst immigration levels in both Leeds and the wider UK have fallen since 2016, it proudly remains a city of sanctuary and equality of opportunity, with integration at the heart of a multi-cultural agenda' (Council of Europe 2020a: n.pag.). Because of a sympathetic Council and a network of third sector organizations, 'The overall rate of achievement of the urban policies of Leeds, assessed as a whole through an "intercultural lens", is higher than that of the model city' (Council of Europe 2020b: 12). Against this background, a number of artistic activists have taken a lead. In 2018, Leeds became the first city in the United Kingdom to have two Theatres of Sanctuary: Leeds Playhouse (the first in the United Kingdom) and Opera North. Both run outreach programmes (including choral projects), and Opera North also promotes a concert programme including high-quality 'world music' artists. Alongside these major players, local residents have organized groups, set up choirs and promoted cultural events.

Perhaps the two major contributions to the musical life of Leeds by people from migrant backgrounds have been the oldest Caribbean carnival in Europe and the Leeds International Piano Competition, established by Fanny Waterman, whose parents were Jewish emigres from Russia. The former is the most multi-ethnic draw on the Leeds calendar and the latter has given a major boost to the careers of many internationally acclaimed pianists. These do not stand alone: for example, the RadhaRaman Folk Festival not only celebrates Bengali music (and dance and poetry) but also offers a platform to performers from other musical cultures whose work may strike a familiar chord or excite similar emotions.

## *The project*

I started from the standpoint of someone who lives in Leeds, enjoys going to gigs featuring music from a wide range of musical traditions, has friends from different ethnic/national groups, works with refugees and asylum seekers and has (with colleagues) written previously about the experiences of new migrants (e.g., see Long et al. 2014). But I needed more than that. Apart from reading widely, I wanted to engage directly with ethnically minoritized people in Leeds to try to understand their position. With the help of Leeds Asylum Seekers Support Network and contacts knowledgeable about local music, I was able to identify initial research participants and then sought repeated referrals. This resulted in 22 interviews as well as more informal discussions conducted over six weeks in the autumn of 2021. While I am extremely grateful to those who gave their time in this way, individual names do not appear here; their quotes are unattributed. Of the interviewees, thirteen identified as male and nine as female, from ethnic groups across five continents. Issues of gender were not raised directly, but there were no obvious gendered differences in participants' responses. Apart from ethnic grouping, participants also varied in migration history, age and the nature of their musical involvement. So, for some, Leeds is a place they are still trying hard to understand; others have lived here all their lives.

Most of the interviews were conducted by telephone or internet call (Zoom), but some participants preferred to speak face-to-face, so we met in a location of their choosing. The interviews lasted between 30 and 90 minutes and were recorded, apart from three for which more extensive notes were taken. I also attended events connected with the themes explored, and suddenly there were books around the house and radio and television programmes speaking to similar issues.

Interviews were then trawled to identify common themes. This confirmed the significance of identity and belonging and also suggested a link to resistance (accompanied by feelings of credibility and legitimacy). Understandably, these are not discrete categories, but instead overlapping 'sets'. Nor should it be suggested that music was seen in these terms by all participants.

## *Music and migration*

Despite the growing recognition afforded world/global/roots music, it is only really some elements of Caribbean and Irish music that have been accepted into the UK mainstream, though there has been some more recent commercial success achieved by Bhangra (partly through Bollywood films), K-Pop and Salsa. It is not only people who are affected by the process of migration but their music too. Some influences may be quite subtle, but some participants were consciously following a path of hybridity to produce fusion music. This is nothing new. It is not realistic to suggest there is something that could be labelled 'West Indian Music', without recognizing the existence of ska, reggae, calypso, bluebeat, soca, rocksteady, dub and others, each of which may have drawn on music from Africa and South Asia with French Creole and Latin influences. Reggae was adapted, as with the addition of strings for example, to make it more palatable to British audiences and in turn enjoyed crossover success to influence British rock; Ska was hybridized through Two-Tone.

I was previously unaware that there is a recognizable Leeds style of Irish music that originated at the border of Sligo and Mayo. Because such a large proportion of the Irish population in Leeds came from there, it was easy for them to perform together in a familiar manner. This was contrasted by participants with the London style (*London Swing*) which had had to adapt to accommodate the musical influences of a more diverse Irish population there. Interestingly, much of the Leeds style was attributed to musicians who had themselves emigrated in the early twentieth century; in their case to the United States where they made early phonograph recordings. Technology had overtaken what had previously been an oral tradition (for some other ethnicities involved in this study the oral tradition retained much of its significance). Another participant observed that while early migrants from the Caribbean, for example, prized imported records, now people have instant access to music from around the world via sites like YouTube and Spotify. Indeed, the web is by far the major source of music for most of those who are not part of a sizeable minoritized ethnic community in Leeds.

Participants from both the Irish and Caribbean communities were able to identify venues that in previous decades had been known for their music. For Irish music, it was pubs like The Regent, The Roscoe or The Pointer (see also Untold Stories n.d.), while those in the Caribbean community looked to places like the Hayfield pub, Strega Blues Bar or the International Club (see also Friar 2018). Few of these remain, either demolished for urban renewal or forced out of business. According to research participants, the relationship of these two ethnic communities with music venues represented rather different processes, as one member of the city's Irish community commented:

> The concept of 'the session' as we know it evolved in London because they couldn't play in the houses where two or three might be sharing a room, so they went to the pub and played a few tunes. It was the same for those who came to Leeds. Up to that point music had been played in the home in Ireland.

Other participants maintained that it was being denied access to dance halls and night clubs that led to Blues/house parties becoming so significant for African Caribbeans. Those from other migrant groups struggled to identify similar venues for their own styles of music, apart from religious music in Gurdwara and recorded Arabic music being played in shisha lounges. It is unsurprising that some performers found it difficult to continue in their new environment with a shortage of potential collaborators nearby with the requisite musical knowledge and techniques.

The diaspora can play its part in keeping the tradition alive, for example the seven times All-Ireland accordion champion, Sean Gavaghan, is from Leeds. Beyond that lies incorporation into the Leeds music scene as this advocate of another genre of music identified: 'I think Indian music has found a home here. If you go to any "Indian" music event, you'll get quite a mixed audience'. Ultimately, there may be a crossover so that:

people with no connection whatsoever are great traditional musicians. In Leeds there was a concentration of the Irish community, but then there was all this alternative culture who wanted to be part of this almost exotic underground culture. The sessions were a melting pot of people.

Similarly, Kibitz is a Leeds klezmer band, with no Jewish members, so they have been challenged over cultural appropriation. I prefer to see such crossovers as acceptance of the legitimacy of the musical form. I do not know if any have Caribbean heritage, but one of their songs is introduced on Facebook with 'its shameless reggae-inspired breakdown'. Previous writers have addressed deterritorialization, taking the music away from its place of origin, and reterritorialization, having typically incorporated new influences in the process (Viladrich 2019). Elements of other musical forms may be incorporated even without a fusion project, simply through a process of absorbing surrounding influences.

When asked what distinguished the music we were talking about from British music, I was surprised how many referred to the importance of poetry and of telling a story, which interviewees saw as being (for the most part) secondary to the tune in British music. Although surprised to be asked, participants were able to identify several benefits flowing from their engagement with music: happiness, fun, calming, healing, therapeutic, relaxation, reflection, memories, connections and education. Several also mentioned its ability to create 'a feeling of home'; it helped to satisfy a desire to 'hold onto as many things of our culture as we can', especially in terms of securing a sense of cultural identity.

## *Identity*

Hargreaves et al. (2002: 1–2) assert that music is 'a significant part of deciding and announcing to people […] who you are' and note that the self is 'constantly being reconstructed and renegotiated according to the experiences, situations and other people with whom we interact in everyday life'. One participant commented that 'musical interest is tied to what kind of identity you're trying to create for yourself'. Identity is not something fixed, but a dynamic process, and a large part of an individual's self-concept comes from their membership in a social group (Tajfel 1973). So, in addition to supporting personal identity, music also makes a considerable contribution to people's social/collective identity (Folkestad 2002), which may be founded in national pride, cultural practices and social norms (Fitzgerald and O'Flynn 2016). Cain et al. (2020) affirmed that the social practice of music-making was central to maintaining a collective cultural identity. This may be particularly important at times of stress as typified by Kurdish research participants, for example, who endorsed the struggle for Kurdish sovereignty.

> Many of us want to hold onto our values in fear of losing who we are, our identity, and doing things we have done all our lives is seen as all right because often British society is seen as multi-cultural even though it may not be true in some areas. There will be some disagreements, but I do listen to English music a lot and I grew up when there was conflict in Iraq and there was English, American and European music played on the radio and I can relate to those songs.

For many people the music they most closely identified with and which they felt identified them was simply the music they grew up with, so it could equally be soul, funk, jazz, blues as anything immediately identifiable with the traditional music of the country they or their forbears came from.

The music/identity relationship varies between individuals. Listening to music we may take what we will in accord with our identity, while those creating music may use it to reflect or obscure their identity depending upon the circumstance. For example, while for some the Carnival was a source of nourishment, others were critical on the basis that it played to ethnic and gender stereotypes that did nothing to advance the welfare of the Caribbean community. One participant, however, noted that just as Carnival has changed over its many years, so has he.

At a local film screening attended by people of diverse ethnicities, there were two films that spoke to musical identity. One of the people in the film *Palestine Underground* (Kelly 2018) saw 'music as therapy for an identity crisis'; and in *The Story of Lovers Rock* (Shabazz 2011), a film about reggae in London in the late 1970s and 1980s, one voice proudly proclaimed that the music 'gave us an identity we hadn't had before'. A research participant talking about Bengalis in Leeds observed: 'Here music is a reason to come together. It's also a statement of who they are. It's related to their identity and here they may have an identity crisis for example and through music they like to reveal themself'.

It is not unreasonable to expect musical relationships to change through the generations post migration, though Gilroy (1993) argues that music can aid transmission of a 'social imaginary' of the minority experiencing everyday hybridity across (national) borders, forging new forms of belonging for second-generation immigrants. A Leeds-born member of the Irish community said:

> Irish music gives me pride in my cultural identity. My Irish identity comes out as soon as I pick a fiddle up and put it under my chin, but I'm equally proud of being from God's own county, as proud of my Yorkshire roots as my Irish roots[...] I think

we've been lucky in Leeds in keeping the musical traditions going. I remember playing at an Irish lad's party in London and he was of that generation that he denied his Irish roots back in the '60s and '70s. He rediscovered his Irish identity in later life because it was OK to do so [as anti-Irish prejudice has declined].

This reflects how our identities are not simply chosen by ourselves but are in part imposed upon us. Disparaging stereotypes of particular forms of music can be involved in denigrating minorities as inferior to others. One African Caribbean participant observed ruefully:

When I hear certain musical forms there is something about identity in there even though I know I'm *being identified* with it. Music does heighten your sense of belonging and heighten your sense of identity. It's not always in a positive sense. If you see something on TV that references 'urban music' you know what that means. When there's reference to urban music there's no reference to someone like me listening to Yo-Yo Ma or even Van Morrison.

Despite not selling in large quantities and in the face of persistent racism, for minoritized ethnic communities their music 'becomes an avenue to counter negative descriptions commonly prescribed to their community' (Cain et al. 2020: 78). Talking about reggae, another participant maintained: 'The identity before Lovers Rock was about the angry young black man, always fighting with a chip on the shoulder. Lovers Rock showed us as fully rounded human beings'.

The interviews suggested that a person's identity owes much to group association through feelings of belonging.

## *Belonging here and there*

Notions of belonging were often associated in the minds of research participants with the idea of home, shared experiences and musical memories: 'when certain soundtracks come on there is a sense of belonging to a certain time, a certain context'. Maffesoli (1996: 10) adopts the term 'emotional community' to represent 'social types that enable a common "aesthetic" to serve as a repository of our collective self-expression'. This is accompanied by a collective emotion and memory. I conclude that in the case of migrants this might refer not just to the emotional community left behind in another country but to an idea of community that impels migrants to try to comply with demands to fit in and demonstrate that they belong in Leeds. At the same time as many in Leeds want to make migrants feel that they belong in the city on their own terms, there are others who taunt ethnically minoritized people generally with 'Go back to where you belong'. Consequently, first-generation migrants in particular 'are faced with the dilemma of whether they should demonstrate their Britishness, retain a distinct heritage or forge some hybrid identity' (Long et al. 2014: 1780).

Güney et al. (2014: 132) argue that 'the idealization of homeland is a major factor in the collective imagination of diasporic communities', with music making the physical separation from home more bearable. The 'sense of belonging to a wider community appears to evoke nostalgia or a mediated sense of the music's historic significance' (Cain et al. 2020: 74). One participant from China commented: 'If it's one [song] I've heard a lot, it takes me back to a time rather than a place. If I hear one that my mother liked that reminds me of home'. Another said: 'I don't listen to reggae music a lot, but when I do it takes me back to my family home'. A third (from France) suggested:

> The music is something that takes you back home straight away – not only the physical space, but the time-space. I share with my siblings for instance the time-space even though we have physical distance. The physical distance of the ex-pat will make the feeling stronger. Living here in England it gives me a sense of connecting with home – a little tinge of nostalgia. In exile there is that sense of loss and the music brings it home.

Clearly, the same music arouses different feelings than for those still 'back home' who have no need to bridge the loss.

Participants also revealed a desire to pass on their heritage, like this from another French respondent:

> When you're away from your home country as a parent you may not feel linked to nursery rhymes in English. So, I've taught a lot of rhymes in French because they have emotions attached to them that English nursery rhymes don't.

Even without the disadvantages attached to being 'the other', it should not be surprising that those who have newly arrived wish to be seen to be accepted as belonging in their new environment, yet if they try to do so they are still reminded by many of their 'difference'; they are not allowed to be 'us'. Clavane (2012) explains how many Jewish immigrants in Leeds pursued a strategy of radical assimilation in pursuit of Englishness. This of course caused tensions with the insistence of others (and sometimes themselves) on the need to remain faithful not just to the Jewish religion, but to Jewish culture. Coming from a Caribbean background, one participant similarly observed, 'We never got a [parental] lecture about how to act in Britain but they did things that revealed how they wanted us to behave in

British culture'. For some the acquisition of certain musical skills might be adopted in order to promote acculturation in the United Kingdom (in the United States, Hwang and Cho [2019] write of Koreans getting piano lessons for their children) in an attempt to assert 'belonging'; here, I'm interested in the music minoritized groups have brought with them to the United Kingdom.

Providing a platform for local musicians affirms that what they do has credibility, but just knowing that they and perhaps more famous musicians are performing in Leeds gives reassurance to others. A promoter commented:

> A couple who came to Mbongwana Star [at Howard Assembly Room] were absolutely buzzing afterwards. Especially when you hear music that does remind you of home there's a connection. They said that they felt more a part of the community of Leeds knowing that bands like that were playing here.

Hearing music from 'home' makes people feel closer to home, and in doing so makes Leeds feel more like home.

### 'We resist in our music'

This was the title given to the film showing at which one of the speakers observed of Palestinian music, 'Their art is resistance, it shows they have a culture that cannot simply be discounted'. Even without revolutionary lyrics music can represent a challenge simply by protesting worth, refusing to accept the role of the inferior and downtrodden. In writing about music fuelling resistance to felt oppression via racism and repressive state structures, Gilroy (1987: 204) noted that 'Black expressive cultures affirm while they protest'. A strong theme of resistance was identified by participants, for example, in the work of Linton Kwesi Johnson, The Specials, The Selector, and early Marley with his political critique of Babylon.

For all its air of colourful celebration, carnival is an opportunity for resistance. As a measure of the insecurity of the West Indian community in Leeds, some expected participants in the first carnival (1967) to be arrested by the police for being on the streets. As calypso, soca and samba played by steel bands/orchestras vie with sound systems, many elements of carnival protest the iniquities of slavery, particularly through satire by parody. Political themes are evident each year, as in 2017 with Mama Dread's 'Migrant Masqueraders' (Farrar et al. 2017). The cultural link provided by music, dance and costume at carnival asserts the right to ethnic diversity in Leeds at the same time as asserting the right to be British (cf. Orlando 2003).

It is difficult to resist without understanding and music can be an educational force as someone originally from Jamaica observed:

> A lot of the songs we were listening to were telling us things that we weren't hearing at school. I researched people I'd only heard about in songs. The first time I heard about Jomo Kenyatta was on a Burning Spear record. The music was our news. I heard about the New Cross fire on records. It was about resistance.

There was a tantalizing postscript to this recollection: 'But Lovers Rock was about healing. You need something to keep you calm'.

It is not just for those from the Caribbean that music often represents resistance to colonial subjugation. One participant from an Irish background described going to a South Asian performance in Chapel Allerton library:

> everyone joined in for one song. Turned out to be about getting together to drive the Brits out of their country. The communists used to do lots of these songs and when I later asked [name of musician] what the song was, he said 'you'll have to be more specific, there's millions of them'. At Armley Museum, he and his friends did a set of anti-imperialist songs.

Of course, it is not only the British who are the bad guys. Particularly for those arriving as asylum seekers, the anger may be directed at the regime they have fled, as for these three participants from Iraqi Kurdistan, Iraq and Chile.

> People like me are attracted to any musical product that highlights the position of Kurdish people speaking for the oppressed.
>
> I was brought up with protest songs [...]. It was always tapes that somebody gave you because that kind of music wasn't allowed in the country during that time.
>
> The people there writing songs, some were killed – it's not safe. So those out of the country record and send songs to friends back there as a gift for the protesters.

I was told that in Ireland, 'Suppression came from within. The music was rejected by its own people. My dad loved the music, but amongst his generation It was just repressed apart from pockets in places like deepest Connemara.' As in some Muslim societies, the very act of playing music can represent resistance.

The 'hostile environment' promoted by the UK government over the past decade and the xenophobia that was stoked by the Brexit debate have given greater salience to songs of resistance. The recent climate has certainly challenged the idea of Britain as a society comfortable with multiple ethnicities, though sadly that is not an unfamiliar story. Recalling the fate of David Oluwale[1] one of the voices from Leeds' Caribbean community observes in Caryl Phillips' *Foreigners*: 'The music and the singing preserved us, and I think without it we'd have been wiped out' (Phillips 2007: 229). Speaking at a very individual level one participant observed: 'It came from something that resembled me and I could relate to, and that gave me the determination to keep going even when I had problems'.

Music may support political action by contributing to feelings of collective identity (Martiniello and Lafleur 2008), as one participant commented:

> BLM [Black Lives Matter] has prompted an awakening in Asian communities as well. Youngsters identify with protests in India (e.g. farmers protesting) as well. My daughter came back from honeymoon on Monday and on Tuesday she was in London protesting against Priti Patel trying to deport a Sikh to India. Desire to learn the music goes hand in hand with trying to preserve the culture.

## *Conclusion*

Should Leeds be considered special in terms of the arguments advanced here? The city certainly offers fertile ground for a case study with some 150,000 residents not considering themselves to be 'White British'. Among them, the sheer diversity of ethnicities excites curiosity and their migration pathways from South Asia, the Caribbean and elsewhere may differ from those in other cities like Leicester, Birmingham or Manchester. However, my goal has been to search between differences to identify what might be held in common, hence the emphasis on identity, belonging and resistance. One of the migrants explained that Kurdish music helped him overcome the unfamiliarity and strangeness of the United Kingdom: 'It's like claiming ownership – it adds flavour to a place – it's like building a sense of belonging to a place. I'm in Leeds, but I still have the music'.

Long et al. (2014: 1783) observe that 'while it may be open to some to derive cultural capital from the assertion of difference, this privilege is rarely extended to immigrants who are expected to reproduce established community norms'. The cultural capital accumulated before they came may be less easily deployed in the United Kingdom where the value of non-British music may go unrecognized. Nonetheless, it is possible for minoritized ethnic groups to generate cultural and social capital through their music; it forms part of their cultural repository. Young people, particularly those at school might be expected to have the cultural capital to discuss the merits of a new artist from Leeds or the rights and wrongs of drill. However, beyond that, those from minoritized ethnic groups who have the cultural capital to allow them to perform may find themselves in a position where it then becomes acceptable, sometimes even desirable to introduce others (like me) to a part of another culture. Unfortunately, as participants recounted, it can be difficult to find a space where they can share their music. Some had been fortunate to find people reaching out to encourage participation in musical ventures; others had persisted in their own efforts. When performed, music allows residents of Leeds to see the minoritized other in a more positive light for what they can add to the creative life of the city. Research participants showed how music emphasizes a person's multiple identities while at the same time helping to negotiate an ambiguous relationship with the United Kingdom.

Particularly for refugees, what their home nation previously represented for them may no longer be satisfied by that place today; forced to flee they must carry that version of their country with them, and music offers one mechanism for doing that. Lidskog (2016) stresses the need for immigrant groups to 'make place', a place in their new home that allows them to feel comfortable. One research participant from Sudan argued: 'Wherever you live you can make it home. In Leeds not all of us enjoy the same music but that's not important for getting on'. True, but music can make a place feel more like home so that migrants 'accepted where they were but remembered where they came from' (Untold Stories n.d.). Music can have a social role in generating feelings of belonging as places are 'claimed' within the larger space of the city. Larger, well-established ethnic groups may now have a network of tangible spaces in which to engage in creating or consuming music; others may be restricted almost entirely to virtual spaces serviced by YouTube and Spotify (most mentioned by participants). Even for well-established groups, their music spaces may be nostalgic re-creations of long-gone pubs or blues/house parties. Whether tangible or virtual these musical spaces offer the chance to relax and find solace, a space of familiar sounds where they are temporarily relieved of the burden of being an outsider. Members of minoritized communities in Leeds now have multiple musical traditions they can claim as part of their identity.

## NOTE

1. David Oluwale arrived in Leeds from Nigeria in 1949. In 1969, after years of being brutalized by the police, his body was found in the River Aire.

## REFERENCES

Cain, Melissa, Istvandity, Lauren and Lakhani, Ali (2020), 'Participatory music-making and well-being within immigrant cultural practice: Exploratory case studies in South East Queensland, Australia', *Leisure Studies*, 39:1, pp. 68–82.

Clavane, Anthony (2012), *Does Your Rabbi Know You're Here?* London: Quercus.
Council of Europe (2020a), 'Leeds, United Kingdom – Intercultural city', https://www.coe.int/en/web/interculturalcities/leeds. Accessed 15 February 2023.
Council of Europe (2020b), *Leeds ICC Index Analysis*, Strasbourg: Intercultural Cities Secretariat, https://rm.coe.int/icc-index-analysis-2020-leeds-united-kingdom-september-2020/1680a0098a. Accessed 15 February 2023.
Farrar, Guy, Smith, Tim and Farrar, Max (2017), *Celebrate! 50 years of Leeds West Indian Carnival*, Huddersfield: Northern Arts Publications.
Fitzgerald, Mark and O'Flynn, John (2016), *Music and Identity in Ireland and Beyond*, London: Routledge.
Folkestad, Göran (2002), 'National identity and music', in R. MacDonald, D. Hargreaves and D. Miell (eds), *Musical Identities*, Oxford: Oxford University Press, pp. 151–62.
Friar, Danny (2018), *Rewind 'n' Come Again – 50 Years of Leeds Reggae*, Leeds Mas Media – Leeds Carnival blog, 27 November 2018, https://leedsmasmedia.wordpress.com/2018/11/27/rewind-n-come-again-50-years-of-leeds-reggae/. Accessed 15 February 2023.
Gilroy, Paul (1987), *There Ain't No Black in the Union Jack*, London: Unwin Hyman.
Gilroy, Paul (1993), *The Black Atlantic*, London: Verso.
Güney, Serhat, Pekman, Cem and Bülent, Kabaş (2014), 'Diasporic music in transition: Turkish immigrant performers on the stage of "Multikulti" Berlin', *Popular Music and Society*, 37:2, pp. 132–51.
Hargreaves, David, Miell, Dorothy and MacDonald, Raymond (2002), 'What are musical identities, and why are they important?', in R. MacDonald, D. Hargreaves and D. Miell (eds), *Musical Identities*, Oxford: Oxford University Press, pp. 1–20.
Hwang, Yoo J. and Cho, Eun (2019), 'Musical parenting and acculturation of South Korean immigrant mothers', *International Journal of Community Music*, 12:1, pp. 57–77.
Kelly, Jessica (2018), *Palestine Underground*, UK: Boiler Room.
Lidskog, Rolf (2016), 'The role of music in ethnic identity formation in diaspora: A research review', *International Social Science Journal*, 66:219&20, pp. 23–38.
Long, Jonathan, Hylton, Kevin and Spracklen, Karl (2014), 'Whiteness, Blackness and settlement: Leisure and the integration of new migrants', *Journal of Ethnic and Migration Studies*, 40:11, pp. 1779–97.
Maffesoli, Michel (1996), *The Time of the Tribes*, London: Sage.
Martiniello, Marco and Lafleur, Jean-Michel (2008), 'Ethnic minorities' cultural practices as forms of political expression: A review of the literature and a theoretical discussion on music', *Journal of Ethnic and Migration Studies*, 34:8, pp. 1191–215.
Orlando, Valerie (2003), 'From Rap to Raï in the mixing bowl: Beur hip-hop culture and banlieue cinema in urban France', *Journal of Popular Culture*, 36:3, pp. 395–415.
Phillips, Caryl (2007), *Foreigners: Three English Lives*, London: Vintage.
Rojek, Chris (2000), *Leisure and Culture*, Basingstoke: Palgrave.
Shabazz, Menelik (2011), *The Story of Lovers Rock*, UK: Verve.

*Soul Music* (2021), 'Take Me Home, Country Roads', BBC Radio 4, UK, 4 August, 9.00–9.30 am, https://www.bbc.co.uk/programmes/m000ydl2. Accessed 14 December 2021.

Tajfel, Henri (1973), *Human Groups and Social Categories: Studies in Social Psychology*, Cambridge: Cambridge University Press.

Untold Stories: The Irish Community in Leeds (n.d.), 'Emigration & The Irish diaspora', *Untold Stories: The Irish Community in Leeds*, http://www.untoldstories.co.uk/articles. Accessed 21 December 2021.

Viladrich, Anahí (2019), 'Think global, act Argentine! Tango émigrés and the search for artistic authenticity', *Ethnic and Racial Studies*, 42:6, pp. 901–18.

# 8

# A Tale of Two Artists: Thinking Intersectionally About Women and Music in Leeds

*Beccy Watson*

Leeds is arguably a dynamic context in which women (those identifying as women) have forged new ground in the city's music scene since the turn of the new millennium. This chapter is based on the experiences and reflections of two women, Sara Garvey and Fuzzy Jones, both prominent Leeds women musical artists and producers. Their accounts span over three decades, highlighting touchpoints from the 1990s through to the early 2020s. Extracts from in-depth interviews with them illustrate and illuminate how gender is an organizing principle in terms of access to opportunities for making music and wider circuits of cultural production and professional status in Leeds. Ann Wenner, Tami Gadir and Sam De Boise (2020) remind us that gender is always in process, whether studying women as composers and writers, challenging the centrality of men (and a gender binary) as the focus of music-related subcultures, or recognizing women as music performers across the world. Wenner et al. (2020) call for engagement with intersectional frameworks in assessing women and music. As Keenan (2018: n.pag.) stated: 'The overemphasis on white, middle-class women's cultural production has historically been a problem for women's and gender studies, and music scholars have too frequently replicated this tendency'. Thinking intersectionally, that is, acknowledging who, how and what questions (epistemological and methodological) we ask, has a direct influence on the knowledge we generate about women and music. In seeking to include different voices, we should not simply impose a diversity strategy on women and music agendas that evades complex power relations (Wenner et al. 2020).

I make no specific claims regarding the history of popular music in Leeds; there are trajectories many can trace in greater detail than I (as this collection is testimony too). I did, however, grow up in Leeds and relate to a city alive with punk, rock, reggae and dub, jazz and jazz funk, hip hop, folk, soul and dance, garage and more. In the early and mid 1980s, like many other youths at the time, music was firmly part of who I was, and going to gigs (as a 'punter') was a major feature of my leisure time. I later lived in a house with a recording studio that my (then) partner owned and ran in the Leeds 6 postcode. It was there, as a new university lecturer and researcher in the late 1990s, I developed a more conscious view of the interrelationships of gender, class and race that impacted women's everyday lives in the city (Scraton and Watson 1998) and a small-scale study of Leeds music followed (Watson 2010). Doreen Massey's (2005) scholarship 'for space' and the interplay with an embodiment that I have explored since (Watson 2018), speaks to my intrigue and feminist sociological imagination regarding women and music in Leeds. I saw first-hand the gendered space of the studio, the 'set up' and recording dynamics, of mixing and mastering, of networking and tour managing, and I continue to be inquisitive about these gendered power relations.

Wider discourses in circulation – patriarchal, capitalist and racist (hooks 1989) – perpetuate forms of sexism and misogyny within the music industries that are not uncommon (Wenner et al. 2020). Focusing on women and music in Leeds therefore requires more than questioning whether or not women are 'making it' in music. Media tend to over-emphasize 'acceptable' role models, constructing success for women in music that reproduces white, heteronormative, able-bodied normativity, celebrating individual success and glorifying 'opportunities' of neoliberal market forces.

In what follows, Sara and Fuzzy, acquaintances I invited to take part in conversational interviews and who want to be known by their real names, speak for themselves and touch on themes of becoming and being a singer, performer and artist; perceptions of Leeds scenes and women's presence therein; challenges and opportunities in collaborations in music; developing over time and moving into production; and interacting with industry. My commentary as an author is offered in the manner of what Les Back and others have termed 'movements of imagination' (Back and Yarrow 2014: 769), as a means to encourage an ongoing engagement with the issues and ideas raised.

## *Starting out*

Fuzzy reflected on how she came to be in Leeds:

> I started my musical journey in Leeds at university, [...] I did a fine art degree, but I'd always wanted to sing [...] my tutor was really into jazz, and said, [...] 'All your art is about music. Do you want to do music?' [...] And I said, 'I love singing but I've never sung in front of an audience,' and she said, 'well, I know a

place called the Victoria Pub, every Thursday they have a band. I know the band. If I asked them, would you get up and sing?' And I said, 'Um, OK, yeah.' I went one Thursday and I got up and sang Summertime, and then they asked me back every week after that.

Sara recollected:

I'd been besotted by music since I can remember; I was that kid that would find something and tape it and listen to it over and over again but I never thought about singing. I remember one time in school, it was music, and I sang, everybody was like, 'wow, you can sing'. [...] But I never really had any interest in becoming a singer if you see what I mean. My first 'band' was at middle school (in Leeds), it was a punk, kind of heavy metal band, [...] there was a vibe, around Nirvana. [...] Mostly when I grew up though, where I was, it was reggae, Lovers' Rock, Rare Groove, soulful kinds of stuff. [...] Nowadays I just identify as an artist because I've got various mediums, [...] I started off as a singer/songwriter – well, and a dancer – I wanted to be a contemporary dancer back in the day. [...] And then DJing and that's led on to producing, but they're not separate from each other.

As the accounts from Sara and Fuzzy further unfold, it becomes clear that Leeds was, and remains, an important backdrop, a springboard to their different encounters as performers and producers, as women artists. Music scenes in Leeds were certainly something they both acknowledged as being connected to the city having a large student population, informing opportunities in different ways for playing and getting involved in popular music scenes. Fuzzy had, in some respects, the privilege of being an art student:

When I moved to Leeds as a student there was this whole new world that opened up to me, I started going to the Underground [club in the city centre]. [...] all the cool nights at Liquid, and the Yardbird Suite and the Sunday Joint, and all these amazing nights. And I met people who were collecting records – and the whole Northern Soul thing, so I got into collecting records, and there was a big hip hop scene as well, drum and bass. It was the era for drum and bass, clubs like Wire, which wasn't called Wire then [...] I just met loads of people who were really into music, that was really exciting.

Sara charted some memorable aspects of her journey as a female artist:

I did a wide range of stuff and I remember when I, with the Up Your Ronson (1990s) thing, it was house and I'd done loads of house records, literally I'd been on hundreds of house records by then because people just asked me where they just needed a little female vocal coming in somewhere [...] then when I met up with Oak they were playing this sort of trip-hoppy stuff and I'd never really been exposed to it. It wasn't something that really was digging where I was from, I guess it's more like a student-type of thing.

Both women had a sense of the contexts of different spaces and scenes, conveyed through assessing their growing involvement. They shared a do-it-yourself (DIY) sense of how their respective craft in music came about, neither having had formal training or lessons. Sara explained:

I never thought about writing lyrics, I was more about melody and sonics and then sound systems taught me about freestyling because it was a culture, competing, it was competitive in a good way. If you had something to say in a cool way that you think people are going to like, you'd jump in and I was encouraged within the community, [...] it was always a tool I had in the bag. I remember people kept knocking on my door, 'I've got this record, can you come and sing on it?' And I'd be like 'Yeah.' It was part of what I did, [...] I guess luckily where I landed in Leeds, where we were brought up, music was a natural part of life. My mum is African and my dad English and in London my mum didn't like it and said 'Listen we're going to go to Leeds – but I can't be in a place where there are no other brown people,' [...] so my dad found a property that was near to more cosmopolitan cultural stuff [in Leeds], I was exposed to West Indian culture and Sound Systems, it's music every single day, people create music just as a natural way of life.

Sara was influenced from a young age by the community and music scenes that were part of everyday life for her (DeNora 2000). She recognized times and places when she started to make more of an investment in time and commitment, to make her presence in music more visible:

People had studios and little hubs. And I remember we had a hip hop scene, a couple of my friends were rappers and another a DJ. We used to go into hip hop clubs and this is when I started to take myself a little bit more seriously, I started to get a bit more invested in singing, and in freestyle, they'd play B-sides of soul records, funk records, my friends would rap over them and then when they'd run out of things to say I'd freestyle [...] that was my first foray into using some of the techniques I'd learned [...] and obviously it was all original stuff.

## *Becoming established*

Fuzzy's recollection of the clubs in Leeds denotes her sense of exploring the city with the freedom that being a student can offer. Whilst starting to find her way musically in the city's jazz scene (initially), she was also coming out as a lesbian and a sense of inclusive spaces was vital for her.

> We used to love it at the Underground. As art students we were in there all the time, I saw Corinne Bailey Rae before she was well-known. Most of the people [...] – we all used to go there, and I didn't know them then – these were people I eventually had (musical) relationships with. [...] I just remember feeling, in all those places like the Hi-Fi and the Underground, that I was accepted and I could be who I wanted to be, wear my '70s clothes, and dance like. And I was also coming out as well, as being gay, so I needed safe spaces, and even in those places, I felt I could be myself. [...] I was studying in London initially, I didn't enjoy it, and my tutor said, 'Why don't you try Leeds?' – I'd heard about it being really good for the arts, [...] I'd always felt a really welcoming, accepting vibe. Even in the early 2000s, I felt safe, I felt like that's the place where I grew and became Fuzzy.

Sara's 'foray' (as she termed it) was before Fuzzy arrived in the city and arguably reflects a changing cultural landscape in Leeds across the 1990s and the 2000s. Sara had begun to spend more time on music and to find ways to develop as a vocalist:

> I never went to uni, well I did go to uni eventually part-time, I left home at 16, was living by myself, a sort of feral way of life, I didn't have a day-to-day job, [...] I remember [a friend on music scene] lent me this big speaker and a mic and I used to wake up in the morning and whack on this speaker and just sing at the top of my lungs, and I thought to myself, 'Do you know what, I'm going to look at doing this a bit more properly.'

Sara went on to comment on the spaces where music was happening, where she was freestyling and singing:

> Lots of clubs [in the centre of Leeds] were playing the naffest music [laughs] that we would never play in our clubs [in the community]. Sometimes we were like, 'What the hell is this?!' So I was never really aware of, and I never thought it was open to me, [...] I didn't see it was open to me. It's not a judgement or it's not an anger thing, it's just a reality of that space and time.

This contrasted with Fuzzy's experiences of some of these spaces as they were open to her in a different way, possibly being a student and being read as a white woman. Research I carried out on leisure and popular music in Leeds (Watson 2010) considered whether and how the city was 'evolving' in terms of its musical genres and becoming more inclusive of different cultural signifiers that represented an increasingly multi-ethnic Leeds. Sara and Fuzzy's accounts here represent important aspects of the genealogy of popular music in Leeds and thinking intersectionally usefully informs the analysis of this. Sara reflected on cultural-spatial aspects of growing up in Leeds, pointing out exclusions across local and global contexts:

> I was growing up around the Harehills and Chapeltown [areas of Leeds considered inner city] and yet Oakwood [a suburb neighbouring Harehills] was kind of closed to me, do you know what I mean, even though I was probably more Oakwood. My peer group, and where I felt included, was in Chapeltown and Harehills, those communities are excluded from the mainstream community [...] because those places are middle class or white and because as black and Asian people (we) were excluded and I'm still a little bit to this day, the whole Black Lives Matter movement is something, back then you didn't go to town, there were no shops for you in town that represented you. So, what you did as kids is you just created your own little community and your own clubs and your own things.

It is the prerogative of researchers, and responsibility (Watson 2018), to craft the voices of participants into meaningful representations to be shared through writing. Fuzzy arrived in Leeds about a decade later than Sara's comments about the 1990s, yet charting key moments and events is rarely offered in precise linear and/or chronological ways, by interviewees or interviewers. A sense of movement across and through time was conveyed by Fuzzy and Sara; I asked both women about their experiences of starting out through to where they are now. Fuzzy described when she became aware of wanting to take more ownership of the production of her music:

> Well, after I'd sung a lot and been the front woman of many bands, I'd done as much as I could singing-wise, I'd written lyrics for drum and bass producers, and I'd sang in big bands who'd headlined at The Wardrobe and things [...] I wanted more ownership but in the beginning, I thought, 'Oh, I couldn't do that. I'm a lyricist and I'm a singer.' I didn't have the confidence. I thought I just needed to work with (other) really great musicians. Then in 2007, after doing a lot of different stuff, trying to find my sound, trying to record in different studios, I met [...] who was really into vintage microphone, reel-to-reels, and stuff like that. I helped him build a studio in Headingley, it's now a record label. I've skipped a bit of time out, because the bit in between, when I was developing, I was going through recording at all these different studios, paying money, I was with an indie band – it didn't go well. I got vetoed on my ideas, I was the singer [...] there was a bit of sexism going on there, I didn't write the music, but I wrote the lyrics and the melody, I got overlooked about how it should be mixed

in the studio, one of the guitarists went in and changed it, I was really upset. It didn't sound anything like it should sound [...] this was like, a big, massive learning curve for my musical education as a woman. I've been to so many studios, music studios where the sound engineer hasn't listened to what I'm saying, or they've put their own ideas instead of mine. I still ask whether that would happen to a bloke as much as a woman.

This passage from Fuzzy's transcript is telling and captures themes highlighted in research and scholarship focused on gendered power relations that are present and persistent in popular music (Keenan 2018; Wenner et al. 2020). Sara also noted how, in her first band 'the boys were seen to do the clever stuff, play guitars and write music'. Examples in both women's accounts illuminate how gender influences various contexts of cultural production and music scenes.

Having been noticed by Leeds club promoters, Sara reflected:

When the Up Your Ronson guys were looking for a vocalist, I'd worked in Music Factory behind the bar so that's how I knew about these people, [...] as it turned out that record label folded [...] but they said 'a friend of ours is looking for a singer' and then he passed it on (my demo) [...] he contacted me and they just played some music and I just freestyled and they went, 'Right, yeah, sweet', and in a few weeks we made a record – all of a sudden I was in commercial record label land and that was how swift it was. And I didn't know that their plan was to get a manager, get a record deal, they'd been in the professional music industry quite a long time, I didn't know any of that then [...] at that point I never really made any money from records because I'd be making little underground house records, there probably had been money on the table, I didn't see any of it and it wouldn't have been enough to be anything.

## *Shaping the scene*

There is arguably little research that looks distinctly at women and publishing rights and women's music production; certainly, much of it fails to address intersectional power relations (Keenan 2018; Wenner et al. 2020). This spurred my interest in documenting how Fuzzy and Sara had experienced Leeds music scenes in this regard. Fuzzy, like Sara, albeit in different ways, went through long periods of self-directed development, from teaching herself to play guitar to mixing and producing her own and other people's music. Fuzzy negotiated ways of working in the initial studio that she helped set up but saw that it held her back in some respects too:

I learnt a lot in those years of being in that studio, about studio craft and vocals, microphones, all that kind of thing [...] but again, I never got really as much involved in the techie side, and I think I felt like I wanted to, but he had more control over that. [...] There was nothing written in contracts or anything like that, so that was half the problem when you start these things.

Sara made several comments about the negotiated acceptance of women in the political economy of music. She stated, 'Music is business. A woman in that business is [still] frowned upon'. Both women demonstrated that they were often in receipt of how, as Sara articulated:

> You're still going to come up against barriers, you're still going to have things where you won't get invited to the 'All Boys Club' where networking really happens, because a lot happens in networking and relationship building where you might not have access to. [...] it's 100% effectively men's terrain and it takes a really, really strong woman with a certain skillset to get through because you have to fight against the cultural norms of what you've been taught.

Leeds is not unique in that (Cohen 1991; Wenner et al. 2020). It was hard to ignore the stark ways that gender impacted opportunities for Sara and Fuzzy charting their respective career paths. This was explicit at times, for instance when Sara was told (by her male manager) to 'not be pregnant' or certainly 'not tell anyone', with the consequence that she kept it a secret from her band (at the time) and record label until seven months into her pregnancy. Then she had to negotiate being a parent and an artist and the challenges and expectations associated with being a mother. Conceptually, it might be appealing to consider how gender binaries are less influential, particularly in the arts and creative industries, yet pervasive heteronormative discourses in operation are hard to ignore. Concurrently, celebrating women's success at overcoming barriers and any increased numbers of women in music acting as role models fails to adequately engage with complex gender relations and differences (Keenan 2018). Sara had commented on previous encounters with male employees at a record label based in London:

> There was an element of colour, a racial element as well. I was just like there in my hoodie or whatever and they'd be like, 'Yo' [trying to sound 'street'] [...] When we went into meetings the mainly males [label employees] spoke to the guys and didn't make eye contact with me at all. [...] except to ask me something, to say how pretty I was and how nice my voice was or, I felt wheeled out as a prop. [...] my sort of acumen and my abilities outside of what I looked like and sound like were not taken seriously. It annoyed the fuck out of me.

The multiple contexts of women and music are interconnected with a myriad of different cultural signifiers that played out, metaphorically and literally, and constituted via and through different facets of identity within differential power relations. The claim here is not one based on diversity but on the difference in power relations. Whereas Sara had felt excluded on the grounds of gender and race she also commented on how her band were noticed and given time at the label because coming from Leeds had something of a buzz to it, it was unique from so many of the acts forming in London in the 1990s. In the early 2000s, Sara became a vocalist with Nightmares on Wax (formed in Leeds in the mid 1980s).

## *Moving into production*

In the early 2010s, Fuzzy moved into paid employment at a community radio station in Leeds (Chapel FM). By this time, she had also started playing more regularly on a folk circuit, having learnt the guitar and writing prolifically. She was gigging in suburban areas (including areas known for being LGBTQ-inclusive) as well as at the radio station. Having increased professional status was significant in her move into music production as well as performance and promotion:

> At Chapel FM I had all the professional equipment; I could practice there whenever I wanted. And then I became centre manager there, and I started putting on Fuzzy's Living Room Presents Female Artists, once a month thing, or once every two months, and it was basically, I'd just set it up like my living room, and invite my favourite female artists to come and play [...] And the connectivity grew because of all the people I met at Chapel FM, and who'd come for gigs, and who'd come to do music workshops and things like that. So I developed more of my own network [...] the camaraderie and the solidarity, and community of working – presenting other female musicians, and 'Oh, why don't we do something together?'

There is vibrancy and agency in these descriptions of becoming more successful on their own terms; success here is used in a qualitative and relative sense (not a count of sales, downloads, bookings or other statistical measures). A sense of continuing DIY enthusiasm, women-focused, self-taught increased technical knowledge being put directly into use. Fuzzy exclaimed:

> I said one morning to my partner, 'I just want to write an album [...]. I'm just going to record it and just release it. Fuck it. I'm not going to be precious anymore', because

people always said to me – somebody said to me once 'Don't make it perfect. Make it now.' So yeah, I just did it.

She linked this sense of being able to take control of her creative processes and practices not only to opportunities she had in a material sense, such as access to studios but also to experiential, less tangible elements that were influential in her musical development. Working with other women musicians, and forming a network, was the key:

When I was working at Chapel FM and I'd gone solo, and I was starting to do solo gigs. I just met all the girls on the scene, really, [...] I knew some of them through other musicians, and then The Sisterhood we organised our own UK tour in 2018. [...] We just wanted to showcase women, to show some kind of solidarity. And it was a sell-out, and people were really interested in seeing four women onstage all playing on each other's songs. [...] it wasn't about being a band, it was about being collective, and we'd be the front singer of our own song, and then we'd all play and do backing vocals on each of our songs. [...] And then we got some funding to do workshops for women, and non-binary and trans people, and we did that. We got funded by Leeds Inspired (not for profit sector).

Fuzzy's confidence and competency in professional-level production were also growing, setting up Women in Music Ableton introductory courses at Chapel FM, teaching herself via Ableton Live (online) and attending a Beth Orton residency course at Leeds Conservatoire.

I forged these relationships, a bigger network of women in music community [...] and it gave me the confidence that I could actually produce music myself. I went ahead and was like, 'I can do whatever I want now. I can do it the style that I want.'

By the 2010s, Sara was pursuing her solo interests:

I started getting little studio set-ups, but I never thought, people didn't expect it from me, I had a long way to go to learn to get to the commercial level, what I was doing was immediate with the vocals. [...] I remember thinking at on point, 'I'm done with music', I had a couple of family tragedies and it makes you look at life different and I'd travelled around the world and I'd done all these amazing things and I thought, 'Maybe I'm done', and then musically, rebuilding, I thought anything I do from now I'm going to do what I want to do. [...] and then my first record, it took me a couple of years, I hired a studio, put my stuff through, learned how to do it and I was like, 'I'm the boss of this', [...] and it went mental, and I was like,

'Wow, maybe' and I mixed it to pre-master mix myself and I got an email from the 'mastering' studio in Berlin saying, 'This is an amazing mix', [...] it took a few years but now I'm where I am and I'm a composer and a mixer and I'm a producer and vocalist and a DJ.

Sara explained, 'DJing led me into production', and that she had been asked to DJ because a promoter saw that having a female DJ would be novel and attract new crowds:

And that's how it started (in Leeds city centre), so there are benefits of being female, you get a leg in quicker and I remember going to a friend of mine who I made music with from Hungary, [...] all of sudden I was getting all these DJ sets and I wasn't very good at mixing, because I hadn't learned it, he used to do it and was able to control and coordinate the EC40 and showed me how to do it on there and I learned from thousands and thousands of hours watching YouTube [laughs] [...] and then I started looping stuff naturally and making little edits. That opened the door of producing, so now I use Ableton and Logic.

It was exciting to hear about Sara and Fuzzy's moves into production, and tell, as in Sara's comments, how significant gender remained in terms of knowledge and scene setting. Age and experience were reflected in both the women artists' sense of self and the wider circuits of popular music. Both have taught themselves production techniques and speak 'Ableton' in ways that demonstrate their ability and their music production 'capital'. Sara reflected on the influence of gender and race that continues to shape women and music discourses:

I went to Ableton Loop conference in Berlin twice and I have spoke[n] about this, that women, some of it is on our toes, we haven't been taught how to push ourselves forward, we are in a competitive industry and competitiveness is what men are conversely over taught (to their detriment). And when I started promoting my inbox would be filled with guys saying, 'I really want to DJ at your event', [...] but a girl will stand back and wait to be asked, wait to be noticed. There has been a massive influx over the last couple of years especially in the DJ world where it's become a thing, diversity, a bit like Black Lives Matter where people are now seeking to not look 'un-diverse', I've got a few gigs off the back of that, gigs I would have got eventually but it might have taken a bit longer had there not been this drive to be looking to be having diversity, and you know when we look in the competitive field, women, we're at a blessed position, if you're a white male in house music it's very difficult to stick out [laughs], whereas if you're a woman and you're half decent, you'll get in the door and then it's up to you what you do in that door.

## Conclusion

Although it resonates with much of what Fuzzy said and Fuzzy also DJs, I wanted to give the last word from the interviews to Sara:

> The first release I did, I curated, I did the campaign for it, I did the artwork for it, I led it in the business side of things and I thought, right I'm going to do that. I think it's really empowering. Once you take that step, once you say I don't care if I fail, then it can happen. Like this year (2022), I obviously do a lot of DJing and I'm making music and I've got my own studio, I'm producing other people. I want to do an album and tour it. [...] When I look back it's a world apart from back then, I'm now a (different) woman and all those experiences have taught me either you stay there or you get better. And it's a constant evolvement. I think there are more women in this space now and more women now are starting to help each other.

Leeds is clearly significant in shaping the routes Sara and Fuzzy have taken, then and now, the city influenced their professional pathways expressed through various aspects of space and embodiment. Their experiences suggest a turn/growth in women's presence as music producers, whilst, as women, pursuing and generating artistic production, the interview data highlights the significance of gendered intersections. Identities negotiated and forged and the interconnection with for instance, leisure pastimes informing more 'serious' sustained professional activity, is a key subplot to the stories and narratives of how Sara and Fuzzy have gone on to be part of a music 'industry' rooted in (and beyond) Leeds. Sustained, professional activity, including opportunities to make a living from, to be taken seriously as, women musicians and producers, reflects intersectional power relations where gender, race and class are notable. Their accounts contribute to understanding how women recognized as cultural intermediaries in the music industry requires acknowledgement and analysis that is more complex than statistical tallies of those involved or lists of barriers to be overcome, including for instance, sales or dominant discursive representations of female artists (Keenan 2018; Wenner et al. 2020). We need to listen to different voices of individual women and gather more accounts, stories and narratives, of both then and now, charting women and music in Leeds. I certainly look forward to both collecting and reading more of those; for now, I am thankful to the artists Sara Garvey and Fuzzy Jones for talking to me.

# REFERENCES

Back, Les and Yarrow, Thomas (2014), 'Writers on writing', *Journal of the Royal Anthropological Institute (N.S.)*, 20, pp. 766–70.

Cohen, Sara (1991), *Rock Culture in Liverpool: Popular Music in the Making*, Oxford: Clarendon Press.

DeNora, Tia (2000), *Music and Everyday Life*, Cambridge: Cambridge University Press.

hooks, bell (1989), *Talking Back: Thinking Feminist, Thinking Black*, Boston: South End Press.

Keenan, Elizabeth (2018), 'Intersectionality in third-wave popular music: Sexuality, race, and class', in *Oxford Handbooks Online*, Oxford: Oxford University Press, https://www.oxfordhandbooks.com/view/10.1093/oxfordhb/9780199935321.001.0001/oxfordhb-9780199935321-e-36. Accessed 21 March 2022.

Massey, Doreen (2005), *For Space*, London: Sage.

Scraton, Sheila and Watson, Beccy (1998), 'Gendered cities: Women and public leisure space in the postmodern city', *Leisure Studies*, 17:2, pp. 123–37.

Watson, Beccy (2010), '"What about us?" Examining popular music, leisure and urban arts policy in the post-industrial city', *Annals of Leisure Research*, 13:3, pp. 459–75.

Watson, Beccy (2018), 'Thinking intersectionally: Fourth wave feminism and feminist leisure scholarship', in D. Parry (ed.), *Feminisms in Leisure Studies: Advancing a Fourth Wave*, London: Routledge, pp. 58–78.

Wenner, Ann, Gadir, Tami and De Boise, Sam (2020), 'Broadening research in gender and music practice', *Popular Music*, 39:3–4, pp. 636–51.

# 9

# Leeds Punk through a Feminist Lens

*Mallory McGovern*

In the politically volatile and declining industrial atmosphere of late 1970s' Leeds, punk music took hold with a uniquely progressive and often feminist impulse compelling the bands and the fans. Under the spectre of violence against women created by the Yorkshire Ripper, and inheriting the sexist structure of UK punk and the music industry at large, the formation of three key groups in Leeds – Gang of Four, the Mekons and Delta 5 – challenged the UK punk establishment. In this often under-recognized scene, Leeds punks embraced anti-racist, anti-sexist and more egalitarian principles that other punks touted but often crudely implemented. As distinctly local and truly punk, the Leeds scene is particularly suited for an investigation of punk challenges to the status quo through the lenses of gender and race.

Before arriving in Leeds, the punk subculture was solidifying in terms of style, sound and, most crucially in the British context, ideology. As post-war political and social cooperation among the British government and public fractured, punk was understood by many Britons as a cultural response – one which both the left and right sought to utilize (Worley 2012: 333). While some bands adopted explicitly political beliefs – like the anarchism of Crass and the Poison Girls or the class politics of Oi! bands – other punks expressed nothing political beyond general social discontent. Often, political statements were overshadowed by a desire to shock and rebel. During a *Slash* magazine interview with British band The Damned, politics were on the radar, but more salacious topics were equally important:

> S: Do you like Margaret Thatcher?
> D: Oh, she's tasty! I'd like to stick my cock in her mouth ... good blow-job she is ... good head, Margaret Thatcher! ...
> S: Would you say England is going down the drain?
> D: It's gone! Nearly finishing. Sinking fast. That's why we are over here.
> (The Damned 1977: 7)

The band's off-colour, sexually explicit response to a political query showed that not all punks were articulating succinct ideological positions. Moreover, while mocking the Conservative politician, the statement was in no way progressive, relying on sexist tropes to communicate their position. If punk was defined by a core stance of rebellion and subversion, this ethos was shaped by standards of sex, gender and race, as well as by locality. As this chapter will explore, in an environment of rampant sexism, violence against women, and rising racist factions, this scene embodied rebellion.

In an effort to evoke the character of a scene analyzed by an outsider, this chapter provides the quotations of those who 'lived it' wherever possible. It presents a critical feminist narrative of the late 1970s drawn from punks turned academics, lyrics, discussions between bands and music journalists, and interviews published in the fanzine *Slash*. Entering punk scholarship in search of women's contributions to popular music, *Slash* (a Los Angeles-based fanzine) provided an entry point to UK punk through its extensive coverage of British bands. As an American scholar looking to work beyond the well-established history of punk London, Leeds presented itself as a city alive with feminist activism, social change and music. In these varying accounts, songs and fanzines, Leeds emerges through the complicated record of punk as a scene that challenged issues of sexism and racism not only in British society but within a subculture that often appeared to forget the egalitarian, open and anti-establishment principles it was supposedly built upon.

## *'Are you sure you should be going out?':*
## *Leeds prepares to enter the 1980s*

From the mid 1970s into the 1980s, Leeds experienced a period of transition alongside the rest of the UK. Political conflict, police corruption and industrial decline plagued the city, as did the acceptance of violence against women and the sexism embedded in the region's working-class masculinity (Wattis 2017a: 1073–74). In January 1981, Peter Sutcliffe – often referred to as the 'Yorkshire Ripper' – was apprehended and convicted of thirteen murders and seven attempted murders against women in West Yorkshire and Manchester. This egregious violence against women was notable, and as Trowell (2015: 70) posits, Leeds at this time can be defined less by its 'ghosts of industrial past' but rather as a city enveloped with the terror created by the crimes of Sutcliffe. Art students, leftists, feminists, punks and politically-minded youth were under an 'extreme cloak of psychological dread merged with more diffuse forces around racial tensions and a culture of violence' (Trowell 2015: 70). Furthermore, tensions were high between working-class locals and students often seen as troublemakers running around the city on the government's dime (Reynolds 2006: 56). This charged environment was crucial to understanding the bands of Leeds as their music and performances directly targeted the city's political and social issues.

Although an improvement from the dominant culture, punk's rejection of traditional, and often sexist, music standards did not result to uninhibited equality for female punks. Feminist punk displays or non-normative femininity in the public sphere was often not respected, and scrutiny of women and femininity across all of Leeds was heightened following Sutcliffe's crimes (O'Brien 2012: 33). In total, thirteen women, among them seven sex workers, would become victims – first, of Peter Sutcliffe's violence, and secondly, of police bias and incompetence (Wattis 2017b: 3). The police case, marked by misogyny and victim-blaming, evoked varying reactions. Fear was understandably common, particularly following the death of Jacqueline Hill, Sutcliffe's final victim and a student at Leeds University. One female university student described the fallout from Hill's murder: 'I think the way I would describe it is that [it] felt like we were under siege. That it was very difficult to go about a normal way of living' (Laura, quoted in Wattis 2017a: 1079). Yet, another local woman described her resilience to the situation:

> It certainly didn't affect the way we dressed or anything [...] still tarted-your-self-up and went out with your skirt up your arse [...] Flashing-it in heels and what-have-you, yeah. Still went to night-clubs, still went to pubs. Not stopping us doing what we wanted to do. Me mother, as me mother didn't go out drinking much [...] 'ooh be careful, are you sure you should be going out?' 'shut up mother, "it's never going to happen to me is it?"'.
>
> (Jessica quoted in Wattis 2017a: 1081)

While female participation in punk can certainly be read as a defiant response along the lines of Jessica's attitude, Leeds also became home to a faction of radical and revolutionary feminists who questioned the society that would allow these crimes to happen.

Taking issue with violence against women, feminists argued that the murders reflected less about the 'mind of the killer' and more so the 'working-class attitudes to what is and is not proper female conduct' (Smith [1989] 2013: n.pag.). In such an environment, feminists contended that the search for justice was hopeless:

> How on earth, given their own attitudes to women and female sexuality, did the police expect to be able to recognize the killer if they came face to face with him? If, as they believed, the man was disgusted by prostitutes – well, so were they.
>
> (Smith [1989] 2013: n.pag.)

Critical reflection into working-class society and strong affective responses came to characterize the feminists of Leeds. This work culminated in the first UK Reclaim the Night marches – public night-time demonstrations by women during a time when public spaces became increasingly associated with female fear (Mackay 2015: 88–89). As Na'ama Klorman-Eraqi's work shows, both the motivations of and the actions taken by feminists and punks during this time found significant resonance with one another. Certainly, both groups presented a contrarian feminine presence. Furthermore, building from feminist scholar Sara Ahmed's (2010) concept of 'affective communities', Klorman-Eraqi argues that affect, chiefly anger, 'shaped the two communities' politicization, their definition of collectivity, and informed the production and spectatorship of their cultural and visual practices' (2021: 357). While the punk performance of anger may be obvious, given their literal performance of music, feminists also showed an unwillingness to shy away from a spectacle.

## *'Ideologically sound': Musical organization and practice in Leeds*

Music journalist Simon Reynolds once described Gang of Four as the Clash but with 'a proper grounding in theory' (2006: 61), a foundation facilitated by the band's university origins. The Leeds punk scene, 'a loose community of musicians that included Gang of Four, the Mekons, and Delta 5 […] who were connected by friendships and a common interest in music' (Reddington 2007: 43), was structured so that musicians not only exchanged instruments and practice space but ideas. The bands' origins were deeply interconnected and born out of conversations between 'friends and girlfriends' (Burnham 1981: 6). In an April 1981 interview, drummer Hugo Burnham is quick to specify that the Mekons were friends rather than a musical influence, while also crediting the Mekons' Andrew Corrigan with Gang of Four's name (Burnham 1981: 6). While the bands may not have been able to form their version of an egalitarian artist collective, they remained aware of the environment that existed off-stage, acknowledged by Gang of Four in an interview with the magazine *Slash*:

> **SLASH:** As I was saying, your lyrics are more socially conscious than most rock songs, and …
> **HUGO:** There was something in the English press in England where Squeeze were interviewed, it's really classic in a way, one of the band members had watched us play and listened to us, and he said 'the things the Gang of Four sing about I don't really want to know about.' It's almost like an admission of his insecurity, about living in his own little world, girls, beer drinking, playing in a rock band, and nothing happens outside that life.

JON: And taking a girl home, calling her a dog, treating her like shit, thinking that's the way you ought to behave yourself.

(King and Burnham 1979: 21)

While rallying cries against the government or leadership were not uncommon in punk music, Gang of Four was concerned with the implications of daily life. Burnham described their message as 'not specifically politics with a capital P which means government politics, it's more the politics of their daily lives. The politics of the way you're trained to think from the day you were born. That's the politics of it' (Burnham 1981: 7). Arguably, the bands' origins and structure laid the foundation for revolutionary messaging. Therefore, the bands were well-positioned to address issues of gender and sexism, racism and power imbalances in society. In Leeds, punks not only stood in contrast to city locals but also differed from other UK punk acts in their political insistences that went beyond mocking the Queen.

Among the bands, Gang of Four and the Mekons stood out for their particularly strong embrace of egalitarian principles in band formation and political messaging within their music. The Mekons were emphatically committed to the punk do-it-yourself ethos and held a unique approach to political messaging, best described by founding member Mark White, in response to the question 'how did the Mekons start?':

Chaotically, as we did everything else. Don't forget also the close links with the Gang of Four. Both bands tackled similar themes in different ways, different forms. I suspect that there was some sort of Gang of Four plan, but the Mekons were not like that at all. [...] It was important to us that the decision-making, song writing, and economic arrangements should follow the political or social constructions that we were trying to develop.

(White cited in Langford et al. 2018: 104)

The intentionality of Gang of Four was confirmed by guitarist Andy Gill, describing the group as one which shunned 'rock spontaneity', a belief which was evident in the political weight of their name – a direct reference to the Maoist 'Gang of Four' faction prominent during China's Cultural Revolution (Reynolds 2006: 55–57). Additionally, the bands also showed a clear socialist underpinning in their exclusion of hierarchy in band formation. Founding member Mark White expressed the band's disdain for 'the hero-led "rock"' leading to the slogan of 'No personalities emerge' (White cited in Langford et al. 2018: 104) among members, echoing the rock critiques common to punks. Regular collective practice, as seen in Gang of Four's joint composition of music, shared publishing rights and equal pay among members (Reynolds 2006: 58) set Leeds apart, particularly from the

London scene which would become increasingly commercialized and commodified into the 1980s.

With a clear Marxist focus and awareness of societal hierarchies, it is unsurprising that feminist theory would be incorporated into the bands' guiding principles and art. As part of an 'ideologically sound' performance, Mekons member Mark White stated: 'When I write I try so hard to make sure the words are sound, that there's nothing sexist in them [...] So a lot of the early songs were written wimpy on purpose' (Reynolds 2006: 66). This 'wimpy' sound is heard in their 1979 album *The Quality of Mercy is Not Strnen*. In the album's second track, 'Rosanne', the singer seems to reverse the patriarchal roles of romantic relationships between men and women, taking on a submissive role:

> If you want Earl Grey tea, I will buy it. If you buy, buy new shoes, I will stretch them. If you have other men, I will like them. If they take, take you home, I'll forgive you. But if they take you away, I will cry.
>
> (The Mekons 1979)

Subservient, self-sacrificing and generous, the song is a clear reversal of the typical male lead singer. While the song's title 'Rosanne' and the male singing voice seem to indicate a heterosexual relationship, the song's neutered lyrics and tone create a sense of gender ambiguity. Mark White – who described the Mekons writing process as a series of 'long discussions' which ultimately left him to write lyrics while other members handled the music – expressed a keen interest in creating music beyond pop conventions as well as sexist predilections:

> Three-minute pop songs deal in generalities and banalities; multi-syllabled, closely argued text doesn't work. How can you make something out of that form which is relevant? [...] I was taken with the Buzzcocks idea that by not gendering the song, you could get away from all the appalling sexism and macho strut that so characterized songs of the period which we all hated. This was why most Mekons songs feature characters who are particularly feeble, or maybe that was just me.
>
> (White cited in Langford et al. 2018: 105)

Combining unconventional gender expression and new methods of musical storytelling, the Mekons were able to create an artistic embodiment of their beliefs.

While Leeds was dominated by all-male groups, it remained a city in which men and women were active participants. Kevin Lycett of the Mekons noted, 'Women were as active as men, and nobody blinked an eye', and despite the challenges women faced in the music industry, the Leeds scene evolved to be more inclusive (Simpson 2019: n.pag.). The music of Gang of Four reflected an understanding of the dynamics between men and women within broader society. Through a feminist reading, the chorus of 'Damaged Goods' reflected the transactional nature of sex, asking for the singer's partner to 'refund the cost', and stating 'you said you're cheap but you're too much', and ultimately suggested the female partner became 'damaged goods' (Gang of Four 1979a). Questioning romantic relationships was part of the broader feminist project many Leeds bands undertook, in part because of their surroundings. As Andy Gill recounted,

> Feminism then was undiluted, with some extreme ideas. You couldn't be in Leeds at the time and not take a view on it. [...] To us, it wasn't an option not to write about this, we had to have a position. That was the Gang of Four – talking about aspects of romance in a matter-of-fact, bold, analytical way. It was refreshing, partly inspired by the debates going on around us.
> (Gill cited in O'Brien 2012: 29–30)

Beyond the Reclaim the Night marches, radical and revolutionary feminists in Leeds were active in the broader exchange of ideas and practice among UK feminists, often presenting the most extreme or experimental suggestions for transforming society. Certainly, punks were aware of these movements, and, unsurprisingly, the politically conscious bands of Leeds took on anti-sexist stances with an active radical feminist faction in town.

In 1979, Gang of Four also released the singles 'At Home He's a Tourist' and 'It's Her Factory', both of which tackled gender norms in British society and wider patriarchal culture. 'It's Her Factory' in particular noted the confinement of women to the home, using the metaphor of addiction and explaining women's housework as analogous to (masculine) factory labour to signal legitimacy. The song spoke of 'housewife heroines addicts to their homes' and a 'paternalist journalist' who 'gives them sympathy because they're not men' (Gang of Four 1979b). The song reflected the wider public recognition of a world in which gender roles were changing but recognized the limits still placed on women. The band not only acknowledged the limitations of women in Leeds during this time but also exhibited the constraints of feminist thinking in their musical practice, most noticeably in their behaviour and performance style. Their 'quasi-violent stage presence' and repressed emotionality typical of both English and Marxist Leftist culture (Reynolds 2006: 68) created a band that was aggressively masculine and anti-sexist. This dynamic permeated the larger scene, according to journalist Simon Reynolds:

> The 'unisex' brand of feminism in vogue on the Leeds scene meant that women became tough minded, assertive, and 'dry.' The men, however, didn't have to get any more moist or androgynous. Jon King [singer-songwriter, Gang of Four] rejected

the notion that men needed to develop their feminine emotional side. 'That sort of resort to the motions is part of the oppression,' he argued. 'If all the time you react to things on an emotional level, you'll never get anywhere.'

(Reynolds 2006: 68)

Even with their shortcomings challenging gender and sex in practice and status as an all-male band, Gang of Four contributed to the feminist conversation in Leeds and ultimately carried the Leeds feminist message beyond the city's university students as their popularity grew.

Gang of Four was the most commercially successful group producing the prominent type of punk that was especially strong in Leeds – that of more political, art-school post-punk bands. Lucy O'Brien (1999: 196) described 'a more intellectual feminist element', growing alongside political campaigns favoured by punks, such as the Anti-Nazi League, Rock Against Racism (RAR) and Rock Against Sexism. O'Brien's own band, the Catholic Girls, formed after the group attended an abortion rights march in 1978 (O'Brien 1999). Leeds-based, mixed-gender band Delta 5 also communicated their dissatisfaction in feminist terms. Their first two singles 'Mind Your Own Business' (1979) and 'You' (1980) addressed harassment and mistreatment. 'You' carried a more conventional message of the singer's disappointment with her partner, but the specific problems listed in the lyrics illuminated double standards by which women were judged in relationships. Complaints, ranging from someone 'who keeps me out when I want to go home' and 'who was seen with somebody else', reflected a partner who was inconsiderate and unfaithful. While this song followed longer musical traditions of recounting troubled romantic relationships, the lyrics of 'Mind Your Own Business' went beyond interpersonal relationship plights to wider social issues.

For female bands performing in Leeds at the time, tensions between leftist and right-wing groups, as well as national conversations on gender and sexuality, made personal identities highly political. Delta 5 faced scrutiny and even violence from the 'macho contingent of the punk audience' and white nationalist groups looking to harass a band active in RAR (O'Brien 2012: 32). But what was possibly most compelling about Delta 5 was their adoption of the subversive love song, a musical choice that echoed the Women's Liberation Movement's rallying cry of 'the personal is political'. Bethan Peters, Delta 5's bass player, made explicit connections, stating: 'Personal relationships are like a microcosm of the whole world in that way we are commenting on things in general' (Reynolds 2006: 66). In addition to utilizing parody, the jarring sounds of punk provided a political opportunity as well. O'Brien described Delta 5's sound as: 'Their voices combined with the discordant guitar [...] and in so doing distilled the sense of alienation felt by young women keen to break away from restrictive models of femininity' (2012: 31). This certainly came across in the band's most popular song 'Mind Your Own Business', in which a jarring chorus of female voices rejected the idea of niceties and asserted the singers' independence, asking the listener 'Why don't you mind your own business?' (Delta 5 1979). While many interpret the song as a woman's reflection on gender relationships, the lyrics were written by a man, Simon Best, who was associated with the Leeds scene (Peters cited by Goldman 2019: n.pag.). Bethan Peters also noted that the song could be interpreted in multiple ways. 'It did apply to the boy/girl thing', Peters explained, 'but it could also be about anyone, which was quite nice' (Goldman 2019: n.pag.). Regardless of the song's target, it rejected traditional feminine standards of passivity and instead encouraged women to create their own rules.

## 'Against the racist poison in rock music': Punk in the face of the National Front

In late 1970s post-industrial northern England, racism touched all corners of public life and culture. Drawing from fascist movements preceding the Second World War, the far-right returned with a vengeance in the late 1960s and 1970s as economic troubles and growing numbers of immigrants in Britain activated nationalist sentiments (Shaffer 2013: 462). While nationalists initially targeted young, male, working-class football fans (Shaffer 2013: 464–65), the primarily white, male punk subculture also provided a pool of disaffected youth. Furthermore, punk's adoption of Nazi symbols and phrases in the London scene seemed to suggest a possible affinity for racist and nationalist ideologies. British punk icons like Siouxsie Sioux and Sid Vicious openly played with Nazi ideology and imagery (Sabin 1999: 208). In a *Slash* interview, Siouxsie justified her past use of swastikas:

> It was just very much a repellent and, I dunno, very much shocking people. I mean, at the time it was a very stale period in music, and there wasn't anything representing any youth at that time and it needed a crude way of knocking it out. […] And that's why it did a lot, cos a lot of people at the time would look and go 'ugh'.
> 
> (Sioux et al. 1979: 26)

*Slash* interviewer Jane Garcia questioned this defence, as Siouxsie had openly worn Nazi armbands multiple times, even before she began performing (Sioux et al. 1979). While punk's flirtations with the far-right were viewed by many as harmless or ironic, these instances complicated the often paradoxical relationship between popular music and race in Britain.

Political organizing entered the punk sphere in reaction to racist and fascist comments from David Bowie and Eric Clapton. In 1976, activists called for an organization to fight the racism and fascism that had now infiltrated the music industry, writing:

> Rock was and still can be a real progressive culture not a package mail order stick-on nightmare of mediocre garbage.
> Keep the faith, black and white unite and fight.
> We want to organise a rank and file movement against the racist poison in rock music – we urge support for Rock Against Racism.
> (Socialist Workers Party 1976: 11)

In a critique of rock music orthodoxy, these activists' aims resembled those articulated by punk. Furthermore, to many punk observers, racism seemed to be embedded in popular music and its purveyors. Yet, in contrast to challenging sexism within rock music, a distinct front formed against racism (although Rock Against Sexism would eventually form as an offshoot of RAR) with greater political coordination enacted through local gigs and large festivals. In 1978, documentary photographer Thomas Blower captured images of the Northern Carnival against the Nazis in Manchester, characterizing the event as one with "no violence, no antagonism, it was one big party with thousands of people in attendance" (British Culture Archive 2021: n.pag.). Following in the footsteps of the first RAR carnival held in London earlier that year, the festival began with over 15,000 marchers meeting at Strangeways Prison where it was believed National Front members had infiltrated prison staff (British Culture Archive 2021: n.pag.). However, local gigs across the country were also crucial to RAR's strategy. Leeds punks became involved early on, with local organizer Paul Furness setting up a RAR club in town to showcase local and visiting bands (Barnett 2016: n.pag.). As Furness noted, 'It was the perfect timing for Rock Against Racism, really – we had punk bands and reggae sound systems, it was highly political' (Barnett 2016: n.pag.).

While typically cultural conservatives, the far-right saw 'a sign of white youngsters coming into their own identity' in punk and quickly began to seek out elements within the subculture that could align with their own beliefs (Worley 2012: 341–42). Many young participants used punk as a way of creating anti-establishment identities – whether this was as a female bass player or by virtue of being a punk fan – but white nationalists were attracted to the movement largely due to its white and working-class identifications. Leeds was thus an obvious site for far-right recruitment. The rationale for promulgating far-right ideologies through punk was articulated by Eddy Morrison, a white nationalist and member of the National Front during the 1970s:

> We either had to condemn Punk or use it. I chose the latter option and started a spoof fanzine called 'Punk Front' which featured a NF logo with a safety pin in it. To my great surprise, 'Punk Front' was a huge success and soon, especially in Leeds, NF members and supporters were going to the biggest Punk Club around – the infamous 'F Club.' I started to regularly go to the club and NF Punks were recruiting other punks.
>
> (Morrison cited in Andrews 2017: n.pag.)

*Punk Front*, as well as recruitment activities at the popular punk venue F Club, drew in Leeds artists (Shaffer 2013: 467); local bands such as the Dentists, the Ventz, Crap and Tragic Magic played songs with titles such as 'White Power', 'Kill the Reds' and 'Master Race' (Sabin 1999: 208). When Rock Against Communism was established in 1979 in response to RAR, the far-right had a pool of supporters and sympathizers in Leeds.

Amidst the rise of nationalist and racist politics, many punks were eager to respond, including one of punk's most popular and politically engaged acts, the Clash. The band notably espoused many leftist political ideals, but their song 'White Riot' was easily misconstrued as a rallying cry for white nationalists enamoured with the sounds of punk. In its review, *Slash* magazine called it a 'classic chaotic call to arms' and acknowledged the back cover art of the album, which featured images from a riot that took place at the Caribbean carnival in Notting Hill the previous summer (Kickboy 1977: 29). The Clash may have referenced this riot as an inspiration for complacent white youths, but the band's specification of a 'white' riot enabled the song's adoption by racists, specifically the National Front (Ambrosch 2018: 910). In their first single 'Never Been in a Riot', the Mekons put a satirical spin on the Clash's call to arms, with the lyrics 'I never been in a riot, I've never been in a fight […] I'm always in the toilet, missing out on the noise' (The Mekons 1978). Their inept, non-violent protagonist completely rejected the Clash's message. As Kevin Lycett of the Mekons explained in a 2015 documentary:

> Mark and I definitely found the Clash's 'White Riot' very offensive. 'I want to riot for us poor downtrodden white people.' So we wrote a song that was actually about, well, what is life like now. And no, I've not been in a riot. In fact, I'm frightened of being in a riot; the police scare the living shit out of me.
>
> (Lycett cited in Angio 2015)

Instead of pretending to understand the relationship between the police and people of colour in England, the Mekons recognized the situation's complexity and their inability to provide a solution. The case of 'White Riot' is one of many short-sighted punk expressions that blurred the lines of anti-racism and racism within the subculture. However, the Mekons counter-protest exhibits the scene's awareness not only at the national level but at the subcultural and local level as bands and fans contended with the genre's shortcomings in an environment where political missteps could prove dire.

## *Conclusion: Remembering Leeds punk*

Acknowledging that Leeds' most prominent punk and post-punk artists were overwhelmingly white and male, the scene's commitment to equitable ideologies, as evident in music and action, surpasses the radical politics of many punks of the period in other cities. Ideologically influenced by both leftist and feminist theory, Leeds bands were deeply invested in how music could affect change. Living in a city marked by the Yorkshire Ripper's extreme violence against women and by the hatred of the National Front, Leeds bands were primed to question the sexist and racist foundations of the UK and the larger culture. In this smaller scene built upon friendships and art-school theories, punks challenged the established norms of both the mainstream and the subculture. Lucy O'Brien (2012: 28) described her band's efforts in feminist terms, stating:

> We were trying to do things differently, trying to faithfully record our emotions as we experienced it. […] We sounded like our physical selves – young, angry teenage girls getting to grips with feminism, driven by a charged energy. It was a point of principle not to make music that had been done before, to write lyrics devoid of romantic clichés, to express the truth of fraught sexual relations.

Threatened by established right-wing organizations in their backyard and continued violence against women, Leeds punks drew on university connections, personal and artistic relationships, and anger to create a scene flourishing in ideas and intentionality. Punk, as a genre, is notoriously difficult to define; however, through social and political awareness and careful consideration of performance, Leeds' punks created a scene to be remembered equally for its punk sounds and aesthetics as for its anti-sexist, anti-elitist and anti-racist principles. Amidst the mayhem, an unapologetically punk and distinctly local scene emerged, immortalized on record.

# REFERENCES

Ahmed, Sara (2010), 'Happy objects', in M. Gregg and G. J. Seigworth (eds), *The Affect Theory Reader*, Durham: Duke University Press, pp. 29–51.

Ambrosch, Gerfried (2018), '"Guilty of Being White": Punk's ambivalent relationship with race and racism', *The Journal of Popular Culture*, 51:4, pp. 902–22.

Andrews, Travis M. (2017), 'Neo-Nazis have rock bands, too – They've been around for decades', *Chicago Tribune*, 23 August, https://www.chicagotribune.com/entertainment/ct-neo-nazi-rock-bands-20170823-story.html. Accessed 20 February 2020.

Angio, Joe (2015), *Revenge of the Mekons*, USA: Music Box Films.

Barnett, David (2016), 'Loved the music, hated the bigots', *Independent*, 19 July, https://www.independent.co.uk/arts-entertainment/music/features/loved-the-music-hated-the-bigots-7138621.html. Accessed 15 February 2020.

British Culture Archive (2021), 'Rock Against Racism Northern Carnival, 1978 | Thomas Blower', 21 April, https://britishculturearchive.co.uk/thomas-blower-rock-against-racism-alexandra-park-1978/. Accessed 10 February 2022.

Burnham, Hugo (1981), 'Interviewed by J. Bach, "Gang of Four Hugo"', *Damaged Goods*, 1:4, pp. 6–7.

Delta 5 (1979), *Mind Your Own Business*, composed by A. L. Riggs, B. Peters, J. Sale, K. E. Knight, R. Allen and S. Best, vinyl, London: Rough Trade.

Gang of Four (1979a), 'Damaged Goods', composed by D. Allen, H. Burnham, A. Gill and J. King, *Entertainment!*, vinyl, London: EMI Records.

Gang of Four (1979b), 'It's Her Factory', composed by D. Allen, H. Burnham, A. Gill and J. King, *Entertainment!*, vinyl, London: EMI Records.

Goldman, Vivien (2019), 'A mosh pit of one's own', *The Paris Review*, 19 May, https://www.theparisreview.org/blog/2019/05/16/a-mosh-pit-of-ones-own/. Accessed 14 February 2020.

Kickboy (1977), 'Albums', *Slash*, 1:4, pp. 26–29.

King, Jon, Burnham, Hugo, Gill, Andy and Allen, Dave (1979), 'Interviewed by Anon: "The Gang of Four Interview"', *Slash*, 2:10, pp. 20–21.

Klorman-Eraqi, Na'ama (2021), 'Radical feminism and punk: Visual cultures of affect and disruption', *Photographies*, 14:2, pp. 357–78.

Langford, Jon, White, Mark, Lycett, Kevin and Corrigan, Andy (2018), Interviewed by R. Bestley, 'Still fighting the cuts: An interview with Mekons 77', *Punk & Post Punk*, 7:1, pp. 103–15.

Mackay, Finn (2015), *Radical Feminism: Feminist Activism in Movement*, New York: Palgrave MacMillan.

O'Brien, Lucy (1999), 'The woman punk made me', in R. Sabin (ed.), *Punk Rock: So What?* London: Routledge, pp. 186–98.

O'Brien, Lucy (2012), 'Can I have a taste of your ice cream?' *Punk & Post-Punk*, 1:1, pp. 27–40.

Reddington, Helen (2007), *The Lost Women of Rock Music: Female Musicians of the Punk Era*, Burlington: Ashgate Publishing Company.

Reynolds, Simon (2006), 'Militant entertainment: Gang of Four, the Mekons, and the Leeds Scenes', in *Rip It Up and Start Again: Postpunk 1978–1984*, London: Penguin Books.

Sabin, Roger (1999), '"I Won't Let That Dago By": Rethinking punk and racism', in R. Sabin (ed.), *Punk Rock: So What?* London: Routledge, pp. 199–218.

Shaffer, Ryan (2013), 'The soundtrack of neo-fascism: Youth and music in the national front', *Patterns of Prejudice*, 17:4&5, pp. 458–82.

Simpson, Dave (2019), 'Pubs, disco and fighting Nazis: How Leeds nurtured British post-punk', *The Guardian*, 19 April, https://www.theguardian.com/music/2019/apr/19/pubs-disco-and-fighting-nazis-how-leeds-nurtured-british-post-punk. Accessed 1 February 2020.

Sioux, Siouxsie, Morris, Kenny, McKay, John and Severin, Steve (1979), 'Interviewed by J. Garcia, "Siouxsie and the Banshees"', *Slash*, 2:9, pp. 26–27.

Smith, Joan ([1989] 2013), *Misogynies*, London: The Westbourne Press Archive, Saqi Books, https://www.perlego.com/book/569371/misogynies-pdf. Accessed 17 November 2021.

Socialist Workers Party (1976), *Socialist Worker*, 2 October, https://www.marxists.org/history/etol/newspape/sw-gb/1976/496-2-oct-1976.pdf. Accessed 2 December 2021.

The Damned (1977), 'Interviewed by Anon., "Exclusive Interview: The Damned"', *Slash*, 1:1, pp. 5–7.

The Mekons (1978), 'Never been in a riot', in *Never Been in a Riot/32 Weeks/Heart and Soul*, vinyl, Edinburgh: Fast Product.

The Mekons (1979), 'Rosanne', in *The Quality of Mercy Is Not Strnen*, vinyl, London: Virgin Records.

Trowell, Ian (2015), 'Hard floors, harsh sounds and the northern anti-festival: Futurama 1979–1983', *Popular Music History*, 10:1, pp. 62–81.

Wattis, Louise (2017a), 'Exploring gender and fear retrospectively: Stories of women's fear during the "Yorkshire Ripper" murders', *A Journal of Feminist Geography*, 24:8, pp. 1071–89.

Wattis, Louise (2017b), 'Revisiting the Yorkshire ripper murders: Interrogating gender violence, sex work, and justice', *Feminist Criminology*, 12:1, pp. 3–21.

Worley, Matthew (2012), 'Shot by both sides: Punk, politics, and the end of consensus', *Contemporary British History*, 226:3, pp. 333–54.

# 10

## Americana and Leeds: Narrating the American South with Northern Grit

*Dave Robinson*

When it comes to sustaining live music scenes, size matters. For diverse and alternative scenes to flourish, a sufficiently large and culturally vibrant population centre is a prerequisite. Such is the case with the musical world that has become known as Americana. Along with Americana's main creative hubs – the music cities of Nashville, Tennessee and Austin, Texas – local scenes are generally concentrated around metropolitan areas like New York and London, and a handful of college towns; with scene participants coming together for annual gatherings at such events as Hardly Strictly Bluegrass in San Francisco and the Kilkenny Roots Festival in Ireland. Americana conforms to what Richard Peterson and Andy Bennett (2004) refer to as a translocal music scene, in which geographically scattered local scenes cohere and communicate around a distinctive form of music and signifying practices.

The Americana scene transcends national borders but is unevenly distributed both internationally and intra-nationally. Celebrating a melting pot of musical styles rooted in the American South, Americana's reach is mainly confined to North America and parts of Europe. Whilst cultural and historical factors have a bearing on the geographical distribution of local live scenes, so too do the roles of particular people, places and practices in particular moments in time. Together, these factors define Americana's symbolic 'sense of place' and what cultural geographer Peter Jackson (1992) refers to as 'maps of meaning'.

Since its formation in 1999, the Nashville-based Americana Music Association (AMA) has branded 'Americana' as an old-time country-folk hybrid for a distinct audience, but here I consider Americana as a more diverse musical world incorporating a broader range of vernacular American styles. In Leeds as elsewhere in the

United Kingdom, it is a musical world embedded in grassroots music practices ever since the urban folk revival became a bridge for trans-Atlantic cultural exchange back in the 1950s. In this essay I discuss how a wide range of musical influences, including Big Bill Broonzy's country blues, Terry and McGhee's Piedmont blues, Bill Clifton's bluegrass music, the Weavers' interpretations of traditional American folk songs and the 'jug band' inspired skiffle craze, all served as sources of musical meaning for Leeds-based musicians and audiences. The Leeds-based punk band the Mekons also came to recognize Hank Williams' abject country sounds as 'music of the people', and in more recent times, local promoters have sought to introduce Leeds audiences to new and innovative Americana artists and sounds.

Whilst folk revival era New York and Austin's 'progressive country' movement serve as historical sources of inspiration for today's Americana scene, local scenes in other places have their own historical points of reference. In post-war Britain grassroots enthusiasm for American music amongst young people was initially taken up in the form of 'trad' jazz and skiffle music, with folk revivalists occupying a more politicized musical space. Jazz and skiffle served as precursors for the mainly London-based British blues movement of the early 1960s, and the emergence of local scenes in cities beyond London, including rhythm & blues (R&B) scenes in Manchester, Birmingham and Belfast, and country scenes in Liverpool and Glasgow.

Leeds was not synonymous with a particular musical style or sound, but the fascination with American roots music was as vibrant, diverse and eclectic as anywhere else. Young Leeds-based musicians were inspired by visiting American artists from Big Bill Broonzy to the Weavers; by imported R&B records; and in some cases by the sounds emanating from American Forces Network (AFN) radio, or by songs printed in *Sing Out!* magazine, as copies were distributed in folk clubs. Whilst the largely pub-based Leeds folk clubs of the 1960s and 70s are long gone, with the notable exception of the Grove Inn in Holbeck, an American roots scene has continued on through a succession of re-births. Along the way, new venues, promoters and musicians have captured moments of musical meaning: Steve Phillips and Brendan Croker's blues club at the Pack Horse in the 1970s, punk's embrace of country music by the Mekons in the 1980s, John Keenan's promotion of alternative country at the New Roscoe in the 1990s, through to the post-millennial scene in which Leeds has become a favourite destination for touring American acts as well as hosting regular sessions for local Americana acts.

The story of Americana music in Leeds is one of a heterogeneous and ever-developing scene that has become embedded in the musical life of the city. What is more, the significance of experimentation and innovation in local musical practices has been largely overlooked: Steve Phillips' intricate country blues guitar picking having a 'profound affect' on Mark Knopfler's own unique guitar style

(MKNews 2021); Nick Strutt and Roger Knowles appearing on BBC Radio 2's pioneering *Country Meets Folk* radio programme; whilst the Mekons turn to country music was at the vanguard of what would become 'Insurgent Country', and which continues to mark out country as music of resistance. In the following sections, I explore the practices, places and people that have sustained this enduring and at times influential live music scene.

## Luminaries and inspirations

During the late 1950s and early 1960s, British audiences were introduced to the music of American folk, blues and country artists through tours organized by such luminaries as British jazz and blues pioneer Chris Barber and American folk and bluegrass ambassador Bill Clifton. In Leeds, as elsewhere, touring American acts stimulated an enthusiasm for these different styles of music and served as formative influences on aspiring local musicians. For a young Steve Phillips, such an influence was country blues singer and guitarist Big Bill Broonzy who Phillips (2021) recalls seeing at Studio 20, a late-night basement jazz club on Upper Briggate (see Meadowcroft, this volume). Roger Knowles' introduction to American country music was through AFN radio in Germany where his father was stationed with the RAF, but Knowles recalls his later visit to a concert at Leeds Town Hall in 1959 being 'hugely influential on my tastes and subsequent interests' (Knowles 2021: n.pag.). The concert in question was part of a tour described by *New Musical Express* as a 'folk, blues and country-and-western package – the first show of its kind ever to tour Britain' (*NME* 1959: 2), and featured the Weavers, the foremost American folk group of the time, along with Piedmont blues players Sonny Terry and Brownie McGhee, as well as Johnny Duncan and the Bluegrass Boys.

A significant feature of this 'first show of its kind' is that it 'packaged' black blues musicians with white folk and bluegrass players. Like Broonzy (and Lead Belly before him), Terry and McGhee had already been embraced by the folk revival, playing to largely white American audiences during the 1950s and recording on Moses Asch's eponymous Folkways Records. Their billing alongside the Weavers – the revival's primary international ambassadors – is thus unremarkable, but Duncan's background was very different. A white hillbilly singer from Tennessee, Duncan had settled in Britain after marrying a local woman whilst stationed in Cambridgeshire with the US Air Force in 1953. After forming the Bluegrass Boys, Duncan had commercial success in the United Kingdom as part of the late 1950s skiffle scene; his band regularly appearing on the BBC Light Programme's *Saturday Skiffle Club*. The 1959 tour thus presented British audiences with a unique mix of music and musicians rarely found together on the same bill in the United States where, as before and since, 'race'/'R&B' and 'hillbilly'/'country' continued to signify separate racially coded markets. And whilst the folk revival served as a vehicle for expressing common cause amongst social and political protesters on either side of the Atlantic, the African-American 'jug band' inspired skiffle craze – an early form of 'DIY' culture – constituted a specifically British mode of musical resistance to the Anglo-American corporate music hegemony.

As elsewhere in Britain, skiffle provided new music-making possibilities for young people in Leeds and surrounding areas. Already familiar with country music from his time spent listening to AFN in Germany, Roger Knowles recalls that 'It was only when the skiffle era began that my knowledge of country was brought to the fore again. The school skiffle group couldn't work out how I knew songs that Lonnie Donegan had supposedly just written' (Knowles 2021: n.pag.).

Even though some of the songs that British teenagers were 'discovering' were anything but new, that didn't matter. What was important was that skiffle was *their* music. Skiffle itself was a short-lived phenomenon but it paved the way for the British blues boom of the early 1960s and galvanized interest in folk music for young people. In the West Yorkshire area, vibrant folk and later blues scenes emerged along a Leeds-Bradford axis. Bradford's Topic Folk Club, founded by Alex Eaton in 1956, is the longest-running folk club in Britain and forms part of that city's radical musical-political tradition; the club's name itself was taken from Topic Records, a label launched by the Workers' Music Association of which Eaton was a member (Eaton 1990). Both the Topic label and the club played important roles in communicating counter-hegemonic meanings for a trans-Atlantic folk revival; Topic Records producing some of the first American blues records available in Britain, whilst Eaton, whose club later organized the Weavers concert at Leeds Town Hall, noted how 'clubs for skiffle were bound to succeed and given that initial push could very well continue as Folk Clubs' (Eaton 1990: n.pag.).

If Bradford's Topic was the first in the area, by the early 1960s folk clubs began to proliferate around Leeds, two of the main ones being the Grove Inn in Holbeck and Johnny Wall's Club Memphis, which, like the Topic, would move venues several times. Playing at Club Memphis was an important moment in the launch of Steve Phillips' musical career. As Phillips recalls:

> I started playing guitar in 1961, mainly rockabilly and country music. I'm also listening to Leadbelly and trying to figure out how to play it on a 12 string guitar. In 1965 I do a floor spot at Johnny Wall's Memphis Folk Club at the Coach & Horses in Beeston. A few weeks later I bump into Pete Boyle who saw me perform at the Folk Club. He had started a Jug Band Club in Hunslet, and would I do the interval

spot for 10 shilling. Eventually I formed my own jug band after doing the interval spot every week, called Easy Mr Steve's Bootleggers, which performed until 1968.

(Phillips 2021: n.pag.)

The use of the term 'jug band' here indicates a deeper interest in American roots music fomenting amongst the pubs and clubs of Leeds. Phillips himself recounts how he 'started to learn more about country blues guitar picking – particularly Robert Johnson, Blind Willie McTell, Blind Blake' (Phillips 2021: n.pag.). But although the emerging scene was distinctively organic and grassroots in character, its creative energy was sparked by the coming together of local music enthusiasts and newcomers to Leeds.

## *Students and the scene*

In particular, the scene drew vitality from the city's expanding student population. In 1962 Roger Knowles and fellow Harrogate resident Robin Dransfield formed the nucleus of what would become the Crimple Valley Boys, a bluegrass band styled on the New Lost City Ramblers. They received encouragement from British-based American bluegrass guitarist Bill Clifton who'd organized European tours for both the Ramblers and Bill Monroe, and when the Crimple Valley Boys broke up in 1966 Clifton suggested that Knowles team up with mandolin player Nick Strutt from Essex who was studying at the University of Leeds. Strutt and Knowles were instrumental in introducing many old-time American songs to British audiences and by 1968 were appearing regularly on Wally Whyton's BBC Radio 2 programme *Country Meets Folk*. As Knowles recalls, 'We did well, getting many gigs and culminating in opening for Hank Snow and Willie Nelson at the Liverpool Empire and London Palladium' (Knowles 2021: n.pag.). They were later joined on banjo by Richie Bull, another Essex native studying at the University of Leeds, and recorded two albums as Natchez Trace before Strutt and Bull briefly joined Bob and Carole Pegg's folk rock band Mr Fox (see Chapter 2 by Karl Spracklen). Knowles and new bluegrass partner Pete Stanley subsequently toured and broadcast across Europe, whilst Bull returned south to join pub rock band the Kursaal Flyers, but Strutt would remain an enthusiastic part of the local folk and country scenes until his death in 2009.

Whilst students brought vitality to the Leeds scene, some also gained musical inspiration from local players. Mark Knopfler first arrived in Leeds in 1968 as a junior reporter for the *Yorkshire Evening Post* before enrolling on an English degree at the University of Leeds in 1970. Knopfler's official fan site testifies to the 'profound affect on Mark's guitar playing' (MKNews 2021: n.pag.) that Steve Phillips had during this time. Phillips himself recalls how in 1969

> I was approached by the *Yorkshire Evening Post* for an interview. A young cub reporter called Mark Knopfler had seen me perform and arranged for me to be interviewed by STEPHEN PHILLIPS who ran the arts & music side of the paper. After this Mark starts coming round to play guitar with me. I also when the fee was good enough took Mark along with me to perform. We were called The Duolian String Pickers.
>
> (Phillips 2021: n.pag.)

It was during this time that Knopfler made his first recording; a demo disc of a self-penned number entitled 'Summer's Coming My Way' (1970), recorded in a converted studio at a house in Pudsey and featuring Phillips on 12-string guitar. After graduating in 1973, Knopfler moved to London to pursue his music career, but years later he would return for a now legendary session at the Grove Inn which would briefly bring the Leeds pre-Americana scene to national attention.

The coming together of local musicians with ones who'd come to Leeds as students was a significant factor in sustaining a vibrant and outward-looking American roots scene in Leeds during the late 1960s and early 1970s. In this respect, the scene displayed something in common with the Austin, Texas scene of a few years earlier where students like Janis Joplin came together with locals at the Chuck Wagon and Threadgill's tavern to play and listen to music spanning old-time country, folk, bluegrass and blues (Malone 2002: 393–94; Robinson 2019: 394–95; Shank 1994: 39–41). Of equal importance in each of these places and moments was the presence of local organizers and entrepreneurs driven by a similar enthusiasm for the music. Bluesville 68, described by Steve Phillips (2021) as a 'really excellent blues club', was started in 1968 by local band manager Dave Stansfield who hosted club nights at both the Meanwood Hotel and the Farmers Inn at Thornbury, featuring emerging local artists like Phillips as well as the cream of British blues from Alexis Korner to Fleetwood Mac. Stansfield was later joined in the Bluesville 68 venture by Dave Foster, a fellow member of 'folk psychedelia' band Moonkyte. In the mid 1970s, Foster opened a specialist record shop called Melgary Music in the Grand Arcade, Leeds, and in the following decade launched the Unamerican Activities record label to promote local blues and country artists (Foster 2021). Nowadays Foster fronts a country blues project called Mister Dodo Bones and the One-Eyed Jacks, who hold gigs at the community-run Headingley Enterprise and Arts Centre ('HEART'), a favourite venue for today's local Americana acts. It was through Foster that Steve Phillips linked up with Brendan Croker, a singer-songwriter and devotee of American roots music from Bradford, to form the blues duo Nev & Norris.

## Fading roots and new shoots

In 1976, Phillips and Croker also started a blues club at the Pack Horse pub near Woodhouse Moor, but by this time the British blues scene was in long-term decline with rock having become the dominant paradigm. So too, country music was taking on a more pop flavour, whilst the British folk movement had lost meaning for younger people following the schism caused by folk rock and the derision with which punk rockers viewed folkies. As for the university scene, broadcaster Liz Kershaw who was studying at the University of Leeds recalled a similar shift away from the 'folky stuff': 'It was so quaint. People took their own cushions to gigs and sat cross-legged. Then around 1977, the lads with long greasy hair and Led Zeppelin albums under their arms decided to cut it all off and go spikey' (Kershaw cited in O'Brien 2021: n.pag.).

Steve Phillips virtually stopped performing in the early 1980s whilst Brendan Croker pursued a solo career, eventually releasing the album *A Close Shave* (1986) on Dave Foster's Unamerican Activities label. But a musical alliance between Phillips, Croker and Mark Knopfler eventually came together when Knopfler, by then famous on the back of the Dire Straits *Brothers in Arms* album (1985), joined the others for an informal gig at the Grove Inn on 31 May 1986. As Phillips explains: 'He is so famous by this time the gig gets reported on the front page of some of the daily newspapers. This is perhaps the start of the NOTTING HILLBILLIES' (Phillips 2021: n.pag.).

The Notting Hillbillies album initially inspired by this gig was eventually produced three years later and released in 1990 as *Missing ... Presumed Having a Good Time*. The album included a mix of traditional country blues numbers and original songs, emphasizing the musicianship of each of the players. Its timing also coincided with the rise of a neo-traditionalist tendency in country music and renewed interest in older performers such as guitarist Chet Atkins, with who Knopfler also recorded an album the same year – *Neck and Neck* (1990). In between time, Knopfler had guested at Croker's Leeds Polytechnic gig in June 1989 with Phillips opening the show; and the Hillbillies toured their album in 1990, including two nights at the since demolished Astoria Ballroom in Leeds.

## Punk goes country

Knopfler's presence in these collaborations helped raise the profile of American roots music in Leeds as it did more widely, but the mid 1980s also saw Leeds punk band the Mekons take a decisive turn to country music with their aesthetically redefining 1985 album *Fear and Whiskey*. This new musical direction neither affected the Mekons' raw punk style nor their radical political consciousness. Moreover, the band's embrace of country music would serve as a far-reaching influence for articulating the notion of 'alternative country' – a then emergent musical world in which punk rockers came to recognize the 'three chords and the truth' simplicity they shared with 'hard' country music.

Formed in 1977, the Mekons were part of the same group of University of Leeds art students as Gang of Four (GO4) and Delta 5, and together formed a radical musical alliance embracing a gender-inclusive and collectivist ethos. Members of both the Mekons and GO4 had associations going back to their time together as pupils at the prestigious and progressive Sevenoaks School in Kent. If this background appears a far cry from country music, their involvement in Rock Against Racism activities in Leeds in the late 1970s and the Mekons' re-grouping at the time of the 1984 miners' strike explains their quest for a more 'functional music'. Studio engineer John Gill introduced the Mekons to an obscure form of folk music known as 'English Country Music' which had been revived in rural East Anglia during the 1960s (Digby 2001; Stradling 2000) and which would have a 'profound affect' on the Mekons' own music. As former Mekon Kevin Lycett explains:

> We were particularly engaged by its artlessness and its sense of being functional music before being 'artistic' music. It was there to do a job; to tell stories, provide oral history and to give people a bloody good time. Not to be worshipped, academically studied, or put in a glass case. It was the music that mattered, not the composers or musicians.
>
> (Lycett 2021: n.pag.)

Lycett (2021) describes how the Mekons recognized much in common with this music of unknown composers and musicians who played for pleasure amongst their own, usually poor, communities. He might as easily be describing what John Street (1986: 187–89, 199–201) identifies as the vital community function that music, and in particular country music, has performed in the American South. But if English Country Music laid the ground for the Mekons' interest in American country music it was Chicago DJ Terry Nelson who would first recognize the connection between the Mekons and American country. As Lycett explains, 'we were blown away by the music Terry sent us, and quickly saw the common ground. As with English Country Music, to paraphrase Wycliffe, it was music of the people, by the people and for the people' (Lycett 2021: n.pag.).

Concluding with a cover of the 1948 Hank Williams/Leon Payne country classic 'Lost Highway', *Fear and Whiskey* has been hailed as a defining album of alternative country and is regarded by many fans as the band's masterpiece. But as Lycett recalls, the Mekons' turn to the country was initially received rather differently by fans:

> Bemusement/derision/distaste [...] A few got it and loved it, but most thought it was some kind of trashy joke and yee'hawed away through our sets, not realising we were in deadly earnest. I don't think any band in the UK was doing what we were at that time. So it was quite a stretch for audiences and fans.
>
> (Lycett 2021: n.pag.)

By this time, the Mekons line-up included violinist Susie Honeyman, multi-instrumentalists Lu Edmonds (previously of the Damned) and Rico Bell, and Leeds-born vocalist Sally Timms, who each added something to the band's new country sound; as did, on occasions, the guesting Brendan Croker. Of the three longstanding original members of the Mekons – Lycett, Tom Greenhalgh and Jon Langford – only Lycett has remained in Leeds, continuing to fulfil the role of 'functional music' with his band the Hill Bandits performing local gigs and supporting causes and events including community music project Cloth Cat and 'An Evening with Caroline Lucas' (Green Party MP). Meanwhile, it was Langford who went on to blaze a trail for what has been dubbed 'Insurgent Country' music through his long association with Chicago-based Bloodshot Records. An enduring creative force on the Bloodshot roster, Langford and numerous collaborators have continued the Mekons' collectivist ethos through such projects as country-punk outfit the Waco Brothers and hard country covers band the Pine Valley Cosmonauts; projects which spearhead Bloodshot's resistance to the corporately controlled country music industry. Thus, a kernel of meaning that took root in Leeds at the time of the 1984 miners' strike continues to inspire counter-hegemonic resistance across a translocal, trans-Atlantic music scene in the 2020s.

## *Americana rising: An emergent scene*

My own introduction to the Leeds scene came in the late 1990s, as I attended gigs by American 'alternative country' artists such as Neal Casal and Jason Ringenberg at the New Roscoe pub and Steve Earle at the Irish Centre. I saw Leeds-born guitarist Stu Page playing blues at the Grove and country at the Haddon Hall pub in Kirkstall, and attended country music nights at Kirkstall Post Office Club. At that time, the description 'Americana' was in its infancy in Britain, and although the Roscoe gigs attracted avid alternative country fans, as elsewhere, there lacked the essence of a unified American roots scene in Leeds. The term 'country' denoted a waning working men's club scene derided by more middle-class folk and blues enthusiasts. And although a few touring singer-songwriters such as Tom Russell, who ex-miner Dennis Collier booked at Castleford's Mirage Hotel, crossed over the country/alternative country divide, these largely existed as separate taste worlds. In 1999, this began to change with the establishment of the AMA in Nashville, whose branding avoided the contaminated 'C word'. As a largely country-folk musical hybrid, Americana became marketable to a more liberal-progressive, middle-class audience on both sides of the Atlantic, including an alternative-identifying cohort of the millennial generation. 1999 also saw the launch of BBC Radio 2's *Bob Harris Country* programme, which gave Harris free reign to redefine what country music was for British audiences whilst keeping one eye on his ageing *Old Grey Whistle Test* audience and also seeking to attract younger migrating listeners from Radio 1 to Radio 2.

In Leeds, as elsewhere, these events helped draw together a cross-generational audience including older alternative country and American roots fans and a growing younger fan base for the hybrid Americana style. It is a scene that continues to flourish and develop to this day. One of the key figures in sustaining the Leeds scene is Tré Mealiff, who relocated from London in 2007, and has been promoting gigs for touring Americana artists (known as the Hee Haw Sessions) ever since. As she recalls:

> At the time, John Keenan was the only person working within these genres [country / folk / Americana]. He was doing a fine job at The New Roscoe and I loved attending those shows. But I felt it wasn't enough, there were artists I wanted to see but they weren't coming to Leeds. So really Hee Haw Sessions was born out of a personal wish to have these artists play in the city that I resided in.
>
> (Mealiff 2021: n.pag.)

Mealiff's comments highlight the crucial role of committed music fans, some operating as small-scale entrepreneurs, in creating, sustaining and revitalizing local live music scenes. Whilst John Keenan is *the* legendary Leeds music promoter across multiple genres, Mealiff has taken up a torch for American roots music once carried by Alex Eaton at the Topic, and by Dave Stansfield and Dave Foster with Bluesville 68. Others who have done so in recent times include Garry Cape and Janet Whisker with their Tumbleweed Americana events at Seven Arts in Chapel Allerton, and Ben Pike, who hosts Afternoon Americana sessions at Northern Guitars Bar on Call Lane.

In terms of Nicholas Abercrombie and Brian Longhurst's (1998: 141) notion of an 'audience continuum', Americana here offers accessible opportunities for the 'fan' and the more committed 'cultist' to become actively involved with the object of their fandom in the roles of 'enthusiast' (e.g. amateur player or event volunteer) or 'petty producer' (e.g. semi-professional musician or part-time promoter). And for some, like Tré Mealiff, Americana's independent, non-corporate business structure offers opportunities to pursue a career in the music industry on their own terms. As Mealiff remarks: 'Like me, lots of music promoters are just music fans on a mission' (Mealiff 2021: n.pag.).

As a primarily acoustic musical category involving many solo artists and duos performing to niche audiences, Americana not only offers opportunities for small-scale producers and entrepreneurs but is also suited to small grassroots music venues and non-traditional performance spaces. In Britain, live Americana scenes are based around both commercially run venues and, increasingly, not-for-profit venues such as arts and community centres and clubs; many of them operated as 'social enterprises' by community interest companies (CICs). The introduction of CICs in 2005 opened up new spaces for live music just as traditional venues were facing mounting financial and commercial pressures due to rising rents and competition from large venue operators. Moreover, the types of spaces CICs operate, the grant funding they can access and the locations they inhabit coincide with Americana's flexible venue requirements, limited financial resources and alternative-identifying 'sense of place'. A vibrant Leeds Americana music scene has flourished amongst mainly not-for-profit venues over recent years. Whilst larger touring acts are accommodated at the similarly not-for-profit Leeds Irish Centre as well as university venues, a grassroots scene has become centred around community-operated venues in North Leeds.

The Brudenell Social Club, a former working men's club, became a CIC in 2007, at which time it was already a live music venue hosting an eclectic range of alternative music. Located in the predominantly student area of Hyde Park, the Brudenell has continued to thrive since incorporating as a CIC, adding a second 400-capacity concert room in 2017 and becoming an iconic venue on the Leeds music scene. It has long been a popular Americana venue, and since 2008 has been hosting many of Tré Mealiff's Hee Haw Sessions. The club also has a reputation as a venue that artists enjoy playing at and are keen to return to; fellow Austinites James McMurtry and Dale Watson being amongst the Americana artists I've seen there multiple times. Run by Nathan Clark, the club serves as both music venue and community hub; its bar caters to both students and locals of all ages. Clark's community focus and DIY ethos are as much an attraction to Americana promoters, artists and fans as the well-equipped venue itself. Mealiff explains why such not-for-profit venues are so important for sustaining grassroots scenes:

> These venues are key to the music eco-system as a whole. They are an important cog in the wheel of developing and nurturing emerging talent. Similarly, they also

provide a space where music fans can truly be themselves and feel a part of it all. Hee Haw Sessions had its beginnings in Santiago [a music bar in Grand Arcade] and shortly afterwards moved to Brudenell where most of our shows reside today. The support these venues give us at the start and the continued support to this day from The Brudenell has made it possible for us to continue bringing shows to Leeds.

(Mealiff 2021: n.pag.)

As to why artists keep returning to Leeds, Mealiff explains:

There are venues in Leeds who really know how to take care of artists. Bonds are formed and those venues become like a home away from home. In addition to the industry side of things, there's the audience response to the artists. There's never a dull night at a show in Leeds!

(Mealiff 2021: n.pag.)

The Brudenell's 400 capacity makes it a relatively large venue for Americana in the United Kingdom, and for some American artists touring Europe, it may be only viable to play one date in the north of England. For such gigs, the Brudenell's catchment is not just local; Americana fans travel from across the north, just as Leeds-based fans gladly travel to Manchester or Tyneside when the only gig's taking place there; each in turn demonstrating their commitment to a grassroots scene operating at a translocal level.

Between 2013 and 2017, the smaller 100-seat auditorium at Seven Arts in Chapel Allerton hosted Tumbleweed Americana, organized by Garry Cape and Janet Whisker who booked mainly touring solo performers and duos. Seven Arts is a multi-purpose arts and performance space set up as a CIC from the outset in 2007 by a group of local residents to 'improve community spirit through involvement in the arts' (Seven Arts 2021: n.pag.). And over in Headingley, the Headingley Enterprise and Arts Centre (HEART), located in a former primary school and operated by a community benefit society since 2011, continues to form a regular venue for grassroots Americana featuring locally based artists of all ages, from Dave Foster as Mister Dodo Bones, to established local blues-man Serious Sam Barrett, and young Texan artist Rachel Laven, temporarily domiciled in Leeds, who I managed to catch at HEART shortly before the March 2020 COVID-19 lockdown. But the grassroots scene is not confined to not-for-profit venues alone. Just up the Otley Road from Headingley, the quirky Hyde Park Book Club and the hip LS6 Café are amongst the small bar venues to have hosted Americana sessions; whilst across Woodhouse Moor is the Lending Room at the Library pub which sometimes serves as an alternative venue for Hee Haw

Sessions gigs. From there right through the city centre to Northern Guitars Bar on Call Lane where Ben Pike has run Saturday afternoon sessions are a trail of small venues which have – more or less frequently – hosted Americana music in recent years. And with the single exception of the Library pub, all these venues are independently run and appeal to a clientele who identify with alternative culture and an anti-corporate ethos.

## Conclusion

When I attended AmericanaFest UK (Americana music industry conference) in Hackney, East London, in 2020, there were moments when the world of Americana appeared to me as little more than a vanity project for a narcissistic society; or what Anthony Giddens (1991: 52) might refer to as a stage for the 'reflexive project of the self'. There, Americana could give the impression of an exclusive musical space – a 'knowing community' – in which social actors crave a stage and an audience without considering what wider meaning their musical world holds for potential fans. This impression may be inaccurate and unfair to many of the mainly southern-based delegates, but it is based on the contrasting attitudes and assumptions I observed between London and the scenes I am familiar with in Leeds and elsewhere in the north of England. In short, a grassroots music scene involves more than just using the term 'grassroots'; and finding an audience involves having something to communicate with them rather than just finding the right platform to get noticed. In the present-day Leeds Americana scene, as with earlier scenes, such assumptions are understood. Whereas some hip London venues like Omeara in Southwark and Paper Dress Vintage in Hackney present Americana as part of a 'cultural brand' to boost the 'night-time economy' in gentrifying districts (see Chatterton and Hollands 2002), the Leeds Americana scene is run *by* fans *for* fans.

## Postscript

Research for this chapter was undertaken during 2021, at a time when COVID-19 restrictions continued to disrupt live music events, and the long-term impact of the pandemic on music venues remained uncertain. In June 2022, I finally got to the Georgia-based Drive By Truckers' (twice-postponed) gig at Stylus, University of Leeds, as well as a gig by the New York-based Felice Brothers at the Brudenell Social Club. On both occasions, it was heartening to find myself at sold-out performances amongst familiar groups of still committed Americana fans. Since the 2020

UK lockdowns, some regular grassroots events appear to have gone by the wayside, but others have survived; notably the Tuesday Night Live events at HEART which regularly feature local and up-and-coming Americana artists. As with folk, blues and country clubs of earlier times, the Leeds Americana scene continues to be run by enthusiasts whose foremost mission is to promote the music they love as members of a close-knit fan community.

## ACKNOWLEDGEMENTS

The author would like to thank Roger Knowles, Steve Phillips, Dave Foster, Kevin Lycett and Tré Mealiff for their invaluable insights and assistance with this project.

## REFERENCES

Abercrombie, Nicholas and Longhurst, Brian (1998), *Audiences: A Sociological Theory of Performance and Imagination*, London: Sage.

Chatterton, Paul and Hollands, Robert (2002), 'Theorising urban playscapes: Producing, regulating and consuming youthful nightlife city spaces', *Urban Studies*, 39:1, pp. 95–116.

Digby, Roger (2001), 'English country music – A personal view', *Concertina*, https//concertina.net/rd_ecm.html. Accessed 10 October 2021.

Eaton, Alex (1990), 'Topic Folk Club: The 30th Anniversary – Memories of the very early days of The Topic', transcribed from *Tykes' News* (Summer, Autumn and Winter editions) by Trevor H. Charnock, http://nawaller.com/topicfc/History/alexeaton.html. Accessed 1 September 2021.

Foster, Dave (2021), e-mail correspondence and telephone conversations with author, 3–19 October 2021.

Giddens, Anthony (1991), *Modernity and Self-identity: Self and Society in the Late Modern Age*, Cambridge: Polity.

Jackson, Peter (1992), *Maps of Meaning*, New York: Routledge.

Knowles, Roger (2021), e-mail correspondence with author, 4 January–12 March 2021.

Lycett, Kevin (2021), e-mail correspondence with author, 7 July–25 August 2021.

Malone, Bill (2002), *Country Music USA*, 2nd rev. ed., Austin: University of Texas Press.

Mealiff, Tré (2021), e-mail correspondence with author, 4 July–2 August 2021.

*MKNews* (2021), 'Mark Knopfler', *MKNews: The Official Mark Knopfler News Website* https//mark-knopfler-news.co.uk/biogs/mark-knopfler/. Accessed 4 September 2021.

*New Musical Express (NME)* (unattributed) (1959), 'Lonnie is a fan of the weavers', 18 September, p. 2.

O'Brien, Lucy (2021), 'Everybody hold on tight', Leeds Alumni Online, https://alumni.leeds.ac.uk/post_punk. Accessed 5 September 2021 [link no longer available].

Peterson, Richard and Bennett, Andy (2004), 'Introducing music scenes', in R. Peterson and A. Bennett (eds), *Music Scenes: Local, Translocal, and Virtual*, Nashville: Vanderbilt University Press, pp. 1–16.

Phillips, Steve (2021), e-mail correspondence and telephone conversation with author, 14–22 August.

Robinson, Dave (2019), 'Austin and Americana music: Sites of protest, progress, and millennial cool', in B. Lashua, S. Wagg, K. Spracklen and M. Selim Yavuz (eds), *Sounds and the City: Volume 2*, London: Palgrave MacMillan, pp. 389–411.

Seven Arts (2021) 'About', *Sevenleeds*, https//sevenleeds.co.uk/about/. Accessed 28 December 2021.

Shank, Barry (1994), *Dissonant Identities: The Rock 'n' Roll Scene in Austin, Texas*, London: Wesleyan University Press.

Stradling, Rod (2000), 'Review of English country music: Record no. 1', Mustard, https//mustard.org.uk/reviews/ecm.htm. Accessed 10 October 2021.

Street, John (1986), *Rebel Rock: The Politics of Popular Music*, Oxford: Blackwell.

# PART 3

## HISTORIES OF POPULAR MUSIC IN LEEDS

# 11

# Leeds City Varieties in the 1950s and 1960s: Decline, Nudity and Nostalgia in the British Variety Industry

*Dave Russell*

In the early 1950s, Leeds City Varieties, while an admired survivor of music hall's Victorian heyday, was essentially just another small regional variety theatre dependent upon 'nude' or 'girlie' shows and operating within an industry in terminal decline. However, in less than a decade, it had attained iconic status within British light entertainment, serving as the location of BBC television's highly successful Edwardian-flavoured variety show, 'The Good Old Days' from 1953 and designated a building of 'special architectural or historic interest' in 1960. It is the venue's unique position as 'the theatre with the double life' (*Daily Sketch*, 14 February, 1969: n.pag.), home to a renowned family entertainment but also a committed provider of a highly controversial cultural form, that makes it such a rich site for study. This chapter explores both the role of these contradictory elements in maintaining the viability of the City Varieties in an exceptionally difficult environment and their wider significance within contemporary debates and discourses surrounding mid-twentieth-century British variety. 'Popular music', considered in terms of genre, style and repertoire, features only modestly with the focus falling instead on the significance of the spectacles that music underpinned.

By 1950, the City Palace of Varieties, or 'The Verts' as it was popularly known, was the country's oldest surviving music hall still in regular operation (see Figure 11.1). It was established in 1865 when Charles Thornton, publican of the city-centre White Swan, replaced his long-established concert room with a fully equipped music hall, advertised as Thornton's Grand New Music Hall and Lounge, but known more prosaically as Thornton's Varieties. Over the next decades, it was subject to frequent changes of both ownership and name – City Varieties first appears to have been adopted in the 1890s – before eventually

FIGURE 11.1: The City Varieties in 1949, viewed from the gallery. Courtesy of Leeds Central Library.

passing to the Joseph family, first, from 1941 until his death in 1962, in the shape of Harry and then his sons, Stanley and Michael, who controlled the hall until its sale to Leeds Metropolitan District Council in 1987 (Mellor 1970: 45–48; Riley 1997). Harry Joseph, born in London to Polish-Jewish emigrants in 1898, had managed and owned several southern and London suburban variety theatres in the 1930s, before moving to Leeds after the bombing of his Lewisham Hippodrome in 1941 (*The Stage*, 3 May, 1962: 4). He arrived at a propitious moment when variety's long-term decline was temporarily arrested by buoyant wartime demand. Prosperity held until the late 1940s but, from that point, the rise in home-based leisure, especially television, initiated a catastrophic decline (Wilmut 1985: 158). In 1950, the leading theatrical trade paper, *The Stage*, regularly listed some 100 venues offering weekly variety performances. By 1960, that number had shrunk to about fifteen, with the introduction of commercial television in 1955 initiating a particularly sharp decline. The Leeds Empire, by then the city's only other variety house, closed in 1961 and by the late 1960s, the City Varieties was one of a mere handful of remaining British venues.

Many larger variety theatres tried to overcome their growing difficulties in the 1950s by attracting younger patrons through the introduction of American or American-influenced pop music. The American balladeer Don Cornell, his compatriot, country artist, Slim Whitman and the British skiffle star, Lonnie Donegan, all headlined national variety tours in 1955 and 1956 which included appearances at the Leeds Empire (*The Stage*, 12 May, 1955a: 2; 12 April, 1956a: 2; 8 November, 1956d: 3). However, while such ventures were feasible for leading syndicate-controlled venues, they were beyond the budgets and capacities of smaller, independently operated theatres such as the City Varieties. The Varieties could only seat about 900, while the Empire, part of the powerful Moss Empire circuit, held almost double that number. Searching for a distinctive and viable staple product, many of these 'number two' halls, the City Varieties prominent amongst them, invested ever more heavily in the female nude show. One commentator noted that the vast majority of the 45 touring revues opening in one week in June 1955, approximately a fifth of the country's entire stage entertainment, included 'varying degrees of naughtiness and nudity' (*Daily Herald*, 13 June, 1955a: 4).

Acts rooted in the erotic display were long established in music hall and variety. Depiction of scenes mimicking classical statuary and history painting, featuring women in flesh-coloured tights and variously called poses plastiques, tableaux vivant or living statues, existed from the 1870s, while the Edwardian vogue for 'classical dance' could excuse scanty clothing and varying degrees of leg display (Mellor 1970: 202–04; Russell 1996: 78–79; Faulk 2004: 142–87). In the late 1930s, the introduction of naked or partially naked living statues into the revues at London's Windmill Theatre and the arrival of various 'exotic' routines based on new American modes of striptease saw nudity become far more a feature of live entertainment. During the Second World War, the Windmill's popularity with servicemen provided erotic entertainment, especially that featuring an overtly Anglicized look, with a patriotic gloss and, thereby, a significant degree of acceptability (Mort 2007: 33–35). Joseph swiftly grasped the potential of nude entertainments in the later 1940s, even replacing the 1949–50 pantomime season with an extended run of 'Peek-a-Boo', featuring Phyllis Dixey, then arguably Britain's best-known striptease artist (Purser and Wilkes 1978; *Leeds Mercury*, 5 December, 1949: n.pag.). In May 1950, he announced his intention 'to make the Varieties the Folies Bergère of the North' (*The Stage*, 25 May, 1950: 4) and adult revue was to become the core of the City Varieties' programmes, only abandoned in 1969 when the successful revival of pantomime suggested other avenues to profitability.

A lack of business records prevents detailed analysis, but, in a profoundly difficult operating climate, nude shows clearly provided Joseph and his peers with significant benefits. Larger syndicate halls had initially eschewed the genre on moral grounds and, although commercial realities softened their stance, they largely left the field open for the smaller venues. More widely, variety theatres for once had a competitive advantage by being able to present material that was completely beyond the moral universe of contemporary television and cinema. While stimulating demand, sexual entertainment also helped ease problems of supply. Although fees for the star performers could be costly, those for the young women providing 'glamour' through group posing, dancing or other support roles were not. The weekly minimum wage for revue artists established by the trade union Equity was between £4.50 and £7, depending on the performer's age and the size of the cast, while nudes could usually earn a marginally more generous £8 (*Daily Herald*, 14 June, 1955b: 4). Costs as well as clothing were thus shed, although profits often remained extremely modest: one (un-named) show in the early 1950s lost money at half of the venues in a twenty-week tour, generating a surplus of only £44. Financial pruning was a constant feature resulting in the twelve-piece City Varieties orchestra of 1952 becoming a quartet within a decade (Mellor 1970: 208–09; Fields 2013: 81). Nevertheless, promoters frequently argued that nude performances drew far larger attendances than their 'standard' equivalents and although their evidence was often anecdotal and self-serving, the loss of audience experienced by the Camberwell Palace and the Chesterfield Hippodrome when public campaigns forced the withdrawal of nude shows, was striking: the former saw a 60 per cent reduction over a six-week period, the latter closed down almost immediately (*The People*, 6 June 1954: 5; *The Stage*, 28 July, 1955c: 3). Quite simply, as Michael Joseph recalled, variety was given a final if brief lifeline by the nude show, 'keeping theatres like ours alive and working' and saving many 'straight' careers (Fields 2013: 14). Rather than being the perversion of variety that many believed it to be, it was its contemporary representative face.

It is important to stress that displays of nudity or near-nudity often formed a relatively small proportion of stage time. This was in spite of titles which, provocatively displayed across colourfully dramatic advertising posters, were sometimes as much a tease as the acts themselves. The popular association of France, and specifically Paris, with extremely liberal sexual mores saw the City Varieties regularly host revues such as 'Folies Parisiennes' (1954) (see Figure 11.2) and 'A Naughty Nite in Paris' (1956), while puns referencing common phrases or elements of popular culture were also used heavily: a section of 'Strike a Nude Note' entitled 'Nudes of the World' (1951), 'Strip, Strip Hooray!' (1950 and onward) and 'Yes we have no Pyjamas' (1955), featuring the 'Naughty Nightie Girls', were amongst the results. Although often labelled 'revues', most shows lacked the unity of theme and structure this implied and were essentially standard variety bills into which some degree of sexual entertainment was inserted. 'Comic Strip', for example, which

FIGURE 11.2: 'The theatre with the double life,' a recording of 'The Good Old Days' interrupts the run of a Paul Raymond nude show in 1954. Courtesy of Leeds Central Library.

played the Varieties in September 1954, included not only 'Those Lovely Naughty Ladies', the Valentine Girls, but Bobbie Wildman who whistled Albert Ketèlbey's hugely popular Edwardian light classical tune 'In a Monastery Garden', played the accordion and bones and did a tap routine (*The Stage*, 24 June, 1954: 5).[1] Although, as will be discussed below, 'nude' and 'family' entertainments were sometimes viewed as strict opposites, most performers moved seamlessly between them. Several cast members from the initial episode of 'The Good Old Days', for example, continued at the Varieties for a full week's engagement where they were joined by Suzette Duprez, the 'Glamourous French Model' (*Yorkshire Post*,

20 July, 1953a: 4). Indeed, one of that group, magician Eric Williams, was soon to develop a parallel career producing nude revue. His attempt to persuade his dancers to appear naked in his show 'Fancy Pants' and their refusal, backed by a threat of strike action, became a brief media *cause celebre* (*The Stage*, 26 April, 1956c: 3; *Sunday Mirror*, 22 April, 1956: 5).

Although mainstream artists were often well-received, it was, however, a display of the female body that drew audiences. The rulings of the Lord Chamberlain's Office, the official censor for live theatrical performance until its abolition in 1968, constrained activities to some extent, although its powers over the variety industry were far from comprehensive (Purser and Wilkes 1978: 42–45). Dancers, in particular, largely eluded controls and, as one commentator noted, 'the addition of two stars and a fig leaf [resulted in] [...] by far the most sexually provocative' of the acts on view (*Daily Herald*, 14 June, 1955b: 4). There was, however, no escaping the injunction that nudes remain motionless and what was often advertised as 'striptease' was actually 'posing', with artists revealed to audiences in a pre-set position via changes in lighting and/or the use of curtains, drapes or revolving sets. Use of body make-up, nipple covers and various forms of *cache-sexe* from pouches and G-strings to sticking plasters – most local authorities, including Leeds, used policewomen to ensure that these were suitably deployed to prevent displays of pubic hair – meant that some performers were not strictly nude (Purser and Wilkes 1978: 42–45, 53; *Yorkshire Post*, 17 June, 1954: 6). Nevertheless, the public display of nudity or near-nudity occurred to an extent and with a frequency previously unknown in mainstream British entertainment.

From the 1940s, a distinct subgroup of *poseuses* emerged within the variety profession. Its earliest stars were Dixey and 'Jane', actually Chrystabel Leighton-Porter, a model for the eponymous *Daily Mirror* cartoon 'glamour girl' and who subsequently built a stage act based upon the character (Saunders 2004). Both were frequent and popular visitors to the City Varieties – 'Jane' chose it for her farewell performance in 1963 – as were future leading lights such as Peaches Page, Blondie 'Godiva' Haigh and Rhoda Rogers. They were expected to augment their nude routines with other more traditional elements, most commonly dance, although song, comedy and, in one unlikely case, fire-eating also featured (Fields 2013: 109). Page, also a key figure in the world of female wrestling and advertised as 'Britain's Biggest Star Without a Bra', impressed one reviewer by managing to move between posing and singing 'the famous aria from *Madam Butterfly* ['One Fine Day'] without [it] appearing the least incongruous' (*The Stage*, 12 September, 1957b: 16; 19 September, 1957a: 4).

Their styles varied considerably with Dixey amongst the more conservative, marrying a certain artful humour with a loyalty to older style depiction of classical scenes (Purser and Wilkes 1978: 96–97, 143–45). 'Peek-a Boo', the knowing but coy title of her show that played the Varieties in numerous iterations, captures something of her approach. Her act was deemed sufficiently inoffensive for her to be chosen to open the Butlin's Holiday Camp booking desk at a Leeds department store in 1949 (*Yorkshire Evening News*, 24 January, 1949: n.pag.). From the later 1950s, as the deteriorating market situation encouraged ever greater sensationalism, erotic entertainment became more prominent within various programmes, with the energetic young promoter, Paul Raymond, increasingly using nude groupings as backdrops for every act, irrespective of content, in his touring revues (Purser and Wilkes 1978: 143). As the familiar stars retired, the City Varieties and the handful of other venues continuing with sexual entertainment increasingly drew on artists who had honed their acts in private strip clubs and who tended to bring with them a harder-edged and more sexually direct aesthetic.

The music hall had attracted criticism from moral reformers from its inception and it is hardly surprising that the nude display added a coda to this history. Hostility took the form of a steadily increasing hum of concern focusing on the immorality of the performances and their promotional material, the financial and emotional exploitation of the young women who took part in them and, perhaps the biggest concern, the degradation of the variety tradition. Nudes, it was commonly argued, had killed the 'family' show and thereby the variety business more generally. In his 1957 play, *The Entertainer*, in which John Osborne used music hall's demise as a symbol for Britain's wider political decline, a character asks, 'why should a family man take his wife and kids to see a lot of third-class sluts standing about in the nude? They'll go once. They won't go again' (Osborne 1959: 15). After visiting the City Varieties to see 'Naughty Nights and Saucy Sights' in 1953, *Daily Mirror* writer, Eve Chapman, overlaid concerns for family audiences with a wider narrative stressing the threat posed by such entertainments (American crooners were also targeted) to the national character and sense of humour. 'The full-bellied laugh in British music halls is fast dwindling to an uneasy snigger', she claimed, arguing that old-fashioned 'vulgarity' was being replaced by smutty innuendo accepted by ever more passive audiences (*Daily Mirror*, 5 March, 1953: 2). Those responsible were swiftly identified. In an age when male youth culture was so often the object of moral panic, it is interesting to see opprobrium fall upon the adult males making up 'the usual seven rows […] in the front stalls' and whose 'sexual repression [and] deep-seated emotional instability', was held by one psychologist to drive demand for nude entertainment (*The Stage*, 5 April 1956e: 3; 17 July, 1958: 4).

The realities were more complex. As already argued, the shows were more symptomatic than the cause of decline. Moreover, there is also evidence that, at least in the earlier 1950s, traditional variety audiences were relatively comfortable with them. Dixey's biographers claim that the City Varieties' audience was 'largely composed of – certainly led by – students' but large-scale student attendance was probably only associated with the annual visit of (male) residents from Leeds University's Devonshire Hall (Purser and Wilkes 1978: 115). In 1952, their rowdiness led to an abandonment of the night's entertainment and a lively debate about town and gown relationships (*Yorkshire Evening News*, 22 January, 1952: n.pag.; *Yorkshire Post*, 23 January, 1952: 3). In the early 1950s and probably well beyond, the venue in fact largely drew from the local working and lower middle-class communities. Its weekly printed programme called upon patrons to bring parties 'from your factory, office or club', a media report from 1950 noted the high number of 'cloth caps and shopping baskets' visible in the entry queue, and another, struck by the low ticket costs, saw the audience as drawn from 'a limited and coherent social range' (*Illustrated*, 8 November, 1950: n.pag.; *The Observer*, 17 December, 1950: n.pag.). Crucially, there is also evidence that, while the male gaze was obviously fundamental to its very existence, at least in the early 1950s when the tolerance born of wartime still had purchase, the nude show could attract something resembling a 'family' audience. A magazine photograph of patrons waiting to see 'Jane of the *Daily Mirror*' in 1950 shows an even balance of men and women aged 30–50, sitting mainly in couples or small groups, as well as a small number of children. 'The presence of children' was commented upon by another visiting journalist and taken as a demonstration of the 'respectable attitude in which patrons view the place' (*Illustrated*, 8 November, 1950: n.pag.; *The Observer*, 17 December, 1950: n.pag.). Corroborative evidence can be found for other venues: as late as 1957, a local reporter noted that, despite frequent assumptions to the contrary, the Leicester Palace was 'packed with families ... [for] yet another leg and bust show' (*Leicester Evening Mail*, 11 June, 1957: 3).

Overall, however, family audiences became much rarer as the decade progressed: audiences were increasingly younger, with Harry Joseph claiming in 1961 that the average age of his patrons had fallen from 50 to 25 in a decade, and male-dominated (*Daily Mail*, 23 November, 1961: n.pag.). By this stage, full striptease was emerging in establishments such as the Raymond Revue Bar, opened by Paul Raymond in London's Soho in 1958, and in some working men's clubs. Freed from the Lord Chamberlain's regulations, these private, nominally, 'members only' venues, could allow movement and ever more blatant sexual spectacle became possible (Mort 2007: 2–53). In such an atmosphere nude shows could no longer serve as broad-based entertainment, but the City Varieties, now, crucially, a listed building which could not be easily repurposed, chose to maintain its distinctive product. The consequences were inevitable. In 1964, a journalist described the audience as 'overwhelmingly male' and that remained the case until 'the nudes' were finally abandoned at the end of the decade (*Yorkshire Post*, 30 March, 1964: n.pag.; *Bradford Telegraph and Argus*, 22 February, 1969: n.pag.).

While live sexual entertainment at the City Varieties epitomized what the hard-pressed variety industry had become, the theatre's hosting of 'The Good Old Days' allowed various imaginings of what it once might have been.[2] Intended as an approximation of Edwardian music hall, it featured a chairman presiding over a variety entertainment performed by contemporary artists in period dress, watched by an audience, similarly attired, and given full licence to be noisy. Lusty chorus singing was encouraged – a rousing version of the early twentieth-century favourite, 'Down at the Old Bull and Bush', usually completed the show – and the chairman was to be heckled: applicants to attend the first programme were informed that they 'must be prepared to stand up and barrack' (*Yorkshire Post*, 11 July, 1953c: 9). First broadcast on 20 July 1953 and initially intended as a short series, it was to run until 1983. Screened only three to five times annually in the 1950s, it was nevertheless sufficiently popular to earn Boxing Day scheduling from 1956. By the early 1960s, with live variety increasingly a memory, it featured far more frequently, shown thirteen times in 1963 and 1964. Although claims were made for audiences of over ten million, official figures for the 1968 Christmas period show it attracting only 6.2 million viewers, still the week's tenth most-watched programme (*Television Mail*, 10 January, 1969: n.pag.).

Re-enactment of Victorian and Edwardian music hall was far from unknown. The Players Theatre, a London-based professional actors' club, had specialized in the genre from the late 1930s and its members comprised the core of the company that presented a season of Victorian music hall performances as part of the 1951 Festival of Britain. Chaired by the charismatic South African-born actor, Leonard Sachs, these shows were later reprised in several leading variety theatres (*Weekly Dispatch*, 1 April, 1951: n.pag.; *The Stage*, 19 April, 1951c: 3–4, 26 April, 1951a: 8; 1 November, 1951b: 14). (Sachs was to become, from the third episode, *The Good Old Days*'s immensely popular chairman). Aware of the success of both the 1951 venture and recent features set in, or focusing on, the City Varieties, BBC executives asked Barney Colehan, the producer of those shows, to develop a programme evoking 'the atmosphere of music hall' (Anon. 1984: 3–5). Colehan, the BBC North Region's newly appointed Head of TV Light Entertainment, was hardly a typical BBC recruit, having been born into a working-class Yorkshire family in 1914 and entering broadcasting via the British Forces Network. Nevertheless, his social background and skill in recognizing the untapped possibilities of engagement with the wider public, made him a highly effective programme-maker at a time when the Corporation was increasingly willing to adopt a more demotic tone. His ability to harness popular energy had already been demonstrated on Wilfred Pickles's hugely popular radio game show, 'Have a Go', 'Works Wonders', a radio programme in which workers entertained their peers, and 'Top Town', an inter-town radio talent contest which moved to national television in 1954 (*The

*Stage*, 3 October, 1991: 23; *The Guardian*, 24 September, 1991: 37). It was to be the audience, drawn substantially from amateur dramatic societies in order to guarantee confidence with period dress and highly intrusive close-ups, that defined the new show and became integral to its popularity.

'The Good Old Days' professed few claims to historical accuracy and those who actually remembered the Edwardian period were ever happy to point out its innumerable inaccuracies. When Dolly Harmer, a veteran of the Edwardian stage, claimed that it offered 'bogus old-time music-hall [...] which made her annoyed', she spoke for a number of her generation (*The Stage*, 22 March, 1956b: 4). It was noted frequently that the chairman had disappeared from all but the smallest halls by the late nineteenth century, the City Varieties dispensing with the role as early as 1878, and that the chairman had, anyway, been a quietly assertive symbol of order and authority rather than a lightning conductor for audience misbehaviour, however benignly intended (Mellor 1970: 45; *The Performer*, 15 January, 1953: 2; 22 September, 1955: 12).[3] The programme also substantially misrepresented the basic atmosphere of the Edwardian halls which were heavily flavoured by management attempts to emphasize respectability and devise mechanisms to facilitate a smooth transition from first to second house necessitated by the recent advent of the twice-nightly performance system. Restrictions were placed on excessive displays of enthusiasm (or disapproval), encores and curtain calls were frequently banned and singers – anyway increasingly marginalized by speciality acts such as jugglers and acrobats – were strongly discouraged from performing chorus songs. Neither audiences nor performers could ever be entirely tamed: the Leeds-born singer, Vesta Victoria, defiantly introduced a chorus song entitled 'Don't sing the chorus' (Russell 1996: 71–72). Nevertheless, the Edwardian variety theatre was a far more restrained place than that of Colehan's creation.

Some degree of authenticity was certainly demonstrated where possible. Colehan was anxious to use speciality acts partly not only because of their intrinsic entertainment value but also because they had been such an integral part of the earlier variety stage. There was, too, a willingness to pay homage to stars of earlier generations, initially through the medium of impersonation but mainly via routines based on Victorian and Edwardian song performed by members of the Players' Theatre who were to be central to show throughout its history. A number of older stars, some of whose careers had begun in the late nineteenth century, also appeared, adding a powerful physical link to past glories, and Colehan provided genuine period monologues and sketches for contemporary acts willing to utilize them. Overall, however, the need to succeed as light entertainment outweighed all other considerations. The programme's makers were fully aware of most anachronisms, happily embracing them as effective televisual devices. The use of a chairman, for example, supplied necessary continuity between acts and facilitated interaction between stage and audience. Sachs specifically developed what became his trademark verbose, alliterative introductions to the performers to prompt a 'reaction from the audience without wasting time' (Anon. 1984: 3–5). Similarly, there was no virtue in replacing an enlivening audience *bonhomie* with the more restrictive ambience of the 1900s. There is, therefore, an enjoyable irony in the fact that the initial broadcast, which was live, fell victim to the very logistical problems that Edwardian management feared. Colehan so successfully coached the audience that its 'cheering and shouting [...] [lost] us half a minute of valuable time on each of the eight turns'. Despite pleas for extra time, he was firmly instructed by London to abandon the planned finale and switch promptly to the International Horse Show. One critic felt the problem went beyond mere timing, claiming that 'the audience overwhelmed the show in every way [...] It was almost as if the stars were overawed' (*Yorkshire Post*, 21 July, 1953b: 10). Colehan quickly learnt his lesson, keeping future audiences under tighter control, a process much aided by a move from live to recorded shows in 1959.

There is only so much interpretative weight that a popular TV entertainment series can bear and much analysis of the programme's impact must remain speculative. For the City Varieties specifically, the programme engendered a new lease of life and sense of purpose. The BBC's fees, although probably modest, paid for much-needed renovation in 1954 and were always a useful source of additional income. The publicity value, however, was priceless with the adjective 'famous' seeming automatically to attach itself to any media references to the theatre by the 1960s. Given the lack of congruence between the City Varieties as seen on screen and its staple nightly fare, the full financial worth of that publicity was only realized in the 1970s as a well of cultural capital became available for the Josephs and later managements to draw upon. Nationally, irrespective of whether audiences grasped the confected nature of the entertainment, that very confection became a successful sub-genre of variety in its own right. Colehan and his colleagues fostered an appetite for 'Olde Tyme' performances on both the professional and amateur stage that remains to this day – not least at the City Varieties – stimulated by the pleasures of dressing up and chorus singing at a time of declining opportunity for informal communal music-making and participating in licensed mild misbehaviour: a kind of pantomime for adults.

Beyond that, the function of 'The Good Old Days' within the wider national culture is harder to divine. Much of its popularity stemmed simply from its energy and it being a showcase for contemporary variety acts, both established and emergent: comedians Ken Dodd and Hylda Baker made their TV debuts in the same episode in 1955. However, it is certainly worth considering that its celebration of an untroubled and rather cosy past in a time of contemporary introspection allowed the programme to serve a deeper purpose. In both in conception and continued popularity, 'The Good Old Days' was part of an inchoate but clearly discernible widening of interest in the history and significance of music hall and variety. That music hall was honoured at the Festival of Britain demonstrated its importance within the national self-image and as the decade continued, the BBC explored and celebrated music hall history through plays, documentaries and features as well as adding 'A Night at the Varieties', a radio version of 'The Good Old Days' also broadcast from the City Varieties, to its schedule in 1959. Several books appeared on music hall's past and the foundation of the British Music Hall Society in 1963 to protect and interpret its written and artefactual record giving some organizational coherence to this growing sensibility. It is in this context that the programme should be interpreted.

As already evidenced by Eve Chapman's criticism of the nude show, the demise of twentieth-century variety generated a decidedly elegiac critical discourse equating it with the wider loss of a dynamic and energizing popular culture. Such views were rooted in a powerful late Victorian and Edwardian narrative defining Victorian music hall as a key repository of a vulgar but authentic English urban working-class culture undermined by the bland commercialism of the emerging 'variety' (Faulk 2004). Over the twentieth century, such sentiment, often wedded to various levels of anti-Americanism, became embedded in critiques of mass culture from both right and left, and took on renewed significance with the collapse of live stage entertainment in the 1950s. One of its most powerful statements came in John Osborne's explanatory note to *The Entertainer* asserting that: 'The music hall is dying, and, with it, a significant part of England. Some of the heart of England has gone: something that once belonged to everyone, for this was a truly folk art' (Osborne 1959: 8). Similarly, the novelist and social commentator, Colin MacInnes, was struck by the extent to which music hall song had penetrated 'folk memory' and was moved by the fact that something 'so charming, innocent, comical and realistic, has gone forever' (MacInnes 1967: 21, 12). Neither writer seemed aware that the twentieth-century 'music hall' they celebrated was the very 'variety' that earlier critics had found so vapid, and their shared use of the category 'folk' was hardly an appropriate label for such a highly commercial product. For them, however, it clearly captured the idea of a widely shared cultural universe that had died before their eyes.

'The Good Old Days' should not be pushed too firmly into this narrative of loss but it clearly had the potential to arouse a sense of regret and nostalgia. At the least, its very title, although coined without ideological intent, must have encouraged some to see the programme as an opportunity to make unfavourable comparisons with the contemporary entertainment industry. Reviewing it in 1955, one critic praised singer Joy Beattie, for getting the audience 'singing with her as if they really were of the former century when the halls were happier places with good family entertainment' (*The Stage*, 11 August, 1955b: 11). Similarly, Chapman was far from alone in describing variety audiences of the 1950s as passive and, although such criticism was not entirely justified, the comparison between supposed contemporary inertia and past engagement as presented on screen, must have encouraged a certain pessimism. In the next decade, Colehan suggested that the 'gaiety, warmth and enthusiasm' the programme engendered might help explain its popularity in an age of 'slick, sophisticated cabaret, beat music and twanging guitars' (Anon. 1965: 6). Beneath the over-enthusiasm of the audience and its interplay with the chairman, the show could, indeed, be quite reassuring, its period costume, historical stage backdrops, familiar songs and musical arrangements carefully crafted so as to avoid modern idioms, combining to provide some older viewers with a safe cultural space (*TV Mirror*, 3 April, 1954: n.pag.).

Irrespective of the exact emotions it engendered, this somewhat cavalier period construction actually gained much of its strength from its location in a building of such genuine historical resonance. Virtually every newspaper and magazine article written about the City Varieties produced a standard roll call of performers including Charlie Chaplin, Harry Lauder, Charles Coborn, Vesta Victoria and many others, who, albeit often in early career obscurity, had played the hall, and viewers were fully aware of the ghosts who looked on. That tangible sense of linkage to a rich performance heritage remains a powerful attraction to contemporary audiences and performers and helps render the City Varieties one of the country's most historically significant live entertainment venues. They and future generations should be grateful for the acute stewardship of the Joseph family, the imagination of an unconventional TV producer, the foresight of a government building inspector and, uncomfortably for modern sensibilities, the work of an army of strippers, dancers and *poseuses*, for collectively sparing the City Varieties the fate that befell virtually every other variety theatre in the 1950s and 1960s.

ACKNOWLEDGEMENT
I would like to thank Lisa Taylor for her helpful comments on an earlier draft.

NOTES
1. Here and in several later instances, reviews refer to performances at venues other than the City Varieties, hence the apparent discrepancy between dates.
2. Plentiful post-1970 examples of the show can be found on YouTube. The British Film Institute holds a very limited stock of episodes from the period studied but these were not available during the period of research.
3. The role was made redundant by the almost universal introduction of theatre style fixed-seating at the expense of substantial numbers of 'cabaret-style' tables and chairs.

# REFERENCES

Anon. (1965), *Good Old Days*, commemorative brochure, Leeds: Leeds City Varieties.

Anon. (1984), *Good Old Days*, commemorative brochure, Leeds: Leeds City Varieties.

*Bradford Telegraph and Argus* (1969), newspaper clipping, 22 February, Leeds: West Yorkshire Archives, WYL 2410/3/3.

*Daily Herald* (1955a), 'Are nude shows offensive? An investigation: There's more sex on the posters than on stage', 13 June, p. 4.

*Daily Herald* (1955b), 'The Nude Shows – final report: They get top billing – but little money', 14 June, p. 4.

*Daily Mail* (1961), newspaper clipping, 23 November, Leeds: West Yorkshire Archives, WYL 2410/3/2.

*Daily Mirror* (1953), 'Pass the ripe tomatoes', 5 March, p. 2.

*Daily Sketch* (1969), newspaper clipping, 14 February, Leeds: West Yorkshire Archives, WYL 2410/3/3.

Faulk, Barry J. (2004), *Music Hall and Modernity: The Late Victorian Discovery of Popular Culture*, Athens, Ohio: Ohio University Press.

Fields, Caroline (2013), *The Book of Memories*, Leeds: First Edition.

*Illustrated* (1950), newspaper clipping, 8 November, Leeds: West Yorkshire Archives, WYL 2410/3/1.

*Leeds Mercury* (1949), newspaper clipping, 5 December, Leeds: West Yorkshire Archives, WYL 2410/3/1.

*Leicester Evening Mail* (1957), 'Small demand for night life', 11 June, p. 3.

MacInnes, Colin (1967), *Sweet Saturday Night*, London: MacGibbon and Kee.

Mellor, Geoffrey James (1970), *The Northern Music Hall*, Newcastle: Frank Graham.

Mort, Frank (2007), 'Striptease: The erotic female body and live sexual entertainment in mid-twentieth century London', *Social History*, 32:1, pp. 27–53.

Osborne, John (1959), *The Entertainer*, London: Evans Brothers.

Purser, Philip and Wilkes, Jenny (1978), *The One and Only Phyllis Dixey*, London: Futura.

Riley, Peter (1997), *The Amazing Varieties*, Leeds: City Varieties Music Hall.

Russell, Dave (1996), 'Varieties of life: The making of the Edwardian music hall', in M. R. Booth and J. H. Kaplan (eds), *The Edwardian Theatre: Essays on Performance and the Stage*, Cambridge: Cambridge University Press, pp. 61–85.

Saunders, Andy (2004), *Jane: A Pin-Up at War*, Barnsley: Leo Cooper.

*Sunday Mirror* (1956), 'The reluctant nude …', 22 April, p. 5.

*Television Mail* (1969), newspaper clipping, 10 January, Leeds: West Yorkshire Archives, WYL 2410/3/3.

*The Guardian* (1991), 'Obituary: Barney Colehan', 24 September, p. 37.

*The Observer* (1950), newspaper clipping, 17 December, Leeds: West Yorkshire Archives, WYL 2410/3/1.

*The People* (1954), 'It's just no good – the nudes are preferred', 6 June, p. 5.

*The Performer* (1953), newspaper clipping, 15 January, p. 2, Leeds: West Yorkshire Archives, WYL 2410/3/3.
*The Performer* (1955), newspaper clipping, 22 September, p. 12, Leeds: West Yorkshire Archives, WYL 2410/3/3.
*The Stage* (1950), 'Variety gossip', 25 May, p. 4.
*The Stage* (1951a), 'Fairs', 26 April, p. 8.
*The Stage* (1951b), 'Leonard Sach's "Song Saloon"', 1 November, p. 14.
*The Stage* (1951c), 'Sach's Song Saloon', 19 April, pp. 3–4.
*The Stage* (1954), 'Mass posing at the Granville', 24 June, p. 5.
*The Stage* (1955a), 'Calls for next week', 12 May, p. 2.
*The Stage* (1955b), 'Life in the old dog yet', 11 August, p. 11.
*The Stage* (1955c), 'No nudes – no business', 28 July, p. 3.
*The Stage* (1956a), Calls for next week', 12 April, p. 2.
*The Stage* (1956b), 'Stage promptings', 22 March, p. 4.
*The Stage* (1956c), 'Variety fare', 26 April, p. 3.
*The Stage*(1956d), 'Variety news and gossip – Bernard Delfont's future plans', 8 November, p. 3.
*The Stage* (1956e), 'Variety news and gossip – "Fancy pants" success', 5 April, p. 3.
*The Stage* (1957a), 'On tour', 19 September, p. 4.
*The Stage* (1957b), 'Round about', 12 September, p. 16.
*The Stage* (1958), 'Too much show in the business', 17 July, p. 4.
*The Stage* (1962), 'Harry Joseph', 3 May, p. 4.
*The Stage* (1991), 'Obituaries: Barney Colehan', 3 October, p. 23.
*TV Mirror* (1954), newspaper clipping, 3 April, Leeds: West Yorkshire Archives, WYL 2410/3/1.
*Weekly Dispatch* (1951), newspaper clipping, 1 April, Leeds: West Yorkshire Archives, WYL 2410/3/1.
Wilmut, Roger (1985), *Kindly Leave the Stage: The History of Variety 1919–1960*, London: Methuen.
*Yorkshire Evening News* (1949), newspaper clipping, 24 January, Leeds: West Yorkshire Archives, WYL 2410/3/1.
*Yorkshire Evening News* (1952), newspaper clipping, 22 January, Leeds: West Yorkshire Archives, WYL 2410/3/1.
*Yorkshire Post* (1952), 'Students' conduct at Leeds theatre', 23 January, p. 3.
*Yorkshire Post* (1953a), 'City varieties, Leeds', 20 July, p. 4.
*Yorkshire Post* (1953b), 'Edwardian TV audience were too enthusiastic', 21 July, p. 10.
*Yorkshire Post* (1953c), 'TV show asks for noisy audience', 11 July, p. 9.
*Yorkshire Post* (1954), 'Phyllis Dixey and her husband fined £25', 17 June, p. 6.
*Yorkshire Post* (1964), newspaper clipping, 30 March, Leeds: West Yorkshire Archives, WYL 2410/3/3.

# 12

# The Evolution of DIY Venues as Dancing Spaces in Leeds from the 1940s to 2020s

*Stuart Moss*

Do-it-yourself (DIY) refers to the behaviours of people who think and act creatively to realize an idea without the need for external professional input (Wolf and McQuitty 2011). Leeds has historically been considered as being more progressive than regional neighbouring cities in terms of fashionability and nightlife (Stringfellow and Lafferty 1996), which has attracted people to the city who have been keen to develop this with their own enterprising ideas. Following a twentieth-century decline in the textile industries and recession in the 1970s, Leeds had a number of mothballed and derelict ex-industrial spaces, which years later would provide an opportunity for DIY entrepreneurs to create new nightlife venues. This chapter provides an 80-year overview of the evolution of DIY enterprise in grassroots 'club' spaces in Leeds. Overarching themes within the chapter showcase how youth cultures, creativity, rebellion and a range of sociopolitical forces including racism, division, violence, drugs and legal challenges contributed to the development of leisure spaces for dancing to music predominantly played by disc jockeys (DJ). Drawn from wider research in the 'Leeds Club History Project' (available at www.leedschp.co.uk), the chapter highlights cases in which this development was unique to Leeds; in other ways, the chapter traces a vast yet largely hidden and underacknowledged history of dance music venues in the city.

### The first 'club' entrepreneur

Jimmy Savile pioneered DIY dance enterprise in Leeds. In 1943, he ran a paid-entry record-only dancing event at The Bellevue branch of the Loyal Order of Shepherds, a member's only club in Leeds. Aged 18, Savile hired an event room and hand-wrote flyers with the name of the event, 'Grand Record Dance', the location, starting time and entry price of one shilling. Savile played records from a gramophone modified with a pick-up attached to a valve radio, which amplified the sound (Davies 2014). Attendees were fascinated by the amplified sound; in the 1940s, dancing to records rather than a live band was a novelty. In a 2004 interview with journalist Frank Broughton, Savile stated, 'what I was doing was causing twelve people to do something. And I thought, I can make them dance quick. Or slow. Or stop. Or start' (Broughton 2011: n.pag.). Haslam (2001) considers this to be the first dance event run by a DJ/promoter in the United Kingdom. Ultimately the event ended in failure when the gramophone partially melted and blew the venue's electrical fuses, but Savile made some money, and this gave him ideas for future ventures (Davies 2014).

Savile went on to organize subsequent events at a range of venues around Leeds, and an afternoon tea dance at a tea-room in Otley, where he played music from a record player attached to a 2½-inch speaker. Savile was given the tea-room free of charge as the owner recognized that whilst there, attendees would purchase refreshments (Brewster and Broughton 2006). Savile earned the money from attendees who paid at the door, an early example of a promoter/venue arrangement in terms of the financial split. In 1951, Savile joined John Swale, a business partner with technical expertise, and earned £2 and 10 shillings to run a record dancing birthday party in Otley (Davies 2014). According to Swale:

> We took what was then the Wharfedale Cafe's upper room for five shillings and put the records on with Jimmy spinning them and chatting – and that was the world's first disco. If I'd patented it I could have made a fortune!
> 
> (cited in Jack 2011: n.pag.)

What Savile demonstrated was enterprise and event management, terms that were uncommon, and disciplines that were not yet recognized, in that era.

Jimmy Savile died aged 84 in 2011 after which reports alleged he had sexually abused hundreds of people, both children and adults throughout his life, leading the police to conclude that Savile had been one of Britain's most prolific predatory sex offenders. His inclusion in this chapter is not to eulogize him, but to acknowledge his contribution to the rise of DJ and promoter culture in Leeds and beyond.

## *1950s: The first DIY rock 'n' roll venues*

Rock 'n' roll culture became popular in the United Kingdom in the 1950s. However, in its early days, its American music and fashions were not universally accepted. In

Leeds, at both the Locarno and The Majestic ballrooms there was a strict policy against jiving or audacious rock 'n' roll dance styles as well as the fashions associated with the newly emerging 'teddy boys'.

> Only traditional ballroom dancing, waltzes, foxtrots & the like were permitted. No jiving / BeBop or Rock'n'Roll, which was becoming very popular with the youth of the day but anyone caught out was very quickly ejected. I think this was because that type of music and dance was somehow seen in those days as undermining the moral values of the time.
>
> (Sanderson 2012: n.pag.)

The seeds of DIY were sown as young people who wanted to dance to rock 'n' roll music began to seek alternative spaces at which to do so. In this decade, the existence of youth culture was recognized, whereby values, fashions, language and music played a part in shaping the new identity category of 'teenagers' (Fasick 1984).

The development and proliferation of the jukebox meant that teenagers could organize their own social dancing events whenever they met at venues that had jukeboxes. Numerous venues in Leeds had a jukebox and became favoured 'hangout' spots for young people to dance, including the Texas Grill in Roundhay, Del Monte Coffee Bar in Meanwood and Expresso Bongo in Morley. Those feeding coins into jukeboxes to play records performed the same functions as the DJ, who would soon become a feature of many venues in Leeds. In order to keep patrons on the premises, some coffee bars cleared the tables and chairs next to the jukebox to allow dancing on the premises. Although they gained reputations as 'dens of vice', with disapproval of visiting them, coffee bars in Leeds became favoured spots for teenagers to dance (Hoggart 1957; Jackson 2008; Secret Leeds 2009).

## *1960s: Aspiration and rebellion*

In 1960s' Leeds, there was a genuine sense of aspiration: Yorkshireman Harold Wilson was elected head of The Labour Party in 1963 and Prime Minister in 1964. Although not a 'Loiner' (someone from Leeds; Wilson was from nearby Huddersfield), he gave hope to the people of Yorkshire that their voices would be heard 'down south'. For young people, role models such as Cilla Black and The Beatles had come from northern, working-class backgrounds and were doing very well for themselves.

The mods were working-class youth and young adults, who dressed in smart Italian suits and flaunted consumer items of prestige. The emerging 'mod' subculture adopted Motown and rhythm & blues (R&B) as its music of choice, retrospectively called 'northern soul'. Northern soul 'all-nighters' started to be held in Leeds. An all-nighter was an organized music event, typically held in social clubs, dance halls and coffee shops. The music would be played by DJs all-night long; consequently, attendees at all-nighters experimented with drugs: 'Black bombers and purple hearts were the ecstasy of the sixties – they kept everyone wide awake and wide-eyed' (Stringfellow and Lafferty 1996: 84). In 1967, Leeds City Police formed a specialist Drugs Squad to attempt to deal with the rise in illegal drug use in the city (Thornton 2013). Thus the early northern soul scene provided opportunities based around a music scene for DJs, promoters and drug dealing cultures, offering a blueprint for what would follow two decades later in the rave scene.

Also in the 1960s, a minor 'beat' scene developed in Leeds centred around the Blue Gardenia coffee shop, which had a live music venue in the basement. The 'beat' counter-culture challenged dominant societal values; men grew long hair and beards, and people wore bright-coloured patterned clothes, flared trousers, kaftans, cheesecloth, sandals and beads. Flowers, peace signs and the Campaign for Nuclear Disarmament logo all became icons associated with the scene. This scene was sympathetic to a range of left-wing causes and championed progressive social and political changes. 'By the mid-1960s, long hair had become an unmistakable sign of rebellion' (Haslam 2007: 19). The media renamed the movement as 'hippies', a throwback to the word 'hip' long-associated with 1950s beatnik poetry and music (Street 1986).

In Leeds, the hippie movement was centred around The University of Leeds, where students and faculty identified with its ethos and adopted its look. At the time, many venues rejected the hippie look and created dress code door policies, banning men from those who had long hair or wore flared trousers or open-toed sandals from entry. Consequently, the student bars at The University of Leeds and nearby pubs became favoured destinations for Leeds hippies who would organize their own music events there, as well as in their homes, primarily in the Woodhouse, Hyde Park and Burley neighbourhoods, setting up a house party scene, which still flourishes 60 years later.

## *1970s: Dancing against division*

The 1970s were turbulent times in Leeds, as in the rest of the United Kingdom, with industrial action, economic recession, urban decay and a three-day working week to conserve electricity, which all had social and economic impacts. Leeds was described as grey, depressing and polluted (Leeds Libraries 2019); social deprivation was widespread, with 20 per cent of the city's residents affected (Thornton 2013).

By the mid 1970s, Leeds was gripped by fear and division. Serial killer Peter Sutcliffe (known as The Yorkshire Ripper) began his killing spree in West Yorkshire in 1975. The National Front (NF), buoyed by social anxieties about the economy, had a visible presence on the streets of Leeds (O'Brien 2009) and laid the blame for a housing shortage on immigrants, with fears over immigrant religion and culture also exploited. NF stickers and racist graffiti-covered buildings across the city, with violence from NF followers commonplace (Rachel 2016). A politically left-wing DIY music scene emerged around The University of Leeds Students' Union and pubs in nearby Woodhouse such as The Fenton, spawning grassroots bands such as Delta 5, The Mekons and Gang of Four as a creative subculture grew and stood against the populism of re-emerging right-wing politics and visible Nazi sympathizers (Simpson 2019). Students in Leeds also became highly politicized, concerned with violence against women and the thuggery and division associated with local racist skinheads (O'Brien 2009).

Academics and students cooperated to form feminist sociopolitical alliances (see McGovern, Chapter 9). Leeds developed a politically charged punk scene as 'a rejection by the youth of Britain of an older generation's fake values' (Spracklen and Spracklen 2018: 38). Predominantly involving live performances, punk was short-lived but followed by a vibrant post-punk scene. Punk and post-punk scenes in Leeds were community-centred (O'Brien 2009). This ethos also underpinned John Keenan's 'F' Club, which started in 1977 as an event called 'Stars of Today' at Leeds Polytechnic Students' Union (LPSU). 'Stars of Today' took place at the end of the academic year when students had returned home and the event space wasn't being utilized. Keenan showcased local and national post-punk bands alongside DJs John Cavell and Claire Shearsby playing mostly post-punk music. The LPSU venue had a limited 300-person capacity, but the event was popular and often sold out, so Keenan made it into a members' club so that the regulars would be guaranteed tickets. In September 1977, after LPSU retained the use of their event space for their own events, Keenan was forced to move his event to The Ace of Clubs in Woodhouse, where it was renamed as 'F' Club, with 'F' standing for 'Fuck' in a riposte to LPSU: 'Fuck the Poly'. Keenan described his communitarian motivations in forming 'F' Club for regular attendees:

> I thought of them as like my children, I began to realise that they were intelligent, bright and inventive [...] we were getting a few regular characters that were really interesting [...] I wanted to keep everyone together and couldn't just let it go.
> (Jones 2020: n.pag.)

'F' Club featured live music and DJ Claire Shearsby who continued to work with Keenan and 'pushed the limits with her playlist' (Deboick 2020: n.pag.). Shearsby became the face of 'F' Club, with one regular attendee saying 'if you had to pick the person that that whole scene rotated around, it was Claire' (Jones 2020: n.pag.). Keenan also used 'F' Club to talk to audiences via a microphone about music, and occasionally politics. 'F' Club was held at different locations in Leeds: The Continental Club on Francis Street in Chapeltown from 1978 to 1979, and then Brannigans on Call Lane in Leeds city centre from 1979 until 1981, when it was renamed 'Fan Club'. The event then ran on an ad hoc basis at The Warehouse and Tiffany's until 1982.

## *1980s: Urban creativity and new music genres*

The 1980s was the most creative decade of the twentieth century in terms of new music genre development (Moss and Henderson 2009); many new genres emerged from the fusion of rock music with electronica. Hip hop music was the most radically different genre to attract attention in Leeds in the early 1980s. Many US hip hop artists including Afrika Bambaataa and Mantronix incorporated sounds of the Roland TR-808 drum machine to produce distinct rhythmic beats. These beats and rhythms made the sound of new variants of electro music immediately danceable. B-boying[1] emerged from this, with the popularity of the music and dancing peaking across the United Kingdom in the early to mid 1980s. In Leeds, hip hop became popular amongst young people in both black and white communities city-wide. Considered fresh, creative and aspirational, hip hop wasn't just about music, but also about fashions, art, language and knowledge (see Little and Stevenson, this volume).

If, in the 1950s, rock 'n' roll culture provided an American-influenced escapism following the difficult 1940s, hip hop did something similar in the 1980s. It provided a taste of American trends, which was anodyne to the dark and turbulent 1970s faced by many Leodisians. Whilst many music scenes in Leeds were divided along racial lines during the 1970s, hip hop brought together black and white youths with a shared appreciation of hip hop culture. A notable division in the hip hop scene was in age, with nearly all of those involved being young teenagers, with older generations treating hip hop with some derision, considering it to be 'too American', 'fake' and 'corny' (Bernard 2019; Emm 2014).

Because most of those who were active in Leeds' hip hop scene were under 16 years old and below the legal drinking age, night-time hip hop events in established venues were rare. Local youth clubs in Leeds' suburbs became DIY 'club' spaces and played an active role in helping hip hop fans hear and dance to the music they loved. In Seacroft Civic Centre, the Tuesday night youth club would play electro music, attracting teenagers from across the city who wanted to dance. Demand for hip hop leisure spaces outstripped the supply of venues offering it. Young people sought their own ad hoc locations to listen to hip hop and dance. In Leeds city centre, Dortmund Square became a popular location for hip hop fans to gather and showcase their breakdancing moves and 'battle' other crews on Saturday afternoons. Other popular locations were The Merrion Centre, which had smooth flooring, and the flat area of pavement in between what is now the First Direct Arena and The Yorkshire Bank building off Merrion Way. It was not uncommon to see young people walking around the city centre and suburbs with a roll of linoleum ('lino'), used as a portable dancefloor to demonstrate their dance moves at any location. Music was played through portable cassette players, known as boom-boxes and ghetto-blasters. There was no need for a DJ and the scene epitomized a DIY attitude and mentality. The Leeds hip hop scene peaked in 1985; by 1987, the sight of breakdancing on the city's streets had largely disappeared (Hip Hop Connection 2014), as sounds changed and new scenes emerged.

The DIY spirit amongst these teenagers had lit a spark which, for some, would burn brightly two years later, when the rave scene materialized. This DIY scene had key components in its development in Leeds, including house parties across the Burley, Hyde Park and Woodhouse suburbs; illegal drinking dens ('shabeens') in the Chapeltown suburb and disused former industrial spaces in south Leeds. Furthermore, the rave scene combined politically anti-Conservative, anti-Thatcherite rebellion with a social ethos of peace, love and togetherness. The music featured electronic genres of house, acid house and techno as its soundtrack, but the drug ecstasy fuelled the scene. Together this generated a transformative scene, where people from all backgrounds and identities could dance together in unity.

According to Evelyn (2018), in the 1980s there were very few black DJs in Leeds, which he described as a city divided by race. Areas within Leeds city centre were unsafe for a black man to be (see also Long, this volume). As the rave scene grew, Evelyn recalled DJing at a house party in the suburb of Burley and noticing the presence of Leeds Service Crew[2] members, as well as black people too. Unusually, everyone was getting along and enjoying the music, which was predominantly hip hop and house, as well as the fusion 'hip house' (house music with rapped vocals); all have similar beats per minute, so the tempo for dancing remained fairly constant. That members of a largely racist football hooligan group were dancing in a venue with black people was quite remarkable at the time. Evelyn put this down to the sudden rise in popularity of the drug ecstasy, which was being taken by many of those in attendance. Under ecstasy's influence, the DJ became a god-like figure who dancers collectively worshipped in a drug-fuelled state of techno-shamanism (Hutson 2000; Anderson 2009). According to Phillips (2009), ecstasy helped to 'feminize' the culture around club spaces, invoking feelings of empathy while raves had a sense of communality. The use of ecstasy made the dancefloor at these events a neutral space of acceptance and togetherness, resulting in social mixing on a level that had not occurred in the city before, with a collective identity between participants in shared leisure spaces (Anderson 2009).

The event in Burley that Evelyn (2018) recalled was part of the rave scene rising in Leeds from the existing free party movement, which was already entrenched in the near city centre neighbourhood of Hyde Park. The DIY ethos of the rave scene had many synergies with punk, where people made their own music, pressed their own records, created fanzines, ran pirate radio shows and hosted their own events (Trailblazers of Acid House 2016). The free party scene associated with raves ran from the late 1980s until 1994 when it was quashed by the Criminal Justice Act, which turned 'party people' into criminals, yet concomitantly pushed the rave scene towards commercial club culture (James 2002).

## *1990s: Commercialism*

With the DIY rave scene effectively outlawed, rave culture was co-opted by city centre nightclubs. 'Joy' was the first unofficial rave event to make the conversion into a rave-themed club night in Leeds city centre venues (Lawson 2007). Although it began as an illegal rave in an old mill in Dewsbury in 1989, 'Joy' became an officially licensed event at Leeds Corn Exchange in 1991.

Some established nightclubs in the city matched this by shifting their existing music policies from soul and commercial pop music to house music. The club night 'Precious' at The Hi-Flyers Club was promoted on its flyers: 'Dress Code: Club Style!! (Strictly no ski hats or trainers) This night is not a rave!'. As the smart casual era of clubbing in Leeds was born, the fashions of baggy trousers, loose t-shirts, trainers and high-visibility vests common at raves were replaced by expensive brands such as Vivienne Westwood, La Coste and Louis Vuitton. As its fashions reflected, the rave scene's ethos of inclusivity became more exclusive in city centre nightclubs.

Dave Beer was an early regular at raves around the city before starting a club event, 'Back2Basics', with Alistair Cooke and DJ Ralph Lawson. The event was held (and continues) at various Leeds city centre venues including The Music Factory and The Warehouse. In 1992 Beer and Cooke won the DMC and Mixmag Award for Best Club, establishing Leeds' reputation as a city with vibrant electronic dance music (EDM) scenes. Back2Basics still runs on an ad hoc basis and is recognized as the UK's longest-running club event, celebrating its thirtieth birthday in 2022. Such success gave birth to other events in Leeds by other entrepreneur-promoters with their own ideas for club nights in the city. In the 1990s, competition for the weekend dance crowd became fierce, as supply rose to meet demand, cementing Leeds' reputation as a clubbing city.

The motivations of nightclub entrepreneurs ranged from purely financial to almost completely altruistic. Suzy Mason and Paul Fryer created a 1950s art-themed club night called The Kit Kat Club at a venue called Arcadia, which featured a cigarette girl, a cage, blue cocktails and cheap champagne, as well as regular variety acts (Mason 2018). This event eventually became club night 'Vague' in 1993, which was held at The High Flyers Club, before moving to The Warehouse and running until 1996. An antidote to the machismo of the Leeds club scene, 'Vague' was as much about inclusivity as it was about performance and partying. 'Vague' was held in a nightclub where the lights were on brightly so everybody could see each other. Those who entered had to sign up for a set of behavioural 'rules' designed to stamp out violence and discrimination within the venue, which embraced gay and straight clubbers (Collard 1994). For Leeds, this broke new ground in terms of further opening up the dancefloor, in the true spirit of 1970s New York disco with a 1990s house and trance sound.

## 2000s: The Millennium effect and student promoters

The Millennium proved a difficult time for nightclubs in Leeds. For the Millennium New Year's Eve event in the city's clubs, sky-high entry charges were put in place and many people stayed away. With nightclubs overpriced, many realized they could have an equally good time having parties in their own homes or local pubs. The house party scene in Hyde Park, Burley and Headingley was buoyed, and in the eyes of many former clubbers, nightclubs ceased to be cool places to dance. After the Millennium, attendance at nightclubs in Leeds was noticeably lower.

When the weekend trade dipped following the Millennium it became an economic necessity for nightclubs to actively target students. Therefore, the early 2000s became the era of the 'student promoter' in Leeds. There had been 'student nights' at discos and nightclubs in Leeds since the 1980s, but now the disposable income of thousands of students was fiercely targeted by nightclubs, many of which played R&B, pop and classics alongside cheap drinks offers to attract cash-strapped students and get them through their doors midweek. Entrepreneurs saw opportunities in the burgeoning student market, for those attracted by cheap drinks offers, reasonable entry prices and guaranteed fun to chart music and pop classics. Former students formed several promotions companies specializing in student-orientated events in Leeds clubs: Dave Gardener-Chan and Matt Winterbottom formed Voodoo Events, and Michael Stoner and Adam Cramp formed Viva. Regular events targeting students took place at major nightlife venues across the city centre. Voodoo Events are still operating today and are the longest-running and most successful student event company in Leeds. These former students gained experience through a combination of attending events at clubs in Leeds and/or work-based learning for already-established promoters. Many others followed with their own brands and student clubbing peaked in the mid to late 2000s. Former students had distinct advantages over older established promoters in that they were of a similar age to target audiences and also had established networks and friendship groups amongst students who could help with event promotion.

## *2010s: Re-birth of cool and electro alternative*

For many who attended nightclubs for the music, some Leeds venues became 'uncool' when much of the night was spent queuing for drinks and the music was considered 'cheesy'. In the 2010s, student promoters adapted some of their nights musically in recognition that house music and electro were once again becoming popular amongst students. Gadir (2016) identified that the music genre in clubs can create a cultural divide on the dancefloor, with RnB and chart pop being considered 'lower' forms of music by fans of EDM, who consider the overtly sexualized dancing styles to pop and RnB as 'cheapening' the club experience.

Student promoters emerged who wanted to create 'cooler' events, with a music and community focus instead of drinking and partying. Adam Lind began to run the event Deep Fever at Musiquarium, an intimate venue in the Leeds suburb of Kirkstall. Deep Fever embraced a range of current and past musical styles, fusing 1970s disco with contemporary electro. Becoming very popular and outgrowing its limited capacity venue, it moved to Mint Club in the city centre, where the event ran from 2013 to 2016. However, with the move, Adam felt that the event had become too commercial and decided to stop running it. Haslam (2021: n.pag.) referred to this in terms of nightlife culture when 'success dampens motivation'.

A love for electronic music and the free spirit of the rave scene re-emerged in student-centred neighbourhoods, particularly in Burley, Headingley and Hyde Park, in a burgeoning house party scene. There, electronic music, drugs and rebelliousness thrived, echoing the subversive origins of 1970s disco and 1980s rave culture (Amin 2017; Harrison 2017). These events often included full sound systems, lighting and DJs. To meet the growing demand for this market, entrepreneurs have established organizations to provide technical equipment and even security. Leeds companies such as Complete Event Solutions, Leeds Party Rig, Crispy Aromatic, Reload Sound System and Elation DJs all specialize in this area. 'These operations are legitimate nightlife alternatives; as considered in execution as any illegal rave – perhaps more so' (Harrison 2017: n.pag.). Leeds Party Rig owner Matty Rush (2018: n.pag.) noted that student parties in the LS6 area of

Leeds are plentiful, with 'enough to go around, so competition is friendly' between party companies.

## 2020s: A nod to the future

The coronavirus pandemic and subsequent lockdowns of 2020 demonstrated that people who wanted to party continued to do so, even if it meant risking the police and their own health. With bars, pubs, nightclubs and gig venues closed due to COVID-19, the unofficial house party scene continued unabated in Leeds' student suburbs. Some students have not returned to clubs as frequently as they used to go. Current fear of spiked drinks has also left some (particularly female) students feeling vulnerable in club spaces where the majority of people are strangers. They have opted instead to attend house parties where they are largely in the company of people they know.

Due to the rising popularity of student house parties within the Headingley, Hyde Park, Woodhouse and Burley areas, Leeds City Council (LCC) set up dedicated noise patrols in 2021 to monitor residential properties where noise complaints had been previously made. The stance taken by LCC has been one of warning first, followed by serving a 'section 80' noise abatement notice. During September 2021, 32 notices were issued in one week. The noise abatement notice limits the level and duration of sound within a property, alongside limiting the hours during which noise can be made. Failure to comply with a 'section 80' can result in a closure order, which legally restricts anyone other than registered occupants from entering the property. Recognizing that many of those being served 'section 80' notices are students, LCC is working with all Leeds universities to appeal to their students as well as work within the disciplinary process of offenders (Garthwaite et al. 2021). Should LCC's stance against house parties in student areas continue, students likely will seek alternative spaces to dance.

According to the British Retail Consortium, the lockdowns in 2020 and 2021 crippled footfall on the high street and it has not yet recovered. With shop vacancy rates 'at 13.7% in the fourth quarter of 2020' (Colman 2021: n.pag.), councils will look towards new usage. This could provide opportunities for new, smaller city centre spaces for dancing, more intimate than clubs. A new generation of entrepreneurs could create DIY spaces where grassroots scenes can be nourished and new music communities will grow. In the words of Haslam (2021: n.pag.) 'a physical venue with like-minded people with shared values is a home, it is about much more than music […] the best club in the world is the one that changed your life'.

## Conclusions

The emergence of youth cultures, youth rebellion and a range of sociopolitical forces including racism, division, violence, drugs and legal challenges have contributed to the development of DIY leisure spaces in Leeds for dancing. From the 1940s to the present day, enterprising individuals have recognized hedonistic demand, particularly in relation to new music, and created spaces throughout Leeds (both official and unofficial) where DJs can play to appreciative audiences. Those choosing to utilize unofficial spaces have sometimes been influenced by the lack of policing in these spaces, allowing illegal activities such as drug-taking to flourish. This eventually attracted the attention of authorities who created legislative obstacles for promoters. Where this has happened, the events have sometimes been moved to more official spaces, such as the movement of the rave scene to city centre nightclubs during the 1990s; some events have simply moved to other premises, as in the case of the house party scene in Leeds student suburbs.

In all of these venues, the dancefloor has provided an escape from everyday life, where people can dance as they please, expressing togetherness and unity. Whilst music and youth cultures change, it is unlikely that the demand for these spaces and experiences will cease, and for DIY entrepreneurs, Leeds will remain an attractive city. For more than 80 years (1940s–2020s) the city has been an important and innovative centre of dance music cultures.

## NOTES

1. B-boying, later became known as breakin', and in the media, 'breakdancing'. Practitioners at the time did not use the word breakdancing.
2. The Leeds Service Crew was (and still is) a football hooligan neo-tribe with affiliations to Leeds United Football Club. Its membership is predominantly white working-class males, many of whom have right-wing political leanings.

## REFERENCES

Amin, Tayyab (2017), 'DIY in 2017: How Leeds, Bristol and London scenes are striving to survive', *Fact Magazine*, 15 June, http://www.factmag.com/2017/06/15/uk-diy-venues/. Accessed 18 July 2017.

Anderson, Tammy L. (2009), *Rave Culture: The Alteration and Decline of a Music Scene*, Philadelphia: Temple University Press.

Bernard, Jesse (2019), 'A brief but in-depth dive into the 40 year history of UK hip-hop and rap', Okayplayer, https://www.okayplayer.com/music/uk-hip-hop-artists-rap-90s-music.html. Accessed 31 August 2021.

Brewster, Bill and Broughton, Frank (2006), *Last Night a DJ Saved My Life: The History of the Disc Jockey*, London: Headline Book Publishing.

Broughton, Frank (2011), 'Jimmy Savile: The world's first superstar DJ', *The Guardian*, 31 October, https://www.theguardian.com/music/2011/oct/31/jimmy-savile-first-superstar-dj. Accessed 0 August 2021.

Collard, James (1994), 'United Kingdom of dance: If the capital's clubs are too cool for comfort, the rest of the country is steaming on a Saturday night, says James Collard', *The Independent*, 19 October, https://www.independent.co.uk/arts-entertainment/united-kingdom-of-dance-if-the-capitals-clubs-are-too-cool-for-comfort-the-rest-of-the-country-is-1443970.html. Accessed 8 June 2020.

Colman, Julian (2021), 'Forget shops: How one UK town ripped up the rule book to revive its high street', *The Guardian*, 21 August, https://www.theguardian.com/society/2021/aug/21/forget-shops-how-stockton-on-tees-ripped-up-the-rule-book-to-revive-its-high-street. Accessed 30 September 2021.

Davies, Dan (2014), *In Plain Sight: The Life and Lies of Jimmy Savile*, London: Quercus Publishing Limited.

Deboick, Sophia (2020), 'A city in music – Leeds: Goth ground zero', *The New European*, 2 February, https://www.theneweuropean.co.uk/brexit-news-city-in-music-leeds-68820/. Accessed 5 February 2020.

Emm, Ali (2014), 'NG83 – Rock City Crew', *Leftlion*, 19 March, https://www.leftlion.co.uk/photos/2014/march/ng83-rock-city-crew-448/. Accessed 31 August 2021.

Evelyn, George (2018), 'Chinwag session with George Evelyn', *One Foot in the Rave*, Leeds Trinity, 29 April.

Fasick, Frank A. (1984), 'Parents, peers, youth culture and autonomy in adolescence', *Adolescence*, 19:73, pp. 143–57.

Gadir, Tami (2016), 'Resistance or reiteration? Rethinking gender in DJ cultures', *Contemporary Music Review*, 35:1, pp. 115–29.

Garthwaite, Al., Pryor, Jonathan and Walshaw, Neil (2021), 'Our latest update on anti-social behaviour across LS6', *Headingley, Hyde Park & Woodhouse News*, 10 September, https://www.facebook.com/640664196015250/posts/4314020672012899/?d=n. Accessed 15 September 2021.

Harrison, Angus (2017), 'House party review: Leeds', *Vice*, 24 March, https://www.vice.com/en_uk/article/nzg3xb/house-party-review-leeds. Accessed 27 March 2017.

Haslam, Dave (2001), *Adventures on the Wheels of Steel the Rise of the Superstar DJs*, London: Fourth Estate.

Haslam, Dave (2007), *Young Hearts Run Free*, London: Harper Perennial.

Haslam, Dave (2021), *Lost in Music*, 16 September, Hull: Wrecking Ball Music and Books.

Hector Jones, Jane (2020), 'From the F Club to Go4 to proto goth: Post punk Leeds: An in depth look at how punk impacted on the city', *Louder Than War*, 12 November, https://

louderthanwar.com/from-the-f-club-to-go4-to-proto-goth-post-punk-leeds-and-in-depth-look-at-how-punk-impacted-on-the-city/. Accessed 15 August 2021.

Hip Hop Connection (2014), 'T-breaks meets … masters of the old school – DMW', *Leeds, Hip Hop Connection*, 7 January, https://hiphopconnection.co.uk/t-breaks-meetsmasters-old-school-dmw-leeds/. Accessed 31 August 2021.

Hutson, Scott (2000) 'The rave: Spiritual healing in modern western subcultures', *Anthropological Quarterly*, 73:1, pp. 35–49.

Hoggart, Richard (1957), *The Uses of Literacy: Aspects of Working-Class Life with Special Reference to Publications and Entertainments*, Harmondsworth: Chatto and Windus.

Jack, Jim (2011), 'Friend of Sir Jimmy Savile recalls the good times', *Wharfedale Observer*, 3 November, https://www.wharfedaleobserver.co.uk/features/9341004.friend-of-sir-jimmy-savile-recalls-the-good-times/. Accessed 17 August 2021.

Jackson, Louise A. (2008), 'The coffee club menace', *Cultural and Social History*, 5:3, 289–308.

James, Martin (2002), *Prodigy*, London: Sanctuary Publishing Ltd.

Lawson, Ralph (2007), 'History of back to basics Leeds', *88to98*, 6 March, https://88to98.co.uk/2019/03/06/history-of-back-to-basics-leeds/. Accessed 8 June 2020.

Leeds Libraries (2019), 'Rock against racism', The Secret Library, 25 October, https://secretlibraryleeds.net/2019/10/25/rock-against-racism/. Accessed 18 August 2021.

Mason, Suzy (2018), 'Chinwag session with Suzy Mason', *One Foot in the Rave*, Leeds Trinity, 1 May 2018.

Moss, Stuart and Henderson, Stephen (2009), 'Music', in S. Moss (ed.), *The Entertainment Industry: An Introduction*, Wallingford: CABI, pp. 39–56.

O'Brien, Lucy (2009), 'Everybody hold on tight', *Leeds: The University of Leeds Alumni Magazine*, Autumn/Winter, pp. 14–19.

Phillips, Dom (2009), *Superstar DJs Here We Go!* London: Ebury Press.

Rachel, Daniel (2016), *Walls Come Tumbling Down: The Music and Politics of Rock Against Racism*, London: Picador.

Rush, Matty (2018), in-person interview with S. Moss, The Skyrack, Leeds, 10 October.

Sanderson, Eric (2012), 'Strictly – Come dancing', East Leeds Memories, 30 August, https://eastleedsmemories.wordpress.com/category/the-mecca-ballroom/. Accessed 3 August 2021.

Secret Leeds (2009), 'Coffee bars in the 60's', SecretLeeds – History, Culture and Architecture in Leeds, 16 August, https://www.secretleeds.com/viewtopic.php?f=27&t=1927&sid=7fc1958b4023eb6973e3a985e03b84d9. Accessed 7 August 2021.

Simpson, Dave (2019), 'Pubs, disco and fighting Nazis: How Leeds nurtured British post-punk', *The Guardian*, 19 April, https://www.theguardian.com/music/2019/apr/19/pubs-disco-and-fighting-nazis-how-leeds-nurtured-british-post-punk. Accessed 26 April 2019.

Spracklen, Karl and Spracklen, Beverley (2018), *The Evolution of Goth Culture*, Bingley: Emerald Publishing Limited.

Street, John (1986), *Rebel Rock: Politics of Popular Music*, Hoboken: Wiley-Blackwell.

Stringfellow, Peter and Lafferty, Fiona (1996), *King of Clubs*, London: Little, Brown and Company.
Thornton, David (2013), *The Story of Leeds*, Stroud: The History Press.
*Trailblazers of Acid House* (2016), Angus McIntyre (dir.), (13 April, UK: Sky Arts).
Wolf, Marco and McQuitty, Shaun (2011), 'Understanding the do-it-yourself consumer: DIY motivations and outcomes', *Academy of Marketing Science Review*, 1, pp. 154–70.

# 13

# Music of the Leeds West Indian Carnival

*Danny Friar*

The Leeds West Indian Carnival (LWIC) is an annual Caribbean cultural event held in Leeds throughout August that attracts thousands of people from across Leeds, the United Kingdom and abroad. LWIC follows in the tradition of carnivals and carnivalesque events of the Caribbean which in turn have their roots in European Lent carnivals, European folk traditions and traditional West African masquerade. This unique combination of European and African traditions is a direct result of the trans-Atlantic slave trade which forcibly transported millions of Africans to the Caribbean where they were enslaved by Europeans. Afro-Caribbean carnivals were originally parallel celebrations held alongside Euro-Caribbean Lent carnivals. After emancipation in 1834, Afro-Caribbean carnivals became celebrations of emancipation from slavery. Caribbean carnival arrived in Britain in the mid twentieth century as a result of mass migration from the Caribbean.

Since its inception in 1967, LWIC has acted as a showcase of Caribbean art, culture, dance, food and music. While LWIC has developed and grown over the past five and half decades, for the majority of its history a number of events, under the LWIC banner, have been held leading up to the main event – the carnival parade that takes place on the streets of Chapeltown and Harehills on August Bank Holiday Monday (the last Monday in August). These events include a Carnival King and Queen Show and a Prince and Princess Show where the best costumes are chosen to lead the carnival parade. At times, the LWIC event line-up has also included a Steel Pan Contest, a calypso contest and Last Lap Dance. Since 1992, a shorter J'ouvert Morning parade, held in the early hours of August Bank Holiday Monday, has also been a part of the proceedings.

Traditional Caribbean music, particularly music associated with the islands of Trinidad and Tobago and St. Kitts and Nevis, has played an important role at all the carnival events throughout its history. LWIC has traditionally incorporated five main Caribbean music genres; big drum and fife bands, string bands, steel bands, calypso and soca. This chapter will explore the involvement of music in LWIC and how music has helped develop the event, and how LWIC has preserved Caribbean music heritage and helped promote Caribbean music beyond LWIC.

The music of the more famous Notting Hill Carnival, held annually in London, has been studied before, notably in Henriques and Ferrara's 'The Sounding of the Notting Hill Carnival' (Henriques and Ferrara 2014). However, the uniqueness of LWIC makes it incomparable to Notting Hill Carnival. Unlike Notting Hill Carnival, which originated as a multi-cultural neighbourhood event that has since been described as 'Europe's largest street festival' (Henriques and Ferrara 2014), LWIC has a much more serious tone. LWIC was founded as, and continues to be, a celebration of emancipation and is unique in that it is the longest-running traditional Caribbean carnival in Europe. Indoor Caribbean carnival celebrations had taken place in Britain as early as 1955 (Friar 2018a) including the Caribbean Carnival Fete held in Leeds in 1966 (Farrar 2017). However, LWIC was the first outdoor event to incorporate all four elements of Caribbean carnival: procession, dance, masquerade (the wearing of elaborate, colourful costumes and masks) and music.

## *The first Leeds West Indian Carnival, 1967*

Arthur France, a migrant from Nevis who settled in Leeds in 1957, played a crucial role in providing platforms for Caribbean musicians in Leeds and surrounding areas in the 1960s. In 1964, he founded the United Caribbean Association (UCA) (Jeffers 2014), a Black-led social and political organization that was responsible for organizing West Indian dances at Leeds Town Hall where steel bands from across the United Kingdom performed (Connor 2011). In 1965, he set up the UCA Steel Band, one of the city's first steel bands (Jeffers 2014). LWIC was founded in 1967 by a group of Caribbean migrants, spearheaded by France. It was France's persistence in involving others in the first LWIC that convinced many to embrace their musical talents (Davis 2017).

One of the talents to be convinced by France to perform at the carnival's Calypso King Show was Artie Davis, a calypsonian who had arrived in England from St. Kitts in 1965. In St. Kitts, Davis had learnt to sing at his local church and had taken up performing calypso with a cuatro (a small stringed instrument, similar to a guitar, used in Caribbean folk music) on street corners. In the style of the calypsonians of Trinidad, Davis had christened himself Lord Kingston, after Jamaica's capitol, to reflect the popularity of Jamaican singers in the early 1960s. It was while performing at a local youth club in Chapeltown that Davis was spotted by France and invited to take part in the carnival which he readily agreed to. It was during rehearsals at the Jubilee Hall that Davis was rechristened Lord Silkey [*sic*] after Willie Robinson's suggestion (Davis 2017).

Following the tradition of Trinidad's carnival, performers taking part in the Calypso King Show wrote songs, especially for the contest. Davis's entry 'St. Kitts Is My Borning Land' was based on Lord Mikes's calypso of the same name with altered lyrics, some improvised on the night (Davis 2017), that embraced England as Davis's new home with the line 'England is my home in every way' (Davis 1967) and celebrated the arrival of the carnival in England with the verse:

*Give three cheers to Arthur France and co*
*For bringing carnival to Great Britain*
*For he has done his very best*
*To make it a big success*
*Carnival is here*
*Let's do the rest.*

(Davis 1967)

Despite being a celebrative song, Davis did not shy away from including political lyrics, as was common in calypso music in the Caribbean, including the line 'we must unite together, yes, that will be Black Power' (Davis 1967). It was perhaps the improvised lines about the carnival and France – one of the judges of the contest, that swayed the judges' vote giving Davis the win, and making him the first Calypso King in Europe (Davis 2017).

Another individual convinced by France to take part in the carnival was Rex Watley. Watley was a steel pan player originally from St. Kitts who had played the instrument for around three years before migrating to England in 1960. He had given up the instrument in England to concentrate on work and raising a family. In 1967, France convinced Watley, and others, to join The Gay Carnival Steel Band (Watley 2017), which had been formed by France and Courtland Carter, especially for the carnival. The band built their own steel drums in a basement on Savile Road but had to find a new location to build and rehearse the instruments after neighbour complaints about noise led to a visit from the police (France 2018). France's original plan for the band was to include a rhythm section. A rhythm section is usually made up of various instruments to help keep the timing of the band. The rhythm section can include tambourines, cowbells, conga drums and the traditional Caribbean instrument of a comb and grater (a type of Güira). The comb and grater proved difficult to find in Leeds and one band member instructed to find it returned with a cheese grater (France 2017).

The Gay Carnival Steel Band was one of four steel bands to take part in the LWIC parade in 1967 that followed a route from Potternewton Park to the Leeds

Town Hall (Farrar 2017). The other three bands were The Invaders from Leeds, The St. Christopher Steel Band from Birmingham and a band from Manchester (Farrar 2017). These steel bands played 'pan 'round the neck' – steel pans attached to a rope hung around the neck with the bass pan being supported by wooden legs (Warley 2017). It was the St. Christopher Steel Band, with their performance of 'Elizabethan Serenade', who took first place at the Steel Pan Contest held in the Leeds Town Hall after the parade (Friar and Pitter 2018).

The parade also included a big drum and fife band – a small band usually made up of three or four players playing a military bass drum or 'big drum', a kettle drum, and a fife or tin whistle. Big drum and fife bands are traditionally used in St. Kitts and Nevis to accompany masqueraders during the carnivalesque Christmas Sports. The band in Leeds was made up of three self-taught musicians; Henry Freeman on big drum, Prince Elliot on kettle drum and Kenneth Browne on fife. They accompanied a group of traditional masqueraders led by 'Captain' Thomas Wenham. Among Wenham's masqueraders was Albert Henry who had learnt to play the kettle drum by ear at the age of 6 while living in Nevis. He would become a member of the band the following year (Freeman and Henry 2017).

## Calypso Kings of Leeds, 1967–1972

LWIC provided the Caribbean community with a platform from which they could launch their musical careers. Davis was the first to take advantage of this opportunity. After winning the Calypso King Contest in 1967 he began performing calypso in venues around Leeds. However, Davis was soon to discover that audiences were more interested in rocksteady reggae than calypso. To tackle this issue Davis added another singer, Granville Short, to his act to perform up-tempo numbers. The pair took off and by 1968 they were receiving bookings across Yorkshire (Davis 2017).

Davis was just one of the Leeds-based calypsonians to enter the Calypso King Contest in 1968. There are no surviving documents to say exactly who entered the contests between the years 1967 and 1972 but in an interview with Max Farrar in 1988 Davis gave the names of three other calypsonians; Lord Prinze, Count Mitzie and The Mighty Chucka, who all entered the contest at least once during that period (Farrar 1988a). A calypsonian called 'Smiley' took the title in 1968 and Lord Prinze was crowned Calypso King in 1969 (Anon. 2012).

Lord Prinze was the alias of Lionel Hewitt (Anon. 2012), a Bajan singer who performed in a variety of genres and had made a number of appearances with Leeds reggae group The Bedrocks during 1968 and early 1969. He was with the band when they made their TV debut on 'Colour Me Pop' in 1968 and performed live across the country with them after the early success of their debut single 'Ob-La-Di, Ob-La-Da' – the first recording released by a home-grown reggae act (Friar 2017b).

The 1968 LWIC saw the debut of the Wilberforce Steel Band who went on to become one of the city's most popular steel bands. The band was formed by Watley using instruments left in his basement by the recently disbanded Gay Carnival Steel Band. Wilberforce won the Steel Pan Contest held at the Leeds Town Hall in 1968 and went on to make their TV debut on Yorkshire Television later in the week (Watley 2017).

Around 1969, Davis put forward the idea of adding another musical element to the carnival. String Bands were a popular form of carnival entertainment in the Caribbean but LWIC lacked one. Davis managed to put together a band but one crucial instrument, the baha, a long metal pipe that is blown to provide bass, was missing. Attempts to make a baha from scaffolding failed, and after a couple of rehearsals, Davis's String Band disbanded. Davis's attempt to form a string band may have failed but his popularity at the Calypso King Contest was unshaken and he won first place three years in a row from 1970 to 1972. Davis was unbeatable and other calypsonians refused to compete against him resulting in the contest being put on a long hiatus. Instead, Davis made regular appearances at the Carnival Queen Show (Davis 2017).

## *Golden age of steel bands, 1970–78*

Steel bands became the dominating sound of LWIC in the 1970s, appearing at all the carnival events. The annual Steel Band Contest was axed from the LWIC programme after 1970; instead, bands were judged based on their performance on the road (Friar 2018b). An average of four steel bands took part in the parade during the 1970s. By 1971, The Caribbeans and Esso Steel Band were regular performers at the carnival and the Paradise Steel Band, formed in 1973 (Anon. 1987b), soon joined the growing list of Leeds steel bands.

Prior to the parade, steel bands entertained crowds in Potternewton Park before being mounted onto homemade floats that occasionally used appropriated shopping trolley wheels. The floats were then pulled along by ropes for the entire route, which went from Potternewton Park into the city centre and back (Friar and Pitter 2018). This was no easy task and required the help of many volunteers, often members of the public, who pulled the floats partly or all of the way around the route. Due to the parade's length and the hard work of pulling the floats, a rest was needed at North Street (Farrar 2017). A highlight of the parade came when the procession reached Regent Street and the steel pans echoed under the underpass (Wenham 2018).

Steel band floats could be dangerous and attendees' feet were often run over by float wheels (Hughes 2017). Floats could also bring the parade to a standstill if a wheel came off (Anon. 1972). Heavy rain could also cause a problem; the steel pans would fill up with rain and had to be turned upside down to be emptied (Wenham 2018). When a carnival troupe from Leeds took part in the fledgling Notting Hill Carnival in 1968 they witnessed another Caribbean musical tradition, the iron band, that was being used as an alternative to the steel pans during heavy rainfall (Farrar 1988b). The iron bands of the Caribbean used makeshift metal instruments made from car rims, frying pans, biscuit tins and other everyday objects. The idea of using an iron band was adopted at LWIC in 1970 (Friar 2018b) and 1974 (Anon. 1974).

During the 1970s, members of the Caribbean community in Leeds made a conscious decision to ensure that the traditions and culture of the Caribbean were passed on to the first generation of English-born children of Caribbean heritage. In 1976, Martha Armstrong founded The Caribbean Children's Folk Group (Pitter 2019) and after a campaign led by Gertrude Paul, St. Clair Morris began teaching steel pans in schools across Yorkshire (Morris 2018). LWIC was also used to encourage Black youths to continue the practice of Caribbean culture and by 1976 the Chapeltown Dance Theatre Steel Band, a band made up of Black children and teenagers, was formed under the guidance of LWIC committee member Ian Charles.

Young Black people found steel bands appealing for a number of reasons; not only did they provide an outlet for creativity but they were a fun and safe activity, belonging to their own culture, which could be enjoyed with others of their own age range. Steel bands also had political elements; they were, usually, Black-led groups made up of all-Black members – an extremely important factor in the racist climate of 1970s England. Similar to calypsonians, steel bands could also act as a form of social commentary. The song 'Don't Stop the Carnival', played by the Wilberforce Steel Band, became an unofficial anthem when LWIC had finical difficulties and risked being cancelled in 1976 (Wenham 2021). Added attractions to the steel pans in this period included live appearances across the city beyond the carnival weekend and the possibility of appearing on television. The Wilberforce Steel Band appeared on the 'Black and White Minstrel Show' in 1976 (Anon. 1976). Although not mentioned by name, the Chapeltown Dance Theatre Steel Band made their TV debut in 1977 on the documentary 'Countdown to the Festival' (Anon. 1977a). There was also a possibility of recording. Ten years after winning the Steel Pan Contest, St. Christopher Steel Band from Birmingham released the album 'Island In The Sun' (Anon. n.d.b). By 1978, Leeds had a number of youth-oriented steel bands including the re-launched UCA Steel Band and the Leeds City Schools Steel Band. These bands, alongside the Chapeltown Dance Theatre Steel Band and Paradise Steel Band, were all showcased at the first Carifesta – an annual festival of Caribbean arts and entertainment held at the Leeds Playhouse between 1978 and 1983 (Friar 2017a).

## *Introduction of reggae sound systems, 1975–80*

For youths who preferred reggae music over the steel band music, finding a way to be officially involved in the carnival proved to be an uphill struggle due to the committee's strict rules regarding reggae sound systems and their inclusion in the carnival. By 1975, Leeds had a thriving reggae sound system culture and although reggae sound systems had been introduced to the Notting Hill Carnival in 1973, LWIC had no plans to follow a similar route (Friar and Pitter 2018). Teenagers who owned reggae sound systems had first approached the Carnival Committee in 1975 with the idea of including reggae in the carnival but had been turned away by committee members who wanted to keep the proceedings traditional. The Carnival Committee would not allow sound systems on the road and by-laws forbid loudspeakers in Potternewton Park (Anon. 1977b). Sound systems playing reggae did appear however, in gardens and on streets along the carnival route. For a period of five years sound system crews campaigned to have reggae accepted by the committee as an official part of LWIC, and in 1980, Mavrick [sic] Sound System became the first sound system to play in Potternewton Park on Carnival Day (Friar 2018c). Steel bands remained a crucial element of the carnival and it would be another two years before a soca sound system, Mackie's Disco, appeared at the Carnival Queen Show (Friar and Pitter 2018). More traditional and more appealing to the Carnival Committee was George Henderickson's string band. Formed around 1980, the string band was comprised of seven players playing flute, banjo, guitar, cuatro, baha, guiro and triangle. They made several appearances around Leeds including appearances at the Carnival Queen Show (Anon. 1990a).

## *Evolution of steel bands, 1984–88*

By the mid 1980s, a number of schools, including Primrose High School in Burmantofts and Foxwood School in Seacroft, had formed their own steel bands under the guidance of Morris (Morris 2018). Morris's own steel band, Paradise Steel Band, appeared on ITV's game show '3, 2, 1' in 1982 before being re-launched as the Paradise Steel Orchestra in 1984 (Morris 2018). In 1985 they became the first steel band from Leeds to record when they contributed the track

'Breeze In' to the compilation album 'Sounds of Yorkshire' (Anon., n.d.a). The re-launching of Paradise Steel Band as a Steel Orchestra demonstrates the new direction in which Leeds steel bands were heading from 1984.

The Leeds Brotherhood of Steel was founded around 1984 with the objective to promote steel band music as a cultural and artistic heritage and teach adults and youths from all cultures to appreciate and play steel pan music. This objective was mainly achieved by the initiative and tireless hard work of three men: Arthur France, St. Clair Morris, and Raymond Joseph – a steel pan tutor from Huddersfield (Roscoe Methodist Church 2011).

In alliance with the Brotherhood, members of Roscoe Methodist Church on Chapeltown Road launched the Roscoe Methodist Church Youth Steel Band in 1984. Steel pan tutor Joseph travelled from Huddersfield three times a week to lead the band's rehearsals. It was due to the hard work of Joseph and the band members that the band was able to archive a significant amount of success in a short time, making regular appearances at Roscoe Methodist Church (2011). Joseph was also involved in the founding of another steel band during this period – The New World Steel Orchestra (NWSO).

NWSO was founded by France and Melvin Zakers in 1984 and was tutored by Joseph (Connor 2011). The band's members were local youths aged 14–22 who had all studied under Morris (Anon. 1988b). Using second-hand instruments bought from London's Ebony Steel Band, the NWSO made their public debut in the summer of 1984 after months of rehearsals in a basement on Francis Street (France 2018). Zakers, the band's 'Captain', had played with various bands since 1981 and was tutoring steel bands in Leeds from 1987 (Anon. 1987a).

The NWSO was one of three steel bands from Leeds, alongside three others from outside of Leeds, to take part in LWIC in 1984 (Farrar 2017). They were joined by Paradise Steel Orchestra, who had recently expanded their membership (Anon. 1987b), and The Caribbeans who added extra players especially for the carnival (Anon. 1990b). All three of these bands had extensive repertoires that included classical music as well as calypso, soca and reggae, alongside pop standards and hits of the day (Anon. 1990b; Connor 2011; Morris 2018). Music on the road was also provided by Captain Wenham's Big Drum and Fife Band (Friar 2019a). While reggae remained an unofficial element of the carnival, Mavrick [sic] Sound System played on Harehills Avenue outside Potternewton Park, pausing the music when the parade left the park and allowing the crowd to hear the steel bands (Friar 2019a). Attendees at the Carnival Queen Show earlier in the week would have enjoyed the Kooler Ruler sound system and live reggae by the duo Judy & Linda from Bradford (Anon. 1984). While Davis still had a role in the Carnival Queen Show it had now shifted from musical to comedic as he became a regular performer in the satirical 'Old Mas' sketches (Friar 2019a).

The NWSO improved immensely during the late 1980s, becoming one of the city's most popular steel bands (Connor 2011). They made regular appearances at the Carnival Queen Show and at the Prince and Princess Show, introduced to the carnival in 1987, as well as at the carnival parade (Connor 2011). The band acquired new instruments in 1986 and by 1987, when they appeared on the TV documentary 'Chapeltown One Year On '; they had new uniforms (Friar 2019b). By the end of the decade, they had performed across Europe and had won serial championship competitions (Connor 2011).

## *The introduction of soca and the return of calypso, 1984–96*

By the mid 1980s, Leeds had a small soca scene. The eight-piece band The Macassars, led by Hewitt, had formed in 1984 and became well-known across Leeds for performing self-composed up-tempo soca, highlife and reggae music. Managed by Tony Burton, the band released a 12" EP on their own Bullfrog label in 1986 and toured Europe later that year (Scott 1986).

Despite this growing interest in soca, prior to the late 1980s, soca was a rarity at the carnival (Friar 2019a). DJ Godfather (Mitch Wallace) played calypso and soca music regularly on the local pirate radio station Rapid 105.8 FM (Farrar 1988a) and was crucial in introducing soca to LWIC. In 1984, Wallace had been the first DJ to play soca music in Potternewton Park on Carnival Day (Friar 2019a). However, it wasn't until 1986 that Tropical Heatwave, a soca band from Manchester, became the first live soca act to perform in Potternewton Park (Friar 2019c).

By 1988, LWIC was attracting international soca stars; Arrow was the headlining act at that year's Last Lap Dance (Anon. 1988a) but traditional calypso was still missing from the event. By 1988, it had been sixteen years since the Calypso King Contest had been a part of the carnival programme and, in an interview with Max Farrar, Davis, fearing the calypso tradition was fading away, expressed his hopes for the return of the contest (Farrar 1988a).

From 1989 Davis returned to performing calypso at the Carnival Queen Show (Anon. 1989). By the end of the decade, Leeds was also home to a solo soca performer named Chevi (Eugene Chiverton) who had recorded soca music in the Caribbean and London before founding Cariba Records in Leeds in 1989. Based on Roundhay Road, Cariba Records incorporated a recording studio, a publishing house, and a management and booking agency. The label's debut, and only, release was Chevi's 'AH-Beautiful Day' released in 1989 (Khanum 1989).

The inclusion of reggae at the carnival was debated throughout the 1980s with many believing reggae should be kept separate from the carnival as it was not considered a traditional Caribbean music form (Farrar 1988a). Despite the introduction of the Leeds Reggae Concert in 1986 (Anon. 1986), which took place in Potternewton Park the day before the carnival parade, reggae sound systems still played music in the park and along the carnival route and were slowly accepted by the general public as an aspect of the carnival. The future of sound systems at the carnival was up for debate in 1990 after a triple murder in Chapeltown after that year's carnival parade was linked to out-of-town sound systems. At the carnival in 1991 sound systems were allocated to marquees erected in Potternewton Park (Farrar 2017).

Despite the debate over reggae sound systems, soca sound systems, on floats pulled by tractors, became an official part of the carnival parade in 1991 after Wallace convinced the Carnival Committee to include one sound system, strictly playing calypso and soca, at the back of the parade to prevent drowning out the sound of the steel bands (Wallace 2017). The following year, Wallace convinced the committee to introduce J'ouvert Morning, a traditional Caribbean early morning parade, to the carnival's programme. The first J'ouvert Morning parade held in Leeds included one sound system, operated by Wallace, playing calypso and soca and, in remembrance of the ancestors, a recording of big drum and fife music (Wallace 2017).

Throughout the 1990s carnival events, particularly the Last Lap Dance, featured international calypso, soca and zouk stars alongside local DJs. The stage in Potternewton Park also featured international soca stars on carnival day (Friar and Pitter 2018). The inclusion of soca sound systems in the parade and live soca performances on stage established soca as the dominating sound of LWIC by the mid 1990s. After a 24-year absence, the Calypso King Contest returned to the carnival proceedings in 1996 (Anon. 1996) and although new talent like Ansell Broderick entered the contest, the crown was taken by carnival veteran Hewitt who had last won the contest in 1969 (Anon. 2012). Davis won first prize the following year, 25 years after his last win (Anon. 2012).

## *The decline of steel bands, 2000–15*

The number of steel bands taking part in the carnival began to decrease in the late 1990s, and by 2000, Foxwood Steel Band was one of a small number of steel bands taking part in the carnival (Anon. 2018). Following riots in Harehills and Chapeltown in August 2011, the Carnival Committee took the decision to ban steel bands at that year's carnival parade (Bellamy 2011). Steel bands returned the following year but the ban had a lasting impact on the carnival. Very few steel bands took part in the parade in the following years with only NWSO performing regularly at the carnival from 2012. It wasn't until the opening of the 'Carnival Village' on

Chapeltown Road in 2015 that Foxwood Steel Band once again began making regular appearances at the carnival, playing to crowds from the stage erected there.

## *The rise of soca, 2005–21*

Since the mid 1990s, other musical tastes have been catered for at LWIC; Pan-African Cultural Group drummers and the Leeds Samba group have taken part in the parade in 1998 and 2017, respectively. Guest DJs from BBC Radio 1Xtra have had a presence in the park since 2006 playing a mix of musical genres (Friar and Pitter 2018). Despite this, steel bands and soca remain the official sounds of LWIC.

A growing number of calypsonians took part in the Calypso King Contest, with a total of six performers taking part in the contest in 2005 (Anon. 2012). For the most part, the Calypso King Contest was a male-dominated event that very few women entered. In 2008 Brenda Farara, under the allies Soca B, became the first woman to win the contest prompting organizers to change the name to the Calypso Monarch Show (Friar and Pitter 2018).

Managed by Davis, Farara entered two self-composed songs into the contest in 2008; 'Women Don't Let No Man Fool You' and 'Guns and Knives' (Farara 2017). The latter reflected her involvement with the activist group Mothers Against Guns (Farara 2017) and acts as a textbook example of how calypso composers use political lyrics. In this case, the song's lyrics called for an end to street violence among young people. The song included a chorus of 'put down the damn guns, put down the damn knives' (Farara 2008). Farara went on to win the contest five times between 2008 and 2014 (Farara 2017). Her involvement in the contest encouraged other female artists, such as Lady Sonia(Sonia Webbe), to enter the contest (Friar and Pitter 2018). Three women entered the contest in 2014, bringing the total number of performers to nine (Anon. 2014). The contest saw its first White contestant, Captain Carnival, in 2015 and the contest was renamed the 'Soca Monarch Show' in 2016 to reflect the popularity of soca over calypso (Friar and Pitter 2018). The opening of the 'Soca Village', an open-air live music venue on Chapeltown Road, in 2016 was a welcome inclusion to the carnival celebrations, bringing international soca acts to Leeds and acting as an unofficial successor to the Last Lap Dance which had been absent from the programme since 2010.

In 2017 and 2018, Leeds-based artists Graft and Boyski RLR both released new soca music catered towards attendees of LWIC. Their joint song 'Recline' was the unofficial LWIC anthem in 2017. Despite the COVID-19 pandemic of 2020–21, which saw live events heavily restricted, LWIC continued to showcase local and international talent on both live and virtual platforms including the 2021 headlining act Graft.

## Conclusion

Since its inception, LWIC has provided an outlet for the musical talents of local people of Caribbean heritage. It has also provided a platform from which local performers have been able to launch and promote their careers in show business as early as the 1960s. The 1970s saw steel bands rise in popularity, going on to tour, make TV appearances and even record. Steel bands went from straight to straight and evolved into steel orchestras in the 1980s. However, the inclusion of reggae and soca sound systems brought about their downfall and almost entirely replaced them by the late 1990s. However, since the 1990s sound systems have helped develop the carnival, being key elements of more recent additions such as the J'ouvert Morning parade. Despite these changes, the re-emergence of live calypso and soca ensures LWIC remains traditional at its core and continues to preserve its Caribbean musical heritage.

## REFERENCES

Anon. (n.d.a), 'Sounds of Yorkshire', Discogs, https://www.discogs.com/Various-Sounds-Of-Yorkshire/release/7900221. Accessed 11 April 2020.

Anon. (n.d.b). 'Island In The Sun', https://www.discogs.com/St-Christopher-Steel-Band-Island-In-The-Sun/release/8334398. Accessed 11 April 2020.

Anon. (1972), 'Caribbean extravaganza', *Yorkshire Post*, 29 August, p. 5.

Anon. (1974). 'Caribbean Carnival takes to rain dance', *Yorkshire Evening Post*, 27 August, p. 8.

Anon. (1976), *Radio Times*, 2738, 29 April, p. 17.

Anon. (1977a), *Radio Times*, 2822, 8 December, p. 67.

Anon. (1977b), 'Leeds Carnival – 10 years on the road', *Chapeltown News*, October, pp. 7–9.

Anon. (1984), *Leeds West Indian Carnival Queen Show Programme*, Leeds: Leeds West Indian Carnival.

Anon. (1986), 'Reggae riot in Rodley', *Leeds Other Paper*, 22 August, p. 2.

Anon. (1987a), 'Profile on Melvyn Zakers – Steelband Achiever', *The Official Carnival Magazine*, August, p. 22.

Anon. (1987b), 'The Paradise Steel Orchestra', *The Official Carnival Magazine*, August, p. 24.

Anon. (1988a), 'Carnival', *Leeds Other Paper*, 26 August, p. 6.

Anon. (1988b), 'The future of carnival lies with the youth', *The Official Carnival Magazine*, August, p. 12.

Anon. (1989), *Carnival Queen Show Programme*, Leeds: LWIC Committee.

Anon. (1990a), 'George Hendrickson – King of Carnival String', *The Official Carnival Magazine*, August, pp. 10–11.

Anon. (1990b), 'The Caribbean Steel Band – 30 Years of Golden Melodies', *The Official Carnival Magazine*, August, pp. 12–13.

Anon. (1996), *Carnival Queen Show Programme*, Leeds: s.n.

Anon. (2012), Calypso Monarchs', Febuary, https://web.archive.org/web/20120213174550/http://www.leedscarnival.co.uk/index.php?option=com_content&view=article&id=158&Itemid=48. Accessed 11 April 2020.

Anon. (2014), *Calypso Monarch Flyer*, Leeds: s.n.

Anon. (2018), 'Brief history of Foxwood Steel', January 2018 https://foxwoodpanyard.com/brief-history-of-foxwood-steel/. Accessed 11 April 2020.

Bellamy, Alison (2011), 'Ban on steelbands in Leeds West Indian Carnival parade', *Yorkshire Evening Post*, 19 August.

Connor, Geraldine (2011), *Pan: The Steelband Movement in Britain*, 1st ed., Leeds: Gbakhanda.

Davis, Arthur (1967), 'St. Kitts Is My Borning Land' [Song], Leeds: s.n.

Davis, Arthur (2017), in-person interview with Carnival Chronicles Team, Leeds, 17 June.

Farara, Brenda (2008), 'Guns and Knives' [Song], Leeds: s.n.

Farara, Brenda (2017), in-person interview with Carnival Chronicles Team, Leeds, 17 June.

Farrar, Max (1988a), 'The cockspur crew', *The Official Carnival Magazine*, August, p. 28.

Farrar, Max (1988b), 'A dream come true', *The Official Carnival Magazine*, August, pp. 24–25.

Farrar, Max (2017), *Celebrate! 50 Years of Leeds West Indian Carnival*, 1st ed., Leeds: Northern Arts Publications.

France, Arthur (2017), in-person interview with Carnival Chronicles Team, Leeds, 17 June.

France, Arthur (2018), in-person interview with J. Williams and D. Friar, Leeds, 5 May.

Freeman, Henry and Henry, Albert (2017), in-person interview with Carnival Chronicles Team, Leeds, 17 June.

Friar, Danny (2017a), 'Opportunity knocks – the Caribbean all steel band 1958–1965', Leeds Mas Media, 1 October, https://leedsmasmedia.wordpress.com/2017/10/16/opportunity-knocks-the-caribbean-all-steel-band-1958-1965/. Accessed 11 April 2020.

Friar, Danny (2017b), 'Rockstead Bedrock – The Bedrocks 1966–1970', Leeds Mas Media, 1 December, https://leedsmasmedia.wordpress.com/2017/12/18/rocksteady-bedrock-the-bedrocks-1966-1970/. Accessed 11 April 2020.

Friar, Danny (2018a), 'Europe's first West Indian Carnival – London or Leeds?', Leeds Mas Media, 1 May, https://leedsmasmedia.wordpress.com/2018/05/27/europes-first-west-indian-carnival-london-or-leeds/. Accessed 11 April 2020.

Friar, Danny (2018b), 'Sun Worshippers: Leeds West Indian Carnival 1970', Leeds Mas Media, 1 April, https://leedsmasmedia.wordpress.com/2018/04/02/sun-worshippers-leeds-west-indian-carnival-1970/. Accessed 11 April 2020.

Friar, Danny (2018c), 'Sound Clash Carnival: Leeds West Indian Carnival 1980', Leeds Mas Media, 1 November, https://leedsmasmedia.wordpress.com/2018/11/02/sound-clash-carnival-leeds-west-indian-carnival-1980/. 11 April 2020.

Friar, Danny (2019a), 'Olympic Carnival: Leeds West Indian Carnival 1984', Leeds Mas Media, 1 March, https://leedsmasmedia.wordpress.com/2019/03/14/olympic-carnival-leeds-west-indian-carnival-1984/. Accessed 11 April 2020.

Friar, Danny (2019b), 'Pan forever: A brief history of the New World Steel Orchetra – 1984–2019', Leeds Mas Media, 1 October, https://leedsmasmedia.wordpress.com/2019/10/16/pan-forever-a-brief-history-of-the-new-world-steel-orchestra-1984-2019/. Accessed 12 April 2020.

Friar, Danny (2019c), 'Where culture waits on the corner: Leeds West Indian Carnival 1986', Leeds Mas Media, 1 April, https://leedsmasmedia.wordpress.com/2019/04/25/where-culture-waits-on-the-corner-leeds-west-indian-carnival-1986/. Accessed 12 April 2020.

Friar, Danny and Pitter, Susan (2018), 'Carnival music & Leeds', Leeds Carnival, 1 June, www.leedscarnival.co.uk/leeds-carnival-50-heritage/carnival-music-leeds/. Accessed 11 April 2020.

Henriques, Julian and Ferrara, Beatrice (2014), 'The sounding of the Notting Hill Carnival: Music as space, place and territory', in J. Stratton and N. Zuberi (eds), *Black Popular Music in Britain Since 1945*, Farnham: Ashgate, pp. 131–52.

Hughes, Felina (2017), in-person interview with Carnival Chronicles Team, Leeds, 17 June.

Jeffers, Debbie (2014), *Details of Nomination – Arthur France*, Leeds: s.n.

Khanum, S. (1989), 'United sounds', *Leeds Other Paper*, 11 August, p. 6.

Morris, Annette (2018), in-person interview with D. Friar, Leeds, 20 October.

Pitter, Susan (2019), *Eulogy*, 1st ed., Leeds: Jamaica Society Leeds.

Roscoe Methodist Church (2011), *Roscoe Methodist Church, Leeds: A Unique History*, 1st ed, Leeds: Roscoe Methodist Church.

Scott, Thomas (1986), 'On the move with the macassars', *Leeds Other Paper*, 11 April, pp. 10–11.

Wallace, Mitch (2017), in-person interview with Carnival Chronicles Team, Leeds, 17 June

Watley, Rex (2017), in-person interview with Carnival Chronicles Team, Leeds, 17 June.

Wenham, Angela (2018), personal conversation with author, Leeds.

Wenham, Leroy (2021), interviewed by L. Gumbs, *Eat Your Greens*, Stable Radio, Leeds, 11 June.

# 14

## Jazz in Leeds, 1940s–50s

*Michael Meadowcroft*

Jazz in Leeds before the Second World War, as, indeed in all of Britain, was very sparse and largely confined to 'hot' soloists with dance bands. The Original Dixieland Jazz Band – in 1917 the first band to record jazz – arrived from the United States and had had a residency in London in 1919 but otherwise the domestic jazz scene relied for its inspiration on a number of American instrumentalists, such as Benny Carter and Danny Polo, or on Fred Elizalde, a Spanish pianist who had learnt his music in the United States, all of whom spent time in Britain. Apart from such individual inspirational musicians, jazz in Britain in the 1930s relied on Rhythm Clubs at which an enthusiastic jazz record collector presented a 'recital' drawn from his collection. Occasionally there was an impromptu 'jam session' with the participation of any amateur instrumentalists who turned up. Even the definition of what was 'jazz' was exceptionally flexible. There were ethnographic lectures, such as those reported on in the *Yorkshire Evening Post* (Anon. 1930: 9) in which 'jazz' was assumed to be any folk or native music played by black musicians, rather than the instrumental music whose evolution from its African roots began in and around New Orleans in the late nineteenth century and is still progressing today from those roots. Others equated jazz with crooning and had to be corrected in the correspondence columns of the local Leeds newspaper (O'Shaughnessy 1934). Even amongst those who had a better awareness, jazz music was very much a minority interest and was under considerable attack from classical music fans who either regarded jazz as degenerate and illegitimate or who believed that the only jazz that was acceptable was the so-called 'symphonic jazz' such as Gershwin's 'Rhapsody in Blue' or Constant Lambert's 'Rio Grande'.

A cryptic advertisement appeared in the local Leeds newspaper in September 1934, 'Jazz Band wanted, 2 nights weekly, for public house' (Anon. 1934a: 2) The pub involved was probably the Compton Arms in Harehills as subsequent advertisements appeared for 'The First Leeds Rhythm Club' there (Anon. 1934b: 2), but it seems to have disappeared by the time of the war. Another 'hot' band called the Blue Aces was based in South Leeds in the 1930s and played at a number of venues across the city (Leeds Libraries 2021). A new 'Leeds Rhythm Club' began in 1941 at the Arcadian Ballroom in the County Arcade (Anon. 1941: 2), and it moved to a new regular venue from early 1942, meeting each Sunday evening at the Morelle School of Dancing, 72 Boar Lane, to which 'All Hot Instrumentalists' were invited to 'take part in Jam Sessions' (Anon. 1942: 7). The live jazz that began soon after the end of the war was catalyzed by the New Orleans revival. Determined young enthusiasts were able to order 78rpm discs from the United States on obscure labels, either from specialist shops, such as Dave Carey's and James Asman's in London or from mail order companies. To ears attuned to the easy-going British jazz of Sid Phillips, Harry Parry and Freddy Gardner the rough earthiness of New Orleans pioneers Bunk Johnson and George Lewis was an attractive shock.

## Early days – The 1940s

Those who absorbed this new but old American music quickly became purists, almost members of a secret cult quite separate from those who enjoyed 'hot' music, which itself had been regarded as not 'proper' music by classical music enthusiasts. There was a rather curious connection between these followers of New Orleans jazz and radical politics and many of the early enthusiasts were Labour activists and even members of the Communist Party. Part of this stemmed from the awareness that the origins of the music were in downtown New Orleans amongst the African American population, plus the clear fact that the purists themselves were largely from working-class communities who happily found common cause with friends and colleagues who were also outside the more middle and upper-class attachment to classical music (cf. Finkelstein 1948).

Across Britain, jazz bands sprung up, largely of enthusiasts who moved from listening to playing. Often they were teenagers who having learnt the rudiments of their instruments immediately got together to struggle through tunes they listened to on the records. These early bands were more enthusiastic than sophisticated, learning tunes by ear and usually relying on one band member with some musical background to set out the chord sequences on which the ensembles depended but which were not always followed. Today we all have large chord books, usually and for obvious reasons, put together by banjo or guitar players, such as the mammoth compilation by the late Alan Noble (2007) which contains 2040 tunes! The existence of these chord encyclopaedias has never stopped band members from arguing over their accuracy. Learning tunes by ear was more difficult than it sounds and was evidence of the innate musical skills of many early British revivalists. Leeds did not miss out and the city's first such local group began in 1946 and was made up of art college students who named themselves the Vernon Street Ramblers after the small cross street between Woodhouse Lane and Cookridge Street where the college was housed. One of its first members was trombonist Ed O'Donnell who continued to play the same New Orleans style in and around Leeds for almost 70 years until his death in 2014 (The Newsroom 2014). This first Leeds 'revival' band probably relied on clarinettist Alan Cooper for its musical base. His later career, not least as a multi-instrumentalist playing the whole range of clarinets, and as a founder member and arranger with the Temperance Seven, demonstrated great musical skill. He went on to become a nationally renowned jazz musician with many acclaimed recordings to his name (The Times 2007).

With various changes in name and personnel, this first Leeds band morphed into the Yorkshire Jazz Band in early 1949 and survived at least until 29 December 1961 when they shared the bill at the Liverpool Cavern with the Beatles (Leigh 2015). The band was formed and led by a mixed-race tuba player, Bob Barclay. By trade, Barclay was a sheet metal worker and like many early postwar jazz musicians was pleasantly eccentric. In his memoir, singer George Melly tells of playing a Leeds gig and staying overnight with Bob Barclay (Melly 2006: 40).

> Bob lived in a cellar in a rotting elegant house near the city centre of which he was officially caretaker. The rest of the house was a small garment factory. I used to stay with him, but this had two disadvantages. For one thing you didn't get to bed until about six because Bob insisted on playing every record the Yorkshire Jazz Band had ever made, and for another thing, when you did get to bed, his large boxer dog used to show how fond of you it was by leaving great snail tracks of mucus all over your face and arms.

The Yorkshire Jazz Band's regular Wednesday evening engagement from early 1949 was at the Yorkshire Jazz Club based at the Adelphi public house on Leeds Bridge, whilst the rival Leeds Jazz Club met on Sunday evenings at the Metropole Hotel on King Street – again with the Yorkshire Jazz Band. Bob Barclay also owned a club, Studio 20 on New Briggate, and this became the Mecca for the region's jazz fans with music every evening (see Figures 14.1 and 14.2). As the Sela Bar it still hosts live music today. In Barclay's time not only did it employ many well-known bands, but it had occasional visits from American stars, including Jimmy Rushing and Sarah Vaughan (Bond 2011). After hours it became a centre for jazz musicians and enthusiasts way into the small hours with Barclay and his wife serving food and drinks.

FIGURE 14.1: A session at Studio 20 in 1954. Courtesy of the Terry Cryer Archive Collection.

The Yorkshire Jazz Band proved to be a recruiting ground for London-based professional bands. Ed O'Donnell had a spell as a professional with Ken Colyer but gave it up after six months to return to Leeds, saying it was impossible to get a decent pint of Tetley's beer south of Wakefield. George Melly's (2006) memoir of the traditional jazz life in the 1950s is a brilliant depiction of the raffish, hand-to-mouth existence on the road, such as discovering how to extract chocolate out of London underground machines without inserting coins, and camping out in bedsits or sofa surfing with other musicians – all of it fuelled by a remarkable intake of beer. For all of them the music was the thing and all the trappings of 'normal' society were subservient to it.

A colleague of Ed O'Donnell in the Yorkshire Jazz Band who epitomized the anarchic jazz life of that period was the brilliant banjo/guitarist Diz Disley who was also recruited by Ken Colyer in 1954 (Vacher 2010). Another student at the Leeds College of Art, Disley's cartoons decorated the walls of Bob Barclay's Studio 20 and also of the prestigious 100 Club in Oxford Street, London. Inevitably he was recruited by fellow Leeds art students into the Vernon Street Ramblers. Unless

FIGURE 14.2: George Melly signing the 'Gallery of Fame for Uninhibited Idealists' at Studio 20, 1955. Courtesy of the Terry Cryer Archive Collection.

a band bus was available, Disley either hitchhiked to gigs or drove a yellow Rolls Royce hearse and, despite his otherwise disorganized life, was said never to have missed a gig though often congenitally late and occasionally forgetting to bring his guitar. Unlike most of his contemporaries, he moved on to broader musical fields, playing skiffle, folk music and touring for ten years with the celebrated French jazz violinist, Stefan Grappelli.

By 1949, the Yorkshire Jazz Band had acquired a new trumpet player, Dick Hawdon (Vacher 2009) who was a much more sophisticated musician than most of his colleagues. As a consequence, the band developed a smoother sound, aided by Alan Cooper on clarinet and Diz Disley on banjo and guitar. Despite his later sojourn with the modernists and despite being more of a technical musician than his fellow band members, Dick Hawdon remained a very congenial and convivial colleague throughout his career. He took the well-worn trail to London in 1951. After a short period in Chris Barber's band, he joined Ian and Keith Christie in their Christie Brothers Stompers, a group committed to developing the repertoire and the traditional style. In 1954 Dick Hawdon astounded his Leeds friends by 'going modern' working with Don Rendell, Tubby Hayes and joining the John Dankworth orchestra on and off between 1957 and 1960. He later returned to his earlier style with various traditional bands. He once told me that had he been able to make a living from it he would happily have continued to play traditional jazz. He played with various studio bands and returned north to lead the house band at the renowned Batley Variety Club. In 1967, Hawdon made a complete career change to move into academia, becoming a lecturer and later Head of Department for the newly established and pioneering jazz course at the Leeds College of Music. He was ideal for this role combining his experience across different styles of jazz, coupled with his considerable theoretical musical skills. The students were almost entirely modern jazz musicians and were dismissive of traditional styles until Hawdon made them form a traditional band for the annual college festival. They then found themselves initially unable to cope with the polyphonic improvisation and developed a greater respect for the music, which was Hawdon's aim. During his time at the College, he maintained his contacts with Leeds musicians and happily 'depped' (i.e. deputized, or 'sat in') in local bands, latterly on double bass.

With the departure of these three key members, the Yorkshire Jazz Band recruited other local musicians for its established New Orleans style. There were certainly a number of other bands in Leeds in the 1940s including Geoff Sowden's Chicagoans which adopted the more freewheeling white jazz that developed from Chicago. Sowden was a trombone player who took his inspiration from the great white trombonist Jack Teagarden who for a time was with Louis Armstrong. Sowden later emigrated to Spain and carried on playing there. One of Sowden's Leeds protégés was a young trombonist Malcolm 'Mac' Duncan. He was very talented and after playing with local bands, including the White Eagles, in 1956 he joined what many regarded as Ken Colyer's best band with Ian Wheeler completing the front line on clarinet. After five years with Colyer, he left to form his own band but his personal health problems prevented him from coping or even settling into a regular band. He eventually took his own life in September 1981. Terry Cryer, one of the key British jazz photographers, was born in Leeds in June 1934 and began as an amateur jazz enthusiast taking photographs at Studio 20 and other Leeds jazz venues before building a national reputation (Wilmer 2017).

## *Development – The 1950s*

Each jazz style had its fierce almost tribal advocates but by the 1950s jazz in Leeds had burgeoned and there were a great number of amateur and semipro bands playing different traditional styles. Trumpeter John Cook of the Leeds' jazz band the White Eagles claimed the distinction on 12 August 1956 of blowing the first notes at The Cavern Club in Liverpool (Leigh 2015), later famous as the home venue of the Beatles. Clarinettist Martin Boland led the White Eagles Jazz Band for decades, playing regularly at the Coburg pub on the corner of Woodhouse Lane and Queen Square and at the Star and Garter at Kirkstall. Boland, a man with a very short fuse, arrived at gigs with his bottle of chilled white wine and a wine glass, both of which he perched on the top of the piano and proceeded to imbibe during the evening. The landlord of the Coburg for many years was Al Potts, a clarinettist who took on the management of pubs to make sure he had a venue for his own band! Potts was another character and he used almost imperceptibly to take his teeth out to sing and to put them back in to play the clarinet. Another band of the day that played at the Peel Hotel on Boar Lane had Dennis Rayworth on clarinet who wandered around the audience whilst playing.

Probably the best-regarded Leeds jazz musician of that period was Jim Fuller, a trumpet player who always wore a cloth cap whilst playing. He was sadly forced to give up playing when he contracted a disease which paralyzed his hands and fingers which made it impossible to play the trumpet. The other particularly brilliant musician was clarinettist Martin Fox whose main band was the Savannah Band based in Huddersfield but who regularly played in Leeds. Another trumpeter with a claim to fame is Enrico Tomasso who aged 6 was taken by his pushy father to the Leeds Bradford Airport when Louis Armstrong was scheduled to arrive for his 1968 residency. Enrico played his trumpet on the airport tarmac for Louis who then invited him to come to his Batley gig each evening. Another stalwart was Denis Armstrong who remained loyal to the cornet rather than trumpet and who led the Yorkshire Post Jazz band during the brief years of its existence. Among the many musicians of that whole period, there were some remarkably talented practitioners, mainly self-taught and often without a real awareness of the musical complexities of what they played, who were able to produce great music, unsung in the wider media but appreciated by the many jazz audiences in Leeds and West Yorkshire.

## *Conclusion*

The jazz boom began to decline in the 1960s. From having recordings in the *Hit Parade* – Humphrey Lyttleton's 'Bad Penny blues', Monty Sunshine's 'Petite Fleur' and Acker Bilk's 'Stranger on the Shore' among them – it slowly began once again to become a niche interest, being replaced by rock music and the immense popularity of groups such as the Beatles and the Rolling Stones. This did not concern jazz adherents who happily carried on playing around the pubs and clubs of Leeds. The City of Leeds College of Music still turns out fine musicians from its jazz course but they are almost entirely in the modern idiom. One of its few alumni who still play traditional jazz is Paul Lacey who graduated from the College back in 1980 and who since 2001 has been leading the Back to Basie Band, recreating the style of Count Basie.

Where those playing this music have failed, including myself (Meadowcroft and Bee n.d.) is to pass on our enthusiasm and instrumental skills to succeeding generations. Today a dwindling group of elderly practitioners double up in different bands, just about keeping the handful of continuing jazz clubs going. The Leeds Jazz Club meets every Tuesday in a West Leeds Working Men's Club with live traditional jazz, and the Seven Arts Centre in Chapel Allerton caters for mainstream and modern jazz. There are a few younger bands in the city but, given the ages of the majority of the musicians, unless those of us still playing make our final gift to the music a deliberate project to take it around to schools and youth organizations it will die. There will have been just three score and ten years of traditional jazz in Leeds.

## APPENDIX: SUGGESTED FURTHER READINGS

Carr, Ian, Fairweather, Digby and Priestley, Brian (eds) (1987), *Jazz: The Essential Companion*, London: Grafton Books.

Chilton, John (ed.) (2004), *Who's Who of British Jazz*, 2nd ed., London: Bloomsbury.

Clayton, Peter and Gammond, Peter (eds) (1986), *The Guinness Jazz A-Z*, London: Guinness Books.

Godbolt, Jim (1984), *Jazz in Britain 1919–1950*, London: Quartet Books.

Godbolt, Jim (1989), *Jazz in Britain 1950–1970*, London: Quartet Books.

Godbolt, Jim (2014), *All This and Slowly Deteriorating Fast – The Memoirs of a Geriatric Jazz Buff*, London: Proper Music.

Harris, Rex (1952), *Jazz*, London: Penguin Books.

Matthew, Brian (1962), *Trad Mad*, London: Souvenir Press.

Parsonage, Catherine (2017), *The Evolution of Jazz in Britain, 1880–1935*, London: Routledge.

Traill, Sinclair, Lascelles, Gerald and Davies, Peter (eds) (1957), *Just Jazz*, London: Peter Davies.

Traill, Sinclair, Lascelles, Gerald and Davies, Peter (eds) (1958), *Just Jazz 2*, London: Peter Davies.

Traill, Sinclair, Lascelles, Gerald and Davies, Peter (eds) (1959), *Just Jazz 3*, London: Peter Davies.

## REFERENCES

Anon. (1930), 'The origin of jazz – Vicar of Leeds tells a tale of the Mississippi', *Yorkshire Evening Post*, 24 February, p. 9.

Anon. (1934a), 'Jazz band wanted, 2 nights weekly, for public house', *Yorkshire Evening Post*, 4 September, p. 2.

Anon. (1934b), 'The first Leeds Rhythm Club', *Yorkshire Evening Post*, 26 November, p. 2.

Anon. (1941), 'Also in Arcadian Ballroom, Leeds Rhythm Club evening session', *Yorkshire Evening Post*, 9 January, p. 2.

Anon. (1942) 'All hot instrumentalists are invited to take part in jam sessions held each Sunday evening at the Leeds Rhythm Club', *Yorkshire Evening Post*, 25 February, p. 7.

Bond, Chris (2011), 'The golden days when jazz brought colour to a grey city', *Yorkshire Post*, 30 June, https://www.yorkshirepost.co.uk/news/golden-days-when-jazz-brought-colour-grey-city-1928564. Accessed 21 February 2022.

Finkelstein, Sidney (1948), *Jazz a People's Music*, New York: Citadel Press.

Leeds Libraries (2021), 'The Blue Aces jazz band, c1930s', Media Library, 19 August, https://news.leeds.gov.uk/resources/kmdn1-l2bbz-jhne6-c59y3-9bhiw. Accessed 21 February 2022.

Leigh, Spencer (2015), *The Cavern Club: The Rise of the Beatles and Merseybeat*, Carmarthen: McNidder and Grace Limited.

Meadowcroft, Michael and Bee, Liz (n.d.), 'Jazz', Liz Bee and Michael Meadowcroft, https://www.beemeadowcroft.uk/jazz. Accessed 21 February 2022.

Melly, George (2006), *Owning Up: The Trilogy*, London: Penguin Books.

The Newsroom (2014), 'Ed O'Donnell', *Yorkshire Post*, 8 March, https://www.yorkshirepost.co.uk/news/obituaries/ed-odonnell-1844133. Accessed 21 February 2022.

Noble, Alan (2007), *Jazz Charts*, Shipley: Alan Noble.

O'Shaughnessy, J. P. (1934), 'More thoughts on jazz', *Leeds Mercury*, 12 May, p. 6.

*The Times* (2007), 'Alan Cooper', 25 August, https://www.thetimes.co.uk/article/alan-cooper-x82vvwl8tbw. Accessed 21 February 2022.

Vacher, Peter (2009), 'Dick Hawdon', *The Guardian*, 14 September, https://www.theguardian.com/music/2009/sep/14/dick-hawdon-obituary. Accessed 21 February 2022.

Vacher, Peter (2010), 'Diz Disley obituary', *The Guardian*, 15 April, https://www.theguardian.com/music/2010/apr/15/diz-disley-obituary. Accessed 21 February 2022.

Wilmer, Val (2017), 'Terry Cryer obituary', *The Guardian*, 21 January, https://www.theguardian.com/artanddesign/2017/jan/20/terry-cryer-obituary. Accessed 21 February 2022.

# PART 4

## POPULAR MUSIC HERITAGE, LEGACIES AND FUTURES

# 15

## *Sounds of Our City* Exhibition: Music and Materiality in Leeds' Abbey House Museum

*Kitty Ross and Paul Thompson*

A growing body of scholarly work on popular music heritage is focused on the area of museums and the ways in which they curate and exhibit popular music (e.g. Baker et al. 2016a, 2016b, 2020; Cortez 2015, 2016; Fairchild 2017; Knifton 2012; Leonard and Knifton 2015; Leonard 2007, 2010, 2014, Mortensen and Madsen 2015; Van der Hoeven and Brandellero 2015). Museums can be seen to have a central role in institutionalizing popular music heritage, displaying 'versions' of the history of popular music through 'temporary exhibitions, permanent displays and dedicated visitor experiences' that have 'actively mobilised sounds, images and objects' to capture the diversity of popular music's material past (Leonard 2014: 357). In their survey of museum collections of popular music, Leonard and Knifton (2017) found that museums have only started to take the subject seriously in the last few decades, something that is mirrored within Leeds Museums and Galleries, but the growing number of popular music exhibitions shows that 'the museumification of popular music heritage is, thus, now well established in both scholarship and practice' (Baker et al. 2020: 435).

This chapter introduces Leeds Museums and Galleries' exhibition *Sounds of Our City* at Abbey House Museum (January 2020–December 2021) and contextualizes the exhibition in relation to recent developments in curatorial practices and displays relating to popular music. A particular curatorial practice of theming particular popular music narratives around individual artists is a common one and can be viewed positively as 'Tribute/Celebration' (Cortez 2015) or more critically as 'canonic representations' (Leonard 2007). These different emphases are directly connected to the context in which they are applied, such as where Cortez's (2015) work relates to curators in museums in Portugal and their attempt to raise the profile of lesser-known artists to challenge Portugal's established history of popular music (310–11). Leonard used 'canonical representations' to denote exhibitions that 'replicate received knowledge about popular music histories by concentrating on events that have already been given high levels of media and critical attention' (2007: 153). The tension here is 'between the celebrated and the overlooked, dominant narratives and hidden histories, and how these should be told' (Knifton 2012: 22), and the curation and representation of popular music in the museum should not be 'determined solely by the music canon and the most celebrated of music "moments" or scenes' (Leonard 2010: 180). For these reasons, the *Sounds of Our City* exhibition took a critical view of both the definition of popular music, which is sometimes characterized as post-1945 commercial hits and the curatorial and exhibition practices of 'Tribute/Celebration' (Cortez 2015) or 'canonic representations' (Leonard 2007). Instead, it focused on 'place' as a way to theme the exhibition and display artefacts in relation to the places and venues in which people have experienced music in Leeds. This helped to avoid focusing on distinct chronological narratives, having to classify items by musical genres, to differentiate between 'popular' and other types of music and, importantly, to make connections across 200 years of Leeds' musical history with the museum collections.

In order to convey the 'intangible nature of music and music cultures' (Leonard 2007: 148), and try to 'properly reflect the experience of listening to music and participating within its associated cultures in the static space of a museum' (Leonard 2007: 148), the exhibition included a number of oral history interviews that were recorded with those involved in the Leeds music scene over the last 50 years. These interviews were accompanied by a digital display of photographs of local gigs that were submitted by numerous musicians, music promoters, fans, collectors and audience members via social media. Mortensen and Madsen contend that 'sound is a difficult phenomenon to contain in an exhibition environment' (Mortensen and Madsen 2015: 251) but Knifton argues it is an essential 'part of an expanded toolkit' (Knifton 2012: 23). For *Sounds of Our City*, the curators included an exhibition playlist that visitors accessed via a jukebox, which was lent by Leeds-based jukebox manufacturers Sound Leisure. It showcased the broad approach adopted in defining popular music and included work from music written by J. Hopkinson in the 1840s through to the Kaiser Chiefs and the Elephant Trees in the 2000s. Beginning first with an introduction to Leeds Museums and Galleries, the following chapter takes the reader through the exhibition's key themes and the types of artefacts and insights within each theme.

## *Leeds Museums and Galleries*

The museum's own collections have developed and changed since the service was founded by the Leeds Philosophical and Literary Society in 1821. The early curators were more interested in bringing the 'wonders of the world' to Leeds rather than collecting material from the surrounding area, but this changed in the twentieth century. Abbey House Museum, which is situated in the suburb of Kirkstall a couple of miles from Leeds city centre, opened as a 'museum of bygones' in 1927 and, from 1953, it expanded to include reconstructed street displays.

A chance encounter between the museum's curator Cyril Maynard Mitchell and Jack Dearlove led to the first important music-related acquisition (LEEDM.E.2011.0443 1964). Jack was descended from a great dynasty of Leeds musicians and instrument makers, beginning with Mark Dearlove whose music shop on Boar Lane was first recorded in directories in 1808. Mark's son, Mark William Dearlove Jnr. (1802–80), exhibited a quartet of model instruments at the 1851 Great Exhibition; two of which Jack Dearlove had shown at the Festival of Britain and then donated to Leeds Museums in 1952. Jack Dearlove subsequently arranged to donate more instruments and archives that had been preserved in the family, which were exhibited in a reconstruction of the Dearlove shop at Abbey House Museum from 1955 and remained part of the displays until 1997. Most of the Dearlove family performed on the popular circuit of dance halls, music halls, seaside promenades and cinemas (see Figure 15.1).

In the following decades, the museum added to its music-related holdings, mostly responding to public offers of donation rather than through proactive acquisitions. The museum has a notable collection of musical boxes, phonographs, gramophones, musical instruments, wax cylinders, gramophone records, sheet music and programmes, which all reflect the general trends in musical tastes and consumption over time, but only a few have a real Leeds connection (beyond having been donated by Leeds residents). The *Sounds of our City* exhibition then provided the opportunity to uncover some of the hidden stories of Leeds from these wider collections, and to commission performances and recordings of music written in Leeds within the collection. With the help of student musicians from Leeds University and Leeds Conservatoire, there are now recordings of the following pieces written by Leeds' composers:

- 'The Blue Belles Quadrilles and Waltz' composed by J. Hopkinson about 1840
- 'Farewell Kathleen', 'Little Nell' and nursery rhyme settings by George Linley (1798–1865)
- 'This is Our Opening Day', composed by J. Williamson, Leeds, 1872 for the opening of Roundhay Park

FIGURE 15.1: The Dearlove Orchestra outside the Royal Baths, Harrogate, *c.*1891. Courtesy of Leeds Museums and Galleries.

- 'Beulah Land', a hymn composed by William Muff, Pudsey, 1881
- 'Grand March Composed in celebration of Leeds being made a City 1893', by William Spark (1823–97)
- 'Reverie', by Frederick Kilvington Hattersley (1861–1946)
- 'The Call to Duty' by Alfred Warrington Lodge ('Blind Alf'), 1922

These recordings can be found in the Leeds Museums and Galleries (n.d.) YouTube channel.

In recent years, the Museum has tried to be more proactive in building collections that reflect the varied histories and diverse cultures of the city and the different communities within it. When the new Leeds City Museum opened in 2008 in the city centre, it was the first time that there had been a gallery devoted to the history of Leeds, and this included a section on music. For this, curators sought to acquire collections directly related to Leeds musicians and bands, which was helped by a flurry of local musicians then riding high in the charts such as Kaiser

Chiefs, The Pigeon Detectives and Corinne Bailey Rae. Kaiser Chiefs seemed particularly proud of their Leeds origins, summed up in a promotional t-shirt with the motto 'Everything is Brilliant in Leeds'. The new gallery also featured singles and albums by earlier bands such as Soft Cell, Chumbawamba, The Sisters of Mercy, The Wedding Present and The Mekons.

A staff restructure at Leeds museums around this time afforded the opportunity to recruit a team of community curators to help engage with local groups and to lead projects that actively encouraged contemporary collecting. Community-led displays were then built into the structure of the Leeds Story gallery as well as a rolling programme of temporary exhibitions, which created an archive of digital photographs, video and oral history recordings that were all accessioned into the Leeds Museum collections. Projects since 2008 have included Leeds Festival collecting project (2009–12), Silver 70s Exhibition (2011), which prompted the museum to search out LPs by the Gang of Four, The Mekons and a copy of The Who Live At Leeds. Leeds Music (2013), which commissioned video interviews about venues such as the Cockpit, Futuresound, Dear Atria at Eiger and Ellen & The Escapades at the Brudenell Social Club. Leeds Museums started collecting Hip Hop objects in 2014 and have hosted a number of Hip Hop Culture Events at Leeds City Museum (see Little and Stevenson, Chapter 16). Leeds Music Sound Bites (2018) was a project that commissioned a Rock Against Racism (RAR) digital film and a donation of RAR and 1970s punk objects by Paul Furness, one of the movement's organizers. Other donations included objects linked to Goth Culture donated by Elizabeth Griffin, objects and a film related to busking, a few Reggae items collected via Marcia Brown and further additions to the growing Hip Hop collection. LGBT/West Yorkshire Queer Stories (2018–21) was a broader project that yielded some musical objects including event posters and 1980s vinyl records from the Leeds/Bradford band Fartown Fruits.

The most recent of these music-related exhibitions is *Sounds of Our City* exhibition (2020–21), which was proposed as a way to bring together elements of previous music-related exhibitions and fill particular gaps in existing collections. Among the items acquired after a callout in 2019 were Leeds International Piano Competition programmes, a ukulele, Jake Thackray LPs, and a Leeds Parish Church chorister's uniform, as well as further gig flyers and tickets. We also recorded twelve audio interviews to both bring some contemporary voices and stories into the exhibition, and to challenge the museum's traditional privileging of the visual (Dudley 2010. The interviewees included: Rod Brooks (of the Dawn Breakers), Hunter Smith (founder of Jumbo Records), Ian De-Whytell (Crash Records), Madeleine Ackroyd (who worked for Vallances Records), Alex Johnston-Seymour (Busker), Steve Trattles and Mark Johnson (Whippings and Apologies creators), Dave Beer (Back to Basics Founder), Chris Czuhra (Recalling the New Romantics), Annette Morris (singer-songwriter), Jabbar Karim (Fever FM) and John Beck (composer and producer).

## The exhibition

As previously noted, the exhibition was structured around the theme of 'place' and the places where people experience or engage with music, instead of using the dominant structuring curatorial approach of 'narrative' (Baker et al. 2020), which can either consciously or unconsciously promote dominant or canonical histories of celebrated individuals or groups. In this way, the objects were: 'left to speak for themselves as autonomous aesthetic objects' (Leonard 2007: 155). The physical space in the gallery too favours a thematic approach because there is no set visitor route and visitors can begin and end wherever they choose. The relative size of the display objects also helped to dictate which themes would occupy which spaces. The spaces in this instance were the existing cases of different shapes and sizes. Abbey House exhibitions are usually changed annually, so are planned over the previous year beginning with a survey of potential exhibits already in the collection (as outlined above) and with due consideration for the existing space and layout. A workable thematic structure is key to this approach as it helps to shortlist objects, which highlights any gaps, some of which were addressed in this instance by loans from private individuals. The condition of the objects is a further consideration and it was ensured that each exhibit was visually interesting and in good condition.

The first two cases featured domestic room settings looking at how music is consumed and experienced within the privacy of the home, including developments in recording technology since the late nineteenth century. A living room set included early devices such as the Polyphon (a musical box with interchangeable discs), phonograph (to play wax cylinder recordings) and a large HMV radiogram from 1930. The room also included music-themed ornaments and souvenirs, from a Beatles pepper pot to a figurine of one-legged black violinist Billy Waters (1778–1823) based on the 1818 print by Thomas Lord Busby.

Facing it was a contrasting set recreating a teenager's bedroom, complete with a 1980s Recor sound system and a 1998 Spice Girl's Official Merchandise doll depicting Leeds-born Melanie Brown. The bedroom was adorned with posters, t-shirts, badges, annuals, fanzines and scrapbooks associated with different bands, both from Leeds and elsewhere (see Figure 15.2). As the objects ranged in date from the 1960s to 2000s, it was obviously not supposed to represent any specific teenage experience but to evoke the personal space where young people honed

FIGURE 15.2: The bedroom displayed in the *Sounds of Our City* exhibition, photographed by Kitty Ross. Courtesy of Leeds Museums and Galleries.

their musical tastes and identities. We also added a few musical toys such as a 1961 Lumar toy gramophone with Kidditunes records and a 1978 Compute-a-Tune toy synthesizer, made for Waddingtons of Leeds.

Both of these cases used the structuring concept of 'nostalgia', which is a traditional 'engagement strategy of museums' (Leonard and Knifton 2015: 163). By adding a bed, a chest of drawers and posters, the exhibition was actively 'designing a "space for the revisit of time"' which for some visitors may act as an 'affective trigger' (Mortensen and Madsen 2015: 251). For younger visitors, who have no direct experience of the objects in the case, creating a mock bedroom for exhibiting popular music artefacts helps to frame them with a 'common emotional ground' (Mortensen and Madsen 2015) so that they can compare and contrast their own bedroom and the ways in which their music technologies, images and objects differ. Here, the use of nostalgia was 'an important curatorial tool' in order to cultivate 'historical understanding' and 'appreciation for the social dimensions' for visitors (Leonard and Knifton 2015: 161) of Leeds' music history within the broader context of popular music history in order to make heritage 'meaningful in the present' (Leonard and Knifton 2015: 171).

## Music in education

An early section of the exhibition looked at music tuition and training in Leeds. The oldest items related to concerts given by pupils in small private schools where one programme advertises a Juvenile Concert at Mr Sigston's Academy for Mr Hopkinson's Pupils, February 1819, which is likely to be the same John Hopkinson who was a music publisher in Leeds in 1835 and later set up a piano-manufacturing firm in London. He also wrote the 'Quadrilles' mentioned earlier in this chapter. Another programme from 1823 announces 'Miss Fryer's Juvenile Concert' and advertisements in the *Leeds Intelligencer* in 1830 showed that Miss Fryer and her sister ran a Ladies Boarding School on Park Lane. This particular item highlighted societal views at the time where music was an important accomplishment for 'refined' young ladies, even though they were not expected to perform professionally.

It was not until 1878 that the first dedicated music college opened in Leeds and the exhibition displayed programmes connected to the Yorkshire Training College of Music, which was situated in Victoria Square, and set up as a subsidiary of Trinity College, London with Mr J. Sidney Jones as musical director. Later, in 1894 Edgar and George Haddock established a Leeds College of Music, now known as the Yorkshire College of Music and Drama, it still thrives as an independent charitable trust and is not to be confused with the similarly named Leeds College of Music founded in 1965 (now Leeds Conservatoire). The exhibition also featured a silver plaque presented by Leeds University students to Thomas James Hoggett in 1906 who taught at both the University of Leeds and the Leeds City School of Music.

This part of the exhibition showed that anyone seeking to study music in Leeds in the early twentieth century had quite a choice of institutions and this continued as Leeds Conservatoire (previously Leeds Music Centre) opened in

1965 and launched the first jazz degree in Europe in 1993 and, in 2004, became the first UK conservatoire to offer courses in Popular Music, Music Production and Music Business.

This exhibition theme sought to showcase music learning at all levels, which included school recorder lessons, Sunday School concerts, local youth orchestras and a ukulele that had been lent to scores of beginners by the Otley Ukulele Orchestra since they were founded in 2011.

## Music shops

There is evidence of music shops in Leeds since at least the early nineteenth century. Some music shops such as Mark Dearlove's establishment (first listed in street directories in 1808 but later advertising claimed the firm dated back to 1797) and J & J Hopkinson piano-making business (1835) are represented in the collection through ephemeral letterheads, business cards and advertisements. However, one example of an Italian-made mandolin sold by Albert Warwick, listed at Woodhouse Lane from 1898 to 1907 also yielded information about the customer too from a label on the case that identified the owners as 'Williams & Daughter, Theatrical Costumes, Leeds'.

Much of the sheet music in the exhibition was also stamped with the name of local retailers, such as Banks Music House (founded in 1911) and Archibald Ramsden (1835–1916), who started his first 'musical establishment' in 1864 and, in 1872, opened a new building on Park Row including a saloon for musical performances. The business survived into the 1950s by adapting to the new era of gramophones and radios.

The museum's collection of records reveals the myriad of early twentieth-century Leeds record shops. Before the advent of glossily printed album covers, most records had cardboard sleeves advertising the retailer. The exhibition highlighted the common practice of shops selling both bicycles and gramophones, for example W. R. Stubbs & Son in Wortley, and R. Broughton & Sons on Waterloo Road. Other shops catered for specific communities, such as S. Nevies on North Street who advertised the 'Latest Hebrew-Jewish & English Records'.

The collection highlighted the separate record departments within department stores such as Lewis's and the Leeds Industrial Co-operative Society and it included objects from two dedicated record stores that survived into the 1980s. Barker's started in Albion Place in 1913, and moved to the Headrow, before finally closing in 1984. Vallances were also on the Headrow from 1934 to 1987 until they were edged out by bigger chain stores. Smaller independent stores still survive in

Leeds and the museum proudly displayed items from Hunter Smith, who founded Jumbo Records in 1971.

## Music in concert venues

This part of the exhibition introduced the history of concert venues in Leeds, beginning with the earliest known public concert, which took place in September 1726 and was held in the 400-seat Assembly Room in Kirkgate. As audiences increased, a larger venue was needed so in 1794, an 800-seat Music Hall opened on Albion Street. Among the objects associated with the Albion Street Music Hall is a picture of Paganini dedicated to Mr Dearlove of Leeds and signed by the maestro himself when he performed there in 1832. Leeds Museums and Galleries also displayed programmes for charity and subscription concerts from the 1830s and for the series of 'People's Concerts' established by William Spark and John Hope Shaw in the 1850s. The Music Hall closed in 1870 and was finally demolished in 1973.

The museum also holds brass tokens advertising the short-lived Royal Casino Promenade Concert Hall, King Charles Croft, built in 1849, which became the Royal Alhambra in 1856 and reopened as the Royal Amphitheatre in 1865 but burned down in 1876. We also displayed tickets from the Coliseum, which opened on Cookridge Street in 1885 complete with organ and raked seating for singers. Within ten years it was converted into a theatre and then a cinema, but more recently was reborn as a music venue as the Town & Country Club and latterly as the Leeds O2 Academy.

The collections include records of concerts held in non-purpose built concert venues such as the Leeds Philosophical Hall (Leeds City Museum) and the Leeds Institute. In the 1960s the Odeon cinema on the corner of the Headrow and Briggate hosted performances by The Beatles, Ray Charles and The Rolling Stones, among others. Leeds newest large concert venue is the First Direct Arena, which can seat 13,500 people, and opened its doors in July 2013 with a sold-out concert by Bruce Springsteen.

## Music at Leeds Town Hall

Leeds Town Hall opened on 7 September 1858, which hosted the first Leeds Musical Festival attended by Queen Victoria, and remains one of the city's most prestigious venues to this day. The need for a larger concert hall was one of the drivers for the opening of the Town Hall, which could seat 4000 people and over 400 performers, and the exhibition included tickets and programmes from the 1858 Festival as well as the conductor's baton used by William Sterndale Bennett. Many famous composers, including Dvorak, Elgar and Vaughan Williams, wrote works for the Triennial Leeds Music Festivals, held intermittently between 1858 and 1985. Samuel Coleridge Taylor, wrote a cantata 'The Blind Girl of Castél-Cuillé' for the 1901 Festival and in 2020 we obtained a copy to add to the exhibition.

The museum collection includes an array of programmes for town hall concerts and events. Many were organized by the Leeds Philharmonic Society, founded in 1870, which invited professional orchestras such as the Hallé from Manchester. The Leeds Symphony Orchestra, founded in 1890, was renamed the Northern Philharmonic Orchestra in 1935. It attracted conductors such as John Barbirolli and Malcolm Sargent and continued to perform morale-boosting afternoon concerts throughout the Second World War.

One of the most high-profile Town Hall events is the Leeds International Piano Competition, co-founded in 1963 by local piano teacher Dame Fanny Waterman. Her archive was presented to Leeds University in 2019 but some duplicate programmes were donated to Leeds Museums and shown in the exhibition. The Leeds Town Hall concert series continues to host a wide programme of both classical concerts and chart-topping acts such as Sophie Ellis-Bextor and Lloyd Cole, who were among the concert flyers collected by the museum in 2019.

## *Music on stage and screen*

Although ballad operas were performed alongside plays at the old Leeds Playhouse in Hunslet (1771–1865), there was nowhere to stage large operas until the Leeds Grand Theatre opened in 1878. This part of the exhibition showed a number of programmes from the Leeds Amateur Operatic Society (founded 1890) as well as from touring companies such as D'Oyly Carte and the Carl Rosa Opera Company. Other theatrical and musical venues represented in the exhibition included the Leeds City Varieties (founded in 1865), Leeds Hippodrome (based in King Charles Croft from 1848 to 1933) and the Empire Palace Theatre on Briggate (1898–1961). The music hall star Vesta Victoria (1873–1951) was born in the suburb of Holbeck and first appeared on stage with her parents at the age of 4. Her biggest hit was 'Daddy Wouldn't Buy Me A Bow Wow' which is why it was one of the tracks chosen to play (on the jukebox) throughout the exhibition. In 2020, the museum was gifted a silver and pearl brooch inscribed to Vesta Victoria by one of her admirers in 1893.

The museum had photographs of another Leeds-born music hall star, George Henry Elliott (1882–1962), but this presented a sensitive historical and cultural challenge because he was one of the many white singers who performed minstrel songs in racist blackface. We took the decision not to display any of his photographs in the exhibition but, instead, selected one of his recordings for the exhibition playlist because he sang these songs with a noticeable Yorkshire accent. We deliberately chose a track 'I'm Going Back Again to Old Nebraska' written by the African-American composer Noble Sissle in 1928, which was digitized from a record in the museum collection.

Francis Laidler's pantomimes at the Leeds Theatre Royal ran from 1909 to 1959 and music was a key ingredient, and the museum recently digitized a small publicity gramophone record for the 1935 Red Riding Hood Pantomime starring Gwladys Stanley and Roy Barbour, which is available on the Leeds Museums YouTube channel.

## *Music in dancehalls and ballrooms*

The rise of the concert hall, where the audience stays seated to listen to a performance, is a relatively recent phenomenon compared to the history of music performance. The Leeds Assembly Rooms, which opened in 1777 in a wing of the Third White Cloth Hall, included a handsomely decorated ballroom and the exhibition displayed a copy of a small book of 'Old English Country Dances', collected by Frank Kidson of Leeds in 1890, which included tunes that may have been familiar in the Assembly Rooms, with local titles such as 'Yorkshire Bite' and 'Kirkgate'. The exhibition also included dance cards and invitations for events held in church halls and institutes around Leeds as well as photographs and documents relating to dance bands such as the Brunswick Dance Band based in Morley, and a stylish 1880s photograph shows members of Bacon's Select Dancing Academy based at 9 Park Lane.

A significant bandleader to come from Leeds was Ivy Benson, born in the suburb of Holbeck in 1913. She rose to fame with her all-female swing band in the 1940s. The museum commissioned a ceramic figurine for the museum collection to commemorate her in 2017 (see Figure 15.3).

From the 1930s, many cinemas doubled up as dance halls, such as the Odeon on Briggate and the Majestic on City Square. One of the most iconic dance venues was probably the Mecca Locarno Ballroom in County Arcade (1938–69) and the exhibition displayed a couple of tickets from Jimmy Cliff's performance there in June 1968.

FIGURE 15.3: Ceramic figure of Ivy Benson and her band, made by Katch Skinner, 2017, photographed by Norman Taylor. Courtesy of Leeds Museums and Galleries.

## Music in pubs and clubs

The division between concert venues, dance halls, clubs and bars can be fluid and venues are often multi-purpose. So, when planning the exhibition, one factor that defined a pub or a club was whether the audience could enjoy a drink when the music was playing. Pubs have long been associated with music, whether just having a piano in the bar or renting rooms for rehearsals and, from 1885, the Guildford Musical Society met over dinner at the Old Green Dragon Hotel (a pub on Merry Boys Hill) as evidenced by medals in the exhibition.

We aimed to represent as many different venues as we could in a small case, with flyers from Leeds West Indian Centre, Joseph's Well, The Cockpit, Leeds Stylus, The Fenton, Leeds Metropolitan University Student Union, The Cardigan Arms, The New Roscoe, The Vine, Basement Nightclub and Bar Phono, HQ Bar and Gatecrasher, among others.

The case displayed accessories worn by Elizabeth Griffin as a 1980s Goth, and a Vivienne Westwood shirt worn to the 'Vague' club at the Warehouse in 1994. It also included the 1970 LP of 'The Who Live At Leeds' and a 2014 copy of Carboot Soul by George Evelyn from Nightmares on Wax.

## Music in the streets

The lives of street musicians often go unrecorded and undocumented, but the Leeds collections included a few glimpses. The exhibition included ballad broadsheets, printed by John Broadbent who was listed as a newsagent on York Street in the 1850s and a poignant collection related to Alfred Warrington Lodge, known as 'Blind Alf', who sang operatic arias and ballads on Commercial Street for over 50 years. An obituary from March 1928 described how he

> managed for years to eke out a living by singing to the strains of the concertina. Sometimes, when fates were unkind, the concertina was missing, but it was not long before 'Alf' had acquired sufficient money to regain it from the custody of the pawnbroker.
> (LEEDM.E.2012.0553.0003 1928)

In 2017, the museum acquired a guitar, busking stool and microphone used by Peter Haughton to entertain passers-by over 80 years later, and the exhibition also included the funeral eulogy for Johnny Walker, another much-loved busker who died in 2018.

This section also explored the music of street parades, including those associated with the Leeds Military Tattoo and Leeds Children's Day. The exhibition included a copy of 'Floreat Loidis' a Children's Day marching song composed by J. Hartley Stones of Savile Green Council School in 1933.

From its beginning in 1967, the Leeds West Indian Carnival has championed traditional Caribbean music (see Friar, this volume). At the first carnival, steel bands and a big drum and fife band entertained crowds in Potternewton Park before processing through the streets on homemade trolleys pulled along on ropes. The exhibition included photographs, ephemera and souvenirs relating to Carnival from its growing collection, which shows its significance in the cultural calendar of Leeds.

## Music in Leeds' parks

Bandstands were a feature of Leeds' parks from the 1860s, and although the metal railings from most of them were melted down during the Second World War, the exhibition included a collection of posters advertising brass band concerts in Armley and Bramley, a tradition that continues in some of the surviving bandstands every summer.

When Roundhay Park was opened to the public in 1872 by Prince Arthur he was greeted by a mass rendition of the specially composed song 'This is Our Opening Day', a copy of which survives in the collection, providing evidence that Roundhay Park hosted large-scale musical events long before the Rolling Stones played there in 1982 (see Mills, Chapter 3).

The exhibition also showed other artefacts from music-related events in Leeds' parks such as Edward German's 'Merrie England' in 1953 in Temple Newsam Park, Opera in the Park and Party in the Park, which were council-funded events and also held at Temple Newsam Park from 1994 until 2014 (see the front cover image). Temple Newsam Park is notable because it was also the initial location for the Leeds Festival when it started in 1999 before relocating to its current home in Bramham Park and the exhibition included an emblematic pair of festival wellington boots.

## *Musical instruments and composers of Leeds*

The largest section of the exhibition was devoted to Leeds-made musical instruments, which was dictated primarily by the size of the objects, which made them an interesting visual focus for the display. The earliest and most intriguing of these is a glass harp made by Joshua Muff in 1820, which creates an ethereal sound from resonating graded glasses set in a wooden frame. We also displayed items from the Dearlove collection including a double bass from 1851, a violin, and some of their exhibition medals (see Heppleston, 2020 for more information). Another unusual instrument on show was a dulcimer made by Leeds music-teacher Walter Stainton Meeson (1866–1928) for the 1888 Workmen's Industrial Exhibition. Leeds was also home to many important organ makers, including William Naylor and J. J. Binns of Bramley.

Also on show were a 1910 gramophone made by Perfectophone Co. Ltd., Kirkstall Road, a 1937 radio made by Pegasus, Lower Wortley, and a 1970s Kestrel electric guitar amplifier, made by Futuristic Aids Limited, Henconner Lane.

The case also featured many of the composers, bands and songwriters who were born or lived in Leeds, which included George Linley, Frederick Kilvington Hattersley, Dorothy Martin (composer of 'Yorkshire Songs' in 1960), Jake Thackray, Jeff Christie, Gang of Four, The Mekons, The Squares, Soft Cell, The Sisters of Mercy, Chumbawamba, Joe 90, The Wedding Present, The Pigeon Detectives, Kaiser Chiefs, Corinne Bailey Rae, Ellen and the Escapades and The

Tenmours. This is obviously not an exhaustive list and the museum hopes to continue to acquire material relating to Leeds-based musicians.

The final section of the exhibition touched on the importance of music in religious worship and the oldest object in the exhibition was a 1769 cello, which provided music in Hunslet Parish Church before they installed an organ. The display also featured church choirs, especially that of Leeds Parish Church, as well as items relating to Jewish cantors and the generous loan of a portable harmonium used at the GNNSJ Leeds Sikh Gudwarah, in the suburb of Beeston.

## *After the exhibition and conclusions*

The *Sounds of Our City* exhibition was originally planned to run through December 2020 but was extended for a second year after the COVID-19 pandemic threatened to cut it short. One fortuitous result was that the exhibition moved online, which gave a platform for the audio content where it could be appreciated more readily than within the physical gallery. This helped to further centre sound as an important part of the exhibition and helped to further challenge the museum's traditional privileging of the visual (Dudley 2010). Data captured by the museum showed that there have been over 3000 visits to the virtual exhibition since it opened on 1 January 2020. Interestingly, the virtual exhibition helped to encourage more visits when the museum eventually reopened and, more importantly, it has also been the catalyst for further projects and collaborations; the most exciting of which was the commission by Music:Leeds (see Thompson and Nicholls, Chapter 18) which resulted in 'Sonic Stops' (Music:Leeds 2021) that featured two soundscape compositions framed around a visualization of bus journeys across a musical map of Leeds.

*Sounds of Our City* is not the last word in displaying the musical heritage of Leeds but has been an important means of bringing together existing elements of the museum collections that reflect and represent the musical life of the city, as well as revealing gaps in the collections. The museum's collections do not exist in a vacuum but complement the important musical archives also held by West Yorkshire Archives, the city's universities and others, all of which help to preserve popular musical heritage (Baker et al. 2020). Private collectors too are important contributors to museum collections that have preserved much of the material culture of popular music (Leonard 2007) and we were fortunate to be able to borrow some of these items for the exhibition. Since January 2020 the *Sounds of Our City* exhibition itself has also encouraged further acquisitions, most notably the prototype Ibanez JGM10 Jon Gomm signature guitar donated by internationally recognized Leeds-based musician Jon Gomm himself in May 2021.

The challenges presented by the COVID-19 pandemic also show that online exhibitions can be a useful way of encouraging more visitors to an exhibition and can provide an outlet for objects, artefacts, audio and visual material that may be more challenging to present in a museum space. Importantly, a supplementary online exhibition can help to make the exhibition process less transitory and display objects, artefacts, audio and visual material beyond the usual lifespan of a time-bound exhibition.

## NOTE

At the time of writing, an online version of the exhibition is available at: https://museumsandgalleries.leeds.gov.uk/virtual-visit/sounds-of-our-city-online-exhibition/.

## REFERENCES

Baker, Sarah, Istvandity, Lauren and Nowak, Raphael (2016a), 'Curating popular music heritage: Storytelling and narrative engagement in popular music museums and exhibitions', *Museum Management and Curatorship*, 31:4, pp. 369–85.

Baker, Sarah, Istvandity, Lauren and Nowak, Raphael (2016b) 'The sound of music heritage: Curating popular music in music museums and exhibitions', *International Journal of Heritage Studies*, 22: 1, pp. 70–81.

Baker, Sarah, Istvandity, Lauren and Nowak, Raphael (2020), 'Curatorial practice in popular music museums: An emerging typology of structuring concepts', *European Journal of Cultural Studies*, 23:3, pp. 434–53.

Cortez, Alcina (2015), 'The curatorial practices of exhibiting popular music in Portugal at the beginning of the twenty-first century: An overview', *Revista Portuguesa De Musicologia*, 2:2, pp. 297–324.

Cortez, Alcina (2016), 'How popular music is exhibited by museums in Portugal at the beginning of the twenty-first century: A case study', *Curator: The Museum Journal*, 59:2, pp. 153–76.

Dudley, Sandra H. (ed), (2010), *Museum Materialities: Objects, Engagements, Interpretations*, London: Routledge.

Fairchild, Charles (2017), 'Understanding exhibitionary characteristics of popular music museums', *Museum & Society*, 15:1, pp. 87–99.

Heppleston, Neal (2020), 'Dearlove conservation', Heppleston Lutherie, https://www.hepplestonlutherie.co.uk/blog/2019/12/1/dearlove-conservation. Accessed 16 February 2022.

Knifton, Robert (2012), 'Popular music beyond text: An academic perspective on popular music in the museum', *Social History in Museums*, 36, pp. 21–25.

Leeds Museums and Galleries (n.d.), 'Leeds museums and galleries', YouTube, https://www.youtube.com/user/leedsmuseums. Accessed 16 February 2022.

Leonard, Marion (2007), 'Constructing histories through material culture: Popular music, museums and collecting', *Popular Music History*, 2:2, pp. 147–67.

Leonard, Marion (2010), 'Exhibiting popular music: Museum audiences, inclusion and social history', *Journal of New Music Research*, 39:2, pp. 171–81.

Leonard, Marion (2014), 'Staging the Beatles: Ephemerality, materiality and the production of authenticity in the museum', *International Journal of Heritage Studies*, 20:4, pp. 357–75.

Leonard, Marion and Knifton, Robert (2015), 'Engaging nostalgia: Popular music and memory in museums', in S. Cohen, R. Knifton and M. Leonard (eds), *Sites of Popular Music Heritage: Memories, Histories, Places*, London: Routledge, pp. 160–73.

Leonard, Marion and Knifton, Robert (2017), 'A critical survey of museum collections of popular music in the United Kingdom', *Popular Music History*, 10:2, pp. 171–91.

LEEDM.E.2012.0553.0003 (1928), *Obituary: Alfred Warrington Lodge*, 3 March (newspaper cutting), Leeds Museums and Galleries.

LEEDM.E.2011.0443 (1964), 'Cyril Maynard Mitchell and Jack Dearlove, interviewed by Dick Gregson', *Home This Afternoon*, BBC, 24 August (Audio recording), Leeds Museums and Galleries.

Mortensen, Christian H. and Madsen Jacob W. (2015), 'The sound of yesteryear on display: A rethinking of nostalgia as a strategy for exhibiting pop/rock heritage', *International Journal of Heritage Studies*, 21:3, pp. 250–63.

Music:Leeds (2021), *Sonic Stops* (art exhibition), Abbey House Museum, 28 April, http://www.musicleeds.com/sonicstops. Accessed 16 February 2022.

Van der Hoeven, Arno and Brandellero, Amanda (2015), 'Places of popular music heritage: The local framing of a global cultural form in Dutch museums and archives', *Poetics*, 51, pp. 37–53.

# 16

# Where You're From *and* Where *They're* At: Connecting Voices, Generations and Place to Create a Leeds Hip Hop Archive

*Sarah Little and Alex Stevenson*

Hip Hop culture emerged in 1970s New York, built on the four elements of DJing, breakdancing, graffiti and rapping. By the early 1980s, Hip Hop, or rap music,[1] became a global phenomenon, and in the United Kingdom, reggae soundsystems[2] started to incorporate US Hip Hop into their playlists. The release of seminal early Hip Hop films such as Wildstyle (Ahearn 1983) gave rise to the first wave of British youth engaging with Hip Hop culture. Despite the common perception of the emergence of British Hip Hop culture being London-centric, cities such as Leeds, with their long-established reggae soundsystems, proved a fertile environment for early pioneers to forge their 'glocal' (Bennett 1999: 1) interpretation of Hip Hop culture. Whilst much of the existing literature on British Hip Hop tends to focus on London (Bramwell 2015; Hesmondhalgh and Melville 2001), a number of studies exploring the role of Hip Hop within other cities and regions across the United Kingdom have recently emerged (see Bennett 1999; Lashua and Owusu 2013; Williams 2020; de Paor-Evans 2020). However, as is the case with many other popular music scenes, Hip Hop in Leeds has been largely overlooked.

Cohen et al. (2014) recognize the trend within recent decades for the preservation and positioning of popular music cultures as sites of 'heritage' through the development of music archives. North American institutions such as Harvard[3] and Cornell[4] both established scholarly Hip Hop archives in 2002 and 2007, respectively. Baker et al. (2016: 8) argue that since then, a significant number of individuals and community-led groups have attempted to establish archives to preserve the material aspects of the music cultures from which they emerged, referred to as 'DIY' (do it yourself) archives (Baker and Huber 2013: 513). As a popular music culture, Hip Hop is no exception to the 'DIY' archive trend. This is perhaps understandable, given Hip Hop's characterization as an art form possessing an enduring ethos of self-facilitation (Little 2019; Speers 2014). Such 'DIY' and community-produced archives aim to preserve and curate the written and oral histories of Hip Hop culture.

This chapter explores the history of the Leeds Hip Hop scene as a site of cultural significance in the emergence and development of UK Hip Hop culture from the late 1970s onwards. It focuses on the planned archival partnership between the community-led group The Hip Hop Historian Society (HHHS) and Leeds Museums as an example of what Baker (2017: 3) refers to as 'community-led, grassroots, specialist archives [...] dedicated to specific genres, artists or locales which are marginalized'.

## *Leeds, Hip Hop and the museum*

HHHS is a Leeds-based community-led collective voluntary group formed in 2018, co-founded by Leeds Hip Hop Graffiti Artist Monks[5] (a.k.a Monkee), and consisting of Hip Hop practitioners and supporters whose aim is to document, preserve and celebrate the history of Hip Hop culture in Leeds. The group has a pre-existing relationship with the Local Authority-funded Leeds Museums. Since 2014, both organizations have collaborated to produce an annual Hip Hop history month community day at Leeds City Museum and HHHS has donated artefacts, which have featured in a number of ad hoc Leeds music exhibitions. Marek Romaniszyn, Assistant Community Curator for Leeds Museums, has been involved in the development of the Leeds Museums' relationship with HHHS since the first Hip Hop celebration event in 2014. He recalls the significance and scale of this event, stating 'it was huge, Afrika Bambaata came down and there was around 3000 people' (Romaniszyn 2021: n.pag.).

In 2019, the HHHS and the museum began drafting an agreement to create a permanent Leeds Hip Hop history archive to be housed at Leeds Museums in order to document and celebrate some of the key events and practitioners involved in the development of Leeds Hip Hop culture. The artefacts are intended to be a blend of material artefacts (including event posters, albums, album artworks and notable press articles) and a recorded collection of oral histories gathered from Leeds Hip Hop practitioners. Despite delays due to the global COVID-19 pandemic, work has continued such as preparing interviews and artefacts to be included in the future archive.

## Methodology

This chapter draws on semi-structured interviews with key artists, promoters, practitioners, community project leaders and Leeds Museums staff to expose a history of Leeds Hip Hop, and to explore the interconnections between generational experiences to investigate how this history might discover and locate its voice through the further development and expansion of the archive. The Interviews explored both participant's experiences of Hip Hop culture in Leeds and their thoughts about the creation of the archive. This approach draws on the process of co-curation to gather data as a means to 'facilitate[ing] different ways of remembering *and* [...] also the invitation to contextualize these memories in different discourses' (Beate 2020: 58, original emphasis).

Initially, one key practitioner from each of the generations since the emergence of Hip Hop was selected for interview based on their age, longevity and engagement with the Leeds scene. A 'snowball' or 'chain' sampling method (Patton 2002) was then implemented to help select further participants, which were based on suggestions from initial interviews until enough information-rich narratives were gathered that covered the past five decades with significant overlap. The findings from these interviews were synthesized to build a history of Leeds Hip Hop, and through this process, the challenges of historicizing a multi-generational popular music culture were investigated.

This chapter does not claim to offer a definitive history of Hip Hop in Leeds, however, the contributions from participants offer new insight into the culture over the last five decades. The findings are structured chronologically to focus on each era, and generation, of Leeds Hip Hop history in turn (reflecting the structuring framework utilized in McNally's 2010 'Home Grown' Hip Hop history exhibition[6]). This supports a valuable dialogue that is in keeping with the long-term ambition to tell the broad and rich story of Leeds Hip Hop through the creation of the planned archive.

## *Mixtapes and sound systems: The late 1970s to mid 1980s*

DJ Weston (2021), a member of the early generation of Leeds Hip Hop artists, has remained consistently active in the Leeds scene and remembers his earliest memories of the emergence of Hip Hop's presence in Leeds. He recalls in the late 1970s and early 1980s mixtapes[7] from the United States beginning to filter through to the United Kingdom, with US Hip Hop tracks occasionally being played at music events and clubs that were otherwise focused musically on playing reggae, dancehall, soul and funk. Khadijah Ibrahim (2021), the founder of the long-established street poetry jam collective Leeds Young Authors, recalls a similar experience of early US Hip Hop tracks proliferating through the playlists for Reggae sound system gigs during that same time period.

At that time, the geographic locus of venues and events interweaving Hip Hop music was concentrated in various Blues and underground clubs around the Chapeltown and Harehills areas of North Leeds. Both Ibrahim and Weston recall Fox's club in Chapeltown as a key venue where early Hip Hop tracks would be played. Weston recalls that Hip Hop could be heard amongst Funk, Soul and Reggae music at Studio One in Sheepscar and the Starlight Ballroom in Shaftsbury. Ibrahim also describes how Hip Hop was played alongside other music genres on the Reggae sound systems in Leeds: 'In Chapeltown, Reggae music was definitely at the heart of what was being played, but […] you'd definitely hear Hip Hop' (Ibrahim 2021: n.pag.).

In 1983, Weston recalls the formation of 'Breakin' the Mould' one of the early street break dancing crews from Leeds, along with 'Connection '84'. The following year, Leeds record store Jumbo Records held a body-popping battle, where Weston remembers 'the energy of the crowd, all pushing through, and closing in, it was amazing' (2021: n.pag.). Weston remembers that this element of Hip Hop culture, at that time in Leeds, was largely a youth culture: '[the] only places you'd hear Hip Hop before 1987 was in youth centres, and you often had to bring your own records' (2021: n.pag.). For Weston and the break dance crews he was associated with, the culture 'died around 1985' (2021: n.pag.) before re-emerging with renewed vigour and presence around 1987. By this, Weston explains that he is referring to a significant downturn in the presence of Breakdance crews and battles/competitions. He remembers this as a national cultural shift, and estimates that it was driven in part by that early generation reaching adulthood:

> I've spoken to old skoolers about what happened […]. My theory is that we all reached an age where we all had to get jobs. Before '86, if you were 18 and a break dancer you were old, that wasn't heard of.
>
> (Weston 2021: n.pag.)

Weston's recollections of this are supported by Hip Hop artist Project Cee, who, reflecting on his experiences in the rural south-west of England, explained 'there were people at that time [mid-1980s] who were probably five years older than us, and they just kind of thought of breakdancing as really childish, and they very quickly moved on' (de Paor-Evans and McNally 2021: 155).

Weston also recalled his simultaneous involvement in graffiti writing, remembering large and active graffiti crews present in Leeds at that time. He began DJing in 1986, going on to DJ for Leeds/York Hip Hop crew New Flesh for Old

(Ninjatune) and Jehst (YnR). Although prior to this time there were few Hip Hop DJs, partly due to the expense of equipment, Weston remembers an influx of Hip Hop DJs in and around Leeds in 1987, which included Bradford DJ John Biddy and (BBoy crew) Soul City Rockers (who went on to co-found the DJ group Nightmares on Wax with George Evelyn and Kevin Harper).

One of the earliest documented video recordings of Leeds Hip Hop artists appears in the BBC Hip Hop documentary *Bad Meaning Good* (BBC 1987), featuring Leeds Hip Hop rapper Daddy Speedo. Weston and Khadijah recall Speedo's emergence in the scene along with fellow MCs Boddy Popper and KD Ranko, all of whom transitioned from toasting in the Leeds Reggae scene to rapping over Hip Hop. In the late 1980s, UK rappers would routinely adopt American accents (Stevenson 2017) and, in Leeds, Hip Hop artist Testament (2021) even admits to continuing to be influenced by the American accent in his lyrical delivery through to the late 1990s. The specific turning point at which Leeds MCs began to rap in their own Leeds accent is difficult to pinpoint, though available recordings of Leeds artists suggest this shift began in the mid 1990s, as evidenced in the unreleased posse track *Drinking Tea with the Lads* (1993) by Progressive Agenda and New Flesh for Old (Emery 2017).

### *The emergence of a homegrown scene: Late 1980s–90s*

The early 1980s saw the emergence of a Hip Hop presence in Leeds through Breakdancing, Graffiti and imported mixtapes; however, the late 1980s bore witness to the development of a distinct Leeds Hip Hop culture through the establishment of Hip Hop nights, Hip Hop DJs and locally produced mixtapes. Weston recalls that around 1987 an increasing number of city centre clubs began to play Hip Hop tracks, as DJs realized that the younger generation, now of club-going age, possessed an appetite for the Hip Hop sound.

One of the first distinct 'Hip Hop nights' in Leeds took place first at Phono and then later in the downstairs room 'Rickys' at the city centre club Coconut Grove, with Soul City Rockers' Hip Hop night called Downbeat. Weston remembers its popularity and that 'other nightclubs started […] seeing the queues outside – they would even send spies down from other clubs to write down the set list so they could go back and play [it] in their club!' (2021: n.pag.).

Though it is challenging to ascertain a specific date when a Leeds Hip Hop scene was established in earnest, a robust approximation can be extracted from interview participants' recollections of the time period when Leeds artists began to produce their own musical material. Whilst this may be considered to signify a shift away from Bennett and Peterson's (2004) notion of a 'Translocal' towards a 'local' Leeds Hip Hop music scene, this would be an over-simplification, due to the glocal nature of Hip Hop participants, who are described by Alim as 'negotiating their identities and memberships in the simultaneously localizing and globalizing imagined world of Hip Hop' (2009: 107).

Weston recalls 1989 as a cultural shift in the emergence of a Leeds Hip Hop scene as artists began to produce their own mixtapes. Around this time some notable Leeds artists also became active in the scene, including Nightmares on Wax (whose broader camp at this time Inner City Leagues, included Shane '10 Tonn' Fenton and others), LSK, Breakin' the Illusion (BTI) – who later went on to found Low Life Records with Leeds artists Braintax (T.E.S.T. and FourNine) and LFO, alongside established sound system crews such as Ital Rockers.[8]

## *A technological evolution: Early 1990s–2000s*

The early 1990s ushered in a new era for Leeds Hip Hop, both in terms of sound, prevalence and shifts in inter-crew relationships. Technological developments including the increasing availability of sampling and home recording equipment played a key role in this shift, which enabled further development in sound and resulted in a shift away from the faster tempo electro-beats (that characterized much earlier Hip Hop) to Boom-Bap, New York-style Hip Hop beats. Weston recalls that changes in the availability of technology also impacted interrelationships between crews and artists in the scene. Historically crews were more closely connected within the Hip Hop community, which was driven by the scarcity of technological resources and the need to share, as well as limited outlets through which to hear and receive new music. However, the 1990s saw crews and artists empowered with the ability to record themselves at home, without the same need to share equipment or source significant funds in order to pay for commercial studio time.

In the late 1990s, UK Hip Hop began to enjoy a further proliferation of artists/crews and further national exposure. Within this creative environment, the next generation of Leeds Hip Hop rappers developed their own style, showcasing their material at various, now regular and established, Hip Hop nights within the city such as Fresh Jive and Drum Major (at The Wardrobe). For Weston, the late 1990s signified a cultural turning point where the commercialization of Hip Hop music led to fragmentation within the scene and shifts in artists' motivations for producing music. The next generation of artists emerged from an environment where commercial endeavour and entrepreneurship were a familiar element of the context of Hip Hop. Monks has a buoyant recollection of the Leeds scene in the late 1990s:

> Jehst was on the Leeds scene [...] after I put on the Therapy nights at Warehouse we formed the Therapy Allstars, which was Tommy Evans, Jehst, DJ X, Agent M, and ADM [...] there was Testament [on the scene], as well as Afro Physiks [...] then we formed Junkyard Tactics [...] there was a lot going on.
>
> (2021: n.pag.)

He goes on to expound on other elements of Hip Hop culture 'during that time [the mid to late 1990s] we painted Way Ahead Records artwork and formed the crew Triple A with graf writer Rocaine and Insa' (2021: n.pag.). Monks also remembers playing the inaugural date of Leeds' long-running community music festival Hyde Park Unity Day, established in 1996 as a response to local civil unrest and street riots.

Testament, Leeds-based Hip Hop artist in the critically acclaimed live Hip Hop band Homecut, recalls his integration into the Leeds Hip Hop scene in the late 1990s. 'I started my degree at the University of Leeds in 1997 and wanted to start a band. [...] We first played youth centres and college events [...] our first paid gig was at The Faversham for [promoter] Tony Green' (2021: n.pag.). Having spent the last two decades delivering hip hop workshops in schools and developing Hip Hop theatre productions, Testament's experiences of the Leeds Hip Hop scenes demonstrated a tapestry of involvement in a number of cultural, Hip Hop-related communities. He recalls that 'as a live band, we [Homecut] had more of that crossover appeal, we got booked for all sorts of different gigs' (2021: n.pag.). Testament, Monks and Weston all recall that Leeds Student Radio (LSR), as well as a number of local pirate radio stations, were supportive of Leeds Hip Hop acts giving airtime to Leeds artists either through offering slots to run Hip Hop shows and/or through playing local Hip Hop.

Later, Testament became MC and host for the regular Leeds Hip Hop night *New Bohemia* (The Faversham), which ran from the mid 2000s for a number of years playing host to a wealth of United Kingdom and local Hip Hop artists including Jack Flash and Tommy Evans. Speaking on notable artists and practitioners who were active in the Leeds scene at that time, Testament remembers Kid Kanevil, BBoy Shane '10 Tonn' Fenton, Monkee (now Monks), and B Girl Firefly, and his involvement with key Leeds Hip Hop collective Invizible Circle.

Invizible Circle were a notable Leeds Hip Hop crew in that they formed as a cooperative in 2001. Inspired by US Hip Hop group the Wu Tang Clan, the perception of the power drawn from belonging to a collective, and following veteran Hip Hop DJ Oddball's proclamation that selfish promotion amongst the Leeds scene must end, founding members including J Bravo, Monks, DJ Combine, Totally Dis-illusioned (T. D.), Kid Kanevil and Agent M would pay subs (subscriptions) to the collective, which were used to record, promote and support the collective's

30-plus members. The collective both proliferated and divided over time, branching off into more discrete projects, including Invizible Circle Records, whose artist roster included Leeds-based acts BTI and Junkyard Tactics; however, Invizible Circle, in name and in its original form, exists as a prominent part of the history of the Leeds Hip Hop scene.

Defenders of Style MC Prys recalls the point in time that he and his fellow crew members first became involved in the Leeds Hip Hop scene:

> I started listening to Invizible Circle, getting passed down tapes that were from the older graf crews, we were really into graf so that got us into the scene. We looked up to the likes of 9ine Lives, Monkee, Double D Dagger, Eliphino, we were just blown away by what they were doing.
>
> (2021: n.pag.)

Promoter Harry Lotta remembers the long-running, community-focused Hip Hop night Lyrically Justified as a similar example of a Leeds-based music collective and platform created to nurture local Hip Hop talent (Lotta 2021: n.pag.). Lyrically Justified, formed with an ethos of promoting love, music and a strictly open mind policy (BBC 2008), was initially set up at Leeds Metropolitan University in 2004 by Harry and fellow collaborator and DJ Ms Sykes, and eventually moved to a regular listing at Leeds city centre club, Carpe Diem until 2011.

What is clear from the interview participants' responses is that intergenerationality in the context of Leeds Hip Hop history is more complex than solely the age of the artist. For example, despite Homecut being active on the scene into the late 2000s, Testament places Double D Dagger, Arro (Miniature Heroes) and Jack Flash into what he considers the 'next generation'. Defenders of Style (who were active from the mid 2000s) cite 'looking up' to some of these artists as the previous generation of established Hip Hop artists, indicating that the level to which an act is established and the degree of critical 'underground' recognition they have received plays a role in defining one generation from the other.

When Weston recalls the earlier days of Hip Hop in Leeds, he states that 'every generation "came through" at the same time in the sense that everyone was into the break dancing. Then, when the clubs became more musically segregated Hip Hop heads pulled back a bit' (2021: n.pag.). Tony Green, a long-established Leeds promoter who has supported emerging Leeds Hip Hop acts through hosting Leeds Hip Hop nights and larger scale gigs in the region, similarly described the Leeds scene 'breaking up' in the early 2010s as the different elements of Hip Hop splintered. From around 1997, Tony established regular Hip Hop nights such

FIGURE 16.1: A Freshjive flyer, c.2010. Courtesy of Freshjive events.

as Freshjive at the Faversham (see Figure 16.1). He mentions that alongside the musical acts at his nights, which would regularly have more than 700 people in attendance, there would also be local BBoys and BGirls such as DMW, Weston, Roy, Andrea, Firefly and Sean from Leeds crew Breakers Unify, as well as many high-profile scratch DJs/Turntablists who had competed in the DMC world DJ championships.

Green recounted the numerous events he put on in partnership with Shane '10 Tonn' Fenton from around 2004, highlighting the importance of ensuring that Hip Hop events in Leeds represented the scene. 'Once I'd started working with him [Shane] […] we got to […] the roots of the culture, and I started to really understand it, and what it meant to the city, and what it meant to kids' (2021: n.pag.). Green described how important the BBoys and BGirls were at their nights:

> the floor, the lights; it was a prerequisite of anywhere we were, so when they walked in, it was like *'this is for me, this is my night'*. We gave them all VIP cards so they never had to pay for anything [...] they were our celebrities.
>
> (2021: n.pag.)

Green remembered the early 2000s as a golden era for Hip Hop in Leeds:

> as a club scene we were potent, we were in the middle of it, and it represented [...] you came to a Hip Hop night and it wasn't 30 lads in a corner just rapping [...] it was big, charismatic, full of all sorts of people, dancing and partying, and that's what Hip Hop was.
>
> (2021: n.pag.)

Monks also recalled working closely with BBoy 10 Tonn and his family's charity movement *Speak to the Streets*. In an interview in *The Guardian* in 2011, Fenton described this scene as being 'about making things happen and bringing people together and empowering the youth' (Slack 2011: n.pag.), highlighting the significant role Hip Hop has played within the communities of Leeds.

### A 'golden era' and the return of the rap battle: The 2000s–10s

Echoing Tony Green's reflections on Leeds Hip Hop's 'golden era', MC Matter remembers the prominence and popularity of Hip Hop in mid 2000s Leeds recalling the *8 Mile* Rap Battle competition series coming to Leeds in 2005, which for Matter was a significant cultural flashpoint: 'Jack Flash entered and all the next Leeds MCs were out in force' (Matter 2021: n.pag.). Matter also recalled that, following this, Leeds club Dr Wu's sat for a period as a locus of Hip Hop activity. For Matter, this prolific period for Leeds Hip Hop inspired his generation of Leeds artists, including 'Defenders of Style, Alphabetix and all of them [...] we did stuff for each other, supported each other' (2021: n.pag.).

Matter also identified the re-emergence and return in popularity of the acapella rap battle scene within Leeds Hip Hop around 2009, with regional artists Lego (York), Dialect (Leeds) and Lunar C (Bradford). For Weston, this re-emergence heralded a welcome cultural turn within Leeds Hip Hop where the characteristics of the battle event demonstrated a return to the raw energy, sense of fun and close crowd proximity of the germinal years of the Leeds Hip Hop scene. Whilst Green also described this as 'the next chapter, all those kids coming through, like Matter, the Don't Flop thing'[9] (2021: n.pag.), he also described how eventually, after the broader appeal of the battle competitions waned, these events become much smaller-scale events with the same 50 or 60 hardcore Hip Hop heads attending, lacking the broader appeal of the party vibe that the previous Hip Hop events offered. Green described how once he stopped putting on dedicated Hip Hop nights that the bigger mainstream clubs and venues 'swallowed bookings up' (2021: n.pag.) leading to a lack of engagement with the local Hip Hop community and limited support opportunities for younger up and coming artists that there had been previously.

## *Conclusions*

Our interviewees highlighted that themes of 'inspiration', 'know-how' and 'a sense of unity' all held a place within inter-crew relationships of the same generation, which encouraged descendant generations of Leeds Hip Hop. Conversely, direct mentorship and the explicit 'passing on of Hip Hop knowledge' between generations played a less significant role. For Weston, whilst older and younger generations inspired, and continue to inspire each other, a stronger sense of connection and mentorship could have been fostered within the scene. Testament remembers mutual love and respect between newer and older generations of Hip Hop culture in Leeds but highlights how eventually younger generations were not necessarily looking up to older generations for support. Matter expounded on his experience of Hip Hop's inter-generational relationships stating 'Hip Hop is a generally belligerent culture that doesn't give a sh*t what anyone says to them, especially the generation before them, but everyone got on, it was all cool, there was no animosity' (2021: n.pag.).

Against these collegial experiences of Hip Hop interrelationships, the scene has not been without its share of disagreement or Hip Hop 'beef'. Monks recalled several graffiti 'wars' over the decades between rival crews, with Green describing the negative impact of graffiti wars at his club night on both himself (e.g. breaking up fights), and the venues and neighbouring businesses who were often caught in the firing line.

These practitioner accounts have highlighted how the interrelationships and connections within Leeds Hip Hop, both across time (intergenerationally) and across the culture, are more complex and nuanced than simply 'one generation following another', or a particular crew or artist being linked to another. There is also both division and interconnection within the culture's elements, demonstrated in Green's account highlighting the fundamental importance of the relationship between promoter and artist. A number of the artists alluded to the sonic shift away from Electro-beat towards the Boom Bap sound (in the 1990s) as a point of distinction within Leeds Hip Hop history. Weston pointed to a similar distinction between an 'old skool' rap style and the subsequent shift to more complex wordplay and multi-syllable rhyming (in the 1990s), and then later to 'Grime' style of rap (in the 2000s) as a means of distinguishing generations.

Most of the histories of Leeds Hip Hop are oral and become manifest only through the memories of lived experience of the individuals and groups involved. Weston recalled numerous practitioners who were fundamental to the development of the scene in its early years whose influence would have been otherwise forgotten due to a lack of physical documentation of their involvement. Much later in the lineage of Hip Hop history, Prys noted the challenge with documentation of the events of Leeds Hip Hop history: 'there was no YouTube or camera phones then […] it was mixtapes' (2021: n.pag.).

Any archive of Leeds Hip Hop history(s) therefore needs to be one which positions the members of its culture and their lived experiences centrally in the curatorial process. Peter (2020: 61) explains that this approach is fundamental to ethical curation: 'If co-curation is to advertise and evidence civic engagement (including that of co-curators), exhibitions have to include, or be the result of, several (and equal) voices'. Leeds Museums curator Marek also positions this approach as key to successful curation

> [in] ethical community collecting the people in that community are the experts, I think they should be able to come to the collections development meetings and say what they would like to be included [in the archive] and bringing their narrative and their stories with the objects […] the museum can facilitate, provide a platform.
> 
> (Romaniszyn 2021: n.pag.)

Marek added the importance of the relationship between the museum and the Hip Hop community developing over time in which

> contemporary community collecting should be people focussed. […] It should be about creating that balance between the Museum being a neutral platform and communities populating it with their stories and things that are important to them. […] It's important that this is a community led, organic and authentic relationship that develops over a long period of time, to build that trust.
> 
> (2021: n.pag.)

Drawing parallels with the structural narrative of this chapter, Weston maintains that a Leeds Hip Hop archive should document the point at which Hip Hop music began to be played in Leeds and its narrative should begin with the earliest

Breakdancers and Graffiti writers, including everyone involved in the culture from that point onwards. Whereas for Ibrahim, intergenerationality in Hip Hop stretches much further back into history. Reflecting Rose (1994), Ibrahim traces Hip Hop's roots back to the griot and the storytelling traditions of West African cultures, which in turn influenced the 'toasting' of the reggae soundsystem culture, suggesting that a Leeds Hip Hop archive must do more than begin its narrative with the inception of the first Leeds Hip Hop artists and recognize its deeper roots.

For the curator(s) seeking to create a Leeds Hip Hop archive, the above insights suggest a need to make connections between generations, phases and time periods in the history of Leeds Hip Hop culture. Whilst on the one hand the interconnections between different generations emerge somewhat organically; in the liminality between the artists, gigs and venues remembered, on the other hand, there is no clear, distinct lineage between generations of Leeds Hip Hop practitioners or definitive phases in its history. The story(s) of Leeds Hip Hop exists as an interwoven, and rhizomatic fabric of histories whose lineages co-exist at the same time as both connected and disparate.

## NOTES

1. There is much contention about the amalgamation of the terms 'rap' and 'Hip Hop', with rap sometimes considered a reductive term, only referring to Hip Hop music, with the term Hip Hop relating a wider culture (Krims 2000).
2. Originating in 1950s Jamaica, the collective term soundsystems refers to both the music amplification and playback system and the people that operate these systems (Woods 2019).
3. The Hiphop Archive & Research Institute, http://hiphoparchive.org/. Accessed 1 December 2021.
4. The Cornell Hip Hop Collection, https://rmc.library.cornell.edu/hiphop/. Accessed 1 December 2021.
5. As a significant proportion of the histories are drawn from oral and lived experience, it is not always possible to verify definitive or correct spellings of artist and Hip Hop practitioner names or monikers; however, every effort has been made by the authors to check and cross reference these.
6. https://urbismanchester.files.wordpress.com/2010/01/home-grown-the-story-of-uk-hip-hop.pdf. Accessed 1 December 2021.
7. The term 'mixtape' refers to a music recording (originally on a cassette tape) containing a number of music tracks often from a combination of different artists, which have been 'mixed' by a DJ to flow from one track to the next.
8. Ital Rockers went on to become Iration Steppas.
9. Don't Flop is a UK rap battle organization established in 2008.

# REFERENCES

Ahearn, Charlie (1983), *WIldstyle*, VHS, New York: Submarine Entertainment.

Alim, H. Samy (2009), 'Translocal style communities: Hip hop youth as cultural theorists of style, language, and globalization', *Pragmatics: Quarterly Publication of the International Pragmatics Association (IPrA)*, Special Issue: 'Translocal style communities: Hip hop youth as cultural theorists of style, language, and globalization', 19:1, pp. 103–27.

Baker, Sarah (2017), *Community Custodians of Popular Music's Past: A DIY Approach to Heritage*, London: Routledge.

Baker, Sarah, Doyle, Peter and Homan, Shane (2016), 'Special Issue: Historical records, national constructions: The contemporary popular music archive', *Popular Music and Society*, 39:1, pp. 8–27.

Baker, Sarah and Huber, Alison (2013), 'Special Issue: Notes towards a typology of the DIY institution: Identifying do-it-yourself places of popular music preservation', *European Journal of Cultural Studies*, 16:5, pp. 513–30.

BBC (1987), *Bad Meaning Good (1987) UK Hip Hop Documentary*, DVD, extended ed., https://www.youtube.com/watch?v=r0ykYAAqLxc. Accessed 29 December 2021.

BBC (2008), 'Justified and not so ancient', 29 December, https://www.bbc.co.uk/leeds/content/articles/2008/12/29/music_lyrically_justified_feature.shtml?fbclid=IwAR2Ftvr4AYOFh53Af4gbqy6qnZf154u2e5HGPmXIBuD-221GB5l6yQJ0hi4. Accessed 29 December 2021.

Beate, Peter (2020), 'Special Issue: Negotiating the co-curation of an online community popular music archive', *Popular Music History*, 13.1–2, pp. 58–76.

Bennett, Andy (1999), 'Special Issue: Rappin' on the Tyne: White hip hop culture in Northeast England – an ethnographic study', *The Sociological Review*, 47:1, pp. 1–24.

Bennett, Andy and Peterson, Richard A. (2004), *Music Scenes: Local, Translocal and Virtual*, Nashville: Vanderbilt University Press.

Bramwell, Richard (2015), *UK Hip-Hop, Grime and the City: The Aesthetics and Ethics of London's Rap Scenes*, London: Routledge.

Cohen, Sara, Knifton, Robert, Leonard, Marion and Roberts, Les (2014), *Sites of Popular Music Heritage: Memories, Histories, Places*, London: Routledge.

de Paor-Evans, Adam (2020), *Provincial Headz: British Hip Hop and Critical Regionalism*, Sheffield: Equinox Publishing.

de Paor-Evans, Adam and McNally, James (2021), 'Project Cee … in conversation with James McNally', *HEADZ-ZINe 'REGIONS-UK' SOUTH-WEST HEADZ*, 1:2, pp. 151–65, http://clok.uclan.ac.uk/38572/1/SW.HEADZZINE.VOL.1.ISSUE.2.pdf. Accessed 29 December 2021.

Emery, Andrew (2017), 'PA Posse feat. DJ Countdown, SADE & New Flesh 4 Old – drinking tea with the lads', *Wiggaz With Attitude*, 31 August, https://www.wiggazwithattitude.com/pa-posse-feat-dj-countdown-sade-new-flesh-4-old-drinking-tea-lads/. Accessed 1 December 2021.

Green, Tony (2021), in-person interview with S. Little and A. Stevenson, Leeds, 26 November.

Hesmondhalgh, David J. and Melville, Casper (2001), 'Urban breakbeat culture – repercussions of hip-hop in the United Kingdom', in T. Mitchell (ed.), *Global Noise: Rap and Hip Hop Outside the USA*, Middletown: Wesleyan University Press, pp. 86–110.

Ibrahim, Khadijah (2021), online video interview with S. Little and A. Stevenson, 18 November.

Krims, Adam (2000), *Rap Music and the Poetics of Identity*, Cambridge: Cambridge University Press.

Lashua, Brett D. and Owusu, Yaw (2013), 'Merseybeatz: Hip-hop in Liverpool', in S. A. Nitzsche and W. Grünzweig (eds), *Hip-Hop in Europe*, Münster: LIT Verlag, pp. 191–206.

Little, Sarah (2019), 'Cultural democracy: A hip hop-ological study', Ph.D. thesis, Leeds: University of Leeds, http://etheses.whiterose.ac.uk/24638/. Accessed 29 December 2021.

Lotta, Harry (2021), online interview with S. Little and A. Stevenson, 24 November.

Matter (2021), online interview with S. Little and A. Stevenson, 25 November.

Monks (2021), telephone interview with S. Little and A. Stevenson, 16 December.

Patton, Michael Quinn (2002), *Qualitative Research & Evaluation Methods*, London: Sage.

Prys (2021), online interview with S. Little and A. Stevenson, 24 November.

Romaniszyn, Marek (2021), online video interview with S. Little and A. Stevenson, 15 November.

Rose, Tricia (1994), *Black Noise: Rap Music and Black Culture in Contemporary America*, Middletown: Wesleyan University Press.

Slack, Jason (2011), 'How breakdancing promotes positive culture in inner city Leeds', *The Guardian*, 29 March, https://www.theguardian.com/leeds/2011/mar/29/how-breakdance-is-promoting-positive-culture-in-leeds. Accessed 1 December 2021.

Speers, Laura (2014), 'Keepin' it real: Negotiating authenticity in the London hip hop scene', Ph.D. thesis, London: Kings College London.

Stevenson, Alex (2017), 'Hip-hop in the UK', in Horn, David (ed.) *Bloomsbury Encyclopedia of Popular Music of the World, Volume 11: Genres: Europe, Bloomsbury Academic*, 1st ed., Bloomsbury Publishing, pp. 394–8.

Testament (2021), online video interview with S. Little and A. Stevenson, 15 November.

Weston, Paul (2021), online video interview with S. Little and A Stevenson, 10 October.

Williams, Justin A. (2020), *Brithop: The Politics of UK Rap in the New Century*, Oxford: Oxford University Press.

Woods, Orlando (2019), 'Special Issue: Sonic spaces, spiritual bodies: The affective experience of the roots reggae soundsystem', *Transactions of the Institute of British Geographers*, 44:1, pp. 181–94.

# 17

# A Splendid Time Is Guaranteed for All: A Psychogeography of Leeds' Popular Music Heritage

*Brett Lashua and Paul Thompson*

In the modernizing spirit of the 1970s, Leeds was once celebrated as the 'Motorway City of the North' (Douglas 2009: 35). With staggering configurations of highways and arterial roads, Leeds is a sprawling metropolis that is, perhaps, not best characterized as a space for walking. Neither is it widely considered a 'music city' (Ballico and Watson 2020) in terms of producing global music superstars nor having iconic venues or vaunted recording studios, which often comprise sites of a city's popular music heritage (Gibson and Connell 2007). In this chapter, we draw these lines together – walking the 'music city' – as we explored Leeds' popular music heritage on foot.

Because both of us have lived or worked in Leeds for over a decade, we followed Lashua and Cohen's (2010: 82) advice that strolling through a city can provide 'important examples of a "discovery of coincidence" (Augé 2002) triggered by walking'. Walking presents embodied ways to experience, remember and discover new understandings of the city, mediated by space and place. In this, we hoped to encounter the materiality of Leeds' musical past through a series of excursions in which the city inspired and impelled our movements. Also described as psychogeographic tours or *dérives* (Debord [1958] 1995), our walks involved drifting or going with the flow of where the city took us. Debord ([1958] 1995: 50) explained:

> In a dérive one or more persons [...] let themselves be drawn by the attractions of the terrain and the encounters they find there. Chance is a less important factor in this activity than one might think: from a dérive point of view cities have psychogeographical contours, with constant currents, fixed points and vortexes that strongly discourage entry into or exit from certain zones.

Psychogeographical walks often involve intentionally 'getting lost' (Lucas 2008: 91) in anticipation of new insights. In such seemingly un-purposeful ambulation through Leeds, our purpose was to explore the following questions: where might we find Leeds' popular music heritage? What tangible materiality provides links to the city's music heritage and history? How do our encounters with this tangible heritage relate to published accounts of Leeds' musical past?

During the summer of 2021, we conducted a series of musical heritage walking tours (Cantillon 2020; Johinke 2018; Long 2014; Sledmere 2018). We wandered and traced lines through Leeds, from sites of historic events and heritage plaques to hallowed pubs, from vanished clubs to (nearly) forgotten venues, and also graves. While some sites are designated with heritage markers (see Draganova and Blackman 2018; Roberts and Cohen 2015), others are what Sadler called 'obscure places' (Sadler 1998: 76; see also Long 2014: 51): the not-quite hidden but easily overlooked sites of the historical and musical city before our eyes and beneath our feet (Lipsitz 2007).

Our psychogeographical approaches were varied, which we recount below as three walks. Along the way, the chapter navigates theories of affective atmospheres, new materialisms and thanatourism as we encountered sites of Leeds' popular music heritage – where it was legible on the city's surfaces. First, we begin with the smattering of texts that have previously mapped Leeds' popular music heritage sites as guides for our explorations. These included Karl Whitney's (2019) account of music in northern English cities, *Hit Factories: A Journey Through the Industrial Cities of British Pop*, a music tourism guidebook, Perry and Glinert's (1998) *Rock & Roll Traveller Great Britain and Ireland: The Ultimate Guide to Famous Rock Hangouts Past and Present*, and a touristic Great British Music Map (2018). These texts offered brief and sometimes ghostly engagements with Leeds; many sites noted in Perry and Glinert (1998) no longer exist, while Whitney aimed to 'trace the life and death of the British music industry through its [often vanished or former] physical locations' (2019: 2). Sometimes our walks involved no maps. Here we drifted in anticipation of surprises, alerted to us in the spirit of Dutch *Stolpersteine* ('stumbling stones'). *Stolpersteine* are brass memorial plaques 'embedded in the street that call on passers-by to remember' events of the Second World War; they also prompt 'a mental "stumbling"' to consider the past (Rankin 2021: n.pag.). One moment of 'stumbling' is central to our second walk, when we encountered an unexpected art installation in a pedestrian underpass. Our final walk began at a site we had heard of but never visited – the grave of Pablo Fanque. Fanque was a Victorian circus star later immortalized in John Lennon's lyrics for the Beatles' song 'Being for the Benefit of Mr. Kite!' (1967). Fanque's grave linked us to other sites in the city; however, it is unremarked in the few published accounts that document the varied sites of Leeds' popular music heritage, where we begin with our first walk.

## Walk 1: 'Atmospheres' and re-mapping popular music heritage

In *Hit Factories: A Journey Through the Industrial Cities of British Pop* (2019), Karl Whitney visited Leeds (amongst other British cities) and walked its streets, starting from Leeds' bus station, ambling along the Headrow, through its universities and student neighbourhoods of back-to-back housing, then looping back into its centre. Whitney sought connections between the city and its music that were 'dark and compelling' and described his search as 'tapping into the atmosphere of a city' (2019: 117). In similar terms, Böhme (2017: 1) referred to the 'tuned space of an atmosphere' (2017: 28) in cities which:

> engages the affectivity of people; it affects their mind, manipulates moods, and evokes emotions. This power does not appear as such, it rather impacts the unconscious. Although it operates in the realm of the senses, it is nevertheless invisible and more difficult to grasp than any other power.

This sensibility chimes with both the physicality of the material urban environment and the intangibility of music. Böhme (2017: 35) adds that, while elusive, affective atmospheres 'constitute real social power' in shaping the relations between people and the materialities of things, places and spaces. Also referred to as 'attuned spaces', atmospheres are *'the sphere of felt bodily presence'* (Böhme 2017: 70, original emphasis) such as dark, cold, gloomy, gothic, decaying or post-industrial characterizations so often (mis)used to describe Leeds. Atmospheres also invoke psychogeographic practice, in attempts to understand relations between moving through material urban environments and the psychic, daily lives of individuals, i.e., the 'feel' of a city.

For Whitney (2019) the dark and compelling atmosphere of Leeds' music is interlaced with its materiality. Whitney is 'fascinated by the physicality of pop [...] communicated through objects – records or posters or magazines' (2019: 97) which fostered his interest in record shops, then ignited questions of the physicality and sense or 'tuned space' of a city. Whitney aimed to 'trace the life and death' of British music industries through their physical locations by 'visiting the venues, the studios, the terraced houses, and the students' unions: the landscape of pop' (2019: 2). Specifically searching outside London, Whitney was drawn to cities in northern coalfields, fringe ports and places once dominated by manufacturing and mills, such as Leeds. He searched for the darker atmospheres (or, perhaps, *detuned* spaces) of the 'post-industrial edges of the country's regional cities' (2019: 11).

The use of former industrial or warehouse spaces for popular music venues is nothing new, with a lineage from Liverpool's Cavern Club (cellars formerly used as produce storage for nearby St. Johns Market) to innumerable venues for disco, house (e.g. The Warehouse in Chicago, where DJ Frankie Knuckles popularized what became known as 'house' music in the late 1970s), techno, acid house and later dance music styles. Leeds also has a longstanding venue (since 1979) called The Warehouse (19-21 Somers Street) and venues in former mills. Walking along the Leeds-Liverpool canal, we passed the now-defunct Canal Mills nightclub. These venues inspired us to reflect on how once-industrial spaces have become (temporary) sites of student nightlife and live music performances. Almost twenty years ago, Chatterton and Hollands (2004: 266) commented on changing perceptions and uses of the city:

> Who could fail to notice that Leeds' city centre has been comprehensively transformed over the last decade or so? [...] A once semi-derelict city centre, known more for its ugly decaying buildings and a smattering of rough pubs and discos has been redeveloped into what people call the 'London of the North', replete with imposing new office blocks, pavement cafés and cutting edge bars and cool clubs, playing music late into the night.

Catering to over 65,000 students attending its universities and colleges, Leeds' more recent civic identity has relied upon a magnetic 'return to the centre' driven by a 'new urban entertainment economy' (Hollands and Chatterton 2003: 363). This included the addition of a 13,500-person capacity arena in 2013, transforming an area of brutalist 1960s-era office blocks and outdated shopping centres into a nascent cultural district branded 'the Arena Quarter'. Not only a symbol of urban renaissance, Leeds Arena also re-established the city's first large concert venue since the closure of Queens Hall in 1989. Queens Hall, described in Perry and Glinert (1998: 250) as 'a now-demolished, freezing old tram shed', was just south of Leeds' central rail station. It is now the site of towering new offices, flats and restaurants where we stopped for refreshment following our first dérive, momentarily unaware that we were on the site of the former venue with nothing there to denote its heritage.

Leeds Civic Trust maintains over 100 official blue plaque heritage markers in the Leeds area, yet only one is related to popular music, designating the site of The Who's 1970 'Live at Leeds' performance at Leeds University's student union. Surveying this space nearly 50 years later, Whitney (2019: 102) reflected:

> I found a large dimly lit hall with a parquet wooden floor whose blocks were arranged in a herringbone pattern. Students were sitting at tables, eating dinner, and I felt slightly confused that the building had functioned as a venue for what had been, in 1970, one of the biggest rock bands in Britain.

During the 1970s, Leeds' colleges and universities were key sites for concerts and musicians. Many Leeds' musicians were 'educated in art schools, including Gang of Four, The Mekons, Scritti Politti and Soft Cell' (Whitney 2019: 102). For students inspired by Marxist perspectives, punk and post-punk produced urban atmospheres that were 'explicitly political' (Whitney 2019: 104) in capitalist critique and subversion. Arguably far less radical now, Leeds has shifted from its social democratic roots and collective ethos to 'burgeoning neo-liberalism [...] new entrepreneurialism [...] and rampant individualism' in a 'new corporate city' (Douglas 2009: 36). Nowhere is this depoliticization more evident than in the reconfigured dream palaces of Leeds' new shopping centres and student-consumer-centred nightlife.

We read Whitney's mapping of Leeds' musical heritage along with two other texts: the Great British Music Map (2018), a fold-out map showcasing selected sites across the United Kingdom; and Glinert and Perry's (1998) *Rock & Roll Traveler Great Britain and Ireland: The Ultimate Guide to Famous Rock Hangouts Past and Present*. We used these resources to (dis)orient ourselves in our walking tours of Leeds, particularly noting longstanding nodes and landmarks, but also absences on the ground versus what was in print. The Great British Music Map (2018) spotlights just five venues in Leeds: The Brudenell Social Club, Leeds University Student Union, The Lending Room, First Direct Arena and Oporto (a small indie venue in the city's central entertainment district). Additionally, the map characterizes Leeds as:

> Home to the Sisters of Mercy and goth rock | Leeds half of the Reading and Leeds festivals | The Who's album Live at Leeds was recorded at the University of Leeds's refectory in 1970 | From Leeds [...] Corinne Bailey Rae, Soft Cell, Chumbawumba, Kaiser Chiefs, Alt-J, Mel B (Spice Girls), The Pigeon Detectives and the Wedding Present | Black Lace, responsible for 'Agadoo', were voted Yorkshire Band of the Year in 1977 by BBC Radio Leeds.
>
> (2018: n.pag.)

This particular and peculiar assemblage of musicians, venues and festivals highlights how Leeds' music heritage is difficult to characterize through a mainstream lens or unifying master narrative (e.g. Liverpool and The Beatles). As Lewis explained, 'people look to specific music as symbolic anchors in regions, as signs of community, belonging and a shared past' (Lewis 1992: 144). In this way, musical scenes are connected to particular towns or cities, which Miller and Schofield (2017: 141) argued 'have the potential to reassign values to a place [...], being constructed through a spatially concentrated infrastructure [...] that develops often from live performance'. Given that so much of Leeds' live performance infrastructure has either disappeared or changed, it is unsurprising that Leeds' musical heritage landscape is one characterized by 1970s punk and post-punk and 1980s Goth, when prominent area bands gained wider recognition.

In their *Rock & Roll Traveller of Great Britain and Ireland*, Perry and Glinert (1998) noted Leeds 'is reputed to have the best club scene outside of London'; however, 'with a lack of music industry in Leeds, groups have always had to look elsewhere' (1998: 248). Many groups are listed chronologically, but only from the late 1970s including Gang of Four, The Mekons, Scritti Politti and Delta 5. Notable groups from the 1980s include Soft Cell, Sisters of Mercy and The Wedding Present. Moving into the 1990s, attention turns to 'gothy' Red Lorry Yellow Lorry and 'March Violet' [sic], as well as 'anarchic' Chumbawumba (1998: 249). Interestingly, attention is also offered to rap musicians Credit to the Nation, and Black Star Liner, acknowledging some of the city's richer musical diversity.

As for venues, Perry and Glinert (1998) identified less than a dozen in which the student unions for Leeds University and Leeds Polytechnic (now Leeds Beckett) University are prominent, as is Roundhay Park (see Mills, this volume). The Town and Country Club is heralded as the city's main venue, along with the Cockpit for indie bands (see Lomax, this volume). Perry and Glinert celebrated The Warehouse as the site of a Stone Roses gig in 1989, although it is now primarily a dance music venue. A few pubs are noted, including the 'sweaty surrounds' (Perry and Glinert 1998: 249) of The Fenton (see Goldhammer, this volume) and The Duchess of York. Although not elaborated by Perry and Glinert (1998), 'The Duchess' (71 Vicar Lane) hosted indie and punk bands from the late 1980s and was renowned for early performances by up-and-coming groups such as Blur, Oasis, Pulp, Coldplay and Nirvana. The sofa in the venue's office where Nirvana's Kurt Cobain slept after their 1989 gig became legendary (Heritage Venue Project 2020). Closed in 2000, the building is now a Hugo Boss clothes store; we walked by and had to turn back, not realizing the address. Oddly, Perry and Glinert (1998) identify the (above-mentioned) Queens Hall; the venue had been closed for nine years at the time of publication and appears on the page like a ghost.

Retracing the mappings produced by these published accounts then showcased connections and disconnections in sites of Leeds' popular music heritage. The texts highlighted where Leeds' popular music heritage has ossified around a few well-known nodes (Cohen 2012), such as The Who's (1970) 'Live at Leeds' concert. They also celebrated vanished landmarks such as Queens Hall and the Duchess of York. The Duchess still has a strong community resonance as showcased by a dedicated Facebook page, 'I Miss The Duchess of York Leeds' (Miller and Schofield 2017). This resonance is part of 'the atmosphere of the city' (Whitney 2019: 117), which is manifest in Leeds' popular music heritage, even if the city is no longer as radical, dark, gothic, decaying or industrial as it once was.

## Walk 2: 'Song Tunnel' and the material city

Starting from one (of five) Leeds venues noted in the Great British Music Map (2018), The Lending Room, we walked south on Woodhouse Lane (A660), past several university campuses, and the pub venue The Fenton. At this point, on the northern edge of the city centre, several arterial roads converge over the city's sunken ring road (A58 Motorway). Here we encountered a brightly blue and yellow tiled underpass, connecting pedestrians (and cyclists) to the city centre and the Arena Quarter. To our surprise, the tunnel houses an art installation by Adrian Riley (see Figure 17.1), commissioned by Leeds City Council, titled 'Song Tunnel' (Riley 2013). With typographic metal panels featuring the names of 60 artists, songs and albums related to Leeds, Song Tunnel is a kind of wall of fame. Its intention is:

> to represent Leeds popular music scene in its widest sense, from early 20th century music hall to contemporary urban music and celebrate both those who 'made it big' as well as the equally important bands and individuals whose music has been an essential part of the character of the city.
>
> (Riley 2013: n.pag.)

Music celebrated in Song Tunnel as part of Leeds' essential character includes 'Power to the beats' from Utah Saints' album *Two* (2000), The March Violets' 'Lights go out' c/w 'Walk into the sun' (1984), Nightmares on Wax 'Time to listen' from 1995's *Smokers delight*, and Sisters of Mercy's 'More' from their 1990 album *Vision thing*.

FIGURE 17.1: Leeds 'Song Tunnel' (left), with close-up view (right). Courtesy of Paul Thompson.

Although typographical and representational, there is also a distinct materiality to the Song Tunnel, which interested us in two ways. First, the Song Tunnel acted as a kind of *Stolpersteine* (stumbling stone), inviting us to pause, remember and reflect on the past. Back and forth we walked through the underpass, stopping to discuss bands we spotted on the walls and taking photos. Secondly, this surprise discovery reminded us of the materiality of popular music heritage, and how relationships between music, place and the past are 'mediated and made tangible' (Stengs 2018: 236).

Within the broader scholarship on materiality (Thrift 2008), there has been a (re)turn to questions of how matter *matters* (Barad 2003). This 'new materialist' turn is a response to a perceived over-emphasis on language and representation. For Barad, the return to materiality arose from 'an important sense in which the only thing that does not seem to matter anymore is matter' (2003: 801). Accordingly, Barad argued for rethinking the relationship between materiality and representation, shifting away from human-centred understandings. Barad (2003) invited attention to 'intra-active' relationships between humans, spaces, temporalities, lived experiences, things and materials. These relational materialities shape human activity, physically, as well as socially and culturally. A city or a music venue has material effects on those who temporarily inhabit it (i.e. dwelling in place); in this sense, the concrete materiality of popular music heritage sites *matters*, too.

In this framework, material objects – such as a pedestrian tunnel's walls – are understood as agentic because they act upon people's movements (e.g. walking), emotions and memories. For Ahmed (2017: 137), an object, such as a wall, 'is a finding. Let me summarize that finding: what stops movement moves'. Here, Ahmed uses the word 'moves' to invoke emotions and feelings. Adapting Raymond Williams' (1977) 'structures of feeling', Ahmed (2010: 216) flips the phrase to 'feelings of structure' to invoke relations between individual emotions or memories that are prompted or conjured by 'bumping into' material things that somehow 'contain' them – buildings, walls and other things (e.g. vinyl records). In the Song Tunnel, which took us beneath Leeds' arterial roadways, we encountered walls as a vital reminder of the city's materiality and a memorialization of artists, songs and albums that are analogously 'beneath' the city's better-known musical heritage. In sync with our psychogeographical tours of the city, we stumbled upon the Song Tunnel as a 'finding' while intentionally drifting. The Song Tunnel not only connected points on the pathways of our walking tours, but it also reconnected us with Leeds, viscerally and materially, as well as psychically and emotionally. The Song Tunnel brings agentic materiality to the affective (atmospheric) presence of music heritage in our everyday lives: it *moved* us as we moved through it.

## Walk 3: Pablo Fanque and Thanatourism

A gravestone is a material heritage marker and visiting sites such as cemeteries has been referred to as a form of thanatourism (Seaton 1996). Because of its associations with death and morbidity, thanatourism is also known as dark tourism (Stone and Sharpley 2008) as well as black spot tourism (Rojek 1993; Sledmere 2018). The graves of many famous musicians such as Jim Morrison's (in Paris) are well-known sites of thanatourism, but other sites include the houses or places near where musicians passed away. Graves-Brown and Orange (2021) highlighted the spontaneous shrine created in a park across from Amy Winehouse's former home in Camden, north London. Fans left flowers, scrawled graffiti on walls and pavements, and decorated trees with messages to the singer. In another Winehouse example, Sledmere (2018) wrote of Winehouse's (2006) song 'Back to Black', with its gothic music video (and ominously dramatized burial of Winehouse) filmed in London's Abney Park cemetery. Offering a 'psychogeographic overview of the cemetery's space', Sledmere (2018: 130) invited a reconsideration of the uncanny relationships between popular music, people and place through the space of a cemetery. This thanatoptic view (Seaton 1996) affords a deeper engagement with the 'dark currents' and 'uncanny resonances' and 'strange coincidence and serendipity' (Sledmere 2018: 117, 131, 118) of life and death to be encountered in the tangible and affective sites of popular musicians' graves, cemeteries and other memorial sites. Here, we turn to our final example, a walking tour to visit the grave of Pablo Fanque. While we had heard that Fanque was buried in Leeds, we were not sure where or why in Leeds.

Born William Darby in Ipswich in 1796 (or 1810), Pablo Fanque was a renowned black Victorian circus owner and equestrian showman (Turner 2003). His circus frequently toured Britain, particularly northern circuits around Lancashire and Yorkshire, through cities such as Bradford, Sheffield, Manchester and Leeds. Although he died in 1871, Fanque re-entered popular culture after his name appeared in John Lennon's lyrics for the Beatles' song 'Being for the benefit of Mr. Kite!' (1967) on the *Sgt Peppers* album. Lennon drew inspiration from an antique circus poster he purchased in January 1967 from a shop in Sevenoaks, Kent whilst making promotional films for 'Strawberry Fields Forever' and 'Penny Lane' (1967). Lennon's lyrics read almost directly from the poster, which advertised a fundraiser for the recently retired circus performer Mr. Kite in 1843. The lyrics make only a brief indirect mention of Fanque, stating 'The Hendersons' will all be there, 'late of Pablo Fanque's Fair'.

Fanque is buried in Leeds' St. George's Field, near his first wife Susannah, who preceded him (see Figure 17.2). Formerly called Woodhouse Cemetery, St. George's Field is both a cemetery and a park, now part of the University of Leeds. Susannah's gravestone reads: 'The beloved wife of William Darby, equestrian manager, professionally known as Pablo Fanque'. Susannah's death was deemed accidental, 'occasioned by the falling of a portion of the circus erected in King Charles' Croft, Leeds on Saturday the 18th day of March 1848' (as written on her gravestone). King Charles' Croft was a short lane in Leeds' city centre just south of a main east–west thoroughfare, The Headrow, bordered by venues including the Theatre Royal and Hippodrome, where a grandstand had been erected (and fell). Fanque (and his circus) would regularly visit Leeds to perform during tours spanning the 30-odd years of his circus career. Otherwise, there doesn't appear to be any further connection or reason why Fanque (who later remarried) should be interred in Leeds. On the ground in front of his first wife's gravestone, Fanque's memorial simply reads: 'Also the above named William Darby • Pablo Fanque who died May 4th 1871 aged 75 years'. While there is widespread interest in sites with Beatles connections, or what Ingham (2009: 235) referred to as 'landmarks of Beatles lore', Fanque's grave remains one of the more obscure places with associations to the Fab Four.

Going one step further by connecting the mappings of Leeds (in walk 1, above), Pablo Fanque and The Beatles, we uncovered another uncanny resonance between Fanque and Leeds. In *Hit Factories*, Whitney recounts that musician Jon King (of Leeds post-punk group Gang of Four) had a chance encounter in 1967, 'running into three of the Beatles as they emerged from the antique shop in which Lennon had bought the poster that would inspire the song "Being for the benefit of Mr Kite!"' (2019: 103). Despite time spent walking in Leeds, Whitney remained one step away from making the connection between Leeds and Pablo Fanque via Jon King and the Beatles. As a site of thanatourism, Fanque's grave then is a peculiar and unique location in Leeds' popular music heritage because it represents a 'strange coincidence and serendipity' (Sledmere 2018: 118) encountered through material heritage and psychogeographic practice.

## *Conclusion*

This chapter has only scratched the surface(s) of popular music heritage during our psychogeographical tours (dérives) through Leeds. Yet, scratching the surface by walking brought us into contact with Leeds' topographies to see, stumble or discover – often in surprise – the physical presence, but also absence, of the city's popular music heritage, on the ground and on its walls. We began by retracing three mappings of Leeds' popular music heritage (Whitney 2019; Great British Music Map 2018; Perry and Glinert 1998) to better understand the 'atmospheres' of Leeds. These mappings provided useful starting points to explore connections and disconnections between the city and its music. Whitney found both to be 'dark

FIGURE 17.2: The gravestones of Susannah (standing) and William Darby (and with Brett Lashua, foreground). Photo courtesy of Paul Thompson.

and compelling' (2019: 117), whilst the Great British Music Map (2018: n.pag.) characterized Leeds through goth rock, rock festivals and The Who's (1970) 'Live at Leeds'. In this, the 'tuned spaces of atmospheres' (Böhme 2017: 28) of Leeds' popular music heritage had become static and essentialized. Walking through the city allowed us to see beyond the heritage discourses produced and reproduced through the mappings in these texts.

During our second walk, a dérive along Woodhouse Lane, we stumbled upon the 'Song Tunnel' (Riley 2013) in a pedestrian underpass. Acting as a vital materialization and memorialization of musicians, songs and albums, the

Song Tunnel connected points on the pathways of our walking tours beneath Leeds' complex road system; it also provided deeper links to popular music heritage that are 'beneath' or not as well-remembered as other artists from Leeds. In this way, the Song Tunnel reconnected us with the city, viscerally and materially, as well as psychically and emotionally; bringing materiality to the affective presence of music in our everyday lives by the way it *moved us* as we moved through it.

Finally, our third walk focused on the materiality of visiting a gravestone as thanatourism (Seaton 1996). Recasting an unfamiliar link to popular music through the Beatles song 'Being for the benefit of Mr. Kite!' (1967), we found the tombstones of Pablo Fanque, the black Victorian circus owner, and his wife Susannah, in Leeds' St. George's Field. This material starting point of discovery connected with other stories and uncovered further links with Fanque and Leeds. In this way, thanatourism is a form of popular music heritage tourism that can lead to 'uncanny resonances' and 'strange coincidence and serendipity' (Sledmere 2018: 131, 118). Fanque's grave allowed us to see beyond the sites and events that have become concretized in heritage discourses in Leeds.

In drifting through Leeds, we searched for tangible and material links to the city's popular musical past. We mapped our encounters vis-à-vis published accounts, and we moved (and were moved) not only beneath its streets but also beneath the dominant narratives of Leeds' musical heritages. We ended at a gravestone that connected us with wider heritages both within and beyond the city. In exploring these sites and stories we sought to expand our understanding of Leeds' popular music heritage – beyond post-punk, goth rock and synth pop, or the nightclub scenes of the 1990s. We found that popular music heritage has a faint physical imprint in Leeds, an almost ghostly presence that nevertheless may (re)appear to those who embrace getting lost, psychogeographically. And for those looking for it, *a splendid time is guaranteed for all*.

## REFERENCES

Ahmed, Sara (2010), *The Promise of Happiness*, Durham: Duke University Press.

Ahmed, Sara (2017), *Living a Feminist Life*, Durham: Duke University Press.

Augé, Marc (2002), *In the Metro*, Minneapolis: University of Minnesota Press.

Ballico, Christina and Watson, Allan (eds) (2020), *Music Cities: Evaluating a Global Cultural Policy Concept*, Cham: Palgrave Macmillan.

Barad, Karen (2003), 'Posthumanist performativity: Toward an understanding of how matter comes to matter', *Signs: Journal of Women in Culture and Society*, 28:3: pp. 801–31.

Böhme, Gernot (2017), *Atmospheric Architectures: The Aesthetics of Felt Spaces*, London: Routledge.

Cantillon, Zelmarie (2020), 'Urban heritage walks in a rapidly changing city: Tensions between preservation and development on the Gold Coast, Australia', *Journal of Heritage Tourism*, 15:2, pp. 149–63.

Chatterton, Paul and Hollands, Robert (2004), 'The London of the North? Youth cultures, urban change and nightlife', in R. Unsworth and J. Stilwell (eds), *Twenty First Century Leeds: Geographies of a Regional City*, Leeds: Leeds University Press, pp. 265–91.

Cohen, Sara (2012), 'Bubbles, tracks, borders and lines: Mapping music and urban landscape', *Journal of the Royal Musical Association*, 137:1, pp. 135–70.

Debord, Guy ([1958] 1995), *Situationist International Anthology*, (ed. and trans. K. Knabb), Berkeley: Bureau of Public Secrets.

Douglas, Janet (2009), 'Cranes over the city: The centre of Leeds, 1980–2008', in P. Bramham and S. Wagg (eds), *Sport, Leisure and Culture in the Postmodern City*, Farnham: Ashgate, pp. 33–62.

Draganova, Asya and Blackman, Shane (2018), 'No blue plaques "in the Land of Grey and Pink": The Canterbury Sound, heritage and the alternative relationships of popular music and place', in S. Holland and K. Spracklen (eds), *Subcultures, Bodies and Spaces: Essays on Alternativity and Marginalization*, Bingley: Emerald Publishing, pp. 219–37.

Gibson, Chris and Connell, John (2007), 'Music, tourism and the transformation of Memphis', *Tourism Geographies*, 9:2, pp. 160–90.

Graves-Brown, Paul and Orange, Hillary (2021), 'Station to station: Rock music memorial roots and routes in London', in L. Mahoney and J. Schofield (eds), *Music and Heritage: New Perspectives on Place-Making and Sonic Identity*, London: Routledge, pp. 222–32.

Great British Music Map (2018), *Fold Out Map: Strumpshaw, Tincleton & Giggleswick's Marvellous Maps*, Honiton: Marvellous Maps.

Heritage Venue Project (2020), 'Duchess of York, Leeds,' Heritage Venue Project, 4 May, https://heritagevenueprojectcom.wordpress.com/2020/05/04/duchess-of-york-leeds/. Accessed 26 November 2021.

Hollands, Robert and Chatterton, Paul (2003), 'Producing nightlife in the new urban entertainment economy: Corporatization, branding and market segmentation', *International Journal of Urban and Regional Research*, 27:2, pp. 361–85.

Ingham, Chris (2009), *The Rough Guide to the Beatles*, 3rd ed., London: Rough Guides Ltd.

Johinke, Rebecca (2018), 'Take a walk on the wild side: Punk music walking tours in New York City', *Tourist Studies*, 18:3, pp. 315–31.

Lashua, Brett and Cohen, Sara (2010), 'Liverpool musicscapes: Music performance, movement and the built urban environment', in B. Fincham, M. McGuinness and L. Murray (eds), *Mobile Methodologies*, London: Palgrave Macmillan, pp. 71–84.

Lewis, George H. (1992), 'Who do you love?: The dimensions of musical taste', in J. Lull (ed.), *Popular Music and Communication*, 2nd ed., London: Sage, pp. 134–51.

Lipsitz, George (2007), *Footsteps in the Dark: The Hidden Histories of Popular Music*, Minneapolis: University of Minnesota Press.

Long, Philip (2014), 'Popular music, psychogeography, place identity and tourism: The case of Sheffield', *Tourist Studies*, 14:1, pp. 48–65.

Lucas, Raymond (2008), 'Getting lost in Tokyo', *Footprint*, 2, pp. 91–104.

Miller, Dan and Schofield, John (2017), 'The "Toilet Circuit": Cultural production, fandom and heritage in England's small music venues', *Heritage & Society*, 9:2, pp. 137–67.

Perry, Tim and Glinert, Ed (1998), *Rock & Roll Traveler Great Britain and Ireland: The Ultimate Guide to Famous Rock Hangouts Past and Present*, New York: Fodor's.

Rankin, Jennifer (2021), 'Amsterdam's "stumbling stones" commemorate gay victims of Nazis', *The Guardian*, 6 August, https://www.theguardian.com/world/2021/aug/06/amsterdam-stumbling-stones-commemorate-gay-victims-of-nazis. Accessed 16 August 2021.

Riley, Adrian (2013–), *Song Tunnel*, installation, Woodhouse Lane pedestrian subway, Leeds, 1 August 2013–present, http://www.songtunnel.info. Accessed 20 October 2021.

Roberts, Les and Cohen, Sara (2015), 'Unveiling memory: Blue plaques as in/tangible markers of popular music heritage', in S. Cohen, R. Knifton, M. Leonard and L. Roberts (eds), *Sites of Popular Music Heritage: Memories, Histories, Places*, London: Routledge, pp. 221–38.

Rojek, Chris (1993), *Ways of Escape*, Basingstoke: Macmillan.

Sadler, Simon (1998), *The Situationist City*, Cambridge: MIT Press.

Seaton, Anthony V. (1996), 'Guided by the dark: From thanatopsis to thanatourism', *International Journal of Heritage Studies*, 2:4, pp. 234–44.

Sledmere, Adrian (2018), 'Amy Winehouse: "Back to Black" and the gothic', *Journal of the International Association for the Study of Popular Music*, 8:1, pp. 117–35.

Stengs, Irene (2018), 'Popular music and commemorative ritual: A material approach', in S. Baker, C. Strong, L. Istvandity and Z. Cantillon (eds), *The Routledge Companion to Popular Music History and Heritage*, London: Routledge, pp. 229–37.

Stone, Philip and Sharpley, Richard (2008), 'Consuming dark tourism: A thanatological perspective', *Annals of Tourism Research*, 35:2, pp. 574–95.

Thrift, Nigel (2008), 'The material practices of glamour', *Journal of Cultural Economy*, 1:1, pp. 9–23.

Turner, John M. (2003), 'Pablo fanque, Black circus proprietor', in G. H. Gerzina (ed.), *Black Victorians, Black Victoriana*, New Brunswick: Rutgers University Press, pp. 20–38.

Whitney, Karl (2019), *Hit Factories: A Journey Through the Industrial Cities of British Pop*, London: Weidenfeld and Nicolson.

Williams, Raymond (1977), *Marxism and Literature*, Oxford: Oxford University Press.

# 18

# Music:Leeds –
# Supporting a Regionalized
# Music Sector and Scene

*Paul Thompson and Sam Nicholls*

Over the last two decades, local authorities and city governance have recognized that 'culture is a key tool for promoting sustainable urban development through the safeguarding of cultural heritage and the promotion of the diversity of cultural expressions' (UNESCO 2016: 3). Culture is used as part of urban regeneration strategies to 'create a new cosmopolitan image. In an atmosphere of growing inter-urban competition, increasing mobility of capital and the waning importance of physical location factors, cities now profile themselves by investing in the cultural and creative sectors' (Van der Hoeven and Hitters 2019: 263). Popular music, and the activity that surrounds it, has become a significant part of these culture-led regeneration strategies (Ross 2017) where music events for example are used to help cultivate inclusivity, promote social cohesion or reinvigorate urban spaces (Cohen 2013; Holt and Wergin 2013). As an extension of one-off or a series of curated events, a 'Music City' is a term that describes an urban environment that has the ideal conditions to take advantage of the cultural and musical fabric to support and nurture its musical economy (Baker 2017; Terrill et al. 2015). A 'Music City' emphasizes elements of creative development and business growth, placemaking and tourism, access to music-making and music events as well as supporting the existing music scene.

Since the formation of Berlin's Club Commission in 2001, and following the dissolution of Regional Development Agencies in 2012, UK local government's remit has expanded to include the stimulation and support of regionalized music sectors and scenes. These support opportunities have taken different forms such as sector-led initiatives and government-imposed leadership structures in order to improve aspects of the music economy such as protecting a city's night-time economy and developing access to music education and a link to the wider skills agenda. Some UK cities have formulated City Region Music Boards (e.g. London, Greater Manchester, Liverpool and Sheffield) to help provide a more formal and unified strategy to influence music policy and provide consultancy on a local level and implement a regional music strategy. The city of Leeds, which is situated in the North of England, originally developed a dedicated culture strategy alongside the region's proposed bid to become the European Capital of Culture in 2023. In light of the UK's exit from the European Union, and subsequently the disqualification of Leeds from the bidding process, Leeds City Council declared 2023 as a year of culture with a determined approach to improve its arts and culture offering. In addressing music as part of this offering, Leeds City Council consulted with the newly formulated independent organization 'Music:Leeds', which has now undertaken a strategic partnership with Leeds City Council in establishing programmes with funding from national bodies including Arts Council England and PRS Foundation, as well as wider support from other major music industry bodies such as UK Music and Association of Independent Music.

This chapter discusses a range of strategies and initiatives that have been implemented across the city of Leeds with a critical evaluation of the ways in which models from other European cities, feedback and opinion from music professionals, consultation from government officials in Leeds and guidance documents from professional bodies and global consultancy agencies (i.e. Sound Diplomacy and the International Federation of the Phonographic Industry) have been implemented in the development of the city's strategy to stimulate music activity around Music:Leeds' three core areas of activity: Creative Development & Business Growth; Placemaking & Tourism; and Access to Music.

*Context*

A city's Creative and Cultural Economy (CCE) has been defined as 'any human activity that embodies symbolic meaning or is shaped by cultural factors that can be construed as contributing to the cultural vitality of the city' (Hutton 2004: 91). Musical activity is therefore part of a broader creative sector that not only includes the arts, design, fashion and bespoke manufacturing (Baird and Scott 2018) but forms a fundamental part of the global CCE agenda. Live music in particular is a central focus for development within numerous city and local authority CCE strategies because it is a significant contributor to the urban cultural economy. For example, the economic value of live music in the UK accounts for almost 25 per cent of the music industry's £4.5 billion contribution to the UK economy (UKMusic 2018: 8). City and local authorities have come to recognize that music activity and specifically live music is a crucial indicator of a city's cultural and economic vitality, a city's attractiveness as a place to live and an important stream of employment for modern musicians and occupations that support music-making in a digital era (Holt 2010).

Strategies around emphasizing the creative sectors of a city have taken many forms over the lifespan of their implementation but have typically centred upon urban live music policy (Behr et al. 2016; Evans 2009; Gibson and Stevenson 2004; Hudson 2006). Some policies around music activity in cities have been shown to be part of a broader cultural strategy (Hutton 2009; O'Connor and Shaw 2014) or form part of an approach to address noise, gentrification or zoning of the night-time economy within a local authority's urban planning policy (e.g. Gibson and Homan 2004; Homan 2008; Homan 2010; Homan 2014; Homan 2017; Strong et al. 2017). There are CCE policies that are often arguably 'neo-liberal economic policies rather than cultural policies' (Atkinson and Easthope 2009: 69). For example, strategies that sideline creators and artists, emphasize short-lived rather than sustainable cultural activities or create further precariousness in an already precarious labour market are indicators of a neo-liberal economic approach that overlook the interconnected cultural factors beyond the purely economic (Koefoed 2013; Pratt 2008; Scott 2006; Vivant 2013; Zukin 1987; Zukin 1995). Consequently, there are different approaches to designing and implementing CCE strategies and this is often because different actors such as policy-makers, consultancy firms and music industry support organizations have differing views and interests when emphasizing the importance of live music within these CCE strategies.

Despite these differences, a number of common approaches, methods and policies have been implemented across the world to create 'Music Cities' in which 'hard' and 'soft' institutional policies are introduced to support live music activity. For example, as part of a $45 million grant, the national music funding body of Canada (Music Canada) developed a series of short-term, medium-term and long-term strategies in which music was integrated with the connected areas of tourism, heritage, city development and urban planning for the city of Toronto (City of Toronto Strategic Plan 2016; Hracs 2009). Live music activity is supported through 'hard' institutional policy which relates to issues of noise for live music venues/zones within new or existing urban developments and 'soft' institutional implementation in which a dedicated live music office was set up as a central point of contact for musicians, venue owners and promoters to access information relating to: 'noise attenuation, liquor licensing, and building code issues. Here government departments, music businesses and non-profit music related entities share space, ideas and strategies at one location' (Baird and Scott 2018: 3).

The city of Brisbane in Australia is unique within its country because it has ring-fenced the Fortitude Valley area of the city as a dedicated entertainment precinct (Burke and Schmidt 2013), which has been described as: 'a bohemian enclave of creative arts, music and culture' (Baird and Scott 2018: 3). In order to preserve the area's character, Brisbane City Council designed the 'Valley Music Harmony Plan' (Brisbane City Council 2004) that allowed the council to monitor noise levels, implement specific plans for infrastructure and deploy more effective approaches for policing. Hard institutional policy included notifying potential residents of the area to expect above-average noise levels and implementing compulsory sound-proofing and additional noise attenuation measures for new residential builds (Baird and Scott 2018).

Finally, Nashville in the United States has already established itself as a Music City and the 'Home of Country Music' but in the face of the economic effects of gentrification and culture-led urban renewal, The Mayor's office of Nashville has taken a hard and soft institutional approach. First, it has created a merchant advisory group that comprises representatives from government, business, non-profit organizations and the heritage and tourism sectors. The advisory group labelled 'The District' focuses on areas and/or buildings of particular cultural significance to the city of Nashville and strives to extend heritage status to them (The District 2015). Second, Nashville's music city council, the Country Music Association and the Nashville entrepreneur centre have joined together under Nashville's 'Project Music' (Nashville Music Council 2016) to distribute start-up grants to small emerging businesses (Nashville Next City Plan 2015).

In their survey of global music cities, Baird and Scott noted that an ideal Music City should include strategies involving the re-regulation of space, imagineering, governance and supply. On this last point, they argue that an ideal music city requires 'deep engagement with musicians and related creative sector professionals. Such supply-side policies aim to refine the human capital of industry actors through education, training and up-skilling' (Baird and Scott 2018: 5). They further explain that 'hard' institutional forms may include 'the development of contestable grants to incentivise music production, videos and touring; or to underwrite festivals and events, industry conferences and professional development' (2018: 5). The 'soft' institutional forms, Baird and Scott argue, work to encourage musicians and associated professionals to think in a more entrepreneurial way. They suggest soft forms that might include 'organizing professional development, industry awareness, networking and performance events, such information sharing' (2018: 5). This '"upskilling" approach they argue can be implemented in conjunction with other arts strategies through community and youth engagement programs' (2018: 5).

## *Mapping the musical economy of Leeds*

Prior to the formulation of Music:Leeds, a mapping exercise throughout 2017 was undertaken by the initial members of the team. This involved first surveying the number of music businesses, organizations or people currently operating in Leeds and the surrounding area. Existing phone or business directories, internet searches, recommendations from managers, promoters, venue owners and musicians alongside a publicized open call to individuals and organizations were all used to compile a dedicated directory of music activity in the region. The businesses, organizations or people that support and work with artists and musicians in Leeds were then categorized using the areas set out by Complete Music Update (CMU 2018):

- Music creation
- Live performance
- Music marketing & fanbase building
- Artist business services
- Music heritage and tourism
- Music education and participation

This data was compiled into a database to create a holistic view of the musical economy of Leeds. The mapping exercise uncovered some notable aspects of the Leeds music economy in particular the area of 'Live Performance', which showed it was a vibrant part of the sector with 215 music venues in operation under a Leeds postcode. The type and function of these live music venues ranged from large venues operated by multinational corporations, full-time independent music venues to suburban pubs with singular weekly live music events.

In the area of 'Artist Business Services' the mapping exercise identified a number of record labels based in the city ranging from large independent labels with a national profile to smaller micro-independent labels. Although a true number of smaller micro-independent labels was difficult to fully determine it was estimated that there were fewer than ten Leeds-based record labels that were recognized as formal businesses or companies supporting less than ten full-time equivalent (FTE) jobs. The mapping exercise identified a large number of self-distributing artists not attached to a record label, which indicated a large number of music creators in the city who were potentially retaining the rights to their work by not contracting it to third parties. Connected to this point it was found that although there are a handful of successful companies managing associated publishing rights in the field of film and television, the commercial popular music sector has no bespoke publisher in the city. The lack of business representation in this area could limit the potential for local music creators to fully exploit their works and gain wider exposure; particularly within the lucrative field of music synchronization, which is not served by PROs, who at least collect performance and mechanical copyrights for music creators. Finally, the mapping exercise highlighted the lack of legal services for musicians and music operations in the city with no music lawyers or representatives. This may indicate that there is not enough work to support a music lawyer in the city and that the primary elements of the music economy are more independent or do-it-yourself (DIY)-centric than commercial.

## *Establishing Music: Leeds*

Data from the mapping exercise was critical in highlighting the wealth of musical activity in the city of Leeds and that despite a lack of formal structure and sporadic local authority economic support, the music sector and scene are prospering. Although there are three principal considerations, first, the consideration of sustainability and the ways in which this bourgeoning scene can be supported long-term. Second, the consideration of representation and the methods by which the interests and issues of music businesses, organizations and people can be represented to local authorities. Finally, cooperation and the means by which a collective approach can be organized and managed to help meet some of the challenges involved in supporting a regional music sector and scene.

There are a number of existing models for establishing a mechanism for supporting the music sector within a city; for example, some UK cities have formulated City Region Music Boards (e.g. London, Greater Manchester, Liverpool and Sheffield) to help provide a more formal and unified strategy to influence music policy and provide consultancy on a local level and implement a regional music strategy. Some cities and regions have created roles within local government such as dedicated music officers or establishing a dedicated music office (e.g. Brighton) that supports music activity in all areas of the economy. Alongside the region's proposed bid to become the European Capital of Culture in 2023, the city of Leeds originally developed a broader culture strategy of which music was only a part. In light of the UK's exit from the European Union, and subsequently the disqualification of Leeds from the bidding process, Leeds City Council declared 2023 as a year of culture with a determined approach to improve the offer of arts and culture across the city. The findings from the mapping exercise were presented to Leeds City Council and used to advocate for developing a more holistic and strategic approach to support music activity in the city. In a bid to be visible, non-partisan and representative of all areas of the musical economy, Music:Leeds was initiated as an independent organization to act as a conduit for consultation between local music businesses, individuals and services, and Leeds City Council to begin to create a framework for support to the music sector of Leeds.

The first of many consultation events managed and run by Music:Leeds was held at Leeds Town Hall in the Autumn of 2017 in which key individuals, business and services from the local music sector highlighted in the mapping exercise were invited to attend. In an attempt to actively engage as much of the music community as possible, representatives from each of the six areas (Music Creation, Live Performance, Music Marketing & Fanbase Building, Artist Business Services, Music Heritage and Tourism, Music Education and Participation) were invited to 'listen, think, shout and contribute to a day that will help develop a mandate to connect and support music in the city at all levels' (Music:Leeds 2017: n.pag.). The event included addresses and provocations from Tom Riordan (Chief Executive, Leeds City Council), Cllr Blake (Leader, Leeds City Council) and Michael Dugher (CEO, UK Music) alongside sector development experts Sound Diplomacy and individuals working to create models to sustain and promote the music sectors of other cities and regions including Amsterdam, Aarhus, Liverpool and Brighton. The large-scale consultation forum further helped to establish Music:Leeds as an independent organization 'to act as a centralised point to support, develop, grow and promote music in the city across all levels, genres and cultures' (Music:Leeds 2017: n.pag.).

## *Engaging the music economy of Leeds*

Following the 2017 event, Music:Leeds created online networks, including social media channels, an e-mail list and online forums to create a framework for communicating future events, opportunities and news from the sector. Throughout 2018, Music:Leeds was able to host a series of events that addressed the issue of gender equality in the music industries, music industry insights and a series of skills workshops for musicians. These events featured a networking element that also provided an opportunity for diverse parties from the local music community to meet and discuss potential collaborations. Further consultation, with representatives from the music economy of Leeds, was undertaken at the 2019 City Music Forum which served as an opportunity for Music:Leeds to present its initial activity and encourage representatives from the sector to present their own topics for discussion within smaller breakout focus groups. In total, twelve distinct topics were put forward for discussion that were then published in a round-up document, which included:

- Funding, education and accessibility
- Stickability: How can Leeds develop more music businesses? How can we keep talent in Leeds?
- Supporting promoters
- Why is music in Leeds so white?
- Combatting groping, sexual harassment and violence at live music events
- Leeds music history
- Music tourism and Leeds
- Access to live music for children and young people
- The relationship between health and music
- Apprenticeships/training routes in music/music-related and creative skills.

These consultation events served to engage the: 'musicians and related creative sector professionals' (Scott 2013) more deeply from across the musical economy of Leeds. The issues, needs and opportunities discussed at events were then further grouped into three specific areas that Music:Leeds could help to address:

- Creative Development & Business Growth in Leeds
- Placemaking & Tourism in Leeds
- Access to Music in Leeds

The first of these, 'Creative Development & Business Growth' was underpinned by findings from the database, which identified clear areas of strengths and areas for development in both volume and scale for music organizations in the city. In particular, the mapping exercise highlighted a lack of music businesses that could support pathways for emerging music industry entrepreneurs and professionals to establish themselves and/or new businesses in the city relating to the music economy. Some participants on the day of the forum argued that an absence of established pathways often leads to a talent drain to other cities; specifically to London and the South East of England.

The second area identified was 'Tourism & Placemaking', which relates to the ways in which a successful music sector can both attract visitors to the city and retain talent within the music sector and across the broader workforce. Engagement with the musical economy of Leeds showed that although Leeds is highly regarded for having strong longstanding relationships with events and brands (e.g. within the House music scene and the Back to Basics club night, the Pop Punk scene and the Slam Dunk festival, the DIY and Punk Rock music scene with Cops & Robbers), it doesn't currently have a clear and cohesive reputation for its music offering. Representatives from Leeds' music scene underlined that there is a need to create a defining narrative that can raise the national profile of the music sector of Leeds, which is not defined by a 'sound' but by a sense of independence, and diversity as a tangible asset.

The final area was 'Access to Music' in which representatives across the city region highlighted three particular aspects of accessibility that should be addressed in Leeds's current provision:

1. Access to music-making and music events. It is typically community, charity or non-profit organizations that lead the way in access to music-making and musical development but there is still a range of musical, geographical, socio-economic barriers and physical barriers for all ages in the city; specifically disabled and impaired music-makers and audience members.
2. Access and representation. Issues of diversity and representation within the musical economy, specifically at leadership level, are vital to help meet the needs of the diverse cultural communities of Leeds and the global workforce more broadly.
3. Access to opportunities. Improving the local musical economy will also increase access to opportunities of development, employment and engagement with the musical economy. This may also include the ability to help recognize opportunities in order to be able to access them.

## Influencing the music economy of Leeds

Strategic engagement with representatives across the musical economy of Leeds allowed Music:Leeds to address particular aspects of the musical economy of 'Creative Development and Business Growth', 'Placemaking & Tourism' and 'Access to Music'. 'Creative Development & Business Growth' is the area in which Music:Leeds has had the most visible influence on the musical economy of Leeds. This is through the early career artist development programme called 'Launchpad', which groups together twenty to thirty local and national music organizations, businesses and live events to support emerging artists. Funding for Launchpad was generated to support this activity from the National Lottery through Arts Council England and PRS Foundation as a Talent Development Partner. This has crucially helped to create a tangible network of support organizations for anyone involved in music in the region. The secondary impact of developing partnerships with such a wide range of local music festival and organizations is that a tangible network of local organizations has become visible to any artists accessing the Launchpad initiative. By artists engaging with these direct and overtly desirable opportunities (e.g. a sought-after festival slot), Music:Leeds has been able to signpost and disseminate a wider range of opportunities, both from organizations within Leeds, as well as national bodies to include major arts / music funders to emerging artists in the region.

Music:Leeds has also contributed to the area of 'Placemaking & Tourism' through strategic engagement with Leeds Enterprise Partnership, Leeds City Council & Leeds 2023. The Leeds City Region European Structural and Investment Funds Strategy published in 2014 only mentions music once – however, through its developing relationship with local government, Music:Leeds has contributed to the music industry section of the city-wide strategy for 2020 onwards. Unlike Liverpool which has focused on the Beatles, or Nashville with Country Music, Leeds lacks a unifying and tangible focus for its music heritage. However, over the last ten years, momentum has been growing with numerous exhibitions including 'Leeds Music History' and 'One Foot In The Rave', with support from Leeds City Council to Leeds Business Improvement District. Music:Leeds's contribution to the city-wide strategy draws upon the key areas of these exhibitions to develop a strategy to create a notable identity for music in Leeds, celebrating its past and present to help profile the city of Leeds as a musical destination for future tourists, audiences, music-makers and those that support the music economy.

Through the building of networks and strategic partnerships to amplify opportunities, Music:Leeds has also contributed to the area of 'Access to Music'. For example, The Launchpad Project was designed solely to have a direct impact on artists in the region, but engagement with the initiative plays a role in building a noticeable network of music industry individuals and organizations in the city, which has contributed to making music opportunities more accessible, whilst establishing role models and developing the sector and artists. Music:Leeds Launchpad also provides opportunities for artists (musicians and music creators) of any genre and style to access support through a combination live performance, studio recording, one-to-one mentoring, conference, talks and workshop aimed at increasing the knowledge and skills of those who attend. Artists are invited to apply via an open call, which was distributed as widely as possible. Strategic partnerships were made with local festivals to provide live opportunities and this encouraged a diverse range of artists to apply and amplify the opportunities that were on offer to a diverse audience.

Music:Leeds has also engaged with specific activity to address widespread issues around diversity and inclusivity and following collaborative events with Brighter Sound, a Gender Rebalance Equality Action & Advisory Team has been convened to increase and promote opportunities for women and people of marginalized gender in the city. This has led to showcase and social events throughout the year and enabled collaboration across different organizations working within the sector. Additionally, through analysis of its database of music businesses, Music:Leeds has helped to engage venues across the city in addressing sexual harassment at live music events (in collaboration with Dr. Rosemary Hill's Healthy Music Audiences project) and improve venues' online information for disabled and deaf audience members in line with Attitude Is Everything's Access Starts Online guidance. Examples include working with Brighter Sound on Both Sides Now to create more opportunities for female music creators, running consultation supported by Attitude is Everything to improve the access information for live music venues in the city and collaborating with Dr. Rosemary Hill on work to address sexual harassment at live music events.

Importantly, the formation of Music:Leeds has provided an opportunity for widespread organizational cooperation in raising the profile of music activity both within the city and at the national level. This has allowed more sophisticated projects to take place with more awareness for our audiences and practitioners.

## Conclusions and further work

A 'Music City' describes an urban environment that has the ideal conditions to take advantage of the cultural and musical fabric to support and nurture its musical economy (Baker 2017; Terrill et al. 2015). A 'Music City' emphasizes elements of Creative Development & Business Growth, Placemaking & Tourism, Access to Music-Making and music events as well as supporting the existing music scene. Supporting the regionalized music sector and scene of Leeds began with a mapping exercise to identify the individuals, groups, organizations and businesses working within the music economy of the city.

Data from the mapping exercise was crucial in highlighting the diversity of musical activity in the city of Leeds and that despite a lack of formal structure and sporadic local authority economic support, the music sector and scene are prospering. However, three principal challenges and issues were highlighted: sustainability, representation and cooperation. After a consultation event in 2017, Music:Leeds was formed and developed a series of regular events to engage the music industries of Leeds and the United Kingdom more broadly. Further consultation was undertaken at the 2019 City Music Forum, which reinforced a number of issues and highlighted three specific areas of development that Music:Leeds can help to address:

- Creative Development & Business Growth in Leeds
- Placemaking & Tourism in Leeds
- Access to Music in Leeds

Music:Leeds has had the most visible influence on the musical economy of Leeds. This is through the early career artist development programme called 'Launchpad' local and national music organizations, businesses and live events to support emerging artists. Through its developing relationship with local government, Music:Leeds has developed the music industry section of the City-Wide Strategy for 2020 onwards to influence the area of 'Placemaking & Tourism' and, importantly, Music:Leeds has helped to increase awareness of issues of access and inclusivity within the musical economy of Leeds through the curation of a diverse range of events across the region. Music:Leeds was able to facilitate this work and maximize the impact of these projects because of the critical engagement with representatives from across the musical economy of Leeds and building relationships with them through consultations in the City Music Forum.

The activity of Music:Leeds activity to date has been informed by mapping data, consultative events and action research through the delivery of its programme tied to its funding. Further work on evaluating these aspects is needed to fully assess the impact of these activities and how they can inform a structure and pathway through 2023 and beyond. These include the need to effectively support and sustain a fit-for-purpose music ecosystem in Leeds that facilitates emerging artists and music industry professionals, a diverse workforce and increasing music activity opportunities. There is also a need to define a narrative for what music in Leeds represents, to create an inclusive identity that all those engaged with music in the city can respond to, and equally project, and that equally harnesses the power of the city's music heritage.

## NOTE

This chapter was developed from an earlier version that appeared as Thompson, Paul and Sam, Nicholls (2021), 'Music:Leeds – Supporting a regionalised music sector and scene', in R. Hepworth-Sawyer, J. Paterson and R. Toulson (eds), *Innovation in Music: Future Opportunities*, Abingdon: Routledge, pp. 432–34. Reproduced with permission of The Licensor through PLSclear.

# REFERENCES

Atkinson, Roland and Easthope, Hazel (2009), 'The consequences of the creative class: The pursuit of creativity strategies in Australia's cities', *International Journal of Urban and Regional Research*, 33:1, pp. 64–79.

Baird, Paul and Scott, Michael (2018), 'Towards an ideal typical live music city', *City, Culture and Society*, https://doi.org/10.1016/j.ccs.2018.03.003. Accessed 2 December 2019.

Baker, Andréa Jean (2017), 'Algorithms to assess music cities: Case study – Melbourne as a music capital', *SAGE Open*, 7:1, pp. 1–12.

Behr, Adam, Brennan, Matt, Cloonan, Martin, Frith, Simon and Webster, Emma (2016), 'Live concert performance: An ecological approach', *Rock Music Studies*, 3:1, pp. 5–23.

Brisbane City Council (2004), *Valley Music Harmony Plan*, https://www.brisbane.qld.gov.au/sites/default/files/valley-music-harmony-plan.pdf. Accessed 8 March 2023.

Burke, Matthew and Schmidt, Amy (2013), 'How should we plan and regulate live music in Australian cities? Learnings from Brisbane', *Australian Planner*, 50:1, pp. 68–78.

City of Toronto Strategic Plan (2016), http://www.toronto.ca/legdocs/mmis/2016/ed/bgrd/backgroundfile-90615.pdf. Accessed 2 December 2019.

Cohen, Sara (2013), 'From the big dig to the big gig: Live music, urban regeneration and social change in the European Capital of Culture 2008', in C. Wergin and F. Holt (eds.), *Musical Performance and the Changing City: Post-Industrial Contexts in Europe and the United States*, New York: Routledge, pp. 27–51.

Complete Music Update (2018), https://completemusicupdate.com/. Accessed 2 December 2019.

The District (2015), http://thedistrictnashville.org. Accessed 2 December 2019.

Evans, Graeme (2009), 'Creative cities, creative spaces and urban policy', *Urban Studies*, 46:5&6, pp. 1003–40.

Gibson, Chris and Homan, Shane (2004), 'Urban redevelopment, live and public space: Cultural performance and the re-making of Marrickville', *International Journal of Cultural Policy*, 10:1, pp. 67–84.

Gibson, Lisanne and Stevenson, Deborah (2004), 'Urban space and the uses of culture', *International Journal of Cultural Policy*, 10:1, pp. 1–4.

Holt, Fabian (2010), 'The economy of live music in the digital age', *European Journal of Cultural Studies*, 13:2, pp. 243–61.

Holt, Fabian and Wergin, Carsten (2013), 'Introduction: Musical performance and the changing city', in F. Holt and C. Wergin (eds), *Musical Performance and the Changing City: Post-Industrial Contexts in Europe and the United States*, New York: Routledge, pp. 1–24.

Homan, Shane (2008), 'A portrait of the politician as a young pub rocker: Live music venue reform in Australia', *Popular Music*, 27:2, pp. 243–56.

Homan, Shane (2010), 'Governmental as anything: Live music and law and order in Melbourne', *Perfect Beat*, 11:2, pp. 103–18.

Homan, Shane (2014), 'Liveability and creativity: The case for Melbourne music precincts', *City, Culture and Society*, 5:3, pp. 149–55.

Homan, Shane (2017), '"Lockout" laws or "Rock out" laws? Governing Sydney's night-time economy and implications for the Music City', *International Journal of Cultural Policy*, 25:4, pp. 500–14.

Hracs, Brian J. (2009), 'Beyond bohemia: Geographies of everyday creativity for musicians in Toronto' in T. Edensor, D. Leslie, S. Millington and N. Rantisi (eds), *Spaces of Vernacular Creativity: Rethinking the Cultural Economy*, London: Routledge, pp. 75–88.

Hudson, Ray (2006), 'Regions and place: Music, identity and place', *Progress in Human Geography*, 30:5, pp. 626–34.

Hutton, Thomas A. (2004). 'The new economy of the inner city', *Cities*, 21:2. pp. 89–108.

Hutton, Thomas A. (2009), *The New Economy of the Inner City: Restructuring, Regeneration and Dislocation in the 21st century Metropolis*, London: Routledge.

Koefoed, Oleg (2013), 'European capitals of culture and cultures of sustainability: The case of Guimaraes 2012', *City, Culture and Society*, 4:3, pp. 153–62.

Music Canada (2016), *The Mastering of a Music City – Key Elements, Effective Strategies and Why it's Worth Pursuing*, March, https://musiccanada.com/wp-content/uploads/2015/06/The-Mastering-of-a-Music-City.pdf. Accessed 2 December 2019.

Nashville Next City Plan (2015), *Arts and Cultural Land Use Planning including Music Row*, http://www.nashvillenext.net. Accessed 2 December 2019.

Nashville Music Council (2016), http://www.nashville.gov/Mayors-Office/Priorities/Economic-Development/Programs-and-Services/Music-City-Music-Council.aspx. Accessed 2 December 2019.

O'Connor, Justin and Shaw, Kate (2014), 'What next for the creative city?', *City, Culture and Society*, 5:3, pp. 165–70.

Pratt, Andy C. (2008), 'Creative cities: The cultural industries and the creative class', *Human Geography*, 90:2, pp. 107–17.

Ross, Sara (2017), 'Making a music city: The commodification of culture in Toronto's urban redevelopment, tensions between use-value and exchange-value, and the counterproductive treatment of alternative cultures within municipal legal frameworks', *Journal of Law and Social Policy*, 27, pp. 116–53.

Scott, Allen J. (2006), 'Creative cities: Conceptual issues and policy questions', *Journal of Urban Affairs*, 28:1, pp. 1–17.

Scott, Michael (2013), *Making New Zealand's Pop Renaissance: State, Markets, Musicians*, Abington: Routledge.

Strong, Catherine, Cannizzo, Fabian and Rogers, Ian (2017), 'Aesthetic cosmopolitan, national and local popular music heritage in Melbourne's music laneways', *International Journal of Heritage Studies*, 2:2, pp. 83–96.

Terrill, Amy, Hogarth, Don, Clement, Alex and Francis, Roxanne (2015), *Mastering of a Music City*, http://www.ifpi.org/downloads/The-Mastering-of-a-Music-City.pdf. Accessed 2 December 2019.

UKMusic (2018), 'Measuring music', https://www.ukmusic.org/news/measuring-music-2018. Accessed 2 December 2019.

UNESCO (2016), *Culture Urban Future Summary – Global Report on Culture for Sustainable Development*, https://unesdoc.unesco.org/ark:/48223/pf000024629. Accessed 8 March 2023.

Van der Hoeven, Arno and Hitters, Erik (2019), 'The social and cultural values of live music: Sustaining urban live music ecologies', *Cities*, 90, pp. 263–71.

Vivant, Elsa (2013), 'Creatives in the city: Urban contradictions of the creative city', *City, Culture and Society*, 4:2, pp. 57–63.

Zukin, Sharon (1987), 'Gentrification: Culture and capital in the urban core', *Annual Review of Sociology*, 1:1, pp. 129–47.

Zukin, Sharon (1995), *The Cultures of Cities*, Oxford: Blackwell.

# Conclusion: Putting Popular Music in Leeds 'On the Map'

*Brett Lashua, Paul Thompson, Kitty Ross and Karl Spracklen*

In *Off the map: Lost spaces, invisible cities, forgotten islands, feral places, and what they tell us about the world* (2014), Alistair Bonnett writes that today's cities are too often characterized as 'non-places' (Augé 1995) – a generic 'nowhere' lacking a sense of place or attachment. In contemporary cities then there is a need for 'geographical re-enchantment' (2014: 1) and many people 'hunger for places that matter' (Bonnett 2014: 2). Searching for places that matter can ignite a desire 'to radically rediscover the landscape around us' particularly (if, perhaps, incongruously) by realizing 'just how ordinary it is' (Bonnett 2014: 5). That is to say, like Leeds, many of Bonnett's lost spaces and invisible cities are hiding in plain sight. Perhaps we fail to see and appreciate their extraordinariness because we perceive them through the lens of the ordinary and unremarkable. A sense of rediscovery is at the heart of this book: to recognize and remark upon Leeds, in some ways an 'ordinary' UK city, yet in other ways an extraordinary one. Although Leeds in Bonnett's terms is a place that may be considered 'off the map' within wider understandings of popular music heritage, this book has aimed to put it 'on the map'. Because 'every place deserves an atlas' (Solnit 2010: vii), this book presents a kind of atlas of popular music in Leeds. Leeds has popular music histories, heritage, people and places that are remarkable and warrant greater recognition.

If an initial impetus for this book was the *Sounds of Our City* exhibition on Leeds' music heritage at Abbey House Museum (2020–21), then its denouement was an art installation at Leeds' Ginger Works gallery in the Spring of 2022. This installation, titled 'Mapping the Book: Re-Imagining Popular Music in Leeds', featured a wall-sized rendering of a map of Leeds. Created by two of the book's editors, Brett and Paul, the mapping was traced across a printout of the book's draft chapters, jumbled together and spread across two walls (and spilling onto the ceiling). Into these layers, they plotted sites, venues and locations mentioned throughout the book (see Figure C.1) – over 150 sites in total. This created a cartographic remapping of the book, while also capturing a visual sense of 'places that matter' (Bonnett 2014: 5), where music is, and has been, part of Leeds. In a city where the places of popular music, their stories, histories and heritage have not been centralized or widely celebrated, this was one way to foreground the musical geography of the city (or 'popular musicscape', Lashua and Cohen 2010).

The mapping shows areas of dense concentration of musical activities, as well as absences and gaps. Because its pages are layered upon the wall in a way that presents them jumbled, overlain and written into (see Figure C.2), reading across the varying layers provided interesting slippages and re-alignments of the texts. Walking by and scanning the installation, one can read that the Leeds West Indian Carnival offered the first UK steel band contest and the first Calypso King competition; there was a blues club at the Pack Horse pub near Woodhouse Moor in 1976; the Cockpit opened in 1992 within the arches under Leeds Railway Station for rave and indie nights; and that by 1950, the City Palace of Varieties was the country's oldest surviving music hall still in regular operation, established in 1865. The mapping, like the book that it draws upon, provides a multi-layered re-imagining of Leeds' popular music histories and heritage. Walking along the walls of the installation is akin to skimming (or perhaps dancing) across the history of popular music in Leeds.

FIGURE C.1: Putting popular music in Leeds on the map; the installation at Ginger Works, 2022. Courtesy of Brett Lashua.

CONCLUSION

FIGURE C.2: A close-up of the mapping at Ginger Works. Courtesy of Brett Lashua.

The mapping's many layers also invoke the diverse, kaleidoscopic character of music in Leeds. This reflects the variety of chapters and range of contributors to the volume, which features chapters by academics, museum curators, local historians and community advocates, bringing a range of voices and views to the collection. This array of contributions helps to showcase something of the complexity and diverse perspectives of the city. For Solnit (2010: vii):

> A city is a particular kind of place, perhaps best described as many worlds in one place; it compounds many versions without quite reconciling them, though some cross over to live in multiple worlds […]. An atlas is a collection of versions of a place, a compendium of perspectives, a snatching out of the infinite ether of potential versions a few that will be made concrete and visible.

In making the city more concrete and visible, we hope – in Bonnett's words – to also re-enchant the city through its rediscovery. And yet, the mapping at Ginger Works, while making some of the venues and histories of popular music in Leeds more 'concrete and visible', is also only a small part of the 'infinite ether of potential versions' that comprise any city, such as Leeds.

The installation at Ginger Works allowed us to visualize the book as a kind of re-imagined whole. Similarly, another purpose of this conclusion is to highlight some of the connections between the book's chapters, and by stepping back, to consider how the different viewpoints presented in the book align or diverge. In several ways, the art installation at Ginger Works helped us to do this.

First, it showed something of the density of sites and venues in Leeds city centre, over time, many of which we (editors) had not heard of before. From the grave of Pablo Fanque (Lashua and Thompson) to underground Jazz clubs (Meadowcroft), and sites of Hip Hop cyphers (Little and Stevenson), the book, like the mapping, is full of surprises and (re)discoveries. This cartographic density not only includes venues that have been 'lost' and closed down but also a number of venues that have survived under a variety of different names, or offered distinctive genres of music over the years, such as the Underground, which became the Town and Country, and then the O2 Academy, as explored in the chapters by Moss, Lomax and also Watson. Other venues have changed names but continue to cater to similar audiences. For example, Studio 20 was a centre of Jazz in Leeds during the 1950s, and now as Sela Bar the location still hosts Jazz gigs, as noted in the chapters by Meadowcroft, and Robinson.

Second, beyond the noticeable density of venues in Leeds city centre, there is equally, as not only befitting a sprawling city such as Leeds but also apt for a city that is (temporarily) home to thousands of university students, a spread of venues (past and present), scattered to the north of the city centre, towards Leeds' primary university campuses and areas of student housing. The significance of university students to the city's urban 'playscape' (Chatterton and Hollands 2002) is on show in a majority of chapters, whether in Leeds' DIY house party scene in the 2010s (Moss), early 1980s post-punk era (Goldhammer, McGovern) or Jazz in the 1940s and 1950s (Meadowcroft). The annual passage and increasing amount of students coming into and through Leeds' musical spaces leaves an indelible imprint on the city. This influx has a concomitant impact on its musical industries, cultural entrepreneurialism and musicians' careers, as seen across a number of chapters too.

Third, while Leeds is undoubtedly a city that has been shaped by global flows of people, goods, services and – of course – music, there is something that remains remarkably 'local' about the city and its residents. Bonnett (2014) may refer to this connection to the city as a 'sense of place' (Basso and Feld 1996) that runs counter to the increasing and intensifying placelessness or generic homogeneity of cities as non-places (Augé 1995). This tension between musical place-making and the erasure of distinctive local sites and venues is evoked in chapters on Americana music in Leeds (Robinson), the chapter by Gowans, Legard and Procter on the city's experimental music scene, and in accounts of Leeds as a city of migration and movement (Friar, Long). These chapters capture something of the changing relationships between the local and the global, or transnational 'glocal' music scenes (Bennett and Peterson 2004).

Fourth, there are also a handful of venues that are remarkably long-lived, such as the City Varieties – spotlighted in the chapter by Dave Russell – but also small venues like the Fenton – which sits at the centre of chapters by Goldhammer, and from a different perspective, McGovern. These venues allow explorations of continuity and change not only in cities such as Leeds but also elsewhere in the world. While scholars such as Gibson and Connell (2007) have noted the importance of historic venues in constructing certain cities as sites of popular music heritage; this narrative is challenged in Leeds, where no single venue can be seen as the city's pre-eminent character-defining concert space (although, as argued by Lomax, perhaps the Brudenell Social Club is worthy of such consideration). As detailed by our contributing authors, these are edgy, unusual, marginal places, with City Varieties hanging on by the skin of its 'nudie' shows (Russell), and the Fenton (40-odd years later) still a very raw and unassuming pub (Goldhammer, McGovern). These are 'places that matter' which we believe Bonnett (2014: 2) would recognize and celebrate, too.

Fifth, as the chapters on migration illustrate, Leeds exists within a larger landscape, showing the city as a product of global flows of people, goods and (not least) music. Several of the chapters locate the city within not only a regional, northern (England) context, but within an 'imaginary' Yorkshire as well. The chapter by Karl Spracklen positions Leeds within a historical sense of place and also a landscape of rural myth and magic. These shape not only the folk music of Mr. Fox but also remain part of the urban imaginary of the city itself. The chapter by Stephen Wagg also locates its central figure – the singer Jake Thackray – as a distinctly regional character, albeit one who struggled with Yorkshire's wider identifications and rural meanings. Other chapters, in their own ways, engaged with Leeds' 'northern-ness' as part of its position in the United Kingdom (Whitney 2019), and what makes its music unusual and distinctive (Thompson and Nicholls, Mills).

Finally, one common link between the chapters is their insistence that Leeds deserves more attention to its popular music histories, heritage, people and places than it has received. Although the city is generally regarded for hosting numerous musical festivals each year such as Leeds Festival at Bramham Park, it nevertheless lacks the attention that has come to other UK cities and their musical heritage. Liverpool is celebrated for Merseybeat in the 1960s and later moments such as the house music scene surrounding the superclub Cream/Nation in the 1990s (Lashua et al. 2010). Manchester is renowned as the site of 1990s 'Madchester' scene (Milestone 2019). Birmingham is known as the home of metal (Long and Collins 2012). Yet, for many, Leeds remains something of a 'non-place' in the UK's wider popular music imaginary. There have been some attempts to recognize the city's musical heritage, not least the *Sounds of Our City* exhibition at Abbey House Museum, as detailed in the chapter by Kitty Ross and Paul Thompson, and art installations including the 'Song Tunnel' centralized in the chapter by Lashua and Thompson, as well as the collaborative archival practices with Leeds Museums and Hip Hop performers noted by Little and Stevenson. Thompson and Nicholls introduced a range of strategies and initiatives that have been employed across the city of Leeds (UK) since 2017 where models from other European cities, feedback and opinion from music professionals, consultation from government officials in Leeds, and guidance documents from professional bodies and global consultancy agencies have all contributed to the development of the city's dedicated and independent organization Music:Leeds. One of Music:Leeds' core areas of activity, 'Placemaking & Tourism', takes up the task of (re)defining Leeds as a music city. This illustrates that there is always more work to do to recognize Leeds, to give it the atlas that it deserves, and to put popular music in Leeds 'on the map'.

## REFERENCES

Augé, Marc (1995), *Non-places: Introduction to an Anthropology of Supermodernity*, London: Verso.

Basso, Keith and Feld, Stephen (eds) (1996), *Senses of Place*, Santa Fe: School of American Research Press.

Bennett, Andy and Peterson, Richard. A. (eds) (2004), *Music Scenes: Local, Translocal and Virtual*, Nashville: Vanderbilt University Press.

Bonnett, Alistair (2014), *Off the Map: Lost Spaces, Invisible Cities, Forgotten Islands, Feral Places, and What They Tell Us About the World*, London: Aurum Press.

Chatterton, Paul and Hollands, Robert (2002), 'Theorising urban playscapes: Producing, regulating and consuming youthful nightlife city spaces', *Urban Studies*, 39:1, pp. 95–116.

Gibson, Chris and Connell, John (2007), 'Music, tourism and the transformation of Memphis', *Tourism Geographies*, 9:2, pp. 160–90.

Lashua, Brett and Cohen, Sara (2010), 'Liverpool musicscapes: Music performance, movement and the built urban environment', in B. Fincham, M. McGuinness and L. Murray (eds), *Mobile Methodologies*, Basingstoke: Palgrave Macmillan, pp. 71–84.

Lashua, Brett, Cohen, Sara and Schofield, John (2010), 'Popular music, mapping and the characterisation of Liverpool', *Popular Music History*, 4:2, pp. 127–46.

Long, Paul and Collins, Jez (2012), 'Mapping the soundscapes of popular music heritage', in L. Roberts (ed.), *Mapping Cultures: Place, Practice, Performance*, London: Palgrave Macmillan, pp. 144–59.

Milestone, Katie (2019), 'Madchester', in B. Lashua, K. Spracklen, S. Wagg and M. S. Yavuz (eds), *Sounds and the City: Volume 2*, Basingstoke: Palgrave, pp. 303–13.

Solnit, Rebecca (2010), *Infinite City: A San Francisco Atlas*, Berkeley: University of California Press.

Whitney, Karl (2019), *Hit Factories: A Journey Through the Industrial Cities of British Pop*, London: Weidenfeld and Nicolson.

# Contributors

DANNY FRIAR is a local historian, researcher and writer who specializes in the history of Leeds's Black community and Leeds West Indian Carnival. He was a member of the research team for the *50 Years of Leeds West Indian Carnival* exhibition at the Tetley in 2017, Zodwa Nyoni's 2017 play *Carnival Chronicles* and Jamaica Society's 2019 *Eulogy* exhibition and book. He has been a member of the Leeds West Indian Carnival Communications Subcommittee and has 'played mas' (masquerade) with Harrison Bundey Mama Dread's Masqueraders and the AAA Team. He was a founding member of the Arthur France Legacy Group and their secretary. He was a regular contributor to the British Beatles Fan Club magazine for over five years and has written for Down Your Way magazine, Community Highlights and various newspapers including the *Yorkshire Evening Post*. He has contributed items and research to exhibitions across Leeds and has contributed research to magazines and books including Max Farrar's 2022 biography of Arthur France *Speaking Truth To Power: The Life and Times of an African Caribbean British Man*. In 2020, he completed the online course 'History of Slavery in The British Caribbean' with the University of Glasgow. He has given lectures on Black history for Leeds Museums and Galleries, Leeds Libraries, The Thoresby Society and the Grammar School at Leeds. His successful 2021–22 project 'Before Windrush: Black People In Leeds and Bradford, 1708–1948' consisted of an exhibition at the Leeds Central Library, a booklet, a series of blog posts, video content and a series of in-person talks. He also curated the 2019 exhibition *Leeds West Indian Carnival: The Early Years' at Leeds Central Library*. Danny Friar has also worked with Heritage Corner, Leeds to produce and deliver Black History Walks. He lives in Leeds with his wife Joanne.

*****

RIO GOLDHAMMER is a Ph.D. candidate at Leeds Beckett University, and a senior lecturer in music business and professional studies at Leeds Conservatoire. A musician with a background in cultural studies and political theory, Rio has fronted the cult Bradford post-punk group 1919 since their reformation in 2014. His role in 1919 was the entry point for his doctoral thesis, 'An ethnography of cultural identity and heritage in the Yorkshire post-punk scene', submitted in August 2022. Works published to date from the thesis include 'Authenticity in an insider-in ethnography of post-punk' (2021) and 'Provincial towns and Yorkshire cities: Post-punk sounds, suburban escape, and metro-hegemony' (2019). Rio contested the Labour candidacy for Mayor of West Yorkshire in 2020 and has written about politics, sport and music for publications including *The Independent*, *The Conversation* and *Novara Media*. In 2022, Rio was a featured contributor to Keith Khan-Harris's book *What Does a Jew Look Like?* (Five Leaves Publications), and he is currently working on the next 1919 release.

*****

THEO GOWANS is a Leeds-based noise musician, art maker and gig organizer based in Leeds. He performs experimental noise, sound collage and free improvised music solo as Territorial Gobbing and as part of the noise-rock band 'Thank'. He has also been part of a plethora of duos, trios and random assortments, and has recorded numerous albums under all these various guises. Theo also organizes do-it-yourself (DIY) gigs for noise, improvised and unpopular music under the name 'Heinous Whining' bringing national and international touring acts to Leeds. Theo currently is part of Wharf Chambers co-op and helped run the now defunct venue CHUNK in Meanwood and is currently pursuing an MA in creative practice at Leeds Arts University.

*****

BRETT LASHUA teaches sociology of media and education at University College London (UCL). He has worked with schools, community centres, musicians and arts organizations in the United States, Canada and the United Kingdom to address questions of youth inequalities, racialized borderlands and urban place-making. His research is underscored by creative and collaborative ethnographic methods including participatory music-making, soundscapes, cultural mapping, documentary filmmaking, podcasting and digital storytelling, as well as making use of archival approaches. He is the author of *Popular Music, Popular Myth and Cultural Heritage in Cleveland: The Moondog, The Buzzard and the Battle for the Rock and Roll Hall of Fame* (Emerald, 2019), and two co-edited volumes of *Sounds and the City* (Palgrave, 2014, 2019). Brett is a commissioning editor (with Prof. Stephen Wagg) for two book series with Liverpool University Press: one is centred on studies of popular music and place; the other series explores the politics of popular culture. Originally from north-eastern Ohio (USA), Brett played drums in several Cleveland-area bands in the 1990s, and later performed with a number of Liverpool groups in the late 2000s in the years surrounding that city's tenure as 2008 European Capital of Culture; he still occasionally makes some noise behind the drums.

❋ ❋ ❋ ❋ ❋

PHIL LEGARD is a senior lecturer at Leeds Beckett University's Leeds School of Arts. He has been involved in Leeds' underground experimental music scene since the early 2000s, performing as Xenis Emptuae Travelling Band and playing with Ashtray Navigations throughout the first decade of the millennium. He currently plays in Hawthonn, an experimental electronic duo with his wife, Layla. Phil's academic work is chiefly concerned with the study of underground music and related subcultures. At the time of publication, he is completing his thesis, which examines autoethnography as a method for the study of folk-influenced music-making embedded in the UK's occult subcultures.

❋ ❋ ❋ ❋ ❋

SARAH LITTLE graduated from the University of Leeds in 2019 with a Ph.D. in cultural democracy and UK hip hop. She has lectured at the University of Leeds in interactive performance and is the author of a number of academic articles in the field of hip hop studies including 'Women, ageing, and hip hop: Discourses and imageries of ageing femininity' in the *Journal of Feminist Media Studies*. She is also a creative practitioner with a long history in the UK hip hop scene as a member of UK hip hop crews Alphabetix and Northern Hostility as well as being a regularly published co-writer for audio production music for clients including Audio Network and the BBC. Dr. Little served on the executive board for Leeds-based organization the Hip Hop Historian Society. A Yorkshire native and long-time Leeds resident, bringing voice to the history of Leeds music scenes and celebrating the history of UK hip hop remains an enduring interest for this author.

❋ ❋ ❋ ❋ ❋

DAN LOMAX is a senior lecturer, UK Centre for Events Management, Leeds Beckett University. He was DJ/promoter at the Town and County (1994–2000), Gigantic (1999–2009) and The Cockpit (2000–2012). Dan arrived in Leeds as a student in 1991 in time to witness the last gasp of the city's goth scene. Within a couple of years, he started DJing and promoting indie and alternative club nights, and in

1994 he earned a DJ residency in the second room at The Town and Country Club which he updated to capture the burgeoning Britpop scene of the time. In 1998, he took over Saturdays in the T&C's main hall, launching the mainstream night Sorted, and also the indie/alternative Thursday night at Leeds University Union (LUU), originally called Smile but soon rebranded as Gigantic. The closure of the T&C and LUU venues in 2000 led to a new chapter as DJ/promoter of Gigantic at The Bassment and as a DJ at The Cockpit, initially at The Garage and then founding The Session from 2002. Throughout the 2000s, Dan worked across a range of venues and was nominated for DJ and Club of the year in 2006 for Gigantic, quite an accolade for awards traditionally dominated by dance music brands. Since retiring from full-time DJing in 2012, he now plays irregular nights at The Woods, a multi-use events venue in Leeds owned by ex-Cockpit empresario Richard Todd. Alongside his professional life in the Leeds music scene, Dan completed an MSc in events management at Leeds Metropolitan University in 2003 and became a lecturer there in 2010, leading to an academic career focused on music events and event production. He is currently researching the ecosystem of the current Leeds music industry and the relationships between promoters, venues and the wider music community.

\*\*\*\*\*

JONATHAN LONG is an emeritus professor at Leeds Beckett University with the Centre for Sport and Social Justice. Throughout his career, he has been researching in the field of leisure with particular interests in sport and leisure policy, social networks and inclusion, cultural capital and racial equality. Within the work on ethnicity, there have been studies of the experience of new migrants and the racialization of leisure and sport places. Most of this programme of research has meant managing external contracts for organizations like the Department for Culture Media and Sport, Heritage Lottery Fund, Sport England, Central Council of Physical Recreation, research councils and Sporting Equals as well as various local authorities and third sector bodies. With Doug Sandle, Jonathan founded the Fields of Vision initiative exploring the interrelationships between sport and the arts, part of which included his own study of Opera Man's cult status among the fans of Leeds Rhinos Rugby League team. He is currently the series editor (with Kevin Hylton) for Routledge Critical Perspectives on Equality and Social Justice in Sport and Leisure. He is also a Trustee of Leeds Asylum Seekers Support Network, where he works on their projects as a volunteer.

\*\*\*\*\*

MALLORY MCGOVERN is a writer, recent graduate student and aspiring full-time employee based in Washington, D.C. Originally from Fort Myers, FL, Mallory attended Florida State University where she received degrees in History and International Affairs. Mallory recieved her master's degree in American Studies from George Washington University in May 2023 where she was a recipient of the Scottish Rite Graduate Fellowship. While at George Washington, she focused on research in popular culture, particularly music and comedy, from a feminist perspective. As a graduate student, she conducted research on George Washington University's student-run radio station WRGW. Her professional background features work in education as well as non-profits, including her role as program coordinator with the Florida Commissioner's Task Force on Holocaust Education and her work with the New America Fellows Program. Following her graduation, Mallory plans to seek out opportunities in educational media and to continue writing and reading about popular culture.

\* \* \* \* \*

MICHAEL MEADOWCROFT's life has been in Liberal politics. He has been a Leeds city councillor, a West Yorkshire Metropolitan county councillor and served as the Liberal MP for West Leeds, 1983–87. He is an Honorary Alderman of the City of Leeds. After his time in parliament, he spent 25 years assisting 36 new and developing democracies across four continents. He formed his first jazz band in 1959 at the age of 17 in Southport where he then lived. He has continued playing clarinet and soprano saxophone whenever and wherever possible since then and his Granny Lee Jazz Band has a regular booking at the Leeds Jazz Club. His sole academic achievement is an MPhil from the University of Bradford for a thesis on 'Transition in Leeds City Government'. He has continued to be an active local historian in the city, lecturing and writing on a range of Leeds people, places and events. He was chairman of the Leeds Library, 2008–16. He served for twelve years as a director of the Leeds Grand Theatre and Opera House. He has also been a freelance journalist since 1987, having been a *Times* and *Yorkshire Post* columnist and is in demand as an obituarist. He also wrote a series of articles for the *Just Jazz* magazine. He has published a number of books on politics, electoral reform, wine, French philately and on the artworks of the National Liberal Club of which he is a vice-president He is married to Elizabeth Bee, an information specialist and book publisher.

\* \* \* \* \*

PETER MILLS teaches and devises all the music courses in the School of Cultural Studies at Leeds Beckett University in the United Kingdom. He has published books on Van Morrison, Samuel Beckett and The Monkees, the last of which, *The Monkees, 'Head' and the 60s* (Jawbone, 2016), was praised by Michael Nesmith, Bob Rafelson and Jack Nicholson. He has also written about a variety of artists and topics, including Hungarian folk music, national anthems, Jake Thackray and The Durutti Column. He is currently researching the history of music in Student Unions in the United Kingdom for a forthcoming monograph. He has written, contributed to and appeared in BBC radio and TV documentaries on musical topics from punk to classical, and hosted World Music events at the Royal Opera House, Covent Garden. He was the singer and lyricist of the band Innocents Abroad who made two albums, *Quaker City* (1987) and *Eleven* (1989); the band recently reconvened to record a new album entitled *Late Spring*, to be released in 2024 (all three albums are on Stormfield Records).

\* \* \* \* \*

STUART MOSS is a senior lecturer in music industry business and management subjects for Leeds School of Arts, Leeds Beckett University, as well as a National Union of Journalists, registered photojournalist and writer. He has been teaching in higher education since 2001. Stuart holds several positions related to the academic disciplines of business, employability and entertainment management. Such positions include vice president digital learning, for the Asia Pacific Institute for Events Management; an advisory board member for the BSc Entertainment Management program at the University of Central Florida (USA); external examiner for business studies at Liverpool John Moores University (UK); external examiner for business studies at Staffordshire University (UK) and external examiner for events and tourism management at Taylor's University (Malaysia). Stuart was previously appointed to the position of visiting professor at the Imus Institute of Science & Technology in the Philippines. He has been working in higher education for twenty years, prior to this, his work background included marketing and human resource positions in visitor attractions, hotels and telecommunications. Stuart has published widely, including two co-authored textbooks on the subject of employability, as well as two edited textbooks about the entertainment industries, and strategic management within the entertainment industries. Besides these, Stuart has written numerous book chapters, journal articles and delivered over 32 international conference keynotes. Stuart's research interests are centred on nightlife cultures, with a particular focus on the city of Leeds, UK. He is currently co-ordinating the Leeds Club History Project (http://www.leedschp.co.uk) as well as working on *Leeds The Movie* (http://www.leedsthemovie.co.uk), which when completed will be the longest film ever made about the city of Leeds (at around 24 hours in length). Stuart is a serial creative, writer, avid film-maker, gardener, chef and experimental home brewer.

\* \* \* \* \*

SAMUEL NICHOLLS, aka 'whiskas', is the founder and director of Music Local/Music:Leeds and senior lecturer in music at Leeds Beckett University, teaching the BA (Hons) music industries management course. Previously, whiskas has run a music venue and live promotions company, founded Leeds-based Dance to the Radio record label and was guitarist in the band ¡Forward, Russia!, who signed to Mute / EMI Records in North America, achieving two UK Top 40 singles. In a bid to create and facilitate conversations in the local music sector, he convened the first Music:Leeds event in late 2017, and later established the organization as a not-for-profit, with the purpose of acting as a centralized point to support, develop, grow and promote music in Leeds across all levels, genres and cultures. Since its establishment, the organization has evolved into Music Local as it now supports the music sector throughout Yorkshire; primarily through Launchpad, which is a talent development programme that has supported over 100 artists and emerging professionals based across the region since its inception in 2019. Music Local is passionate about supporting local music scenes and has worked with a range of partners and local authorities including Bradford Council, Rotherham Council, South Yorkshire Mayoral Combined Authority, Yorkshire Sound Women Network, Sage Gateshead and Coventry City of Culture. Whiskas is also a director of Come Play With Me, and acts as an advisor to major music funders PRS Foundation, Help Musicians UK and Youth Music.

*****

DAVE PROCTER is a sound artist living on the island of Hammarö in western Sweden where he also teaches English as a second language for the ABF organization and is an academic proof-reader for Karlstad University. He performs all over Europe under a number of musical pseudonyms in acts covering spoken word, folk, post-punk, ambient, drone and noise. He runs the small DIY record label DRET Skivor (https://dretskivor.bandcamp.com/) which attempts to advertise and collectivize artistic output locally in the county of Värmland and more internationally across the continental Scandinavian countries. He is a member of the Värmland art organization, Swedish Experimental Music and Film (SEMF), which curates the Syntax series of multimedia concerts and is a member of the Arvika art collective Kolonin.

*****

DAVE ROBINSON was awarded his Ph.D. by Leeds Beckett University in 2016 for a neo-Gramscian study of country music as contested culture in post-9/11 America. A late-career academic, since 2017 he has worked as a part-time lecturer at Leeds Beckett University and currently leads modules on music, politics and society and mass media. Born in 1957, the son of a professional violinist, Dave's early memories of Leeds include Balmforth's music shop on Merrion Street, the green room at Leeds Grand Theatre when his mother was playing in the pit orchestra, a summer job at Kitchens music shop in part of what is now the Victoria Quarter, and playing second flute in the rehearsal orchestra at the City of Leeds College of Music (the first college to offer a diploma in 'light music'). Eschewing any further thoughts of a musical career, Dave moved to London in 1981, where he worked in a variety of roles but always sought-out live music in his spare time – from Ronnie Scott's in Soho to the Mean Fiddler, Harlesden. After returning to Yorkshire and completing an Open University degree in the 1990s, Dave's interest in country and Americana music was encouraged by his wife Liz; and it was from their trips to Tennessee and Texas in the early 2000s that the idea of doing academic research on the subject took root. Dave's more recent research publications include collaborations with Leeds Beckett University colleague Karl Spracklen on music and alcohol-related leisure, and he is currently writing a book (to be published with Liverpool University Press) on the wider world of Americana music.

\* \* \* \* \*

KITTY ROSS has worked as a museum professional and curator since 1991. Having studied history at Girton College, Cambridge (1986–89), she completed an MA in museum studies at Leicester University in 1990 and is an associate of the Museums Association. As a student she gained volunteer experience at St Albans Museums, The Geffrye Museum (now Museum of the Home) in Hackney and work placements in Lincoln and Leeds. After posts at the Harris Museum, Preston and Clifton Park Museum, Rotherham, she has worked for Leeds Museums and Galleries since 1997. As curator of Leeds and Social History, she is responsible for a large and wide-ranging collection of over 100,000 objects, helping to develop the collections through active acquisition and research and a regular programme of changing exhibitions. She has been involved in two major museum redevelopment projects, that of Abbey House Museum (1998–2001) and Leeds City Museum (which reopened in 2008). She is an active member of the Social History Curators Group, having presented several conference papers and written journal articles. She has worked on many partnership projects with Leeds University, Leeds Beckett University, Leeds Trinity University and Huddersfield University and has supervised student placements for over 25 years. Her role also involves giving talks to local groups on a wide range of subjects drawn from the museum collections and exhibition programme. Beyond the museum, Kitty has been a member of the Sheffield Bach Society since 1992 and is currently their treasurer.

\* \* \* \* \*

DAVE RUSSELL studied history at the University of York at both undergraduate and postgraduate level. He taught in secondary schools in Bradford and Leeds, at the University of Central Lancashire where he was eventually professor of cultural history and head of the institute of football studies, and at the former Leeds Metropolitan University from where he retired as a professor of history and northern studies in 2010. He is now an independent scholar. An historian of nineteenth and twentieth-century popular culture, his particular interests fall in the fields of music, sport and the role of culture in constructing notions of northern English identity. Publications on music include *Popular Music in England, 1840–1914: A Social History* (Manchester University Press, 1997, second edition), as well as essays and articles on the brass band movement, militarism in Victorian music hall, the emergence of the Edwardian variety industry, cabaret clubs in 1960s England, sport and music, popular listening cultures, the history of the music profession, and British opera singers in the nineteenth and twentieth centuries. His current research centres on the cultural history of the guitar and other fretted instruments in twentieth-century Britain.

\* \* \* \* \*

KARL SPRACKLEN is a professor of sociology of leisure and culture in the School of Humanities and Social Sciences at Leeds Beckett University. He is the current editor-in-chief of *International Journal of the Sociology of Leisure*, published by Springer for Research Committee 13 (Sociology of Leisure) of the International Sociological Association. He was one of the co-founders of the International Society for Metal Music Studies, and the first principal editor of its journal *Metal Music Studies*, published by Intellect. He is an interdisciplinary scholar with roots in leisure studies, popular music studies and sociology. His main research interest remains the intersections of communities, identities, inequalities and the meaning and purpose of leisure spaces. He has written hundreds of research outputs, including eight research monographs, edited collections, book chapters, special issues of journals, and journal articles. Most of his research interests – extreme metal, rugby league, drinking subcultures, Scottishness, SF and fantasy fandom, goth culture – drive from his own passion as a fan and a consumer and a tourist; though he is also interested in social justice in the criminal justice system, the far-right and their presence online, and the new work and the new leisure. He was born in Leeds and has not really ventured far from it or the upper reaches of Airedale, apart from three years spent doing his first degree at a university down south. His Ph.D. explored the complexities of the imaginary and imagined communities associated with rugby league in the north of England. This symbolic identity is written into the myths told about class, gender and the north, and nothing since he finished his Ph.D. has changed his mind.

*****

ALEX STEVENSON is the course director for the BA (Hons) music performance and production and BA (Hons) music industries management courses in the Leeds School of Arts at Leeds Beckett University where he predominately teaches modules in creative studio production, production analysis and mixing practice. He is a fellow of the Higher Education Academy and member of the Association for the Study of the Art of Record Production. Alex has published and presented on topics related to UK hip hop, popular music education, mixing practice, music performance and electronic music. He is currently undertaking a Ph.D. in musicology at the University of Oslo, exploring the performance of machine aesthetics in popular music. Alex also has experience as a freelance musician, producer and engineer, and has worked with a number of British hip hop artists including Shameless, Low Key and Plan B, and record labels including All City Records and DAT sound. He has performed for live radio broadcast for XFM and BBC Radio 1 at Maida Vale Studios and performed at venues across the United Kingdom such as Fabric in London and the O2 Academy in Bristol.

*****

PAUL THOMPSON is currently reader in popular music in Leeds School of Arts at Leeds Beckett University where he is programme leader for MA music production and teaches studio production skills, creative music production and popular music history and heritage. His first book *Creativity in the Recording Studio: Alternative Takes* was published in early 2019 by Palgrave MacMillan. His second book *Paul McCartney and His Creative Practice: The Beatles and Beyond* was co-written with his mentor and friend, Professor Phillip McIntryre from the University of Newcastle, and was published in late 2021 also by Palgrave MacMillan. His on-going research interests include music and audio education, popular music heritage, creativity and cultural production in popular music. Paul continues to work as a professional recording engineer and his work has been played on BBC 6 Music, BBC Radio 2, BBC Radio 4 and on independent radio stations across Europe and the USA. He has worked with local, national and international artists including Sam Airey, Stereo Mike, Marcus Bonfanti, The Medieval Baebes, Ian Prowse, The Wedding Present and Utah Saints. His most recent work includes engineering on *One Hand on the Starry Plough*, the latest studio album from Ian Prowse for Kitchen Disco Records (2022). He is a senior fellow of the Higher Education

Academy, an associate member of the Institute of Acoustics and a member of the Music Producer's Guild.

*****

STEPHEN WAGG was a professor in the Carnegie School of Sport at Leeds Beckett University from 2008 until his retirement in 2019, during which time he lived in Bramley, West Leeds. He has written widely on the politics of sport, of childhood and of comedy. While at Leeds Beckett he and his colleague Peter Bramham published *Sport, Leisure and Culture in the Postmodern City* (Ashgate, 2009), a collection of essays about life in post-industrial Leeds. The following year saw the publication of *Sporting Heroes of the North* (Northumbria Press), which he edited with Dave Russell, another colleague and a contributor to this book. In 2014, together with Brett Lashua and Karl Spracklen, also colleagues at Leeds Beckett and editors of this book, he edited *Sounds and the City: Popular Music, Place and Globalisation* (Palgrave Macmillan). This book, about the relationship between music and place, had a sequel in 2019 and is in part the inspiration behind the present volume. The previous year his book *Cricket: A Political History of the Global Game, 1945–2017* was published by Routledge and was shortlisted for the Cricket Writers' Club Annual Award in 2018. His book *The History and Politics of Motor Racing: Lives in the Fast Lane* (edited with Damion Sturm and David L. Andrews) will be published by Palgrave Macmillan in 2023. He is currently planning to write a book on comedy and politics in Britain and the United States. He is an honorary fellow in the International Centre for Sport History and Culture at De Montfort University in Leicester, UK.

*****

BECCY WATSON is a reader in the Carnegie School of Sport at Leeds Beckett University. She is an active researcher within the Centre for Social Justice in Sport. Her research interests focus on gender and leisure, feminist epistemologies, social inequalities and intersectionality. Beccy has published material that reflects sustained involvement and interest across various leisure and sport contexts. She has co-edited several collections with a range of international scholars. Beccy has close to 30 years teaching experience at undergraduate and postgraduate level from media and cultural industries modules to applied social theory in sport. She has been a course leader and staff lead and has led the development of new social science and sport courses. Beccy was a managing editor for the Routledge journal *Leisure Studies* between 2007 and 2014 and is currently on the Editorial Board of *Annals of Leisure Research*. She was an associate editor and board member for

*Leisure Sciences* and is a member of the Leisure Studies Association. She reviews for a wide range of journals and has university wide responsibility for training new Ph.D. supervisors. Her own Ph.D. student completions span a wide range of topics including women and climbing, acid house culture, Islam and dance, post punk, and various aspects of sport for change. Watson has a keen interest in researching dance and masculinities and works closely with community-based organisations that deliver dance and physical activity opportunities across the city of Leeds, UK. She remains an enthusiastic discussant of Leeds popular music scenes, both as academic and gig goer.

# Index

1919 (post-punk band) 18
24-hour city 2–3

**A**

Abbey House Museum 8, 217, 219, 222, 279, 284
Adelphi, The 21, 24–25, 71, 207
Alt-J 66, 254
Americana 5, 7, 144–45, 149, 152–57, 282
Arcadian Ballroom 206
Arctic Monkeys 66
Arts Council England 265, 272
Assembly Rooms 226, 228
Astoria Ballroom 150
Austin, Texas 144–45, 149, 154

**B**

Back to Basics/ Back2Basics (Dave Beer) xiv, xv, 61, 183, 221, 272
Bailey Rae, Corinne 3, 121, 221, 231, 254
Bar Sela 207, 282 *see also* Studio 20
Bassment 59, 64
Beatles, the 9, 178, 207, 211, 222, 226, 251, 254, 258–59, 261, 273
Beer, Dave xv, 183, 221 *see also* Back to Basics
Belgrave Music Hall 68
Big Bill Broonzy 145–46
Birmingham 1, 5, 91, 93, 113, 145, 194, 196, 284
Black Lives Matter (BLM) 113, 122, 127

Blue Gardenia coffee shop 179
Bourdieu (Pierre) 59
Bradford 17–18, 31–35, 38–39, 72, 147, 198, 211, 221, 239, 244, 258
Bramham Park 231, 283 *see also* Leeds Festival
Brannigans xiv, 181
breakdancing 182, 187, 235, 238
Brexit 79, 112
British Broadcasting Corporation (BBC) 43–44, 51–52, 87, 90–92, 96–97, 102, 146, 148, 158, 161, 169, 171–72, 201, 239, 242, 254
British Music Hall Society 172
Bruce Springsteen xiv, 6, 47, 50, 53, 226
Brudenell Social Club 4, 59, 66–68, 154–56, 221, 254, 283
Burley Park 77, 79

**C**

calypso 5, 105, 111, 191–96, 198–202, 280
Calvert, Kit 31, 39
Canal Mills 68, 253
Cardigan Arms, The 229
Caribbean, Caribbean music 3, 7–8, 103, 105–06, 108–10, 112–13, 191–200, 202, 230
Caribbean carnival 6, 8, 104, 140, 191–92
Catholic Girls, The 7, 137
Cavern Club (Liverpool) 207, 211, 252

Chapel Allerton 112, 155, 212
Chapel FM (radio) 125–26
Chapeltown 20–21, 41, 49, 122, 181–82, 191–92, 194–201, 238
Chumbawamba xiv, 3, 61, 221, 231
Chunk 73–74, 76, 80
City Region Music Boards 265, 269
Clash, The xiv, 65, 133, 140
Club Memphis 147
Coburg pub 211
Cockpit, The 7, 55, 59, 62–67, 211, 229, 255, 280
Coconut Grove 239
Coliseum 226
Continental Club 181
Corn Exchange 65, 183
COVID-19 55, 79–80, 82–83, 155–56, 186, 201, 232–33, 236
Crash Records 58, 221
Cryer, Terry (photographer) 208–10
Cud 61

D
Dando, Mike (Con-Dom) 71–73
Deaf Forever festival 70, 73, 76
Dearlove music shop/ Dearlove collection 219, 225–26, 231
Del Monte Coffee Bar 178
Delta 5 1, 6–7, 15, 22, 27, 130, 133, 137–38, 151, 180, 255
diaspora/ diasporic 23, 53, 106, 110
DJs/ DJ culture xiv, 1, 5, 7–8, 58–60, 62, 64–68, 119–20, 127–28, 151, 176–180, 182–83, 185, 187, 199–201, 235, 237–39, 241–43, 247, 253
do-it-yourself (DIY) 5, 8, 15–16, 19, 63, 73, 77, 80–81, 83, 120, 125, 147, 154, 176, 178–86, 236, 269, 272, 282, 288
Duchess of York, The (The Duchess) xiv, 4, 59, 61–64, 67, 255

E
Elland Road (football ground) 20, 25, 28, 45, 48
ethnography/ ethnographic 16–18, 27, 205
European Capital of Culture 265, 269
Experimental music 7, 70–77, 283
Expresso Bongo 178

F
F Club (also F-Club) 16–17, 20–21, 25, 30, 140
Fanque, Pablo 251, 258–259, 261, 282
Faversham, The 22, 26, 58–59, 61, 66–67, 241, 243
feminist/feminism 7, 73, 98, 100, 118, 130–42, 180
Fenton, The 4, 6, 15–28, 58–59, 61, 180, 229, 255–56, 283
folk music 1, 3, 5–6, 31–41, 88–89, 94, 98–100, 104, 118, 125, 144–53, 157, 172, 191–92, 196, 205, 209, 283
Fox's club 238
France, Authur 192–93, 198
Futurama festivals 15
Futuresound 54–55, 62, 66–68, 221

G
Gang of Four 1, 3, 6–7, 15–17, 19–20, 22, 24, 27, 61, 65, 130, 133–37, 151, 180, 221, 231, 254–255, 259
Garvey, Sara 7, 117–29
Gavaghan, Sean 106
gentrification/ gentrifying/ gentrified 4, 32, 156, 266–67
Gill, Andy 1, 16, 20, 134, 136 see also Gang of Four
Ginger Works 9, 279–82
Gipsy, The (album) 31–32, 35, 38, 40
Goth 1, 3, 18, 57, 61–62, 66, 221, 230, 254–55, 260–61
Gramsci (Antonio) 16
Grove Inn, The 145, 147, 149–50

# INDEX

**H**

Headingley (neighbourhood) 25, 34, 155, 184–86

Headingley Enterprise and Arts Centre (HEART) 149, 155

Hi-Fi Club, The 59, 65–66, 68, 121

Hip Hop Historian Society (HHHS) 9, 236

hip hop 3, 5, 8–9, 63, 118–20, 181–82, 221, 235–47, 282, 284

Hippodrome (Leeds) 227, 259

Hyde Park Book Club 155

Hyde Park neighbourhood (LS6) xiv, 26, 154–55, 179, 182–84, 186, 241

**I**

Ibrahim, Khadijah 237–38, 247 *see also* Leeds Young Authors

indie music xiv, 1, 7, 57–68, 71, 122, 254–55, 280

industry/ industrial/ industrialization 2–4, 31–32, 34, 43, 91, 130–31, 176, 179, 182, 251–53

    post-industrialization 5–6, 15, 17, 40, 138

industrial music 70–72

International Club 106

International Federation of the Phonographic Industry 265

intersectional/intersectionality 7, 117, 123, 128

Irish music/ Irish communities 7, 23–24, 38, 103, 105–09, 112

Irish Centre, The 59, 152, 154

**J**

Jackson, Michael 6, 49–50, 52

Jamaica 102, 112, 192

jazz xiv, 3, 5–6, 8, 24, 62, 65, 71, 108, 118, 121, 145–46, 205–12, 225, 282

Jewish communities/ Jewish music 7, 103–104, 107, 110, 162, 225, 232

Jones, Fuzzy 7, 117–28

jukebox 58–59, 178, 218, 227

Jumbo Records 58, 221, 226, 238

**K**

Kaiser Chiefs 1, 3, 15, 53, 65–66, 218, 221, 231, 254

Keenan, John 4, 15, 25, 61, 145, 153, 180–81 *see also* F Club

King, Jon 136, 259 *see also* Gang of Four

Kirkstall xiv, 34, 79, 89, 152, 185, 211, 219

Knopfler, Mark 145, 148–50

Kurdish music 108, 112–13

**L**

Labour Party 33, 89, 91–92, 178, 206

Ladyfest 73

Leeds Arena/ First Direct Arena 4, 67–68, 182, 226, 253–54, 256

Leeds Asylum Seekers Support Network 104

Leeds City Council (LCC) 44, 52, 186, 256, 265, 269–70, 273

Leeds City Museum 220–21, 226, 236, 294

Leeds City Varieties/ Leeds Music Hall 8, 161–73, 227, 280, 283

Leeds Club History Project 176

Leeds College of Music/ Leeds Conservatoire 62, 126, 210, 212, 219, 224–25

Leeds Empire 162–63, 227

Leeds Festival 221, 231, 254, 283 *see also* Bramham Park

Leeds Grand Theatre 227

Leeds International Piano Competition 104, 221, 227

Leeds Jazz Club, The 207, 212

Leeds Metropolitan University/ Leeds Beckett University/ Leeds Polytechnic xiv, 59, 162, 229, 255

Leeds Museums and Galleries 217–20

Leeds Playhouse 104, 197, 227

Leeds Polytechnic Art School 61
Leeds Polytechnic Students' Union (LPSU) 180
Leeds Town Hall 43, 146–47, 192, 194–95, 226–27, 270
Leeds United (football club) 24, 103, 187
Leeds University 59, 63, 132, 168, 219, 224, 227, 253–55 *see also* University of Leeds
Leeds West Indian Carnival (LWIC) 8, 49, 191–202, 230, 280
Leeds West Indian Centre 229
Leeds Young Authors 238 *see also* Khadijah Ibrahim
Lending Room at the Library pub 155–56
Lennon, John 251, 258–59
LGBT/LGBTQ 125, 221
Light Night 73
Live at Leeds (festival) 66–67
*Live at Leeds* (1970) 221, 230, 253, 254–55, 260 *see also* The Who
Liverpool 1, 3–5, 79, 145, 148, 207, 211, 252–54, 270, 273, 283
Locarno Ballroom, The 178, 228
Lovers Rock 108–09, 112, 119
Lycett, Kevin 20, 24, 135, 140, 151–52, 157 *see also* the Mekons

## M
Madonna 48
Majestic Ballroom, The 178, 228
Mama Dread 111, 287
Manchester 1, 5, 15, 26, 44–45, 65, 98, 113, 131, 139, 145, 155, 194, 227, 258, 265, 269, 284
map/mapping 1–2, 4, 6, 9, 33, 39, 232, 251, 254–56, 259–61, 268–71, 274–75, 279–82, 284
    maps of meaning 144
March Violets, The xiii, xiv, 6, 15, 22, 256
Marxism/Marxist 17, 135–36, 254
Meanwood Park 78

Mekons, The 1, 3, 6–7, 15, 17, 19–22, 24, 61, 130, 133–35, 140–43, 145–46, 150–52, 180, 221, 231, 254–55
Melly, George 207–09
Merrion Centre 182
migrants/migration 2–3, 7, 33, 102–14, 180, 191–93, 283
Mint Club 185
mixtapes 237, 239–40, 246–47
mods 278
Mr Fox (Bob and Carole Pegg) 6, 31–42, 148
museums 2, 6, 8–9, 95, 112, 217–33, 236–37, 246, 279, 281, 284
music industry 35, 43, 53, 60, 63, 66–67, 118, 123, 127–28, 130, 135, 139, 152, 154–56, 251, 253, 255, 265–67, 270, 273, 275, 282
    entertainment industry 172
    variety industry 161, 169
Music:Leeds 2, 232, 265, 268–75, 284
myth/ mythology/ myth-making 5–7, 16–18, 22–23, 26–28, 31, 87–89, 283 *see also* place myth

## N
Nashville 4, 144, 153, 267, 273
National Front 15–16, 19–20, 25, 138–41, 180
Nazi/ Nazism/ Neo-Nazi 20, 72, 82, 103, 138–39, 180
    Anti-Nazi League 21, 137
*New Musical Express (NME)* 146
New Roscoe, The/Roscoe, The 106, 145, 152, 229
Nightmares on Wax xiv, 125, 230, 239–40
Nirvana 61
No-Audience Underground 70–82
Noise/Power electronics (genres) 5, 7, 70–82
Non-place 279, 282, 284
Northern Guitars Bar 153, 156

northern soul 119, 179
Northern/the North 6, 8, 32–33, 44, 89, 92, 138, 178, 251–52, 258, 283
nostalgia 76, 102, 110, 172, 223–24

O

Ó Dubhshláine, Melanie 73, 76, 82
O'Brien, Lucy 15, 19, 137, 141, 180
O2 Academy 67–68, 226, 282, 296 see also Town & Country Club
Odeon 226, 228
Oluwale, David 113–14
Opera North 104
Oporto 254

P

Pack Horse, The 59, 145, 150, 280
Palestinian music 111
Peel Hotel 211
Phonographique, The/ Bar Phono 58–59, 61, 229, 239
Pigeon Detectives, The 66, 221, 231, 254
pirate radio 183, 199, 241
place (musical) xiii, xv, 3, 5–9, 37, 41, 63, 71, 73, 77–82, 107, 114, 218, 222, 254, 257–58, 280, 288
 place (and the city) 1–2, 57, 252, 266, 281
 place (and identity) 7, 9, 40, 102, 113, 120–22
 placemaking 264–65, 271–75, 282, 288
 place myths 16–18, 23, 89, 283
 place (obscure places) 251, 259
 place, sense of 144, 154, 279, 282
Pleasure Rooms, The xiv
popular musicscape 7, 280
post-punk 1, 3–7, 15–19, 21, 27, 61, 64–65, 137, 141, 180, 254–55, 259–61, 282
Potternewton Park 193, 195, 197–200, 230
Prince of Wales, The 21

psychogeography/ psychogeographic 9, 251, 257–59, 261
punk 1, 3–4, 7, 12, 16, 20, 25, 28, 57, 61, 117, 119, 130–132, 134, 136–41, 145, 150–52, 180, 183, 221, 254–55, 272

Q

Queens Hall 253, 255

R

RadhaRaman Folk Festival 104
rave xiv, xv, 8, 51–52, 61–62, 66, 179, 182–83, 185, 187, 273, 280
Reclaim the Night (marches) 133, 136
Red Lorry Yellow Lorry 25, 255
regeneration 2, 4, 264
Regent, The 106
reggae 105, 107–10, 118–19, 13, 194–95, 197–200, 221, 235, 237–39, 247
Reynolds, Simon 16, 133, 136
River Aire 3, 32, 34, 114
Rock Against Racism 15, 25, 137, 139, 221
Rolling Stones, The 43, 46–47, 211, 226, 231
Roundhay Park xiv, 6, 43–45, 47–55, 178, 219, 231, 255
Royal Park, The xiv, 70, 73
Royal Sovereign Pub 34
RadhaRaman Folk Festival 104
rave xiv, xv, 8, 51–52, 61–62, 66, 179, 182–83, 185, 187, 273, 280

S

Santiago bar 155
Savile, Jimmy 50, 176–77
Scarborough Taps, The 21, 25
Scritti Politti 1, 254–55
Seven (arts centre) 153, 155, 212
Sheffield 1, 4, 5, 32, 66, 81, 89, 258, 265, 269
Sheeran, Ed 6, 43, 54–55
Simpson, Dave 15, 19–21

Sisters of Mercy, The xiv, 1, 3, 221, 231, 254–56
skiffle 145–47, 163, 209
Slam Dunk Festival 63, 67, 272
soca 105, 111, 191, 197–202
Soft Cell 3, 19, 61, 221, 231, 254–55
Song Tunnel 9, 256, 257, 260–61, 284
Sound Diplomacy 265, 270
Sound Systems 111, 120, 197, 200, 202, 238
*Sounds of Our City* (exhibition) 2, 5, 8–9, 217–33, 279, 284
Strega Blues Bar 106
Studio 20 8, 146, 207–10, 282
Stylus (University of Leeds Student Union) 156, 229
subculture 17–18, 61, 72, 117, 130–31, 139, 141, 178, 180

T
teddy boys 178
Temple Newsam Park 231
Termite Club 7, 70–77, 82
Thackray, Jake 7, 87–99, 221, 231
thanatourism 251, 259, 261
Theatre Royal 228, 259
Three Johns, The xiv, 6, 15, 22–24
Town and Country Club 7, 59, 62, 226, 255, 282 *see also* O2 Academy
translocal music 144, 152, 155

U
U2 xiv, 6, 46, 50–51
UK Music 265, 270
Underground, The 62, 65, 119, 121
UNESCO 264
University of Leeds xiv, 9, 19, 26, 148, 150, 156, 179, 224, 241, 258 *see also* Leeds University
Utah Saints xii, xiv, 1, 3, 256

V
Vallances Records 221, 225
Vernon Street Ramblers 207–08
Victoria Pub 119
Victoria, Vesta 170, 173, 227
Voodoo Events 184

W
Wardrobe, The 122, 240
Warehouse, The 59, 61, 181, 183–84, 230, 241
Waterman, (Dame) Fanny 104, 227
Weavers, The 145–47
Wedding Present, The xiii, 1, 3, 61, 221, 231, 254–55
Well, The/ Joseph's Well 7, 59, 63–64, 229
Wensleydale 33, 39
Weston, Paul (DJ) 237–246
Wharf Chambers 73–74, 76, 80–82
Who, The 230, 253–55, 260
Wilberforce Steel Band 195–96
Williams, Robbie 52
Wire/ Mex/ Milo's 59, 65, 68, 119
Woodhouse Lane 16, 19, 26, 207, 211, 256, 260
Woodhouse Moor 78, 150, 155, 280
working–class 3, 131–33, 138–39, 169, 172, 178, 187, 206

Y
Yard Act 3
Yorkshire (region) 6, 7, 18, 32, 37–38, 40, 44, 54, 64, 75, 87–89, 95, 98, 108, 131, 147, 178, 194, 196, 211, 228, 254, 258, 283
Yorkshire County Cricket Club 103
Yorkshire Dales 6, 31–39, 41
*Yorkshire Evening Post* (YEP) 48–52, 148–49, 205
Yorkshire Jazz Band 207–10
*Yorkshire Post* 46, 165–99, 171, 211
Yorkshire Ripper 6, 15, 19, 41, 130, 141, 180
Yorkshireness 22, 31–41, 89

Milton Keynes UK
Ingram Content Group UK Ltd.
UKHW030249281023
431468UK00004B/31